# Organizing the Transnational

*Edited by Luin Goldring and
Sailaja Krishnamurti*

# Organizing the Transnational:
# Labour, Politics, and Social Change

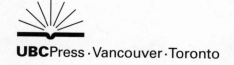

**UBC**Press · Vancouver · Toronto

16 15 14 13 12 11 10 09 08 07   5 4 3 2 1

Printed in Canada on ancient-forest-free paper (100% post-consumer recycled) that is processed chlorine- and acid-free, with vegetable-based inks.

---

**Library and Archives Canada Cataloguing in Publication**

Organizing the transnational : labour, politics, and social change / edited by Luin Goldring and Sailaja Krishnamurti.

Includes bibliographical references and index.
ISBN 978-0-7748-1407-2

1. Immigrants – Canada. 2. Transnationalism. 3. Asians – Canada. 4. Latin Americans – Canada. 5. Ethnicity – Canada. 6. Social change – Canada. 7. Community organization – Canada. I. Goldring, Luin II. Krishnamurti, Sailaja, 1976-

| HD8108.5.A2O73 2007 | 303.48'271 | C2007-904260-0 |

---

Canadä

UBC Press gratefully acknowledges the financial support for our publishing program of the Government of Canada through the Book Publishing Industry Development Program (BPIDP), and of the Canada Council for the Arts, and the British Columbia Arts Council.

This book has been published with the help of a grant from the Canadian Federation for the Humanities and Social Sciences, through the Aid to Scholarly Publications Programme, using funds provided by the Social Sciences and Humanities Research Council of Canada.

UBC Press
The University of British Columbia
2029 West Mall
Vancouver, BC V6T 1Z2
604-822-5959 / Fax: 604-822-6083
**www.ubcpress.ca**

# Contents

# Acknowledgments

Edited book projects such as this one are collaborative: they are made possible by diverse forms of collaborative work and support from several sources. We would like to acknowledge Peter Vandergeest, Director of the York Centre for Asian Research (YCAR), and Viviana Patroni, Director of the Centre for Research on Latin America and the Caribbean (CERLAC), for their generous support and encouragement. The idea for this volume was sparked by a workshop, the first at either centre on a topic involving immigrant and diaspora populations in Canada. Peter Vandergeest led in organizing and securing funding for the fruitful event, which was fairly unique in bringing together immigrant activists, the director of an immigrant social service agency, a labour leader, members of several immigrant communities active in transnational activities, policy analysts from the government and NGO sectors, as well as academics from several disciplines. We are also grateful to Susan Henders and Judith Nagata for sharing their ideas and supporting the initial development of this book.

We are particularly grateful to each of the authors for their willingness to work with us on this volume. They have been patient with our queries and the lengthy time frame. Two anonymous reviewers provided valuable comments for which we are also grateful. A number of people stepped in at crucial moments to assist in the preparation of the manuscript. Susan Henders "lent" research assistant support during the early copyediting phase. Lauren Turner and Hanna Caplan provided excellent and cheerful copyediting and editorial assistance, juggling those tasks with the demands of their own graduate studies. Tony Zeng provided key formatting advice and editorial assistance. We also acknowledge support from David Dewitt, Vice President of Research and Innovation at York University, Robert Drummond, Dean of Arts, and the YCAR for supporting preparation of the final manuscript. Last, but certainly not least, we are grateful to Emily Andrew, our editor at UBC Press, who was extremely enthusiastic and encouraging throughout the process, and to Darcy Cullen, our production editor.

# Organizing the Transnational

# Introduction: Contextualizing Transnationalism in Canada

*Luin Goldring and Sailaja Krishnamurti*

It has become a cliché to note that we live in an increasingly interconnected world. What happens in a Canadian metropolis such as Toronto or Montreal, or in smaller cities such as Sudbury, Moncton, or Prince George, is likely to have repercussions in a wide array of countries: from Hong Kong, Sri Lanka, and China to Sudan, Somalia, and Ghana; from Haiti, Guyana, and Jamaica to Colombia, El Salvador, and Peru; or from Afghanistan, Pakistan, and India to Poland, Portugal, and England. Similarly, what happens "over there" can have a strong impact on people and communities in Canada.

How do we understand the interconnectedness of people and localities around the globe? Most of us are aware that macrolevel processes and institutions such as international trade, international relations, and multilateral trade agreements are somehow responsible for orchestrating many of the economic, political, and cultural connections between countries, regions, organizations, and communities around the world. Many of us are also aware that technology plays an important role in helping people to stay in touch with people whom they do not see on a regular basis and that the media also help people to keep up with news and trends "back home." Globalization is a term we often use to describe this collection of processes, although we may have only a general idea of what the word means. What is becoming increasingly clear to more people, including activists, politicians, and social scientists, is the fact that international migration, and the personal and institutional networks and practices that people forge as they move, settle, and perhaps move again, is also deeply implicated in the social, cultural, political, and economic dimensions of how people and places are interconnected across space and time.

In Canada, we see evidence of these migrant-led or migrant-related connections or transnational engagements in news reports covering a wide range of events and processes. They include fundraising for natural disasters that affect immigrants' homelands; immigrant or native-born Canadians returning to a personal or ancestral homeland to take on political office; the rising popularity of "foreign" films or musical genres associated with particular immigrant or so-called ethnic communities; the periodic arrival of religious leaders who travel to minister to groups in the multilocal diaspora; the earnings that workers send home; political campaigns that include stops in Canadian cities by aspiring candidates running for office outside Canada; or visits by foreign political authorities who, in addition to meeting with their official counterparts in Canada, make time to meet with members of their expatriate communities.

Canadian academics in a number of disciplines have taken up the conceptual challenge of analyzing newcomers both as immigrants and refugees intent upon settling and as people with varying intensities and kinds of ties to their homelands[1] and other regions outside Canada.[2] This is a relatively recent shift, compared to a longer history of scholarship on transnationalism and diasporas in other immigrant receiving countries, such as the United States. In Canada, there is certainly an established body of research on migration, immigrants, and subsequent generations. Much of the early work was framed in the language of ethnic studies or ethnic and race relations, adopted paradigms of assimilation or cultural pluralism, and focused on the assimilation or integration of newcomers into Canadian society.[3] After changes in immigration policy, citizenship legislation, and settlement policies during the 1970s, Canadian immigration patterns shifted from a narrow and racist policy-driven concentration on European source countries to include a wider range of source regions and countries.[4]

The entrance of *new* newcomers, a majority of whom would come to fall under the Canadian label "visible minorities," expanded the coverage of ethnic studies to include non-European ethnicities. As part of the promotion of Canadian multiculturalism, ethnic customs and practices were certainly deemed worthy of study. However, the immigrant experience continued to be studied within the Canadian context and generally did not include "home" other than as a site of history, origin of cultural practices, or nostalgia. The language of race, antiracism, racialization, and diaspora studies came later still, as more scholars from racialized and diasporic groups, particularly South Asian and Caribbean, entered academia. This necessarily sketchy outline of migration and immigrant studies provides the context for situating the relatively recent entrance of transnational studies, diaspora studies, and cultural studies in Canadian work on migrants, refugees, immigrants, and their children.

This collection is intended as a contribution to the emerging body of empirically based and theoretical scholarship on transnationalism and diasporas in Canada. The volume has several features that make it unique in the current Canadian context. First, it attempts to articulate a cultural politics of transnationalism rather than focus separately on economic, political, or social aspects of transnationalism. Second, the concentration on Asian and Latin American migrants in Canada adds depth as well as breadth, as the literature on Latin American transnationalism is scarce compared with that on immigrants from Asia (and other parts of the world). Third, the chapters cover a wide array of institutions, institutional actors, and forms of mobilization that contribute to shaping transnational engagements and spaces. This goes beyond the literature's focus on migrants and states as key actors and institutions shaping transnational spaces. Fourth, and perhaps most uniquely, the book presents a diverse set of perspectives by including work by activists from the immigrant advocacy and NGO sectors as well as academics.

Alejandro Portes and József Böröcz (1989) use the term "context of reception" to describe the wide array of policies and institutions that shape the incorporation of newcomers.[5] This volume contributes to conceptual discussions about transnationalism and diasporas in the Canadian context of reception in several ways. First, the book broadens discussions of citizenship and legal status and their relationship to transnational engagements. Current discussions concerning social exclusion and transnationalism that include attention to legal status rarely consider the case of temporary workers.[6] Second, the collection does not make assumptions about whether transnational identities and practices are widely prevalent, desirable, or to be celebrated. Rather, we include work that raises critical questions about transnational engagements from a variety of perspectives, including those of immigrant advocates, activists, academics, and others. Third, the volume contributes to comparative discussions regarding the role of different contexts of reception in shaping transnational engagements. This is accomplished, for example, in a chapter that examines one group (Salvadorans) in more than one context. More generally, the chapters offer material for subsequent comparative analyses.

We hope that attention to the Canadian context and the specificity of Canadian policies will contribute to Canadian discussions and policy making in the areas of immigration policy, immigrant settlement, and the relationship between incorporation and homeland ties. Finally, we hope to contribute to dialogue between communities (immigrant, ethnic, national, and transnational communities), activists, scholars, and policy makers in Canada.

This introduction proceeds with a section that provides a discussion of terminology and background on the literatures on migrant transnationalism and diasporas. The last section situates the key contributions made by the volume's authors in the context of questions and debates found in the literature on political and sociocultural transnational engagements.

## Transnationalism as a Field of Study and Conceptual Approach

Social scientists and theorists use terms such as transnational social fields, transmigrants, transnational communities, diasporas, transnational citizenship, transnationalism from below, diaspora politics, and long-distance nationalism to describe multisited social networks, practices, organizations, and communities that span national borders. Related terms, such as deterritorialized nation-states and transnationalism from above, point to nation-state responses to im/migrant and civil society transnational engagements.[7] These terms cut across disciplinary boundaries and genres; many of them have been taken up in literature, activist discourse, popular writing, government documents, policy papers put out by international financial institutions, and so forth. The terms invoke identities, belongings, memberships, networks, forms of social organization, social processes, and state policies aimed at citizens, all of which, rather than being contained by national borders, spread out beyond national boundaries and territories. Such processes may originate with migrant organizations, federal governments, local governments, parties, or other institutional actors. Regardless of their origin, they generate responses and tend to become multiscalar, multisited, multidirectional, and transnational.

The concepts of diaspora on the one hand, and transnationalism and transnational communities on the other, have distinct origins and trajectories but are now converging. In the contemporary context, use of the term *diaspora* has centred on the humanities, cultural studies, and political science, while the term *transnationalism* first gained currency among anthropologists and sociologists before spreading to other disciplines. Contemporary usage finds them used almost interchangeably, in a wide range of disciplines, fields, and settings. A brief sketch of the different origins and convergence of the concepts is in order. Diaspora is the older term (Tölölyan 1991; Cohen 1997; Van Hear 1998). Some have argued for a narrow application of the term to "victim diasporas" – people displaced and then dispersed from a real or putative homeland, through ethnic or religious persecution or conflict – but it has come to be used for other "scatterings" of people. Typologies of diasporas include, but are not limited to, groups that originated in or were formed by trade, slavery, indentured labour, colonialism, and political exile (Cohen 1997).

Other theorists have rejected such typologies and use diaspora as a broad theoretical lens to focus on migration, culture, and identity (Safran 1991). As a result, diaspora now refers to collectivities of people living in multiple national contexts who identify as having a common history or identity based on language, ethnicity, racialization, and/or religion. Thus, we now hear references to the Caribbean, African, Indian, Philippine, Hindu, Muslim, Chinese, South Asian, Kurdish, Tamil, Mayan, and Mexican diasporas as well as the classical Jewish and Armenian diasporas. In some cases, diasporic identities are framed as hybrid, creolized, or in other ways "mixed," the product of movements and exchanges between peoples. In other cases, the concept retains a primordialist connotation, although the ethnicity in question may have become a panethnicity. The term usually applies to multiple generations, so that people may identify with a particular diaspora without having active ties to a homeland. Furthermore, people may identify as members of a particular diaspora and live lives firmly rooted in and confined to a single nation-state.

In their agenda-setting book *Nations Unbound: Transnational Projects, Postcolonial Predicaments, and Deterritorialized Nation-States,* Linda Basch, Nina Glick Schiller, and Cristina Szanton Blanc (1994) defined transnational migration as "the process by which immigrants forge and sustain multi-stranded social relations that link together their societies of origin and settlement" (6). While additional and more specific definitions have been developed (see below), the term *transnationalism* is generally used to describe people who feel that they belong to and/or organize their daily lives around more than one nation-state. Thus, in contrast to diaspora, transnational communities, transnationalism, and transnational living are terms that generally emphasize more tangible and contemporary connections between people in societies of destination and origin and perhaps transit. Recent work also emphasizes the importance of including nonmigrant members of transnational social spaces (Levitt and Glick Schiller 2004).

The term *transnational communities* is used somewhat loosely to describe national as well as subnational collectivities. The term could refer to migrants from the same town, region, ethnic group, or country.[8] The concept of transnational social spaces is more general and emphasizes identities, relationships, exchanges, practices, and institutions that arise in the process of transnational migration (Pries 1998; Faist 2000). Peggy Levitt and Nina Glick Schiller (2004) proposed a further distinction between *ways of belonging* transnationally and *ways of being* transnational in order to distinguish transnational identities (ways of belonging) from specific transnational practices (ways of being). They point out that people may feel a sense of transnational belonging without engaging in transnational practices and vice versa. This distinction becomes particularly important when we consider that mobility is not always possible, depending on constraints associated with social location (gender, class, racialization) (Pratt and Yeoh 2003), political affiliation, or the political situations in homeland regions – all factors that may make contact or return difficult for refugees, exiles, and others (Al-Ali, Black, and Koser 2001; Nolin 2006).

This discussion of terminology is not aimed at establishing clear boundaries between diasporas and things transnational. Rather, it draws attention to the potentially large overlap between the two terms. Diasporas may or may not have active transnational communities. For example, overseas

Chinese do not experience their diasporic identities in a uniform fashion, nor do they all feel that they belong to, or act as though they belong to, Chinese transnational communities. Similarly, Jews express their identities in diverse ways, and second- and third-generation black Canadians may share experiences of racialization but may or may not feel connected to transnational communities or social fields, and if they do, these may be rooted in different "home" lands. At the same time, active transnational communities from various origins may or may not have sufficient historical depth, geographical breadth, and ongoing production of identity and solidarity to warrant being called diasporas.

The chapters in this volume focus largely on "the transnational," although the language of both transnationalism and diaspora is used by the contributors. The authors examine a multiplicity of institutions and actors involved in shaping and organizing the transnational. Together they generate a set of analyses showing that a wide variety of actors and institutions organize transnational spaces; some social actors do so in the pursuit of livelihood, others work directly for social change, while others search out avenues for affirming identity and status. Institutional actors include states and organized migrants, but they also include international law, the media, NGOs, organized labour, and immigrant advocates. As such, the volume joins Levitt and Glick Schiller's (2004) call for a reconceptualization of society using the lens of transnational studies. This approach involves understanding society in general, and not only immigrants, as constituted by transnational engagements at various levels and scales. For the purpose of this volume, it involves framing the study of Canadian-based transnationalism beyond the study of im/migrants and states to include a broad set of networks, practices, policies, and institutions.

### Situating Transnational Studies

The growing literature on migrant transnational engagement reflects several interrelated transformations, of which we highlight three. The first involves qualitative and quantitative changes in migrant practices; a second is related to changes in sending and receiving country policies that affect the membership or citizenship status of emigrants in the former and immigrant settlement in the latter; a third rests on conceptual shifts in the study of international migration and includes scholarship on transnationalism and diasporas. Of course, these three kinds of changes must be understood as taking place in the broader context of macrostructural changes commonly referred to as globalization, which includes but is not limited to changes in the role of nation-states, including their relationship to international financial institutions and multilateral organizations; the growth of suprastate governance structures of various sorts (from the EU to the WTO); transformations in civil society responses (antiglobalization movements, transnational advocacy networks, etc.); and sometimes unpredictable changes in the mobility of capital, the international organization of production, and patterns of circulation and consumption – not only of goods but also of images, identities, values, and practices.

## Changes in Migrant Practices

The first set of changes rests on transformations in what Manuel Orozco describes as the five Ts of transnationalism: telecommunications, transportation, tourism, trade (especially for home-country goods consumed by immigrants), and money transfer mechanisms (2003, 2005). Changes in these sectors make it easier and cheaper for more people to be in touch with and maintain active relationships with individuals and institutions in personal or ancestral homelands (Vertovec 2004). They also facilitate transnational business activity, which may be an important economic strategy for im/migrants (Landolt 2001; Wong and Ng 2002; Portes, Haller, and Guarnizo 2002). Noting these changes does not imply any claim about the novelty of transnational engagements, as scholars have documented the historical depth of these processes (Foner 1997; Smith 2003b). Rather, it highlights that these processes have become more widespread, dense, and frequent, to the point of becoming institutionalized at various levels. It also means recognizing that one feature of the current context of globalization is that it is marked not only by the increasing mobility of capital and people but also by changes in the facility with which people develop and maintain social, economic, and political relationships across borders. Migrants at the turn of the twentieth century wrote letters home, and many migrated back to their countries of origin. However, letters and passengers took time to cross the ocean, as did news. The simultaneity of visual, audio, and text-based contact offered by contemporary technologies, and the speed of travel, are simply unprecedented.

## Changes in State Policies

Largely in response to the changes just outlined, nation-states with high proportions of emigrants, immigrants, or both have instituted policies and regulations aimed at redefining membership in the nation. In the case of sending countries, particularly worker-exporting countries, there is a trend toward adopting double nationality and/or citizenship legislation, thus expanding membership in the nation beyond the territorial boundaries of the state (Basch, Glick Schiller, and Szanton Blanc 1994; Itzigsohn 2000). A growing number of countries allow their overseas citizens to vote in federal elections. The right to vote gives emigrants a concrete way of expressing ongoing attachment to their homeland. It also allows states to benefit from the expertise of the diaspora and perhaps an ongoing flow of remittances. The latter, of course, can contribute to the balance of payments.

In the case of destination countries, responses to immigration have been more mixed and contradictory. Most destination states have heightened border control (Heyman and Cunningham 2004). Some, such as the United States, have built fences, invested more in enforcement, and formally and informally militarized the border. Others, such as Canada, have made modest increases in enforcement while using immigration policy to exercise greater control and selectivity over "who gets in." In this way, Canada maintains relatively high immigration targets while in practice reducing the number of refugees and immigrants allowed to enter and increasing the number of temporary workers who are not considered immigrants or members of the nation (Simmons 1998; Sharma 2001).

Policies regarding citizenship, dual citizenship, the settlement of immigrants, and the management of cultural difference also vary in receiving countries (Castles and Miller 2003; Reitz 1998). Canada has relatively high naturalization rates and allows naturalized citizens to hold dual citizenship (i.e., to retain their prior citizenship). In contrast, the United States has been more suspicious of the dual loyalties of the foreign born. Legally, naturalized citizens are supposed to renounce their prior citizenship when they swear their new citizenship oath (Bloemraad 2005). Irene Bloemraad argues that Canadian openness to new citizens retaining dual citizenship, and other policies such as official multiculturalism, has actually facilitated their incorporation.

Canada has had official multiculturalism policies and programs in place since the 1970s. They have sought to affirm a certain amount of cultural difference while at the same time managing it by channelling it through approved avenues such as government support for panethnic and other immigrant organizations, cultural festivals, "heritage language" classes, and so forth. Multiculturalism has been critiqued from several perspectives, including the argument that it inhibits immigrant incorporation and instead ghettoizes immigrants based on ethnic or cultural groupings (Bissoondath 2002), the antiracist position that multiculturalism "can't end racism" (Philip 1992), feminist critiques of how state policies label, discipline, and limit the power of racialized women (Carty and Brand 1993), the argument that multiculturalism is more ideology than policy (Kallen 1995), and analyses that point to the way in which multiculturalism and diversity are used to market Canada and the Canadian workforce (Abu-Laban and Gabriel 2002).

The Netherlands and other northern European countries have implemented their own versions of multicultural policies, some quite different from the Canadian version (Østergaard-Nielsen 2001b). Other countries, such as the United States, have experienced long-standing tensions between ideologies of cultural pluralism (and related metaphors such as the cultural mosaic or the "salad bowl") and cultural assimilation and Anglo-conformity (Americanization or the melting pot). In countries characterized by emigration and immigration, policies in these areas may be extremely contradictory, with active policies in one area, usually emigration, and absent or weak policies in the other. Italy, for example, went from the denial of immigrant settlement to a steep learning curve in terms of immigration policy, while Mexico continues largely to ignore its southern border while at the same time militarizing it in ways that contradict critiques raised about the US treatment of Mexicans at the northern border. Other cases may be less well known. For example, India is prominent in the literature as a country of emigration (see Bose in this volume). However, there are also immigrants from Bangladesh, Kashmir, and other nearby countries who lead precarious and marginal lives in India (Samaddar 1999; Sujata Ramachandran, e-mail, June 2005).

## Conceptual Shifts in Migration, Immigration, Transnationalism, and Diaspora Studies

While empirical realities are changing in complex ways, the field of migration studies, and the related areas of immigrant and ethnic studies, have attempted to capture these changes through several conceptual shifts. First was a shift during the 1980s away from Marxist or neo-Marxist structural models as well as orthodox neoclassical economic models of international migration. The former approach was criticized for ignoring human agency, while the latter approach downplayed or disregarded history and political economy.

Second is the move away from seeing migrants as people who sever ties or simply lose contact with their homeland and toward recognizing the multiple and sometimes contradictory loyalties, identities, practices, and forms of belonging that people may have, whether they are migrants or nonmigrants, mobile or immobile members of transnational collectivities and arenas of engagement. This recognition of the "transnational" also draws on contributions from postmodern and postcolonial theories that not only questioned fixed and primordial ethnic and other identities but also opened up the possibility of recognizing cultural and other commonalities among postcolonial subjects in disparate geographical locations.

Third is a recasting of "ethnic" and "ethnic and racial" studies, as well as traditional area studies, into frameworks and language that recognize transnational and diasporic formations and identities and postcolonial legacies. In the United States, ethnic and racial studies moved first toward the study of specific national, ethnic or panethnic, and sometimes hyphenated groups (Native-American, African-American, Chicano, Boricua, Italian-Canadian, Latino, or Asian-American studies) and then to the more recent diasporic, transnational, and postcolonial framing of ethnic studies. However, tensions remain between advocates of broader versus narrower labels (e.g., Dominican studies versus Latin American and Latino studies). In Canada, where British scholarly trends have been followed more closely, the shift was reflected in a move away from "Commonwealth studies" toward postcolonial and cultural studies during the late 1980s and early 1990s. This change also drew upon critiques of multiculturalism. Despite these differences, there is some convergence in that ethnicity is increasingly framed in relation to historical and diasporic processes and identities, current transnational connections, and attention to postcolonial legacies and racialization. This turn is reflected in the recent establishment at universities in Canada and around the world of departments and research centres devoted to diaspora and transnational studies.

## Two Key Approaches

These empirical and conceptual changes lie at the root of the literature of migrant transnationalism and related work on diasporas. However, these literatures are not monolithic. In addition to disciplinary variation, there are differences in definitions employed, methodological approaches, conceptual and theoretical orientations, and findings. It is worth distinguishing two distinct "schools" within the field of transnational studies, mainly in North America.[9] The first approach follows the lead of Basch and her colleagues in the analysis of transnational social fields, spaces, and flows (Basch, Glick Schiller, and Szanton Blanc 1994). This approach has tended to be interpretive, qualitative, institutional, and often historical and comparative. Work in this tradition provides analyses of transnational collectivities at local (transnational villages) and national (transnational social formations) levels, generally through an interweaving of individual narratives with multisited transnational "case" studies developed through participant observations, interviews, and analyses of existing documents, including archival material. As Peggy Levitt and Ninna Nyberg-Sorensen (2004) note, the "transnational turn" in migration studies calls for shifting the focus of research away from sending or receiving contexts per se and toward an examination of the processes and networks used in structuring and maintaining transnational social spaces (2, 3). Focusing on transnational social fields and social spaces (Pries 1998; Faist 2000; Levitt and Glick Schiller 2004) and how they are constituted has the advantage of including migrants as well as nonmigrants and a wide array of institutions. Furthermore, it encourages grounded empirical research that attempts to recognize and analyze transnational engagements (rather than either ignoring or assuming them).

The second approach is exemplified by the work of Portes and his associates. They define transnationalism as occupations and activities that "require regular and sustained social contacts over time across national borders for their implementation" (Portes, Guarnizo, and Landolt 1999, 219), and they measure it largely at the individual level. These authors have grouped transnational activities as falling into three broad categories: sociocultural, political, and economic. From this approach, individual-level data grouped by national origin (and other variables) can be analyzed to determine variation in types and levels of transnationalism and to test hypotheses regarding the determinants of particular kinds and levels of transnationalism (Itzigsohn and Giorguli Saucedo 2002; Portes, Haller, and Guarnizo 2002).

Scholars working in both of these traditions have contributed to clarifying the terminology of transnationalism. Transnational activity can be described as broad or narrow depending on prevalence, frequency, and intensity. Broad transnationalism describes the case when a large proportion of people (from a given country or locality) engages in a particular practice upon occasion (e.g., attending fundraising events organized by hometown associations), while narrow transnationalism refers to situations in which a small proportion of people is involved in a regular, frequent, and intense activity (e.g., long-term participation in the leadership of a hometown association) (Itzigsohn et al. 1999). Levitt (2001b) notes that people may engage in some but not all or necessarily the same constellation of transnational activities. Thus, for example, one might be in contact with family members and send money home but not engage in political transnationalism. Similarly, a person may hold dual nationality, vote from abroad, and attend rallies by homeland politicians but not send remittances or be involved in other forms of sociocultural or economic transnationalism.

Both of these approaches have contributed to shaping Canadian-based research on transnationalism, although in terms of methodology the social spaces approach has been more widely used. Few surveys have been designed to explicitly examine immigrant transnationalism and incorporation (Hiebert and Ley 2003), but surveys that include items on homeland contact do exist (StatsCan 2003). For the most part, scholars have produced interpretive case studies on a growing number of national and ethnic groups.[10] While most focus on a group in a single Canadian setting, some studies, such as Catharine Nolin's (2004, 2006) work on Guatemalans and Audrey Kobayashi et al.'s (2000) collaborative project on immigrants from Hong Kong, involve research on a particular group in several Canadian locations.

## Transnationalism and Interdisciplinary Cultural Studies

Research on diaspora and transnationalism has generated interest in interdisciplinary approaches to these areas of study. In the humanities, analyses of transnational and diasporic cultural productions have generally been routed through literary studies and cultural studies. In literature, interest in diaspora is often understood as a kind of natural outgrowth of postcolonial theory's interest in the migrant and "cosmopolitan" subject. Theorists such as Rey Chow (1993), Homi Bhabha (1994), and Gayatri Chakravorty Spivak (1996) have connected concepts of diaspora and cultural hybridity to post-colonial migration and self-expression. The theorization of diasporic hybridities in literature and feminist studies has also been strongly influenced by theorists such as Gloria Anzaldúa (1987) and Chela Sandoval (2000), who write about cultural, spatial, and ethnic hybridities of *mestizaje* in the Americas.

Cultural studies as a field of inquiry greatly contributed to interdisciplinary studies of diaspora, particularly through the research of thinkers such as Stuart Hall (1990) and Paul Gilroy (1992) on the middle passage, Caribbean migration, and black cultures in the United Kingdom. Cultural studies draws on theories of film, literature, and semiotics to understand the complex ways in which diasporic people negotiate life and produce culture "in between" cultural and geographical boundaries. These boundaries intersect and operate at multiple scales and levels (identity, the body, the social), with attention focusing on postcolonial subjectivities and collectivities in global cities and landscapes.

The unique Canadian context of migration and multiculturalism has provided a rich backdrop for exploration of diasporic literature and culture. A large number of acclaimed diasporic writers such as Rohinton Mistry, Dionne Brand, and Austin Clarke are situated in Canada, which has led to a focus in Canadian literary studies on diasporic literatures. Canadian diaspora and transnational studies has been inspired by the critical issues raised by these writers and their critics; these questions have prompted or informed significant research on Canadian immigration, antiracism, and critiques of multicultural social policy (Dei 1996; Bannerji 2000).

Interdisciplinary research on diaspora and transnationalism has in this way been concerned with connecting the analysis of cultural representations with the lived social and historical contexts of migrant people's lives. Avtar Brah's book *Cartographies of Diaspora: Contesting Identities* (1996) is situated in the discipline of sociology but draws a great deal on theorizations in literature and cultural studies. More recently, literary theorist Shalini Puri (2006) has argued that studies of diasporic and migrant culture and literature should incorporate social scientific approaches such as fieldwork and that a strong historical and social context is necessary.

The interplay between social scientific and humanist methodologies in approaching diaspora and transnationalism has resulted in provocative contributions to the theorization of these subjects. These analyses ask questions about how migrant people experience diaspora or transnationalism with longing, memory, and ambivalence (Agnew 2005) and about how transnational people reflect on and represent their experiences of racism, work, and family and community life.

## Organizing the Transnational

This volume has been prompted by some of the key questions and insights raised by the literature on transnationalism and diaspora. What is the relationship between immigrant incorporation and transnational engagements? Do transnational practices and identities end with "successful" incorporation? Are social exclusion, racism, and alienation the main explanations for diasporic identities, transnational engagements, and/or continued nostalgia and desire for "home"? What roles do sending country and receiving country policies play in generating or sustaining various forms of transnational engagement? How do class, education, gender, racialization, occupational trajectory, time in the host country, life cycle, and other social locations and variables interact to shape transnational ways of being and belonging?

These are the kinds of questions that research on transnationalism in the United States has been addressing and that work in other contexts, such as Europe and Canada, has examined as well. The chapters in this volume address these questions. They also broaden the range of discussion by analyzing the role of nonmigrant and nonstate actors in shaping transnational spaces and engagements. This move brings other institutions, policies, regulations, and processes into the analysis. For example, several authors examine the role of civil society organizations in host countries, as well as that of institutions such as the media and international law, in shaping transnational engagements.

## Institutions, Policies, and Identities

Research on migrant transnationalism and diaspora has demonstrated the importance of state policies and migrant agency in shaping transnational spaces (Basch et al. 1994). While globalization and capital flows provide an overarching context (Kearney 1995), states and their policies (or lack of policies) (Itzigsohn 2000; Goldring 2002; Smith 2003a), and im/migrants, particularly their organizations, social networks, remittances, and business activities, have occupied a privileged position in the literature (Portes, Guarnizo, and Landolt 1999; Landolt 2001; Portes, Haller, and Guarnizo 2002).

We join Levitt and Glick Schiller (2004) in arguing that transnational studies should include a broad set of institutional actors and processes.[11] The field will undoubtedly retain a focus on immigrants and state policies. However, just as Levitt (1998a, 2003) has argued for increased attention to religious life, the field can be pushed to include other institutional actors and more attention to contested meanings, identities, and the cultural politics of transnational life. Consistent with this agenda, the first part of this book raises theoretical questions and provides empirical analyses of state and nonstate institutional actors, arenas, and processes and the ways that they contribute to organizing identities within transnational spaces.

In the opening chapter, Myer Siemiatycki and Valerie Preston examine state and media constructions of Hong Kong–Canadian transnational spaces. Their analysis incorporates an overlooked institutional actor: the media. While the media and representations of immigrants have been prominent in cultural studies and diaspora studies, they have been less prominent in analyses of transnational social spaces. Siemiatycki and Preston analyze the English- and Chinese-language press and compare their representations of Hong Kong–Canadian transnationalism in Vancouver and Toronto during the period preceding and following Hong Kong's 1997 return to Chinese sovereignty. Siemiatycki and Preston find that "transnationalism 'reads' differently in the mainstream and newcomer community press." Their analysis shows the complex relationship between changes in immigration legislation, press coverage, and responses in the Hong Kong and mainstream communities. Here we see the contradiction between policies that attract a select group of immigrants and a mainstream public response that is not very welcoming. In the midst of this, immigrants cope with living in two worlds while they try to *fit in* in Canada.

Shifting to a supranational level, Susan Henders argues that international law is an arena where state-bound citizenship is being contested. She analyzes four types of postnational citizenship and considers their implications for transnational living and organizing. Henders shows that international law concerning human, indigenous, and minority rights and European citizenship may be incipient, but she demonstrates multiple ways that people make substantive citizenship claims, thereby pushing to expand citizenship in and through institutional arenas not bound by the state.

Sarah Wayland examines Tamil ethnic conflict and argues in favour of expanding the concept of political opportunity structure to include transnational actors. Her analysis shows that transnational networks have enabled the Liberation Tigers of Tamil Eelam (LTTE) to continue their insurgency against the Sri Lankan army. She also shows how immigrants and refugees settled in liberal democratic states such as Canada can play active roles in the international scene given their freedom of movement and their ability to raise funds and channel them and other resources. In an innovative move in the post-9/11 security context, Wayland closes with the suggestion that diasporas can become effective partners in the management of homeland conflict.

Uzma Shakir, an immigrant advocate, analyzes Canadian immigration and settlement policies. She argues that these policies, together with Canadian racism, have led to transnational engagements that are not only reactive (a response to marginalization) but also somewhat involuntary. Although she does not use this phrase, *forced transnationalism* would be an apt way to describe the homeland connections maintained with family members whose entry was made impossible by exclusionary and racist immigration laws, including the head tax and the continuous journey stipulation (as was the case for Chinese and South Asians in the first half of the twentieth century). While not so forced, there is also a degree of involuntary transnationalism when professionals maintain ties because of difficulties with credential recognition or employment or because social exclusion and racism make one feel a perpetual longing to go "home." Shakir's view that contemporary South Asian immigrants' engagement in Canadian politics is limited by transnational commitments differs from that of other contributors to this volume. Sarah Wayland, Aparna Sundar, and Philip Kelly argue that the Asian immigrant groups whom they work with or write about are, in diverse ways, actively engaged in community politics in Canada and with Canadian political institutions. Shakir's position as a community-based activist offers a different perspective on political and social engagement and a unique way of interpreting the concept of the transnational.

The last chapter in this section, by Leela Viswanathan, offers the perspective of someone who crosses the boundaries between activist and researcher in her daily life. Viswanathan raises provocative questions about academic research and ethics. For example, she questions the use of terms such as transnationalism, arguing that immigrants in the racialized communities with whom she has worked are more interested in incorporation than in homeland ties. With respect to research ethics, Viswanathan's experiences as a community social planner and then doctoral student confirm her advocacy for greater effective collaboration between community organizations and researchers in all phases of the research process.

## States, Transnational Labour, and Diasporic Capital

Part 2 of this volume focuses on emerging dynamics and relations between state actors and policies, migrants and their organizations, and Canadian civil society. Three chapters analyze the experiences of women and men admitted to Canada on temporary work visas (Díaz Barrero's chapter on exotic dancers and chapters by Kerry Preibisch and Ofelia Becerril on the Seasonal Agricultural Workers Program). One chapter presents an interview with Stan Raper, a labour organizer who works on campaigns regarding noncitizen workers. The other two chapters in this section provide analyses of labour and refugee-exporting states (Pablo Bose on India) and migrant organizations (R. Cheran on Sri Lanka).

The three chapters on temporary workers show that women and men choose to enter Canada in one of the few legal means available to them in order to support themselves and their families. Because economic and social conditions in their places of origin do not offer them opportunities to earn enough to lead lives with dignity, they endure separation from children and partners. Because they enter legally, but on limited-term visas that are only good for the individual worker, their social marginality is produced through immigration and employment policies that prevent family migration and limit their rights and then reproduced through employment relations and conditions that frame them as temporary and not needing or deserving protection equal to that of citizen workers. These three authors' findings are consistent with work on domestic and temporary workers in Canada (Bakan and Stasiulis 1997; Sharma 2001; Basok 2002). In addition, they offer methodological innovations and theoretical insights. Preibisch broadens the customary analytical lens of both Canadian labour and transnational studies to include workers from Mexico and the Caribbean as well as Canadian civil society. Her analysis goes beyond findings of social exclusion to show that community organizations have begun to organize with and for the workers. In doing so, Preibisch challenges conceptions of isolated agricultural workers with little or no connection to Canadian society. Instead, we see the emergence of transnational social fields that include not only the workers and their families back home but also the communities in which they spend significant parts of their working lives.

Díaz Barrero adds to this literature by examining the relatively unknown and short-lived temporary worker program for "exotic dancers." She identifies the strong transnational familial commitments maintained by the women, because the only way that they can enter Canada is through a program that does not permit them to bring their families. At the same time, she provides evidence of their desire to organize to change their living and working conditions, and she offers recommendations for those wishing to engage in such organizing. Becerril's contribution lies in her gender analysis of both employer strategies and worker responses as well as her incorporation of organized labour and other civil society responses to the macrolevel political economy of agricultural production and labour supply in the horticultural sector in southwestern Ontario. Her framing around the concept of "cultural struggle" recasts class-based approaches to worker responses by emphasizing the cultural terrain in which practices are given meaning.

Raper's account of the Canadian labour movement's response to seasonal migrant agricultural workers provides insights into the development of this civil society response to state efforts to support the industry through the temporary workers program. Raper describes how organized labour has pushed the Canadian state to expand the rights and benefits available to seasonal workers through a series of court challenges and, at the same time, worked with other civil society actors to provide services to these workers in southwestern Ontario. This is obviously an ongoing story, one worth watching as the state expands and modifies temporary worker programs to other countries, such as Guatemala, and other sectors outside agriculture (e.g., construction).

The chapters on the state and capital's construction of temporary workers, and the various transnational social fields generated by people living transnational work lives, are interspersed with two chapters that examine another node in the state-capital-labour nexus. The chapters by Cheran and Bose illustrate different sets of relations between states and emigrants. Both chapters emphasize the important contributions made to development activities by transnationals. However, in Bose's analysis of Indian policy, the state's initiatives are aimed at courting the overseas population, whereas in Cheran's discussion of Tamil networks it is clear that they operate against the state. These chapters serve to drive home the importance of distinguishing between cases in which migrants leave as refugees opposed to the regime and those in which migrants are not in opposition to the state. Both chapters draw attention to the costs and challenges associated with diasporic investment and engagement.

Cheran's chapter on Tamil community networks in Canada (and beyond) analyzes the social capital and other resources that these networks mobilize for development activities in their politically contested homeland. His analysis echoes findings from work on Mexican hometown organizations that emphasizes the social capital of transnational migrant associations and their ability to mobilize resources to help finance roads, schools, and other community infrastructure. However, as he points out, Tamil village and alumni networks do not work with the Sri Lankan state or other institutions. Rather, they avoid the state and generally work with the opposition. His chapter provides an alternative conceptualization of the social capital of transnational Tamil networks as including not only financial flows sent by diasporic organizations but also all the expertise, equipment, and other elements involved in reconstruction, relief, and development work. Cheran's discussion shows how, in this diaspora, transnational engagement is shaped primarily by shared political minority status, politicized collective identities, opposition movement networks, and the political context in the homeland rather than by social exclusion in Canada or Europe, homeland state policies courting emigrants, or other factors.

Bose analyzes a very different state-diaspora relationship that gives rise to a particular form of transnational engagement: the involvement of Indians in the diaspora in several development activities in India. He examines national and subnational (Gujarat and Kerala) efforts to attract diasporic capital for development, and he provides a case study of an urban development project in Kolkata that has substantial ownership by nonresident Indians (NRIs) and persons of Indian origin (PIOs). His work shows how investments by Indians in the diaspora may have negative outcomes from a social injustice perspective. Diasporic capital invested in hydroelectric dams may displace local populations, and housing developments may offer amenities to the wealthy but further marginalize the rest of the population.

Bose's work makes two important contributions. First, it provides evidence of transnational engagements among relatively well-off immigrants. In addition to noting socioeconomic and regional differences within the Indian diaspora, Bose demonstrates that economic exclusion is not the only explanation for transnational engagement among Canadian immigrants – although, read together with Shakir's and Viswanathan's chapters, we must remember that wealth does not necessarily mitigate racism. Second, it joins scholarship that questions the celebratory tone of some of the literature on transnationalism by pointing to some of the real costs of this engagement, particularly for less geographically and economically mobile sectors of the population.

**Transnational Organizing and Social Change**
The chapters in the third section of this volume examine a variety of ways in which transnational networks and diasporic communities in Canada (and elsewhere) organize to effect social change in various geographical and institutional sites and scales. In many ways, this section continues themes that are present in the second section. However, the chapters in this section deepen the discussion by drawing attention to the comparative analysis of different contexts of reception, transnational civil society organizing, and diverse challenges associated with the transnational and "national" political participation of migrants and refugees.

Patricia Landolt's analysis of Salvadoran refugees in Los Angeles and Toronto provides an excellent model for studies that compare how different receiving contexts, particularly their immigration and refugee policies, and the institutional landscape in general, produce distinct patterns of network development, settlement, incorporation, and transnational engagements among apparently similar refugee populations. Differences between the two countries and the two cities contributed to the development of strong transnational organizations and identities in Los Angeles, whereas in Toronto Salvadorans became involved in different types of organizations, and institutionalized transnational engagements were not long lasting.

Aparna Sundar addresses the theme of difference *within* diasporic or transnational communities in the context of an activist organization. She describes the activities of the South Asian Left Democratic Alliance (SALDA), an organization of people from different parts of the region who share a political agenda: organizing for democracy and human rights and against the Hindu nationalist political party in India. The group organizes transnationally (regarding India) and does a great deal of "local" work among South Asians in Canada in an effort to educate youth and others. Sundar's analysis pushes the usual boundaries of "the transnational" by focusing on another form of locally and translocally engaged transnational community. The group itself, and the region with which members identify, present opportunities as well as challenges, which Sundar analyzes with critical reflexivity. In particular, she notes the challenges of working with a "community" that is divided in terms of generation, religion, politics, national origin, political culture, et cetera. This chapter and the earlier one by Bose provide excellent antidotes to romantic views of transnational engagements.

Philip Kelly analyzes the political participation of Filipinos in Toronto. He argues in favour of using a broad definition of political participation that includes nonelectoral activism and takes into account homeland political involvement and affiliation. His chapter shows how political divisions related to homeland politics (pro- and anti-Marcos positions) generated divisions among Filipino immigrants in the Toronto area, limiting opportunities for broad-based mobilization and electoral representation. At the same time, these positions fostered alliances among people who later worked in the context of Canadian political institutions. Thus, his work shows that transnational political engagement may have mixed effects with respect to political integration in the society of settlement. It also shows the importance of understanding class, political, and other divisions within a "community" that is usually treated as homogeneous.

Rusa Jeremic shows how a Canadian coalition of labour, churches, students, international development NGOs, and other social organizations joined the Hemispheric Social Alliance (HSA), a broad-based network of national coalitions and regional networks from many countries in the hemisphere. Together these groups have organized transnationally to challenge the Free Trade Agreement of the Americas (FTAA). Jeremic's chapter convincingly shows that civil society organizations can operate at local and national levels, as well as transnationally, to work to prevent international trade agreements considered to have negative consequences for civil society in all of the affected countries. These activists are embedded in a form of transnational community that is based not on common nationality, ethnicity, religion, et cetera but on a common social and political agenda. While some might argue that these groups are best seen as social movements and discussed in a separate literature, we argue that, if we are seeking an understanding of Canadian transnationalism as complex and multilayered, then there must be room to include the transnational engagements of civil society, not only those of immigrant communities.

The last chapter in this section presents the experiences of two Peruvian immigrants living in Toronto who have participated in the Peruvian government's Council for Peruvians abroad. This council is an example of the institutions being created by some emigrant-producing countries to channel the participation of emigrants – some would argue in order to foster good relations and maintain remittance flows. The firsthand account of the two Peruvians' experiences with this council speaks to the interest that migrants have in participating in home country institutions as well as to the tensions that arise in that process.

## Conclusion

The range of countries from which newcomers come to Canada is extremely diverse.[12] There is consensus regarding the crucial role of contexts of departure and reception in shaping immigrant incorporation. If we extend the argument to include transnational engagements as well as incorporation, then it should not be surprising that there is variation in the transnational and diasporic engagements and identities of immigrants from Asia and Latin America in Canada. Taken together, chapters that present case studies of immigrants or temporary workers from countries such as India, Sri Lanka, the Philippines, El Salvador, or Mexico demonstrate the variety of reasons and opportunities for, and constraints on, transnational engagements. Landolt's chapter makes the additional contribution of showing how changes in different receiving country contexts shape different patterns of incorporation for people from the same country.

These chapters make several contributions to the literature on transnationalism. First, the book presents analyses of more and less voluntary forms of transnational engagements among several groups of migrants and immigrants in Canada. Read alongside the existing literature, the chapters highlight the continuing presence of transnational communities and diasporas in Canada. Historically, Chinese and South Asian immigrants kept in touch with family members who could not emigrate to Canada. Currently, temporary workers in precarious labour markets do the same thing. At the same time, middle-class Filipinos, Tamils, successful Indian immigrants, and activist South Asians are involved in a variety of transnational engagements.

This suggests that it is important to go beyond binary questions such as whether transnationalism is more prevalent among groups that experience systematic social and economic exclusion or whether transnational engagements are associated with successful immigrant incorporation.[13] The alternative is to develop complex, multi-path, and multi-outcome models that take into account the contexts of departure and reception, including refugee policies, political relations with the home state, media portrayals, interaction between civil society and im/migrants, and so forth.

Second, the chapters point to the importance of taking into account institutions and institutional actors that include, but are not limited to, states and migrants. The media, international law, NGOs, unions, and other civil society organizations can play important roles in the construction of transnational social fields and spaces and in the process of incorporation.

Third, it is useful to balance academic analyses with work produced by activists, particularly immigrant activists. They may have a less sanguine view of transnationalism as they work to reduce social exclusion and make a more secure and meaningful "place" for themselves in Canadian society.

Fourth, the specificity of the Canadian context, and that of other contexts of reception, needs to be taken into account in discussions about diaspora and transnationalism.[14] US and northern European contexts of reception differ from the Canadian context, not only in terms of policies, but also in terms of "who gets in" and under what conditions. The diversity of source countries and not sharing a border with a poorer country, as the United States does with Mexico, make for different configurations of immigrant and diasporic communities. Further research is needed in order to compare pathways to incorporation and transnationalism in the Canadian context. This volume is one contribution toward that goal.

### Acknowledgments
We are grateful to Peter Vandergeest and Alissa Goldring for comments on an earlier version of this introduction.

### Notes
1 In many cases, transnational activities are oriented toward a real or putative homeland. However, conflict, migration patterns, and other factors may contribute to a decentring of transnational engagements to other regions of settlement of diaspora populations. Examples include the experience of Guyanese whose main corridors of activity are in the United States and Canada, with little return to or involvement in Guyana, and Kurds in various countries in Europe who, despite organizing politically around the project of establishing a Kurdish homeland, engage with several states of settlement and origin.
2 See Winland (1998) and Hyndman and Walton-Roberts (2000) for early articles on Canadian-based transnationalism, and see Satzewich and Wong (2006) for a recent compilation on the topic.
3 The journal *Canadian Ethnic Studies* began publication in 1969 and is indicative of these trends.
4 Simmons (1998) refers to this change as a shift from racist to neoracist immigration policy. He argues that changes introduced under Pierre Trudeau in the 1970s reflected Canada's concern with its standing in the world system of states, which pushed Canada to adopt colour-blind immigration policies. He also argues that the policies did not go as far as being antiracist since they did not involve measures to explicitly work toward eliminating racism from immigration and settlement policies and related practices. Vilna Bashi (2004) makes a similar argument.
5 The context of reception can include immigration, citizenship, and settlement policies; education systems and policies toward immigrant children and youth; prevailing attitudes, practices, and legislation regarding racism; access to language training; access to services such as health; patterns of residential concentration; and so forth (Portes and Boröcz 1989).
6 See Basok (2002) and the work of Díaz Barrero, Preibisch, and Becerril in this volume and elsewhere for examples of work that addresses issues of transnationalism among temporary workers. Authors such as Sharma (2001) and Ruth Magali San Martin (2004) analyze the experiences of temporary workers and their rights but not in the context of the literature on transnationalism or diaspora.
7 See the introduction to Michael Smith and Luis Guarnizo's (1998) collection on *Transnationalism from Below* for an excellent discussion of transnationalism from above and transnationalism from below, which are distinguished by differences in power and agency. While this distinction is quite useful, scholars also recognize the interrelationship between state- and migrant-led initiatives as well as the roles of other institutional actors.
8 Bridget Anderson (2001) used "transnational community" to describe a London-based association of domestic workers from several countries. This innovative use of the term

stretches the often single-country or monoethnic use of the term *transnational,* a semantic problem not lost on some critics of transnationalism (Waldinger and Fitzgerald 2004).

9 While it is useful to distinguish between these traditions, it is important to note that some individuals have engaged in both kinds of work. Work conducted in Europe has followed a different trajectory.

10 The number of studies is not large; however, the range of national and ethnic groups covered by transnational studies in Canada is impressive. For example, see Winland (1995, 1998) on Croatians, Hyndman and Walton-Roberts (2000) on Burmese, Walton-Roberts (2001) on Punjabis, Waters (2002) and Wong and Ng (2002) on Chinese, Nolin (2004) on Guatemalans, Wong (2000, 2003) and Owusu (2003) on Ghanaians, Duval (2004) on Eastern Caribbeans, Sherrell and Hyndman (2006) on Kosovars, and Landolt (in this volume) on Salvadorans.

11 We are mindful of the concerns raised by Glick Schiller's (2005) critique of methodological nationalism: assuming that nation and nationality are key in organizing migrants' identities and forms of social organization and using nationality as a taken-for-granted starting point and unit of analysis in migration and immigration research. At the same time, we consider it important to study how nation and nationality become significant in organizing the transnational. This approach allows our contributors to analyze the organization of the transnational through Canadian policies aimed at specific countries of origin, such as the Seasonal Agricultural Workers Program, as well as sending state policies, for example in India and Peru. Levitt and Glick Schiller (2004) clearly resonate with our insistence on considering the role of nonstate actors and institutions in organizing the transnational.

12 The foreign-born population in the United States is dominated by a single group: Mexicans account for nearly one-third of this population. In Canada, the country that leads the "top ten" list of source countries is the United Kingdom. Approximately one-tenth of all immigrants come from there (MPI 2004d).

13 Hiebert and Ley (2003) conducted one of the few surveys of Canadian immigrant transnationalism in Vancouver, documenting varying levels of economic and sociocultural transnationalism. They found that transnational activity was more likely to be found among respondents with lower indicators of incorporation in Canadian society (e.g., less time in Canada, lack of identification with Canada, and citizenship only in the country of origin). Overall, the longer respondents had been in Canada and the more they identified with Canadian society, the less likely they were to engage in transnational activities. The authors concluded that, unlike in the United States, where transnational engagement can occur alongside incorporation and can thus be interpreted as a subset of incorporation, in Canada transnationalism is an alternative to incorporation since it is associated with a lack of incorporation.

14 Hiebert and Ley's (2003) findings suggest that there is something about the Canadian context that, over time, discourages transnationalism or attenuates the need for it. It was not within the scope of their study to investigate *why* transnationalism appeared to decline with incorporation, but the findings imply either that immigrant selection, settlement policies, attitudes toward immigrants, and/or other aspects of the Canadian context of reception encourage the entry of people who are less likely to engage in transnational activity in the first place or that newcomers experience incorporation in Canada in a way that reduces transnational tendencies over time. It is also possible, however, that the overwhelmingly East Asian sample is not generalizable to localities where the immigrant population differs in terms of national origin concentrations, recency, immigrant class, or other factors. (The ethnic origin of Hiebert and Ley's sample had the following breakdown: 42 percent East Asian, 28 percent European/Canadian, 17 percent South Asian, 7 percent Southeast Asian, and 2 percent each for Latin American and Arab/West Asian.)

# Part 1
# Institutions, Policies, and Identities

# Part 1
# Institutions, Policies, and Identities

# 1

# State and Media Construction of Transnational Communities: A Case Study of Recent Migration from Hong Kong to Canada

*Myer Siemiatycki and Valerie Preston*

By the late twentieth century, talk of transnationalism was no longer confined to academic circles. In Canada, both recent migrants and longtime residents were increasingly coming to reflect on the meaning of living in "the transnational moment" (Tölölyan 1996), as people more intensely than ever maintained "sustained ties of persons, networks and organizations across the borders of multiple nation-states" (Faist 1999, 2). Canadian media showed particular interest in reporting the migration story of Hong Kong newcomers to Canada. For eleven consecutive years – from 1987 to 1997 – this British colony of scarcely 6 million people constituted the largest single source "country" of newcomers to Canada.

Speaking to reporters, recent Hong Kong migrants to Canada expressed both the complexities and the ambiguities of their transnational lives. Milton Wong, the Vancouver-based CEO of a multibillion-dollar investment fund management firm, emphasized to the *Globe and Mail* of 19 November 1997 how transnationalism was recasting citizenship norms: "There will always be a shuttle back and forth from Hong Kong now," Wong explained, since across the Pacific Rim "a new citizenship concept is emerging – a foot in two places – and Vancouver is one of those places" (D3). Kitty Cheung told the *Toronto Star* of 10 July 1997 how disorienting living with "a foot in two places" could be: "We're confused. We can feel it from our hearts. There are little pieces of Canada, Hong Kong and China inside us. But we just don't know where our home is" (SC 4).

Meanwhile, English-language media discourse frequently contended that Hong Kong migrants were insufficiently attached to Canada. Writing in the *Toronto Star* of 14 June 1996, University of Toronto professor John Crispo complained that Canada's immigration policies were allowing Hong Kong migrants to buy their way into Canada, without "making a meaningful commitment to real Canadian citizenship" (A13). And in a letter to the *Vancouver Sun* of 2 July 1997, Dal Wagner complained that for some Hong Kong migrants to Canada "loyalty to country and pride of citizenship apparently are nothing more than a ledger sheet ... What a sad day for Canada that we tolerate such attitudes and such people!" (A14).

How did the Hong Kong experience of transnationalism in Canada become so contested and charged? The large migration from Hong Kong to Canada during the 1980s and 1990s provides compelling evidence of the potent roles of state and media in framing and interpreting transnational behaviours. Hong Kong immigrants were aggressively recruited by the Canadian state on terms that promoted strong transnational ties. Eager to attract wealthy Hong Kong immigrants, the Canadian government promoted a highly commodified regime of immigration and citizenship. Yet if the state could be instrumental in its selection of newcomers, media and the government would often hold immigrants themselves to a higher standard of obligation to the receiving society.

In this chapter, we explore tensions and contradictions in state and media constructions of the Hong Kong–Canadian transnational experience. Government policies initially advantaged the entry of business class migrants; later, the state reexamined its citizenship policies related to transnational behaviour. This occurred in a climate where leading English-Canadian newspapers were problematizing the transnationalism of Hong Kong migrants. Interrogating this image of the Hong Kong community, we examine the Chinese-language press, where we find a newcomer community actively engaging in Canadian society – and debating how best to live with "a foot in two places." A significant finding of our work is that transnationalism "reads" differently in the mainstream and newcomer community press. An examination of proposed changes in citizenship policies suggests modifications that respond to the criticisms of transnational behaviours raised in the English-language media. Ironically, the proposed changes in legislation also encourage the Hong Kong community to be politically engaged, confirming the community's views of itself as wanting to participate fully in Canadian society.

## The Transnational Trajectory of Hong Kong Migrants

Hong Kong's modern history bred a transnational sensibility among its residents. Hong Kong embodies an extraordinary legacy: as a British colony destined for reunification with China, as an economic powerhouse with global reach, and as a site of both substantial immigration and emigration (Pan 1999). By the end of the twentieth century, residents of Hong Kong had developed a multiplicity of civic identities: Hong Kong resident, Chinese ethnicity, and British subject. There was also a finely tuned predilection to seek security in the face of perceived danger. The colony had on several occasions experienced dramatic population shifts. During four years of Japanese occupation in the Second World War, the colony experienced massive return migration of its residents to China. Conversely, the postwar period saw even greater numbers move from China to Hong Kong in the wake of Communist rule. The uncertainties and anxieties preceding Hong Kong's reunification with China on 1 July 1997 would prompt another spike in emigration.

Throughout the twentieth century, Hong Kong evolved from a regional trading hub to a major global city. David Meyer describes Hong Kong as "the pivot of decision-making about the exchange of capital within Asia and between that region and the rest of the world" (2000, 1). The thriving city's credentials include the world's largest container port and air cargo port, the largest Asian site for regional headquarters of multinational firms, the world's fourth largest gold market, and the fifth biggest foreign exchange trading centre in the world (Meyer 2000, 207-21). Hong Kong has clearly reaped great advantage from its position as the West's entrée to the world's largest market. Hong Kong is also typical of global cities with a highly polarized population, home to large numbers of both wealthy and impoverished residents (Sassen 1994). Writing on the eve of the colony's return to Chinese sovereignty, Roger Buckley observed that "Hong Kong is glamour and misery" (1997, 146). As we will see, it was Hong Kong residents enjoying the former not latter lifestyle that Canadian immigration policy focused on attracting.

In the dozen years prior to the colony's reunification with China, Hong Kong lost about 10 percent of its population to emigration. Some 600,000 residents left the city-colony between 1985 and 1997 (Meyer 2000, 220-21). Fears over the consequences of reunification were the chief factor in emigration. The impending transfer conjured up the "incongruity of combining a rich, capitalist city-state with an impoverished nation ruled by a Communist Party hierarchy" (Meyer 2000, 220). A recurring theme in the literature on Hong Kong's "Appointment with China" is the anxiety that it unleashed among local residents and their desperation to secure a foreign passport "as an insurance policy against things going wrong after 1997" (Skeldon 1999, 69; see also Buckley 1997; Tsang 1997; Meyer 2000).

Yet fear of reunification with China was not the only prompt for the great Hong Kong migration. Beyond anxieties felt at home lay opportunities abroad. Ronald Skeldon regards Hong Kong's migrants not simply as fearful political refugees but also as harbingers of a new world economic order: "Hong Kong migrants are as much bold pioneers in transnational commerce as they are reluctant exiles. The emigrants are part of a global movement of the highly skilled that is linking centres of economic dynamism around the world" (1999, 68). Indeed, the literature on the Hong Kong migration widely echoes Meyer's characterization of the preponderance of those who left Hong Kong in the 1980s and 1990s as an "emigrant elite" (2000, 243; see Buckley 1997; Tsang 1997; Li 1998; Ng 1999). As we will see, it was the immigration policies of receiving countries such as Canada that determined the socioeconomic composition of the Hong Kong migration and therefore shaped its transnational experience.

During the 1980s and 1990s, Canada was the destination of choice for Hong Kong migrants. From 1987 through 1997, more than 314,000 immigrants to Canada cited Hong Kong as their last "country" of permanent residence. This accounted for more than half of the total emigration flow from Hong Kong in this period and comprised over 13 percent – almost one in seven – of all immigrant arrivals to Canada in these years (Citizenship and Immigration Canada 1997; Meyer 2000, 220-21). The vast majority of these newcomers settled in the Vancouver and Toronto metropolitan areas, home to over 80 percent of Canada's Hong Kong community by 1996. While Toronto had a larger number of Hong Kong-born immigrants than Vancouver – in 1996, the respective totals were 110,995 and 86,210 – the community's relative urban impact has been greater in Vancouver. By 1996, Hong Kong was the birthplace of 13.6 percent of all immigrants living in the Vancouver metropolitan area, compared with only a 6.3 percent share of the Toronto metropolitan area's immigrant population. In Vancouver, almost one in every four immigrants arriving between 1991 and 1996 came from Hong Kong; in Toronto, the ratio was one in ten. So, although Hong Kong immigrants were the single largest group of immigrants to settle in the Toronto area between 1991 and 1996, they comprised only one of many large immigrant flows into the city. In Vancouver, in contrast, immigrants from Hong Kong outnumbered all other recent arrivals by a substantial margin (Statistics Canada 1997).

## Sold on Canada

Canada's success in attracting immigrants from Hong Kong owed much to the aggressive recruitment campaigns initiated by Canada's federal and provincial governments. Particularly helpful was having a Business Immigration Program already in place, aimed at luring foreign entrepreneurs and investors to Canada. In 1978, the Canadian government added "Entrepreneur" and "Self-Employed" categories to the Independent Immigrant Class of admissions to Canada. In 1986, Brian Mulroney's government introduced a third "Investor Category." Eligibility required applicants to have a proven business track record, a minimum net worth of $500,000, and commitment to invest $250,000 to $500,000 over a three- or five-year period depending on which province they intended to settle in. With few educational and language requirements, the new categories constituted an exclusive high-speed laneway into Canada for those who might otherwise not have qualified (Li 1998; Ley 2003). Trevor Harrison has described this "commodification of immigration policy" as driven by the Canadian state's fiscal, economic, and political goals (1996, 9). According to the government's calculation, wealthy immigrants would stimulate the economy and create employment

– without requiring social assistance or invoking public skepticism over the arrival of needy newcomers.

Linking immigration overtly to capital investment, the Canadian state explicitly transformed immigration and citizenship into an instrumental transaction. Canada would give preferential entry to those who would invest capital in the country. The government's motivation was expressed in a parliamentary report from the Standing Committee on Labour, Employment, and Immigration stating that "not enough attention has been paid to the potential for using immigration policy to facilitate economic and labour-market growth, to maintain, or enhance, current Canadian living standards for old and new Canadians, and to help smooth out economic and labour market fluctuations" (cited in De Mont and Fennell 1989, 93). The aim of the new approach was to attract immigrants "with substantial capital and business experience to Canada" (Li 1998, 131).

Leaving little to chance, Canada aggressively set out to recruit a business class of immigrants by offering an open door and citizenship in exchange for promises of investment. Nowhere did Canada make this pitch with greater zeal than in Hong Kong. Margaret Cannon described Hong Kong in the late 1980s as "a most-favoured hunting ground for corporate and governmental wolves from Australia, Singapore and Canada, all of whom are licking their chops over all that money and all those rich emigrants Communism is likely to scatter across the globe on or before July 1, 1997, when the British hand over the colony to the PRC" (1989, 11). Canada's recruitment campaign was in a league of its own. "No other Western country has engineered such a blatant grab for Hong Kong's elite and their wealth," two Canadian journalists wrote (De Mont and Fennell 1989, 81). To be sure, Canada had much to offer prospective Hong Kong migrants: political stability, a reputation for embracing multiculturalism, continued links to Britain under the umbrella of the British Commonwealth, a fine school system, and one of the quickest citizenship acquisition protocols in the world, requiring residency of only three years. Teams of Canadian federal, provincial, and municipal officials went to work in Hong Kong – with ample reinforcements of immigration lawyers, accountants, and real estate agents primed to sell Canada to nervous businesspeople and professionals in the colony.

Hong Kong proved by far to be the greatest source of entrants to Canada under the business class (Ley 2003). Canada took in far more worldwide business immigrants during the 1980s and 1990s than Australia or the United States (Wong 2004, 125) and considerably more immigrants from Hong Kong in particular than any other country (Pan 1999). Indeed, in some years, the proportion of total Hong Kong emigrants headed for Canada was estimated as high as 60 percent, as Paul Watson noted in the *Toronto Star* of 16 April 1996 (A2). Although most Hong Kong migrants entered Canada through either the Independent Immigrant ("point system") or the Family

Unification class, between one-quarter and one-third of Hong Kong migrants to Canada entered under the business class (Skeldon 1994, 33). Importantly, Hong Kong immigrants predominated among Canada's business immigrants. Between 1986 and 1996, Hong Kong accounted for 47 percent of all investor category entrants to Canada, 40 percent of all entrepreneurs, and 17 percent of all self-employed admissions (De Mont and Fennell 1989, 133). Vancouver was the preferred destination for business class immigrants, who were less educated and less fluent in English than the other categories of Hong Kong immigrants to Canada (Ley 2003).

Canadian immigration policies and practices served to construct a hyper-mobile and commodified form of transnationalism. Yet the same attributes that made Hong Kong immigrants so attractive to the Canadian state (their wealth, business experience, and economic assets) also raised a number of tensions that unfolded after they were admitted to Canada. If migrant investors with business experience and capital from their homeland were being recruited to Canada, could they be expected to spend significant time away from their Hong Kong investments? If employment and business prospects in Canada proved disappointing, wouldn't some return to work back home? What impact would these patterns of travel have on Hong Kong migrant families? How would potential absentee adult migrants fulfill their residency requirement for securing Canadian citizenship? What claim should the Canadian state have on income earned by migrants on their foreign assets in Hong Kong? These were some of the redefinitions of "belonging in Canada" that unfolded from the Canadian state's instrumental approach to Hong Kong migration between 1986 and 1997.

## Media Representation of Hong Kong–Canadian Transnationalism

The media played a crucial role in public debates about Hong Kong immigration and Hong Kong immigrants' citizenship rights (Lee et al. 2002, 3). The image of wealthy Hong Kong investors buying their way into Canada quickly took hold in the Canadian media by the late 1980s. The titles of two early books about Hong Kong migration to Canada suggest the ambivalence with which Hong Kong immigrants were being presented to Canadians. Appearing simultaneously in bookstores in 1989 were Margaret Cannon's *China Tide: The Revealing Story of the Hong Kong Exodus to Canada* and *Hong Kong Money: How Chinese Families and Fortunes Are Changing Canada,* by John De Mont and Thomas Fennell. Developed from earlier articles in leading Canadian magazines (*Canadian Business* and *Maclean's,* respectively), the publication date of these books attests to how quickly the Hong Kong migration was registering as a matter of national import in Canada.

Both books characterized Hong Kong migrants to Canada as super rich, "the richest immigrants in Canadian history," arriving "in Gucci shoes and

Giorgio Armani suits." "The new Hong Kong immigrants," Cannon predicted, "are going to be making money eighteen hours a day" (1989, 11, 10, 26). This would simply be business as usual, according to De Mont and Fennell, since "the vast majority of Hong Kong immigrants entering Canada under business and investor immigration categories are millionaires, with a few billionaires thrown in for good measure" (1989, 19).

While both books emphasized the economic benefits that Canada could derive from Hong Kong migrants, they also warned about potential pitfalls. Concerns were raised particularly over the extent of business migrants' commitment to Canada. "The cold truth," Cannon asserted, "is that some Hong Kong Chinese want Canadian citizenship but do not necessarily want Canada" (1989, 217). The claim that these newcomers were pursuing Canadian citizenship if necessary, but not necessarily a life in Canada would be the recurring criticism levelled against Hong Kong migrants in the English-language press.

Our examination of English-language press coverage of Canada's Hong Kong community is bounded by time, space, and source. We have focused on the period from 1995 to 2000, which spans the years immediately preceding and following the 1997 reversion of Hong Kong to Chinese sovereignty. The largest-circulation local newspapers in Toronto (the *Toronto Star*) and Vancouver (the *Vancouver Sun*) were selected for analysis.

Relying on content analysis as our principal research method, we searched two databases (The Canadian News Disk and Dow Jones Interactive) for all articles containing the terms *immigration* and *Hong Kong*. Upon review, 231 stories were selected as relevant, 156 from the *Vancouver Sun* and 75 from the *Toronto Star*.[1] The flavour and emphasis of much of what appeared in print may be captured from headlines appearing in 1996. Readers of the *Vancouver Sun* that year learned, "Rising Hong Kong Influx Predicted: That Doesn't Mean Vancouver Will Become Hongcouver, an Immigrant Adviser Says"; "Investor-Immigrant Program Altered to Halt Abuse"; "Wealthy Asian Immigrants 'Set to Flee' over Taxes"; and "Give Chinese Immigrants Due Credit." In a similar vein in 1996, *Toronto Star* headlines declared, "Canadian Banks out to Woo Wealthy Hong Kong Immigrants"; "Hong Kong Money Likes the GTA" (Greater Toronto Area); and "New Canadians with Global Connections."

Through content analysis, we identified and quantified transnational themes discussed in the press. We assessed the prominence of each theme by counting the number of lines of news text devoted to it. Admittedly a rough estimate of the relative importance assigned to a topic, the count provides an initial means of identifying what the media found of interest in the Hong Kong migration. Transnational dynamics of return migration, "astronaut" lifestyles, business class migration, and taxation predominated.

Nodes related to return migration from Vancouver generated a total of 1,176 lines of news text coverage, and the comparable figure for Toronto was 140 lines. "Astronaut" lifestyles generated 561 lines of text in Vancouver and 13 in Toronto. Business class migrants are the subject of 1,115 lines of text in Vancouver and 44 in Toronto. Criminal activity in the Hong Kong community received 755 lines of coverage for Vancouver and none for Toronto. Coverage of Canada's offshore assets declaration law was extensive in Vancouver, where it was discussed in 864 lines, but it was completely absent in Toronto. Negative stereotyping was also more prevalent in Vancouver. Stories portraying Hong Kong migrants as rich globetrotters, as abusers of Canadian citizenship, or as negligent toward their families generated 928 text lines in Vancouver and 248 in Toronto. Vancouver also generated the most text regarding the positive economic impacts of Hong Kong migration: 1,372 lines versus 407 in Toronto. Diversity within Canada's Hong Kong community was discussed rarely, leaving a monolithic impression of the Hong Kong diaspora as a wealthy, hypermobile community minimally rooted in Canada.

Several points emerge from this survey of press coverage of Hong Kong transnationalism. A first point is its considerably greater play in Vancouver than Toronto. Several factors may explain this contrast. Part of the discrepancy may reflect a newcomer community that commands attention by virtue of its *relatively* larger size in Vancouver than Toronto. Editorial orientation may be a second contributing factor. Central to the *Toronto Star*'s outlook, image, and marketing strategy is its self-promotion as the progressive champion of diversity in Toronto (Hackett and Gruneau 2000). This "multiculturalism-positive" perspective may incline the editors to avoid stories that cast newcomer communities in a negative or suggestively disloyal light. Conversely, criticism of Canada's immigration policies and their outcomes was characteristic of Hollinger-chain papers (including the *Vancouver Sun*) at this time (Hackett and Gruneau 2000). Differences in press coverage may also reflect stronger transnational ties among Hong Kong migrants in Vancouver than Toronto. Immigrants who plan or need to return to Hong Kong regularly are more likely to settle in Vancouver. It is one of the western world's leading hubs for flights to Hong Kong. By air, the Pacific city is five hours closer than Toronto to Hong Kong. Despite having a larger Hong Kong–origin population than Vancouver, Toronto also had half as many regularly scheduled direct flights to Hong Kong. In the summer of 2000, Vancouver had twenty-eight direct flights per week to Hong Kong compared with fourteen from Toronto. The large number of direct flights from Vancouver to Hong Kong exceeded those of cities such as Paris, Frankfurt, Zurich, Los Angeles, San Francisco, and Chicago (Airport Authority, Hong Kong 2000).

A second theme in the Vancouver and Toronto press coverage was the instrumentality of transnationalism. If Hong Kong migrants made the news, they were often depicted as standard-bearers for rootless self-interest. The media narrative began with a rather unflattering version of exodus: Hong Kong migrants bought their way into Canada to secure a citizenship parachute in the event reunification with China turned out badly; sojourning in Canada, they lived in expensive homes, often leaving children parentless as they continued to run businesses back home; they took affront at Canadian government policies that taxed their wealth; and, at the first signs of stability in Hong Kong, they returned home – ever ready to use their passports to return to Canada should danger arise again.

Very few stories in the English-language press examined the Hong Kong community's engagement with Canada: its civic participation, philanthropy, and voluntarism. Few sought to explore the diversity within the Hong Kong community by questioning whether rich investor immigrants represented the entire Hong Kong community. Few interviewed poorer segments of Hong Kong society to ask about their interest in migrating to Canada or their views of Canadian immigration policy. And few held the Canadian state to account for setting the terms under which business class immigrants could enter the country. Instead, the press often seemed to be highlighting Hong Kong migrants' failure to demonstrate sufficient commitment to Canadian society. The Canadian state could be instrumental, choosing immigrants on the basis of financial criteria, but the same newcomers could not pursue their own economic interests if they were located outside Canada. A more complex image of Hong Kong transnationalism in Canada was portrayed in Canada's Chinese-language press.

### *Ming Pao* Coverage of Hong Kong–Canadian Transnationalism
The Chinese-Canadian community is sufficiently large to support three Chinese-language daily newspapers in Canada: *Ming Pao, Sing Tao,* and *World Journal.* Together these papers boast a weekly Canadian readership of just under 600,000 (Szonyi 2002, 39). We selected *Ming Pao* as our case study of Chinese press coverage of the Hong Kong migration in Canada. The paper is Canada's largest circulation Chinese daily published *by* Hong Kong–based media, primarily *for* a Hong Kong–origin population in Canada. *Ming Pao* began publishing in Canada in 1993, producing separate editions in Toronto and Vancouver, under local editorial control. Since the Chinese-language press is not available online, our research was based on the Toronto edition.

As Table 1.1 below indicates, *Ming Pao* gave prominent coverage to four themes related to transnationalism: business class immigration, return migration, astronaut families, and citizenship. A review of these stories reveals

*Table 1.1*

**Ming Pao news coverage of Hong Kong–Canadian transnational issues, 1993-99**

| Issue | Number of stories | Number on front page |
|---|---|---|
| Business class immigration | 47 | 17 |
| Citizenship | 77 | 33 |
| Return migration | 52 | 17 |
| Astronaut lifestyles | 11 | 4 |

a striking candour. *Ming Pao*'s treatment of the four issues did not always cast the Hong Kong community in the best light. Stories discussing business class immigration refer to bribes given to Canadian immigration officers and noncompliance with the terms of admission to Canada (*Ming Pao*, 19 August 1996; 21 September 1997; 13 December 1999). Articles referring to citizenship issues quote newcomers who refer to the three-year residency requirement as "immigration prison" (*Ming Pao*, 30 June 1996; 14 July 1997). Such unfettered reporting reflects well on the civic integrity of both the paper and the community it serves.

At the same time, articles submitted to *Ming Pao* by its readers reveal a community committed to full participation in Canadian society. Once a week *Ming Pao* publishes a full page of invited "op-ed" commentary from its readership on a designated forum page. Every week two opinion-/editorial-style articles are published, appearing in both the Chinese and the English languages. These articles are the sole English-language content in the paper and are written by nonjournalist community members – typically academics and other professionals. We reviewed 309 articles that appeared on the pages of "Forum" between 1995 and 2001 – approximately half the total number of forum articles published in the six-year period. Michael Smith has argued that the contours of transnationalism may be probed by asking "to what events do today's transnational migrants and refugees pay attention?" (2001, 155). The forum articles in *Ming Pao* reveal what Hong Kong–origin residents of Toronto felt strongly enough to write about and bring to their community's attention.

The forum op-ed articles reflect a transnational sensibility while emphasizing a sense of belonging to Canada. The single largest category of articles dealt with international affairs. Interestingly, the focus was typically global politics rather than events in Hong Kong. Canadian federal politics were the second most frequent topic, dominated by discussion of upcoming elections and appeals to readers to be sure to vote. The third most frequently addressed issue in the forum articles was education, a common motivation for the move from Hong Kong to Canada (Waters 2003). Many Hong Kong–

Canadians place great weight on their children's education. Next was commentary on provincial politics – particularly the controversial policies of the Mike Harris Conservative government, which often elicited critical commentary. Rounding out the "top five" list were articles related to negative comments made by Markham deputy mayor Carole Bell regarding the settlement of large numbers of immigrants in the town of Markham. Other topics addressed in *Ming Pao* could be found on the op-ed pages of any Canadian newspaper at the time. Recurring topics included Toronto municipal politics, the Canadian economy, the healthcare system, multiculturalism, Quebec's place in Confederation, and racism and discrimination in Canada. The opinions expressed in many articles often contradicted the image of a community characterized as uniformly rich and acquisitive. Articles appeared condemning the removal of rent controls (10 September 1996, A7), supporting a strike by municipal employees (written by a community member on strike) (4 April 2000, A7), and advocating support for gay and lesbian rights (4 June 1996, A7).

Lively debate and a variety of perspectives flourished on the forum page of *Ming Pao*. Few issues have exercised Hong Kong migrants more than taxation. Canada has a considerably higher income tax rate than Hong Kong. And in 1996 the federal government introduced a foreign assets reporting requirement into the tax system. The intent was to allow Canada to tax the income that Canadian residents derived from foreign-held properties, businesses, and investments valued at over $100,000. The move caused outrage in segments of Canada's Hong Kong community. Many had left Hong Kong to protect their assets; now the Canadian state was requiring their disclosure and taxation. *Ming Pao*'s forum coverage of taxation issues was balanced, with some articles giving voice to community frustration while others supported Canadian tax policies. Thus, Wan Fun Ng in an article titled "Less Means More" argued that Canada would be better off economically by reducing its high marginal income tax rate of over 50 percent to bring it closer to Hong Kong's 15 percent rate (21 March 2000, A7). An earlier article by H.K. Luk argued that higher taxes were a fair trade-off for Canada's superior social service and healthcare system (3 June 1997, A7). Regarding the contentious foreign assets declaration, Andrew Kwok argued that taxing assets accumulated abroad "through years of hard work and investment" was unjust and would drive Hong Kong immigrants out of Canada (14 October 1997, A7). Accountant Alexis Yam countered by reminding readers that the declaration requirement was not targeted at the Asian community but sought to strengthen fairness in the tax system so that wealthy Canadians could no longer avoid taxation by transferring assets abroad. Yam also expressed doubt that the new tax measure would prompt a return migration, since Hong Kong migrants "have chosen to come to Canada for things that other places cannot offer, for example, the quality of life and political stability" (14 October 1996, A6).

*Ming Pao* was clearly a contested site of community self-definition. In her headline-tells-all article – "Not All of Us Are That Rich" – Janet Lo complained of the "misrepresentation and stereotyping" that she encountered as a recent immigrant from Hong Kong. "Contrary to what is said in newspaper articles and reports, a majority of Hong Kong immigrants here in Canada have been and still are wage earners," she wrote (17 December 1996, A7). Nor did forum writers see any necessary contradiction in feelings of attachment to both Canada and Hong Kong. The centrepiece of Alexis Yam's 2 July 1996 article titled "Happy Birthday, Canada" (A7) is a trumpeting of a major recent Canadian sporting achievement. It is a triumph, he contends, that ranks with Paul Henderson's goal in 1972 and the Blue Jays' first World Series win in 1992. Just a week before Canada Day 1996, a Canadian dragon boat team became the first non-Asian team to win the Hong Kong Dragon Boat Festival. "It is like a Chinese hockey team coming to Canada and trying to win the Stanley Cup," Yam explained. Confessing his strong feelings for the dragon boat teams of both China and Canada, Yam described himself as "extremely elated" over Canada's victory, concluding that "most Chinese Canadians would probably support teams from both countries and an individual's passion for one team should not be viewed as a lack of loyalty to another." In such fashion do identities stretch and reveal themselves.

### The Unfinished Project of Hong Kong–Canadian Transnationalism

Canada's Hong Kong community grew dramatically in the last fifteen years of the twentieth century. Shaped by the state's immigrant selection policy, Canada received a large number of wealthy, entrepreneurial Hong Kong migrants in this period. Their experience confirms Philip Kelly's observation that "transnational practices var[y] across different immigrant groups" (2003, 213). For the Hong Kong community more than other immigrant groups, transnational living meant affluent lifestyles, the means and need to spend extended time in the homeland, high expectations of employment and earnings in the country of migration, a dynamic homeland economy as an alternative place of work or business, and an unpredictable homeland political environment hovering between stability and threats of repression. These dynamics have created a distinctive form of transnationalism now characterized by substantial temporary and permanent return migration (Ley and Kobayashi 2005).

As chapters in this volume illustrate, unique impulses motivate renewed diasporic ties to homeland across different communities. For example, the Indian state has been particularly aggressive in promoting return investment and migration of its Indo-Canadian diaspora as a strategy of homeland economic development (see Bose in this volume). By contrast, the state in Hong Kong has exerted minimal direct influence over its diaspora's transnationalism. Instead, Hong Kong–Canadian transnationalism is more typically based on migrants' personal and familial calculations of well-being.

The contradictions between the notions of immigrants as settlers with a singular attachment to Canada and current transnational behaviours raise important questions for Canadian immigration, settlement, and citizenship policies. Historically, as David Miller (2000) observes, citizenship has always been spatially bounded and contained – whether in city-states or in nation-states.

Analysis of Hong Kong migration to Canada crystallizes many of the citizenship issues that need to be reconceptualized in an age of transnationalism. Two important examples involve the acquisition of citizenship by children born abroad to Canadian parents and the residency requirement for immigrants to Canada wishing to become naturalized citizens.

Hong Kong is now home to many return migrants holding Canadian citizenship who could at any time exercise their rights of return and rights to sponsor immediate family members for migration. As long ago as 1995, Richard Gwyn reported estimates that up to 250,000 Hong Kong residents could arrive in Canada in this fashion (*Toronto Star,* 19 July 1995, A17). Until then, a sizable number of Hong Kong–Canadians will be residents in Hong Kong. The most recent proposed amendment to Canada's Citizenship Act was Bill C-18, introduced in 2002. This bill would significantly limit the automatic transmission of Canadian citizenship to children born abroad to a Canadian parent. Current policy automatically extends Canadian citizenship to any person born abroad to a Canadian citizen. The sole constraint on this practice of derivative citizenship is that such foreign-born Canadians lose their citizenship unless by age twenty-eight they have established Canadian residency for a year prior to applying to register their Canadian citizenship. This approach permits the world's Canadian diaspora to renew its Canadian citizenship relatively easily, generation after generation. Bill C-18 would end this unlimited transmission of citizenship across the generations by specifying that only the second generation born abroad to a Canadian citizen may acquire Canadian citizenship. Moreover, the applicant would be required to demonstrate a longer period of attachment to Canada by establishing a three-year residency in Canada prior to applying.

Bill C-18 also significantly redefines the meaning of residency for citizenship applicants. Current provisions of Canada's Citizenship Act confer citizenship on immigrants who have resided in Canada for three of the four years prior to applying. However, since the 1970s, the courts have ruled that "physical presence" was not required to demonstrate residency. Instead, the courts contended, residency could be inferred from attributes such as a Canadian home, bank account, club membership, et cetera (Dolin and Young 2002). Awareness that some immigrants, particularly those from Hong Kong, have been absent from Canada for long periods each year has contributed to the perception that immigrants have become citizens without having lived very long in Canada. The new provision set out in Bill C-18 explicitly requires three years of physical residency in a six-year period in order to be eligible for naturalized citizenship. The contradictory pressures of transnationalism on the Canadian state are evident in the new formula. Recognizing that immigrants may need to spend extended periods of time outside Canada, the period available to demonstrate residency has been extended from four to six years. But fearful that immigrants may be receiving Canadian citizenship without spending sufficient time in the country, lawmakers now require physical presence for a three-year period.

In 2003, the Canadian government held public hearings on Bill C-18. The Chinese Canadian National Council (CCNC) – Canada's foremost organization representing Chinese Canadians, with twenty-eight chapters across the country – was particularly critical of the bill. The CCNC contended that proposed changes to derivative citizenship acquisition were discriminatory since they establish different rules for children of Canadians born in Canada and abroad. In addition, the CCNC noted that "mobility is an increasing reality that affects migrant populations in the 21st century. This is particularly the case within the Chinese community" (CCNC 2003, 3). The CCNC also rejected Bill C-18's redefinition of a physical residency requirement for citizenship acquisition. Questioning whether physical presence itself was a factor in creating a good Canadian, the council contended that "it is also important to take into account the changing global economy, which requires people to travel frequently in order to be globally competitive. Canada must balance the need to rub shoulders amongst Canadians and the changing world economy and as such there is a need to maintain a flexible definition of resident in Canada" (1). At the time of writing, the proposed revisions to the Citizenship Act have not been approved by Parliament.

The debate about Bill C-18 illustrates the contradictions inherent in current immigration policies. On the one hand, people applying for admission to Canada as business immigrants are courted because of their entrepreneurial and financial success, which often derives from businesses located outside Canada. Skeptical about transnational migrants, the English-language media emphasize their mobility and question their commitment to Canada. In the Chinese-language press, the community itself expresses interest in Canadian politics and a desire for full participation in Canadian society. The contradictions between policies that attract transnational migrants and public responses to immigrants' transnational behaviours are mirrored in the contradictory views expressed in the English-language and Chinese-language media. The contradictory responses to transnational behaviours raise important questions about citizenship. To what extent can or should citizenship be separated from a territorial imperative? The Hong Kong–Canadian experience brings this question into particularly sharp relief. Ultimately, the contradictions and tensions revealed by our analysis suggest that, while states and the media attempt to restrain this emergent transnationalism, the actions and agency of migrant communities themselves will leave their mark.

**Note**

1  The electronic retrieval of articles permitted their analysis using QSR N5 software. It allows for highly detailed categorization of news content on a line-by-line basis by coding text into tree-like classification nodes.

# 2
# Emerging Postnational Citizenships in International Law: Implications for Transnational Lives and Organizing
*Susan J. Henders*

This chapter examines evidence of an emergent postnational citizenship in international legal norms. It considers what this still tentative, contested development might mean for people with transnational lives. Activists, policy makers, and scholars have pointed to the many problems with state-centric, or national, citizenship. It is questionable that it ever made sense to define a citizenry in formal, state-bounded ways – as if human identities are primarily defined by state frontiers; as if the rights and obligations of belonging should be given only to those with nationality in the state; as if state laws and regulations alone determine who fully belongs and participates in society. Nowadays such an approach makes less sense than ever. People have become more mobile; individuals and communities are more economically, ecologically, culturally, and politically interconnected across state borders; individuals experience identity as linked to multiple and shifting political communities simultaneously; and they live within a web of political authorities extending from the local level to the global level. In this fluid, amorphous context, state-bound ways of understanding citizenship are a barrier to building just, inclusive political communities where all who live within them – and who are affected by them – enjoy meaningful membership and participation. At issue is the moral and functional disconnection between state-centric ways of belonging and the transnational, multirealmed, *lived* experience of increasing numbers of people (see Soysal 1994, 2000). The need to rethink the bases and sources of citizenship has never been more urgent.

This chapter identifies international law as a site where exclusionary statist, or national, citizenship norms are being challenged by more inclusive postnational understandings of the rights and obligations of membership in political communities. It identifies evidence of several emergent postnational citizenships in contemporary international agreements on human, minority, and indigenous rights as well as on European citizenship.

I have termed these forms of postnational citizenship human rights citizenship, multirealmed citizenship, denizenship, and transnational citizenship. This is not to suggest that states are no longer a major locus of individual identities and entitlement claims or that postnational citizenships are uncontested or fully formed. Nevertheless, these embryonic postnational citizenship norms matter. They reveal the cracks and tensions in the state-centric understandings of international law, understandings that policy makers often use to exclude migrants from the benefits of citizenship. They are partly the product of activism and thus signal what has been achieved. Moreover, they are potential political resources in ongoing efforts by migrants and nonmigrants to overcome the ways in which the national citizenship model in its pure form leaves many people outside the very political communities in which they live, work, and maintain meaningful ties.

## Citizenship and International Law

In its simplest terms, citizenship refers to the rights and obligations of members of a political community. As an ideal type, state-centric, or national (also known as modern), citizenship assumes that human loyalties and identities are primarily vested in and bounded by the state. As traditionally understood, international law largely reinforces this state-centric view. The principle of sovereignty is a key reason why. It holds that states are the primary actors in global politics and that they have final decision-making authority in their own territories and over their own peoples – their *nationals*.[1]

In international law, nationality is the formal legal link between the individual and the state. In traditional international legal norms, nationality is an attribute of sovereignty, its primary purpose being to help the state system run smoothly. It aims to prevent conflicting sovereignty claims between states in three ways: by attempting to distinguish between the rights of nationals and those of foreigners or nonnationals; by controlling access to nationality – who is recognized as a national; and by limiting dual nationality (see Brubaker 1989; Sassen 2003). When states designate the people who are their nationals, they are carving out a realm where other states cannot interfere. Noninterference in the domestic affairs of states, including in the ways states treat their nationals, is central to the norm of sovereignty (Preuss 2003).

The principle of nationality does offer protection to nonnationals but only in ways that reinforce sovereignty. States have a right to provide consular protection to their nationals living abroad, and international law obliges "host" states to treat nonnationals according to international legal standards. Until recent decades, these standards were narrowly defined. They did not protect the right of nonnationals to stay in or be readmitted to their host state, even if they were legal residents there. They also mainly emphasized the *negative* rights of nonnationals: that is, they required that host states refrain from interfering with the individual liberties of foreigners, such as those related to free speech or association, obligations often honoured more in the breach. There has been even less recognition in international law of the obligation of host states to respect the *positive* rights of nonnationals (and often of nationals), such as their entitlement to free schooling or healthcare (Bauböck 2002).

A "realist" view of global politics appears to justify the exclusionary state-centric citizenship norms associated with nationality. Policy makers sometimes see the state system as highly dangerous precisely because it has no overarching political authority to maintain peace and order. Each state has to look after its own security and cannot but view nonnationals as potentially threatening fifth columns of other states and other dangerous outsiders (Ryan 1990). In this way, the principle of nationality and realist analyses of global politics reinforce and legitimate state-centred, national understandings of citizenship. Both justify the freedom of states to set their own rules of belonging, subject only to the need to avoid conflicts of nationality with other states.

Notably, the term *citizenship* rarely appears in international law, leaving the sovereignty-centred principle of *nationality* to structure the rules of belonging relatively unchallenged. Nevertheless, in the domestic laws and practices of some states, reflecting the transnationality of many of those within their borders and the activism of migrants and nonmigrants, states do not necessarily conflate. As we will see, some international legal agreements are also pushing for more inclusive forms of belonging that go beyond this state-bound approach.

### From National to Postnational Citizenship

The concept of nationality shows why, following Rainer Bauböck (2002), it is dangerous to begin an analysis of citizenship by identifying the formal rules for membership in states. If our main concern is an ethical outcome that maximizes substantive inclusiveness, we should instead begin with other questions. What concept of political community and what concept of belonging best support substantive citizenship for those who live in, work among, and have meaningful ties with a particular political community as well as those who must bear the consequences of the political decisions made within that community even if they live elsewhere?[2]

What I will call postnational citizenship is one such concept of belonging. Its approach to citizenship rejects the state-centrism and formalism of national citizenship models in which people can only belong to a single political community, the state, and in which the allocation of membership, rights, and obligations is solely a state prerogative, achieved through its laws and regulations. With postnational citizenships, individuals have multiple identities within and beyond states. Moreover, *meaningful* or *substantive* belonging in political communities requires more than the formal legal status conferred by the state (Bauböck 1991; Bottomore 1992; Brubaker 1992). The focus is instead on the *practices* of citizenship and on achieving substantive equality of participation *in addition to* equal legal status. For vulnerable groups and individuals such as many migrants, postnational citizenship requires the recognition of their distinctive transnational lives and a right to participation and influence beyond the formal political realm, extending to civil society, economic spheres, and the family. State laws and regulations matter, but so do the actions of substate governments, international public authorities, and nongovernmental actors, including employers, family members, and religious communities. As several chapters in this volume demonstrate, each of these actors helps to determine who fully and meaningfully participates in and can influence the choices that communities make and the values that they promote (Marshall 1992; Wong 2002). Postnational citizenships thus potentially promote a deeper form of citizenship that encompasses the civil and political, as well as the economic, social, and cultural, dimensions of belonging in both the public and the private spheres.

## Postnational Citizenships in International Agreements

The traces of postnational citizenships visible in the interstices of some international agreements are not entirely new. The state has never fully been the sole locus of citizen belonging. Still, many analysts argue that postnational practices and claims have a new intensity and urgency in our times (see Yuval-Davis 1999a) and not only because the demands of increasingly transnational individuals and groups appear to be on the rise. As other writers in this volume point out, states themselves also sometimes promote postnational citizenships to legitimate the effects of multirealmed governance on their populations, to confront the impact of interdependence, and to maximize the contributions of migrants and nonresident nationals to the state's economic and political goals (see Bose in this volume). "Home" states may view the achievement by nonresident nationals of nationality and substantive citizenship in the "host" state as enhancing these goals over the long term (see Isin and Wood 1999; Bauböck 2002).

Like states, international legal norms are paradoxically both agents of postnational citizenships and barriers to their realization for vulnerable individuals and groups. The examples of human rights citizenship, as well as multirealmed citizenship, denizenship, and transnational citizenship examined below, are limited to illustrating the ways in which international legal norms facilitate postnational ways of belonging. Although they are intertwined and overlapping in practice, I have separated these postnational citizenships here for analytical clarity.

## Human Rights Citizenship

Human rights are radical ideas in a state-centric world, for they assert that each individual belongs first and foremost to the global human community and has rights and obligations flowing from that membership. Rights and obligations associated with membership in a state or other political community are secondary and can be "trumped" by those derived from membership in the human community. In the liberal conceptualization of human rights, an individual can claim these rights against states regardless of whether he or she is the national of that particular state. Human rights citizenship norms are evoked to justify the demands for inclusion by numerous communities and groups, defined by gender, age, sexual orientation, ability, immigration status, and culture or way of life (see Soysal 1994, 2000; Tully 1995).

Since the Second World War, states have increasingly accepted that universal human rights are a legitimate international political concern. Although debates over specific norms, underlying philosophical justifications, and legal forms continue (Taylor 1999), and although enforcement remains weak, governments have been intensively developing global and regional human rights standards and codifying them in international agreements. These agreements express the ongoing and unresolved conflict between the postnational spirit of human rights norms and the continuing dominance of the sovereignty-based national conceptions of citizenship.

The International Bill of Rights itself – the Universal Declaration of Human Rights, the International Covenant on Civil and Political Rights (ICCPR), and the International Covenant on Economic, Social, and Cultural Rights (ICESCR) – clearly expresses this tension (UN 1948, 1966a, 1966b). On the one hand, these agreements require states to treat nationals and nonnationals equally. On the other, they effectively affirm the right of states to discriminate between them. An example of the latter tendency is ICCPR Article 25, which contains one of the few explicit mentions of citizenship in international law. Article 25 provides political participation rights to "citizens" only, including the right to participate in public affairs, vote, run for public office, and access the public service. Moreover, other aspects of the International Bill of Rights effectively undermine substantive postnational citizenship by devaluing the importance of economic, social, and cultural rights. Liberal democratic states such as Canada as well as some other states tend to regard the civil and political rights standards in the ICCPR as binding and justiciable but to see the social, economic, and cultural rights in the ICESCR as nonjusticiable and nonbinding standards to which states are obliged *to strive* (Craven 1995). This disparity undermines efforts to hold governments *legally* accountable for providing the social, economic, and cultural conditions necessary for meaningful, substantive citizenship for nationals and nonnationals alike.

Nevertheless, "citizen" electors can, theoretically, still hold governments *politically* accountable for such citizenship failures. However, the nonnational – who has no right to vote under the International Bill of Rights and still rarely under domestic law – has little political recourse when he or she is excluded from entitlement programs essential to the enjoyment of full citizenship. Canada is among the majority of states whose domestic laws restrict the right to vote to nationals (Blais, Massicotte, and Yoshinaka 2001). However, as discussed below, there is a trend toward extending voting rights in local elections to resident nonnationals, particularly among European states but also in a few US and Japanese municipalities (Hiwatashi 2004; Bauböck 2005). As discussed later, European international legal norms are also moving ahead of their global counterparts to begin recognizing this shift in domestic law.

## Multirealmed Citizenship

The fundamental principle that all individuals are equal members of the human community is in many ways the basis of all postnational citizenship claims, including forms of multirealmed citizenship. In this form of postnational citizenship, belonging is understood as diffused and divided among multiple political communities and authorities simultaneously. Sometimes these communities and authorities are *nested*, fitting together like Russian dolls. Other times they are *horizontal*. In the latter case, individuals make citizenship claims in more than one nonnested polity at the same time. Both varieties of multirealmed citizenship find some support and reflection in international law.

### Nested Multirealmed Citizenship

The nested version of multirealmed citizenship is a consequence of two developments after the Second World War that, like human rights norms, weaken the state's claim to be the sole and primary locus of citizen loyalty and rights (Henders 1997). First, many states have become more internally decentralized and have granted local autonomy and group-differentiated rights to distinct communities within their borders. Second, states have created many international intergovernmental organizations, agreements, and regimes, with authority in almost all policy areas once the exclusive prerogative of states. The result is *multirealmed governance* where decision making is divided and diffused among local, state, and international public authorities. The most robust examples of emergent nested multirealmed citizenship are in Europe, though they are but partial and contested (Linklater 1998). The successes and failures of these norms will have important demonstration effects for the development of postnational citizenships in Canada and other parts of the world.

The key example is European citizenship, primarily a product of the expansion and deepening of intergovernmental and supranational cooperation through the European Union (EU) and the Council of Europe. Central to EU citizenship is the right of all nationals of EU member states to freedom of movement in the union and to vote and stand as a candidate in local and European elections in the member state where they live on the same conditions as nationals of that state (EU 2002, Art. 18, 19). They also have the right to be represented by another EU member state consular authority in a third country if their own state cannot provide such protection and according to the same conditions as nationals of the state providing consular representation (EU 2002, Art. 20). Additionally, the institutions of the European Union and of member states must respect the fundamental rights guaranteed by the European Convention for the Protection of Human Rights and Fundamental Freedoms (Council of Europe 1950; EU 2002, Art. 6[2]). Under this convention, the individual nationals of Council of Europe member states can in some circumstances directly appeal the rulings of state courts to the European Court of Human Rights, whose decisions are binding (Council of Europe 1950, Art. 25-34).

Coupled with European citizenship "above" the state is a growing recognition of regionalized identities "within" states. The two realms have become linked: regional and local authorities in EU member states have gained an advisory role in EU decision making through the Committee of the Regions. The creation of substate citizenship rights has also been supported by the Council of Europe. Its European Charter for Regional or Minority Languages demands that signatory states protect individual and group claims related to the right to culture and identity (Council of Europe 1992b).

Multirealmed citizenship claims and practices tie together the constitutive units of federalizing polities and facilitate power sharing among multiple realms of government with jurisdiction over the same individuals and communities (Bauböck 2002). They integrate the individual's experience of identity as simultaneously transnational, state bound, and local, with the claims of international and regional human rights norms. As Yasemin Soysal describes it, "when they make demands for the teaching of Islam in state schools, the Pakistani immigrants in Britain mobilize around a Muslim identity, but they appeal to a universalistic language of 'human rights' to justify their claims. And, they not only mobilize to affect the local school authorities, but also pressure the national government, and take their case to the European Court of Human Rights" (2000, 4).

However, contestation for supremacy among the vertical multiple realms of citizenship is still evident. This is partly a holdover from national citizenship, which presumed a single *primary* political authority or sovereign. At the same time, the indeterminate and contested nature of multirealmed citizenship may be one of its most useful characteristics. As Andrew Linklater puts it, in Europe, suprastate, state, and substate citizenships coexist in a fluid relationship. At times, they compete; at others, they cooperate. The hierarchy shifts, potentially allowing for each to check the oppressive, exclusionary excesses of the other. This fluidity may help to establish "the normative ideal of forms of political community which release societ[al] potentials for achieving levels of universality and difference" (1998, 181).

### Horizontal Multirealmed Citizenship

A horizontal version of multirealmed citizenship is a result of the increasing movement across borders of people, particularly workers, professionals, and managers, characteristic of contemporary capitalisms. Here individuals make citizenship claims not only on their "host" states but also in their "home" and other states where they have economic, political, cultural, or other ties. Focusing on relatively privileged technical, professional, and managerial migrants, Aihwa Ong (1999) has used the term *flexible citizenship* for the claims and practices associated with those who select different spaces for investment, work, and family relocation. As Siemiatycki and Preston in this volume illustrate, Hong Kong's mobile managers are the archetype, working and/or investing in China while simultaneously seeking nationality, education for children, and opportunities to diversify economic risk in (mainly democratic) states such as Canada *and* maintaining family and business presences in and often strong attachments to Hong Kong (Ong 1999).

International law reflects these trends in limited but significant ways. To recall, international law has typically enshrined a right to nationality and discouraged multiple nationality, thereby inhibiting horizontal multiple citizenship practices that potentially weaken state sovereignty and create conflicts with other states. International and regional human rights standards typically recognize a right to nationality but not to *multiple* nationality. For instance, Article 20(2) of the American Convention on Human Rights provides that "every person has the right to the nationality of the state in whose territory he was born if he does not have the right to any other nationality" (Organization of American States 1969). This right is particularly important for the children of migrants who are denied nationality in their country of birth and are threatened with expulsion to their parents' or even grandparents' country of origin (see Laroche 2001). However, such a right does little to recognize the identities and needs of those whose lives are entwined in multiple states at once.

More generally, the acceptance by states of dual nationality is on the rise (Bauböck 2002), a change also reflected in the increasing support for multiple nationality and horizontal multirealmed citizenship in international law. Canadian law since 1977 has permitted multiple nationality (Government of Canada 2004). In Europe, amendments in 1993 to the 1963 Convention on Reduction of Cases of Multiple Nationality and Military Obligations in Cases of Multiple Nationalities, Second Protocol, under the Council of Europe, loosened restrictions on dual nationality in certain cases, particularly when people of different nationalities marry as well as for the children of such marriages. Noting the large numbers of migrants and second-generation migrants in signatory states, the amendments declare that the "conservation of the nationality of origin," along with acquisition of a second nationality, is important to "encourage unity of nationality within the same family" and to encourage migrants and second-generation migrants to *"complete their integration ... through the acquisition of the nationality of the state"* (emphasis added). Although integration is the goal of states, by permitting dual nationality the convention indirectly supports horizontal multirealmed citizenship.

The support is more direct but still ambiguous in the 1990 International Convention on the Protection of the Rights of All Migrant Workers and Members of Their Families (hereafter the Migrants Convention; UN 1990), which came into force in 2002 despite the refusal of all major migrant-receiving states, including Canada, to ratify the agreement. Among its provisions, the treaty protects the political participation rights of migrant workers in their country of origin, including the right to vote (Art. 41), though notably not in the "host" state. The Migrants Convention also recognizes the migrant's right to transfer earnings and savings out of the "host" state (Art. 47). The availability of remittances, particularly for a migrant's family members still living in the "home" state, may be crucial to their ability to enjoy meaningful citizenship, even if it also eases the economic difficulties of "home" state governments.

## Denizenship

There are at least two routes to dealing with the citizenship deficit of migrant workers and immigrants. One is to maintain the national citizenship model but to allow, encourage, speed up, and facilitate the ability of nonnationals to acquire nationality in their state of residence or work. The other is to depart from the national citizenship model and extend citizenship rights and obligations to nonnationals (Bauböck 2002). The latter route – sometimes called denizenship – is controversial but incipient in some international legal norms.

The Migrants Convention itself goes some way toward recognizing denizenship. Among those economic and social citizenship rights the convention extends to migrant workers with documentation are the rights to form trade unions and associations (Art. 40); to participate in public affairs but not to vote (Art. 41); and to access education, social and health services (if they meet state requirements), vocational training and guidance, and housing, including social housing (Art. 43). Additionally, migrants have the rights to be protected against dismissal, to access unemployment benefits and public works schemes, and to make claims to authorities if an employer breaches the conditions of employment (Art. 54). Undocumented workers fare poorly by contrast. The agreement affirms the right of states to exclude irregular or undocumented migrants and their families from enjoying particular citizenship rights. The treaty also affirms the right of states to determine through their laws how far even documented migrant workers and their families will have a right to equal treatment with nationals in employment (Art. 27) as well as whether they enjoy political rights such as the right to send freely chosen representatives to institutions and processes, the right to consultation, and the right to other participation at the local community level (Art. 42). The only unrestricted economic and social citizenship rights for migrant workers are access to urgent medical care (Art. 28) and access to education and preschool education for children (Art. 30).

Despite the limited nature of the denizenship rights set out in the Migrants Convention, states have been slow to sign and ratify the agreement. In a world where national citizenship is still considered the norm, governments worry about the political and financial costs of implementing the agreement (see Taran 2000). This is the major reason for the reluctance of migrant-receiving states to ratify the agreement (December 18 n.d.), although the Canadian government's publicly declared justification is that "Canada does not have a class of Migrant workers per se"; it argues that Canadian immigration policies in this regard are consistent with international law because nonnationals working legally in Canada are protected by the same legislation and can access the same government programs and services as Canadian workers (Government of Canada 2003).

As noted earlier, European law recognizes somewhat more expansive denizenship rights. Article 6(1) of the 1992 Convention on the Participation of Foreigners in Public Life at the Local Level, in force since 1997 under the Council of Europe, states that nonnationals resident for five years have a right to vote and run for office at the local level. However, Article 9(1) allows states to restrict such rights "in time of war or other public emergency threatening the life of the nation ... to the extent strictly required by the exigencies of the situation" (Council of Europe 1992b).

The proposed EU Constitution (EU 2004), whose future has been in doubt since French and Dutch voters rejected it in referendums, also sets out a range of rights, including those belonging to all individuals in the European Union regardless of nationality and to documented workers and other legally resident non-EU nationals. It also affirms the right of member states legally to restrict access to some citizenship rights, such as through eligibility criteria. The cornerstone of an emergent European denizenship is Article

II-21(2), which explicitly recognizes a right to nondiscrimination based on nationality. However, this right is restricted to claims in those areas subject to the EU Constitution and cannot prejudice other provisions of that document. Thus, most labour rights are available to everyone in the European Union, as are the rights to association and assembly, including for political, trade union, and civic matters (Art. II-12). The same equal treatment exists for the rights to education and vocational training, including "the possibility of receiving free compulsory education" (Art. II-14). By contrast, access to social security and social assistance is subject to the limits in EU and national laws (Art. II-34), as is access to preventative healthcare and medical treatment (Art. II-35), meaning that nonnationals cannot necessarily claim these services *as rights*.

Under the proposed European Constitution, denizens also have limited political rights. The right to stand for office and to vote is limited to EU citizens. However, all EU residents regardless of nationality have the right to good administration (Art. II-41), such as the right to have one's affairs dealt with impartially and fairly and to be heard on matters that affect one's life; the right to access EU documents (Art. II-42); the right to refer cases of maladministration to the EU ombudsman (Art. II-43); and the right to petition the EU parliament (Art. II-44). Symbolically important is the fact that political citizenship rights for both EU nationals and non-EU nationals are located in a chapter of the EU Constitution entitled "Citizens' Rights," suggesting some movement away from a purely national approach to belonging.

## Transnational Citizenship

The right to identity and to associate or organize across borders – what might be called transnational citizenship – remains contested in many authoritarian states. In China, for instance, the government makes extensive efforts to restrict access to Internet sites that it deems subversive. As discussed elsewhere in this volume, the tenuousness of transnational citizenship in democratic states has also become more apparent since the events of 11 September 2001. Despite these tensions, transnational citizenship rights are emergent in international agreements and declarations on minority and indigenous rights, coexisting with statist conceptions of citizenship that sometimes restrict cross-border association and organizing.

This ambiguity is a serious issue for members of minority and indigenous groups, who, like many First Nations citizens in Canada, often understand themselves as belonging to communities that span more than one state. Article 27 of the ICCPR (UN 1966a), arguably the most authoritative statement on minority rights in international law, effectively assumes that minority communities are bounded by the state: "*In those States in which ethnic, religious or linguistic minorities exist,* persons belonging to such minorities shall not be denied the right, in community with the other members of their group, to enjoy their own culture, to profess and practise their own religion, or to use their own language" (emphasis added). The state-centric framing of minorities in this treaty, to which Canada is a party, reflects the desire of governments to minimize threats to state stability and territorial integrity, such as might be caused by conflicts with other states over border-spanning minorities. State-centric understandings of security and belonging assume that state identities and loyalties are primary and that transnationality is threatening or inconsequential.

However, more recent formulations of minority and indigenous rights make room for, and in some cases affirm and protect, the transnationality of human communities and individuals. For instance, Article 1(1) of the UN Declaration on the Rights of Persons Belonging to National or Ethnic, Religious, and Linguistic Minorities speaks of the "national or ethnic, cultural, religious and linguistic identity of minorities *within their respective territory*" rather than within the state (UN 1992; emphasis added). The declaration, which was adopted by the UN General Assembly without a vote but does not yet have the authority of a treaty, also recognizes the right of individuals belonging to minorities "to establish and maintain, without any discrimination, free and peaceful contacts with other members of their group and with persons belonging to other minorities, *as well as contacts across frontiers* with citizens of other States to whom they are related by national or ethnic, religious or linguistic ties" (Article 2[5]; emphasis added).

Notably, it appears that transnational citizenship rights encounter the least resistance from states when they are in cultural fields, perhaps because governments regard cultural transnationalism as less threatening than transborder associating and organizing for more overtly political purposes. Especially since the end of the Cold War, international norms have begun to recognize transnational citizenship for "national minorities," who typically are relatively long-standing nationals of the state in which they live. There are several examples.

The 1990 Copenhagen Document of the Organization for Security and Cooperation in Europe provides that "persons belonging to national minorities ... have the right ... to establish and maintain unimpeded contacts among themselves within their country as well as contacts across frontiers with citizens of other States with whom they share a common ethnic or national origin, cultural heritage or religious beliefs ... [and] to establish and maintain organizations or associations within their country and to participate in international non-governmental organizations" (Art. 32[4] and [6]). The European Charter for Regional and Minority Languages of the Council of Europe has, as one of its stated purposes, "the promotion of appropriate types of transnational exchanges, in the fields covered by this Charter, for regional or minority languages used in identical or similar form in two or more States" (Art. 7 [1][I]). State parties are supposed to "foster contacts between the users of the same language in the States concerned in the fields of culture, education, information, vocational training and permanent education" (Art. 14[a]). The 1995 Framework Convention for the Protection of National Minorities, also under the Council of Europe, goes further, providing for rights to unspecified types of associating across borders. The preamble states that "the realization of a tolerant and prosperous Europe does not depend solely on co-operation between States but also requires transfrontier co-operation between local and regional authorities without prejudice to the constitution and territorial integrity of each State." Article 17(2) provides for the right of national minorities to participate in the activities of nongovernmental organizations within the state and internationally. However, transnational identity is defined in primarily cultural terms, even if the types of relations permitted across borders are not limited to cultural matters. Article 17(1) states that people belonging to national minorities have a right "to establish and maintain free and peaceful contacts across frontiers with persons lawfully staying in other States, in particular those with whom they share an ethnic, cultural, linguistic or religious identity, or a common cultural heritage."

Outside the European context, at the global level, the emergent transnational citizenship rights in the Draft Declaration on the Rights of Indigenous Peoples are more expansive (UN 1992). The draft declaration does not restrict the participation rights of indigenous peoples to the state but implies their belonging to multiple political communities simultaneously: "Indigenous peoples have the right to participate fully, if they so choose, *at all levels of decision-making* in matters which may affect their rights, lives and destinies through representatives chosen by themselves in accordance with their own procedures as well as to maintain and develop their own indigenous decision-making institutions" (Art. 19; emphasis added). Article 35 more explicitly embodies transnational citizenship rights and goes well beyond cultural ties across state frontiers. It even creates obligations for states to facilitate the exercise of rights to transnational belonging. The article reads, "indigenous peoples, in particular those divided by international borders, have the right to maintain and develop contacts, relations and cooperation, *including activities for spiritual, cultural, political, economic and social purposes,* with other peoples across the borders. States shall take effective measures to ensure the exercise and implementation of this right" (emphasis added). While encouraging in terms of the development of transnational citizenship norms, these draft provisions do not have the force of a treaty and are subject to ongoing international negotiations involving, among other participants, Canadian First Nations and government representatives as well as their counterparts from other indigenous communities and states.

For migrants, emergent international legal norms are also pushing toward transnational citizenship rights. However, again, the emphasis is on recognizing a right to *cultural* association and organizing across borders. Here Article 31 of the Migrants Convention (UN 1990) expressly requires states to respect and promote the cultural transnationality of migrant workers and members of their families and to refrain from stopping them from maintaining cultural links with their "home" states. While the Migrants Convention does not expressly provide a right to political organizing across state frontiers, such activities are not expressly prohibited under Article 26. This article requires states to recognize the right of migrant workers and members of their families to organize to protect their economic, social, cultural, and other interests, including through trade unions. However, as a reminder of the ongoing tendency to cast the outsider as dangerous, Article 26 states that the state can limit the exercise of these rights by law if it is deemed necessary "in a democratic society in the interests of national security, public order (*ordre public*) or the protection of the rights and freedoms of others."

## Implications for Transnational Lives and Organizing

Resistance to recognizing human rights citizenship, multirealmed citizenship, denizenship, and transnational citizenship continues. It is fortified by the power of national citizenship discourses to legitimate the claim that formal, legal membership in a single state – nationality – fully encompasses the human experience of belonging in political communities. It is reinforced by employers who, too frequently with the complicity of states, exploit migrant workers as a reserve supply of cheap, flexible labour often unprotected by the health and safety, minimum wage, and social security standards accorded to "citizen" workers (Taran 2000). Racism and ethnocentrism, and the association of nonnationals with criminality and threats to the security and livelihood of states and citizens, help to entrench these exclusionary norms. This tendency is more evident than ever since the events of 9/11 and its aftermath. Despite movement toward recognizing and protecting postnational citizenship in international law, a good deal of international intergovernmental effort still goes into reinforcing national citizenship norms.

At the same time, international agreements on human, minority, and indigenous rights and European citizenship reveal the fruits of activism aimed at going beyond state-centric belonging. These postnational citizenship norms are still scattered and fragmentary and do not all enjoy the widespread support of governments. These norms are weakened by the lax and uneven enforcement of international human, minority, and indigenous rights standards more generally and their tendency to apply mainly in a narrowly defined public sphere. One of the paradoxes of the state system is that postnational citizenship norms depend on the willingness of governments to translate these emergent standards into domestic law and practice. After all, these standards challenge the claims by governments that states are the primary focus of citizen identity and loyalty as well as the claims by state-level governments that they need to protect their nationals against the security and economic threats posed by nonnationals and transnationals. These issues of international and state enforcement are crucial subjects for further research and activism.

Despite these limitations, emergent international postnational citizenship norms are important for transnational lives and organizing in at least two ways. First, they are usable political resources in efforts to formulate and claim meaningful citizenship rights within, among, and beyond states. Second, the tentative recognition in international agreements of plural, overlapping, and transnational identities and belonging in diverse political communities is evidence of the fluid and contingent nature of citizenship itself. As Engin Isin and Patricia Wood (1999) point out, there is nothing "natural" about the modern, or national, conception of citizenship. Citizenship is a fluid political process. The current dominance of national citizenship is the result of political struggles in particular historical times and in particular places, just as emergent postnational citizenship norms and practices are a consequence of political contestation and struggle (Giddens 1982). Because of inequalities of power, dominant groups will always have the ability to impose their views on others, using conceptions of citizenship strategically to exclude others from belonging in the polity. Nevertheless, the tensions between citizenship's language of inclusion and universality, and its practices of exclusion, open important political spaces in which those excluded and their advocates can and do struggle for more just and inclusive outcomes. As several chapters in this book show, they sometimes do so with the support of states. The present chapter has exposed international legal discourses as one of the crucial but contested sites in which the struggle to postnationalize state-based citizenship is well under way, shaped by and in turn shaping Canadian-linked transnationalism.

**Notes**

1   The meaning and practice of sovereignty is more ambiguous and contested than the traditional and "realist" views suggest (see, e.g., Knop 1993; Krasner 2000; Ossiander 2001).

2   On the latter point, which is important but not developed in this chapter, see Young (2000).

# 3
# Transnational Nationalism: Sri Lankan Tamils in Canada
*Sarah V. Wayland*

This chapter presents an empirical case study of Sri Lankan Tamils as diasporic or transnational ethnic actors. Building upon the emerging dialogue between international relations and contentious politics or social movements scholarship (Tarrow 2001; Khagram, Riker, and Sikkink 2002), I highlight the nexus of domestic and transnational politics by demonstrating how actors form ethnic networks and utilize transnational opportunities to pursue political goals in various states.

Sri Lankan Tamil ethnic networks are transnational in two senses of the word: first, they have a common identity that spans state borders; second, they engage in substate relations by forming political networks across state boundaries to influence policies. The first usage is consistent with how "transnational" is applied in most chapters in this volume. It refers to individuals whose identities and relations span national borders. Researchers focus on persons, mostly migrants, whose lives subsume two or more languages and cultures and who have frequent contact with ethnic kindred ("co-ethnics") in other locations. Transnationalism involves the creation of new identities that incorporate cultural references from both the place of origin and the place of residence. The second usage of the term *transnational* is the one employed by political scientists. Transnationalism refers to organizations or institutions below the level of the state but whose activities transcend national borders. In the 1970s, transnationalism was mostly associated with economic relations, especially those of transnational corporations (Keohane and Nye 1971). By the late 1990s, however, political science usage of transnational was extended to nongovernmental organizations and "transnational advocacy networks" united by shared values, the use of a common discourse, and extensive information exchange among like-minded activist organizations (Keck and Sikkink 1998).

Sri Lankan Tamils comprise a particular type of transnational ethnic network, one that exists largely because of ethnonationalist conflicts and persecution in the homeland.[1] Sri Lankan Tamils thus comprise a diaspora, defined as an ethnically distinct community that has been dispersed from its homeland and whose identity hinges on a will to return or a "myth of return."[2] Diasporic communities such as the Tamil ones are composed of refugees and exiles whose movements were spawned by circumstances in their home countries rather than solely by the wish to forge a new life abroad. As such, even those migrants, and especially their children, who desire integration into receiving societies may be active players in the conflicts left behind.

## Transnationalism in an Era of Globalization

Many scholars working on issues of culture, ethnicity, and identity have gravitated to the concepts of diasporas and transnationalism in the context of globalization, arguing that economic factors and social networks of migrant communities are transforming the nation-state. In an oft-quoted passage from the inaugural issue of the journal *Diaspora,* the editor hailed diasporas as "the exemplary communities of the transnational moment" (Tölölyan 1991, 5).[3] One variant of this research is the postnationalist approach, which posits the decline of sovereignty and the belief that the nation-state is an outmoded political formation. Arjun Appadurai, an influential writer in this genre, argues that the nation-state is in "terminal crisis" and that the rise of electronic media in conjunction with migration will give rise to "diasporic public spheres" that will be the "crucibles of postnational political order" (1996, 21-22).[4] According to Appadurai, "one major fact that accounts for the strain in the union of nation and state is that the nationalist genie, never perfectly contained in the territorial state, is now itself diasporic [and] is increasingly unrestrained by ideas of spatial boundary and territorial sovereignty" (160-61). Nations are thus "unbound," operating with fewer constraints in a globalized world (Basch, Glick Schiller, and Szanton Blanc 1994). Other scholars in this vein even criticize the term *diaspora* as an extension of an outmoded nation-state model that assumes congruence between territory, culture, and identity (Soysal 2000). In brief, postnationalist approaches emphasize the power of diasporas at the expense of states.

Most scholarship on transnationalism, however, acknowledges the ongoing importance of nation-states. Drawing on research from political science, sociology, anthropology, geography, and other disciplines, a growing literature situates diasporic politics and transnational communities within states and localities (Smith and Guarnizo 1998; Vertovec and Cohen 1999).[5] This literature considers how sending and receiving states, regions, and localities promote or hinder the creation and maintenance of transnational social networks. Its treatment of the political emphasizes the impact of grassroots activities in the context of national-level policies. This genre of research focuses on the interplay between nonstate and state actors and how diasporas become international political actors through a variety of types of interaction with states: when diasporas engage directly or indirectly in homeland politics; when actors in the homeland – government officials, opposition groups, co-ethnics – actively seek their support; when actors in the homeland provide diasporas with economic or political support; when actors in the homeland deny or discredit the legitimacy of the diaspora; and when the diaspora forges ties with sympathetic third parties such as other ethnic groups, nongovernmental organizations, political parties, or international organizations (Østergaard-Nielsen 2000, 2001a, 2002; Adamson 2002).

In this chapter, I argue that the formation of ethnic networks in the Tamil diaspora has enabled the Liberation Tigers of Tamil Eelam (LTTE), or Tigers, to engage in protracted insurgency against the Sri Lankan government army. I illustrate how traditional conceptions of collective action are insufficient explanatory variables of ethnic conflict in Sri Lanka. In particular, I discuss how our understanding of "political opportunity structure" can be extended to include the role of transnational actors operating from liberal democratic states. I follow this discussion with a case study of expatriate Sri Lankan Tamils and their involvement in homeland politics.

## Transnational Opportunities and Diasporic Politics

Scholars of contentious politics generally agree that the confluence of three broad sets of factors accounts for the emergence and development of social movements and more militant forms of collective action (McAdam 1982; Tarrow 1994; McAdam, McCarthy, and Zald 1996). First, insurgents require *mobilizing structures,* the informal and formal organizational forms available to them. Second, contention depends on the presence of successful *framing processes,* the conscious attempts by individuals to fashion shared worldviews and sets of common grievances that justify collective action. Collective action frames are what attract persons to a cause and keep them there (Snow et al. 1986). Third, in combination with organizational or internal resources, latent grievances are activated by changes in the broader political context or *political opportunity structure* (POS). Opportunity structures are "consistent – but not necessarily formal or permanent – dimensions of the political environment that provide incentives for people to undertake collective action by affecting their expectations for success or failure" (Tarrow 1994, 85). In other words, they are factors external to a movement that influence the movement's emergence and chance of success. Political opportunity structures help to explain why a challenger's chances of engaging in successful collective action vary over time and why similar challenges may meet with very different results in different places. Most research on opportunity structures has focused on variables such as the openness or closure of political institutions, the stability of elite alignments supporting a polity, the presence of influential allies, and the state's capacity and propensity for repression (McAdam 1982; Tarrow 1994; McAdam, McCarthy, and Zald 1996).

If these three sets of conditions – mobilizing structures, cultural framings, and political opportunities – must exist in tandem for insurgents to instigate and maintain challenges to the state, then the case of Tamil insurgency in Sri Lanka presents a puzzle for scholars of contentious politics. By definition, ethnonationalist groups already contain many of the internal factors requisite for mobilization: shared identity, common grievances, and organizational resources. In the case of Sri Lankan Tamils, their organizational structure has been consolidated in the form of the LTTE, now recognized even by the Sri Lankan government as the voice of the Tamil people. Common language and ethnic identity have also contributed to the existence of informal networks. Moreover, the collective action frames within an ethnic population sharing a strong sense of collective identity and grievances formed as a reaction to ethnically motivated persecution are particularly strong.

But the political opportunities have not been favourable to Tamil challengers. In terms of the POS factors outlined above, Tamils were virtually excluded from the political process; Sinhalese elites were united in their support for a unitary state; no influential allies supported the Tamil cause in Sri Lanka; the state engaged in frequent acts of repression; and there was little vulnerability of the "closed" government to outside pressure.[6] Yet insurgency has existed at fairly high levels since 1983. What accounts for the tenacity of Tamil rebels in Sri Lanka?

I posit that a comprehensive understanding of Tamil insurgency can be achieved by extending our understanding of POS to include *transnational* factors that influence a given domestic political situation. A consideration of ethnic groups acting in the diaspora reveals how political actors can act within several opportunity structures at once. More importantly, it reveals how, despite unfavourable conditions in the home country, factors abroad may protract an otherwise nonexistent or short-lived insurgency. Such factors constitute a "transnational opportunity structure."[7]

By transnational, I mean the ability of political activists to traverse the boundaries of a state, using resources and opportunities available from persons living in numerous polities.[8] My research indicates that, in the case of Sri Lankan Tamil mobilization against the Sinhalese government, the impetus and resources for the collective action come largely from the Tamil diaspora. In employing a transnational opportunity structure framework to analyze Sri Lankan Tamil insurgency, I draw on the POS dimensions outlined above to identify two dimensions of transnational opportunity: openness or closure of political institutions in other states, and the presence of allies in other states and in the international arena. In the case of diasporic politics, these two dimensions are necessarily intertwined: migrants settled in new states remain active in homeland politics. Diasporic groups constitute *transnational ethnic networks* that are then mobilized to aid co-ethnics in the homeland, especially with financial resources.

The movement of immigrants and refugees from a situation of persecution and absence of political rights to open societies characterized by democratic governance, freedom of expression, and antidiscrimination laws has profound political implications. Persons who migrate from a closed society to an open one are able to capitalize on newfound freedoms to publish, organize, and accumulate financial resources to an extent that was impossible in the homeland. In some countries of settlement, public funding even supports various forms of ethnic media and organization. Migrants and their descendants can then mobilize in the host country to publicize their cause as well as to lobby decision makers to obtain additional political rights for their co-ethnics in the sending country.[9] Open opportunity structures can even facilitate the creation of distinctive ethnic identities and secessionist movements in the diaspora.[10]

Although Tamil identity is very strong in Sri Lanka, there are limits to its expression in that Tamils have been persecuted because of their ethnic affiliation and have been excluded from holding political office. Indeed, ethnic persecution became the primary cause of migration out of the country, and many Tamils were accepted in liberal democratic host countries with refugee status. In the diaspora, it became possible to explore and express Tamil cultural, linguistic, and religious identity as never before. Associations were formed, with an eye both toward facilitating integration in the host country and toward maintaining ties with the homeland, namely through supporting the quest for Tamil independence. Migration from Sri Lanka has resulted in Tamil identity building from abroad as well as material support for the creation of a separate Eelam.[11]

Tamil elites have mobilized diasporic identity networks around a variety of activities that ultimately impact the conflict in Sri Lanka. These include (1) exchanging information within the Tamil community via Tamil-language newspapers, radio, the Internet, and ethnic organizations; (2) spreading awareness of the Tamil struggle through marches, conferences, and lobbying government officials; and (3) lawful as well as illegal fundraising. All three types of activities – intra-Tamil communication, outreach from the community, and fundraising – reinforce a proud, independent Tamil identity. Ongoing exposure to propaganda about the Tamil struggle and sacrifice in Eelam may also invoke feelings of guilt among those in the diaspora. The impact of these activities, in turn, has been crucial to the perpetuation of the war for an independent Eelam on the island of Sri Lanka. These activities are outlined in the following sections, with a particular emphasis on diasporic politics in Canada, likely the largest Sri Lankan Tamil diaspora in the world.

## Tamil Ethnic Networks

Sri Lankan Tamils are literally scattered around the world, but they are concentrated in certain states. Between 110,000 and 170,000 live in the Tamil Nadu province of southern India, whose coast is less than fifty miles from the northern Sri Lankan Tamil heartland. From a population of fewer than 2,000 Tamils in 1983, Canada's Tamil population has grown to between 110,000 and 200,000 persons, 90 percent of them in Toronto.[12] There are at least 200,000 Tamils in Western Europe, primarily in Britain, Germany, Switzerland, and France.

Britain has been the most important site of the LTTE's overseas political activity. Until antiterrorism legislation passed in Britain on 28 February 2001 banning the LTTE, the Tigers' international secretariat had been located in London. Anton Balasingham, one of the LTTE's most visible leaders and the chief LTTE negotiator at the September 2002 peace talks, resides in London as well.

## Information Exchange

The richness of Tamil diasporic networks is evidenced in the blossoming of outlets for Tamil expression, information exchange, and, generally, the rise of Tamil social capital in Toronto over the past two decades. Today there are ten weekly Tamil-language newspapers, five of them free. Four Tamil-language radio stations broadcast seven days a week and feature very popular phone-in and talk shows. Three cinemas show Tamil-language films, and Toronto is home to the largest Tamil video and music store in the world (Cheran 2001, 181-82). There are at least six Hindu Tamil temples as well as several Roman Catholic congregations. A Tamil community directory has been published since 1990 and has grown to several hundred pages in length. The directory lists businesses as well as social service, political, cultural, and business organizations. The Tamil Eelam Society (TES) is the largest ethno-specific provider of social services to Tamils in Ontario. Since the late 1980s, its board of directors has had close ties with the World Tamil Movement, allegedly a front organization for the LTTE. Because the Canadian government has become more aware of the links between the Tamil Eelam Society and the LTTE, the TES has disassociated itself from political activities and is cultivating its image as strictly a social service provider.

No matter where a person lives, however, access to the Internet provides access to news about Sri Lanka. Indeed, the Internet has been an important means of communication among Tamils around the world. Websites provide analyses of current events with a Tamil perspective, chronologies of the Tamil-Sinhalese conflict, and nonpolitical items such as classifieds and software information.[13] These media outlets are sometimes the only source of information about events in the battle zones due to government censorship.

The extent to which the LTTE itself has utilized communications technology to disseminate a nationalist Tamil message is revealed by the annual Heroes' Day celebrations. Every November LTTE leader Velupillai Prabhakaran gives a speech commemorating Tamil martyrs and pronouncing on the progress of the war. Tamils in the diaspora gather together in public spaces for their own commemorations. Increasingly, the homeland is linked with the diaspora during these events. Minutes after the conclusion of the annual address, Tamils around the world are able to hear Prabhakaran's speech broadcast by private Tamil radio stations. Within thirty minutes, the text of the speech and photos of the event are posted on the Internet in English (Sambandan 1999).

Within the context of a struggle for ethnic autonomy in the homeland, political divisions within the Tamil diaspora are not openly expressed. In contrast to diasporic communities characterized by political factions around homeland issues, such as discussed by Kelly regarding Filipinos in Canada (in this volume), it would be difficult to find Tamils in Canada who publicly criticize the LTTE.

## Public Demonstrations and Lobbying

Tamil identity networks are reinforced by political mobilization in the form of conferences, marches, and various types of advocacy or lobbying. In Toronto, for example, in 1995 and again in 1998, as many as 20,000 persons marched on the Ontario legislature to protest the treatment of Tamils by the Sri Lankan government. In the late 1990s and early part of this decade, Tamil marches and conferences were routinely attended by local, provincial, and even federal politicians.

Lobbying by Tamils in Canada is primarily conducted by the Federation of Associations of Canadian Tamils (FACT), an umbrella organization of ten Tamil associations that has a pro-secessionist stance. The role of FACT, according to one of its leaders, is to "coordinate activity so that they [the Canadian government] could get one voice from Tamils." FACT sends correspondence to public officials and meets with civil servants on issues of concern to Tamils. In 2000, then-finance minister Paul Martin attended a FACT-organized gala dinner celebrating the Tamil new year. Subsequently, members of the Canadian Alliance Party incorrectly alleged in the House of Commons that Martin had attended fundraising events for terrorists. Then-prime minister Jean Chrétien quickly replied that such labels should not be applied to entire communities (see *Globe and Mail*, 22 February 2001).

Formed in 2000, the Canadian Tamil Congress (CTC) has become an important voice for the new generation of Canadian-educated Tamils. Modelled on the influential Canadian Jewish Congress, the CTC has been engaged in domestic as well as transnational issues. Another vehicle for transnational involvement is the Student Volunteer Program, created in Toronto in 2002 to enable second-generation Tamils to learn firsthand about their homeland by engaging in temporary work projects (often teaching) in Sri Lanka. Both of these organizations provide venues for younger Tamil-Canadians to express their concerns to Canadian decision makers.

## Financial Support

According to an article in the *Economist,* "The War the World Is Missing" (2000), the funding for Tamil websites and newspapers comes from contributions by expatriate Tamils as well as from business profits. Indeed, the Sri Lankan government estimates that the Tigers overseas fundraising reaches $80 million a year. Tamil leaders dispute this figure, claiming that it is impossible such a newly formed diaspora could raise such a large sum, a sum that would require average annual contributions of more than $100 from every Tamil individual living overseas. It is the case, however, that the LTTE employs fundraisers abroad.

Another means of fundraising is the production and sale of Sri Lankan-made videos in the diaspora. They feature footage of the war, the hardships of life under the Sri Lankan government, and pro-LTTE events. Tamils may also be asked to buy items to support the separatist cause, such as calendars listing Tamil holidays as well as names of those martyred in the struggle. Finally, Tamils may be pressured to shop at Tamil stores that support the Tigers and even to buy certain products and newspapers.

Tamil leaders have argued that these accounts are exaggerated. Representatives of FACT, for example, have claimed that Tamils in Canada simply do not have the means to donate as much money as some law enforcement officials claim and that most money that goes back to Sri Lanka is sent to family members and relief organizations (Morris 1995, 29; author's interviews). Indeed, remittances from Sri Lankans abroad constituted the largest single source of foreign currency for the country in 1994, around $33 million (Research Directorate 1996, 15). Official figures underestimate the actual remittance amounts since Sri Lankan Tamils are known to use middlemen to transmit money back to relatives. When interviewed, most Tamils state that fundraising for Eelam does occur but that it is generally for relief work in war-ravaged areas.

Even if money is indeed sent back in the form of remittances and relief aid, Tiger involvement in either activity cannot be ruled out. First, a share of these funds may still go to the Tigers. Second, the majority of relief work in the area is conducted by the Tamil Rehabilitation Organization (TRO), which has the status of a nonprofit organization (though not a charitable organization) and is closely linked to the LTTE. Certainly, some or most of the TRO funds support legitimate relief efforts but only those in keeping with the wishes of the LTTE leadership.

## Host State Control over Diasporas

The above accounts illustrate how Tamils in the diaspora have been able to operate transnationally to support an ethnic struggle in the homeland. Although much of this activity occurs without the express consent of the states in which they reside, it is not the case that diasporas are able to bypass states altogether. Diasporas constitute deterritorialized networks in the sense that identity and organization can transcend state borders, but their members do reside in states and target state policies. As a result, states have some modicum of power over diasporic activities.

Several recent examples illustrate the efforts by states to limit particular types of Tamil diasporic activity. Both Britain and the United States have labelled the LTTE a terrorist organization and restricted its activities on their soil. In the aftermath of the 9/11 attacks in the United States, Canada and its neighbour passed antiterrorism legislation similar to what had been signed into law in Britain in 2000. In addition, two antiterrorism initiatives by the United Nations have impacted the ability of the LTTE to operate in various states: the International Convention for the Suppression of the Financing of Terrorism (in force 10 April 2002), and UN Security Council Resolution 1373 requiring UN member states to adopt strong measures against terrorist financing (adopted 28 September 2001).

## Conclusion

Members of the Tamil diaspora are linked by a common identity that is rooted in ethnic persecution; the shared trauma of migration, including guilt at having left family, friends, and a country behind; and economic and social marginalization in the receiving society, particularly in the first generation. Politically motivated ethnic elites are able to capitalize on this shared identity to generate financial and other types of support for co-ethnic insurgents in the homeland. As described above, these networks engage in three broad categories of activity: information exchange within the Tamil community, outreach to the broader society and state about the Tamil struggle, and fundraising. Many Tamils in the diaspora may not actually support the LTTE, but their presence at Tamil public functions lends legitimacy to the separatist cause. Moreover, their financial support has been crucial to the perpetuation of the civil war in Sri Lanka.[14] Whereas Tamils in Sri Lanka have limited opportunities to travel, assemble, express themselves politically, and accumulate wealth, allies in the diaspora have been able to circumvent these constraints and to assist ethnic actors in the homeland. The war is being fought within Sri Lanka, but Tamil efforts are supported by transnational ethnic networks.

This research contributes to a small literature that uses a POS approach to examine immigrant and diasporic politics (Wayland 1993; Ireland 1994; Koopmans and Statham 2000; Østergaard-Nielsen 2001b). First, I have extended existing POS variables outside the domestic sphere so that their transnational dimensions may be included: the openness or closure of political institutions in other states, in this case migrant-receiving states, and the presence of international allies, namely co-ethnics living in the diaspora. Whereas most research on immigrant politics has focused on dynamics in receiving states, my research considers how the POS in receiving states may influence politics in sending states. Second, I have included formal as well as informal dimensions of politics in the concept of transnational opportunity structure. Intragroup communication, publicity efforts, and fundraising by transnational ethnic networks are informal activities that can have significant political ramifications in both sending and receiving states.

Transnational networks sustain ethnopolitical conflicts, and diasporas can play a major role because the resources they provide can upset the existing balance of economic, political, and military power in the homeland. This research lends support to the idea that immigrants and refugees – once thought of as weak victims and politically voiceless – can be important international actors. Settled in liberal democratic states and facilitated by the broader processes of globalization, they can have a significant impact on civil conflicts on the other side of the world. In the case of the Tamil diaspora, the LTTE has set up political offices abroad as well as engaged in extensive fundraising campaigns that have enabled the Tamil insurgents to sustain their quest for an independent homeland. Mobilization by other ethnonationalist groups in the diaspora might also be analyzed from a transnational opportunity framework. Contemporary examples include diasporic activities by Jews and Palestinians aimed at Israel as well as mobilization by Kurds, Sikhs, Kashmiris, Serbians, Croatians, Greeks, and the Irish.

Transnational networks sustain ethnopolitical conflicts, but they may not provide enough resources to definitively change the outcomes of ethnic wars. In the case of Sri Lankan Tamils, support from the diaspora has not enabled the LTTE to secure its ultimate goal of Tamil independence. Indeed, evidence of a military stalemate between the LTTE and the government of Sri Lanka existed by the late 1990s.

A different set of international influences is now affecting the civil war in Sri Lanka. The crackdown on terrorism by Western states in the aftermath of 9/11 and the hardening of public opinion against political violence constricted the transnational opportunity structure for the LTTE's international network. In combination with domestic factors such as the military stalemate and the opportunities opened by the election of a new government in December 2001, this crackdown pushed the LTTE and the government of Sri Lanka to the negotiating table in the fall of 2002.

Remarkably, the ceasefire was still holding when major disaster struck on 26 December 2004 in the form of a tsunami. The devastation brought upon many Tamil areas of the island generated renewed attention and fundraising from the diaspora and around the world, this time with a focus on relief and rebuilding. Unfortunately, it also deepened distrust between Tamils and Sinhalese as many Tamils accused the government of withholding relief aid to Tamil-controlled areas of the island.

This chapter has drawn attention to the role of transnational ethnic networks in *sustaining* ethnopolitical conflicts. Investigation into how various transnational actors might work to *manage* conflicts is just as important and is likely to reveal far different intragroup dynamics and motivations.

**Notes**

1 Ethnonationalist conflicts are characterized by disputes between groups that have claims to a particular territory within an existing state or straddling several states. In this chapter, I also use the broader terms *ethnic conflict* and *ethnopolitical conflict* interchangeably. The use of these terms is not meant to imply that ethnicity itself is the source of the conflict. Rather, ethnic differences often correspond to social, economic, and political cleavages, thereby facilitating mobilization along ethnic lines. See Gurr (1993).

2 There is considerable debate about what exactly constitutes a diaspora, but the more limited definition – drawn from the prototype of the ancient Jews – focuses on a forced or involuntary dispersal from the homeland. Influential analyses of the diaspora can be found in Safran (1991); Cohen (1997); and Østergaard-Nielsen (2001a).

3 For a critique of "celebratory" or "emancipatory" approaches to transnationalism, see Guarnizo and Smith (1998, 3-6).

4 For an attempt to bring anthropological understandings to debates within the field of international relations, see Mandaville (2002).

5 For a critique of the state-centric focus found in some of these works, see Nagel (2001).

6 Due to space limitations, I am unable to provide an overview of the ethnic conflict in Sri Lanka. For more detailed treatment of ethnic identity and political developments in Sri Lanka, see Manogaran and Pfaffenberger (1994); Bose (1995); and Wilson (2000). For personal, anthropological accounts, see Tambiah (1986); and Daniel (1996).

7 An emerging literature on transnational political mobilization, using transnational in the second sense outlined above, is captured in Smith and Johnston (2002).

8 Although beyond the purview of this chapter, states, intergovernmental organizations, and nongovernmental organizations have also actively monitored – and even intervened in – the Sri Lankan conflict. For their role, see de Silva and May (1991); and Werake and Jayasekera (1992).

9 This phenomenon is reminiscent of the "boomerang effect" in which domestic advocacy organizations facing an unresponsive state search out international allies to pressure that state on their behalf. See Keck and Sikkink (1998, 12-13).

10 Sikh mobilization from an independent Khalistan originated in the expatriate community rather than from within the Punjab itself. See Tatla (1999). Many Kurds from Turkey became aware of their Kurdishness only after immigrating to Germany.

11 One Sri Lankan scholar asserts that "certain Tamil nationalist myths which had been politically latent began to be openly expressed [since 1983]; there was a deliberate and conscious attempt to create a ... political identity." The impulse came not so much from the Tamil centres of Madras and Jaffna "but from the expatriate community, who have begun to write extensively on Tamil history and ideology. Their writings are circulated widely and have an important effect on [Sri Lankan] Tamil consciousness" (Coomaraswamy 1987, 77-78).

12 This estimate is based on an analysis of immigration data, census data, and figures given by Sri Lankan Tamils and those who work with Tamils. Most Sri Lankan Tamils entered Canada as refugees or were sponsored by immediate family members who first arrived as refugees and then gained landed immigrant status. The asylum claims lodged with the Canadian Immigration and Refugee Board between 1989 and 1993 had an average acceptance rate of 90 percent, compared to 50-60 percent for asylum claims overall. See Aruliah (1994).

13   Some websites are of interest to particular Tamil communities. *Tamil Canadian,* for example, contains news items as well as listings of Tamil associations and suggestions for contacting government officials in Canada. The *World Mirror,* a fortnightly Tamil newspaper published in Canada, has a web edition. The Tamil Circle listserv distributes news items daily as well as commentaries and queries by subscribers. The Tamil Circle focuses on events in Sri Lanka, but items about events in Britain, Canada, Australia, and elsewhere are also posted periodically. In addition to these English-language sources, some sites are written in Tamil script that can be read with specialized software.

14   This is openly acknowledged by the LTTE. For example, at a Tamil music festival organized by the LTTE in Paris on 1 May 2003, the following statement from LTTE leader Prabhakaran was read to the crowd by the director of the LTTE's television network: "Without your support and financial assistance [the] Tamil Eelam struggle would not have been possible. Please continue to support us."

# 4

# Demystifying Transnationalism: Canadian Immigration Policy and the Promise of Nation Building
*Uzma Shakir*

I have been an advocate for immigrant and refugee rights in Canada for over fourteen years, and I work at an advocacy and social-planning organization called the Council of Agencies Serving South Asians (CASSA). CASSA is an umbrella organization of approximately sixty agencies, groups, and individuals providing social services to the South Asian community in the Greater Toronto Area. Our mandate is to support and advocate on behalf of existing as well as emerging South Asian agencies, groups, and communities in order to address their diverse and dynamic needs. The organization's goal is to empower the South Asian community. CASSA is committed to the elimination of all forms of discrimination from Canadian society.

As part of this work, over the past six years we have been mobilizing and organizing internationally trained immigrant professionals and workers and advocating with them for equal and fair access to their professions, trades, and employment; to fight for the rights of nonunionized workers of colour who are being exploited in their workplaces; and to challenge racist and discriminatory structures in Canadian society, particularly those impacting immigrant communities. We have challenged the lack of credential recognition of immigrant qualifications and skills, the insistence on having Canadian experience in order to secure employment, and the underemployment and precarious employment of immigrants in insecure and nonunionized workplaces.[1]

This chapter is not a theoretical formulation of transnationalism but an experiential exposé of what, in my estimation, produces transnationalism. I am working with a relatively simple definition of the term *transnationalism* that is based more on my experience than on any academic inquiry. In my experience, transnationalism is integral to immigrant experience in Canada, though the reasons and forms may have changed with time. It appears that earlier in Canadian history, immigrant nonwhite workers were forced to retain transnational links to their countries of origin because, although they found work in Canada, they were not allowed to bring their families here or to create stable communities here. Today's immigrants, who are mostly nonwhite and come from nontraditional source countries, can bring families (at least immediate family members) here and even establish communities, yet lack of access to stable and livable work often forces them to leave their families here and seek work elsewhere, including their countries of origin. Some have even abandoned their dreams of building a life in Canada and have returned "home." In either situation, transnationalism is the outcome of nonwhite immigrant experience in Canada.

In basic definitional terms, transnationalism seems to refer to the relationships and ties that immigrants continue to hold with their countries of origin even when they have been "settled" in another society over a long period of time. Obviously, the nature of these transnational ties varies depending on the length of separation and relocation. However, in my experience, transnationalism is not simply about relationships; it is also a product of degrees of racism and racialization experienced by immigrants in the country of their destination, in this case Canada.

I envisage transnationalism in Canadian society to be a function or outcome of immigrant experience in the country of destination, as opposed to some temporary stage of settlement or romantic notions of "homeland." In my experience, race and racialization are critical in understanding the structural inequities that are embedded in Canadian society and that historically have shaped the immigrant experience of transnationalism for some Canadians. I believe that two factors have influenced, and continue to influence, the nature of the transnational ties that Canadian immigrants either actively cultivate or inadvertently experience: first, the degree of marginality produced by Canadian legislation on patterns of immigration; second, the level and degree of racialization and marginalization experienced by immigrants themselves here in Canada. I argue that racialization and marginalization are in fact entrenched in Canadian society and are perpetuated historically through legislation, thus perpetually creating what I call "transnational communities." Furthermore, I argue that this racialization through legislation manifests itself best in the history of Canada's immigration policy as well as through the licensing barriers faced today by immigrants in society.

## Canada's Early Immigration History

According to popular wisdom, newcomers to a country would hold stronger ties to their country of origin than to their adopted country because their immediate families may still be in the country of origin, they may continue to hold property and other relationships in their country of origin, and their feeling of being "strangers" in a new location may remain acute. It is assumed that, once time elapses and immigrants "settle" down in their chosen country of residence, those transnational ties become weaker, though it is now often recognized that immigrants and their descendants may continue to have psychological or emotional ties to a real or "imagined" homeland in which they may have never lived (Rushdie 1991). Although some communities retain such ties for historical/political reasons, as others in this volume and elsewhere discuss, my experience tells a different story.

Seventeen years ago, when I first arrived in Canada, I remember having a conversation with a second-generation Italian friend about the immigrant experience in Canada, and he made a rather curious comment: "We [Italians] used to be the blacks of this society." At the time, I was confused by this statement, but in retrospect and with the advantage of experience I find it quite interesting. It seems to imply two things: (1) that racialization can be constructed by *degrees:* there seems to be a necessity to racialize some in order to maintain the privilege of others in Canadian society, and this seems to be characterized through the relative categories of "whiteness" and "blackness"; (2) that there is movement in this racialization: these categories may shift and change over time. Those once marginalized by degrees of racism might actually move into the privileged category of whiteness over time. This possibility is implied in our multicultural thinking that is premised on the belief that immigrants struggle initially, but over time they become "integrated" into the Canadian norm. But what about the persistence and thus perhaps the necessity of such categories of race? I would argue that, given that the marker of marginality is "blackness," some might never enter this "promised land" of privilege because they will never be white enough! An examination of Canadian immigration history and contemporary experience seems to bear this out.

In my view, Canada's immigration strategy has always been predicated on three important factors: claiming the right to the land, nation building through European immigration, and importing nonwhite cheap labour to service the nation. The first two factors form the basis of the "official" immigration strategy and its accompanying legislative history, which begins with the Sifton Plan of 1896, a policy developed consciously to encourage immigrant settlement in Canada, particularly the west, by giving land to European immigrants. This policy was designed as an immigration strategy to build a nation, though its antecedents lie in an earlier history of European colonization of North America.

The underlying philosophical justification of the Sifton Plan was that the land was "empty" and needed to be "improved" by the industry of white settlers. This fiction could be sustained only by ignoring or eliminating the claims, or indeed the presence, of indigenous peoples. Thus, the "incentive-based" immigration strategy of Clifford Sifton appears to have been predicated on the reality of usurping Aboriginal lands either through "treaties" or by outright settlement. That the land being parcelled off to European immigrants had been owned by the indigenous peoples and in fact had to be taken away from them to be given to European settlers merely reinforces the impression that racialization (in this case as part of colonization) through legislative enactment is entrenched in Canadian immigration history. The violation and usurpation of Aboriginal lands and rights through "treaties" are still being challenged by Aboriginal peoples.

My focus, however, is on the third historical component of Canadian immigration strategy: while indigenous peoples' land was being parcelled off to European settlers, the entry of non-European, nonwhite people was restricted; this restriction necessarily rendered them transient and increased their potential to be used as cheap labour. Right from its inception, Canada has used immigration to meet its labour and economic needs, particularly as the economy has been restructured. But while Europeans have also been part of the nation-building agenda it is interesting to note that nonwhite people have not been part of that agenda – irrespective of whether they were indigenous to the land or arrived here after European colonization. The Aboriginal peoples, early African arrivals fleeing from slavery in America, and Chinese and South Asian immigrant labourers have all had a remarkably persistent history of marginality in society that defies their different histories of arrival, their claims to the land, or indeed their contributions to society. Ostensibly, the Canadian rulers have not viewed or allowed non-Europeans to be active participants in the nation-building experiment but have instead allocated to them a circumscribed role of either serving the nation builders or remaining marginal to society.

This reality seems to play itself out in different forms throughout history. An example is found in the history of Canada's immigration policies, which first explicitly and later implicitly "encouraged" European settlers to build communities but at the same time prohibited American blacks, Chinese, South Asians, and other racialized groups from doing the same. Canada did not have an immigration policy until after Confederation in 1867, but once it was articulated, almost for the next century "most immigration laws were designed to prevent certain groups from entering Canada" (Baldwin 1996, 9). Immigration policies favoured people from Great Britain, the United States, and Western Europe as they were in keeping with the nation's white European identity. A Canadian Policy Research Network publication states that "the central policy issue was how to balance the country's need for people – to settle the land and fuel the economy – with the need for citizens who would help to build Canada as a 'British nation' and a white society" (CPRN 2005). Thus, while immigrants as nation builders were sought from Western Europe and the United States, nonwhite immigrants were recruited merely as contract labour and were discouraged from immigrating with families. A notorious example is the case of the Chinese head tax. Nearly 16,000 Chinese workers were recruited to work on the railway in the nineteenth century, but "in 1885, as soon as the CPR was finished, the federal government imposed a $50 Head Tax on every Chinese immigrant entering the country. This policy forced many Chinese Canadian men to live as 'bachelor husbands' because they could not afford to bring their wives to Canada. In 1904 the Head Tax was increased to $500 and, in 1923, the Chinese Immigration Act all but closed Canada to Chinese migrants. This ban was finally repealed in 1947, thus allowing many women and children to reunite with their male family members in Canada for the first time" (CPRN 2005).

Such policies ranging from outright prohibition to restrictive legislation made it difficult if not impossible for some communities of colour to take root in Canada. For example, the continuous journey stipulation of 1908 required immigrants to prove that they had arrived in Canada without breaking their journey, while the Immigration Act (1910) demanded "proof" of legitimacy of marriage in order for families to come to Canada. These legislative requirements seemed to be designed by the social engineers of the time to bar non-Europeans, particularly those coming from South Asia, from establishing communities in Canada. Thus, for instance, the early South Asian community, just like the Chinese and other Asians, can be seen as a "bachelor society" (Ku 2000, 8) since they often migrated alone, though many men were married with their wives and children still in British India (see Das Gupta 1994). Furthermore, given the discriminatory legislative implications of the continuous journey stipulation for immigrants coming from as far away as South Asia, the migration pattern of South Asians remained sporadic and disjointed. As one commentator notes, "the unjust continuous journey law of 1908 combined with the $200 per person requirement virtually eliminated Sikh immigration to Canada. It was a plan to undo the damage of having let 5,000 Sikhs into the country already. From 2,623 immigrants allowed into Canada in 1907, only 6 were allowed in 1908. In fact Canada would not see new Indian immigrant numbers approaching the 1907 level until 1966, 59 years later when 2,233 East Indians entered the country" (Singh Brar 1997, 1).

The Chinese head tax (1885), the Chinese Immigration Act (1923),[2] and the continuous journey stipulation appear to have been legislative mechanisms to make it difficult if not impossible for nonwhite people to enter Canada as anything but contract labour. Those who did enter became an unfree, vulnerable source of cheap labour for the nation-building project initiated by the Sifton Plan. The monetary and travel restrictions were specific mechanisms to keep these non-Europeans from becoming *the* Canadian nation by establishing rooted communities in Canada. Therefore, those Chinese and South Asians who were able to enter Canada in these early years in effect became transient workers – that is, unable to establish communities in Canada and forced to retain transnational links. The Alien Labour Act of 1897 was meant to control even the importation of contract workers (namely Asian labour), but railway companies effectively ignored this law. This practice by railway companies of recruiting Asian contract workers not only reinforced the transnational reality for Asian immigrants but also made them vulnerable to economic exploitation (see Green and Green 1993).

The so-called labour market needs that ostensibly drive immigration policy in a sense mask an underlying social-engineering component in Canadian immigration policy. This is an important point to remember since it manifests itself in various ways even today. The fact that degrees of racism are historically embedded in Canadian nation-building design and in public attitudes of the time is well documented.

> For the most part ... there was a hierarchy of preference ... The welcome was very different for immigrants from Southern, Central and Eastern Europe, principally Ukrainians and Italians. They met with prejudice and often open hostility. Much of this hostility was directed at the "foreign navvies" – unskilled male labourers – who sought work in Canada's growing resource and industrial sectors. Their presence raised the spectre of class-based social and political unrest rooted in what were thought to be insurmountable ethnic differences. The small number of immigrants from Asia – mostly male workers from China, Japan and India – excited even more extreme reactions, especially in British Columbia, where a quarter of the province's labour force at the beginning of the century was of Asian origin. The tenor of the racism directed at them was nothing short of vitriolic. (CPRN 2005)

Even the non–English-speaking European immigrants who landed in Canada after the Second World War ended up creating a problem for Canadian policy makers and social engineers of the time. There was a social and political backlash against Italians, Ukrainians, Jews, and others, the targets of discrimination and exclusion. But over time even the "nonpreferred" Europeans, actively recruited as cheap labour after the Second World War (from Southern and Eastern Europe), were able to form communities through access to sponsorship rights – a right not easily accessible to Asians. This access meant that rooted communities could be formed in Canada and that those Europeans once marginalized by degrees of racism could eventually build their communities and their capacity to organize in unions, guilds, and politics. However, the experience of nonwhite labour seems to have been different. Initially, it was marked by a persistent inability to establish rooted communities and therefore to organize, and historically this increased its propensity to be exploited as cheap labour.[3]

Thus, it is not an accident of history that, even though Asians have been in Canada for more than 100 years, some continue to display symptoms of what is termed rather euphemistically "the immigrant experience" – that is, they are disengaged from the Canadian milieu, marginalized in Canadian history, unable to establish strong communities and thus retaining strong transnational links. Peter Li (1998) calls it the "delayed second generation syndrome" with reference to the Chinese community, referring to restrictions imposed by discriminatory Canadian law on the reunification of families for Chinese male workers in Canada, thus leading to delayed second-generation growth today. Furthermore, even those who have been in Canada close to 100 years continue to experience some of the same challenges as "new" immigrants – namely, persistent settlement issues, lack of adequate social support, lack of a mainstream voice, cultural marginality (as a deviant to the mainstream norm), and strong transnational links.

## Canadian Immigration since the 1960s

Canada has relied throughout its history on immigration to meet its labour needs, and economic restructuring has usually fuelled this strategy. Canada enacted this strategy in 1867 by opening the doors to immigration, especially to farmers in Western Europe, to settle lands in western Canada under the Sifton Plan. Then, as the economy shifted structurally from initial settlement and farming to a growing need for industrialization, Canada actively recruited people in Southern and Eastern Europe to meet the needs of the postwar boom and to form settled communities through sponsorship rights. By the 1960s, technological changes began to dictate the need for a new type of skill set that could no longer be met by earlier arrivals. At this time, Canada turned to the point system to recruit skilled labour, as with engineers (Bambrah 2005). Until the point system in 1967, the country of origin of prospective immigrants continued to be a significant factor in immigration policy.

Changing labour market needs led Canada to abandon a restrictive immigration policy and to develop one of the most liberal immigration policies in the Western world. As Valerie Knowles points out, "because of the quickening pace of technological innovation, certain acquired skills were becoming obsolete and workers needed periodic training to keep up" (2000, Chapter 6, 4). The government produced a white paper on immigration, tabled in Parliament in 1966, noting that immigration had "made a major contribution to the national objectives," but as Knowles points out, "to prevent an explosive growth in the unskilled labour force, the paper proposed the government tighten up the sponsorship system and admit more independent immigrants (immigrants who applied on their own initiative and had skills required in the labour market)" (2000, Chapter 6, 4). The point system was introduced "as a method designed to eliminate caprice and prejudice in the selection of independent immigrants. In the points system, immigration officers assign points up to a fixed maximum in each of several categories, such as education, employment opportunities in Canada, age, the individual's personal characteristics, and degree of fluency in English or French. The points system was incorporated into new immigration regulations that went into effect in 1967. Other features of these regulations included the elimination of discrimination based on nationality or race from all classes of immigrants and the creation of a special provision that allowed visitors to apply for immigrant status while in Canada" (Knowles 2000, Chapter 6, 5).

As a result, Canada began accepting two categories of immigrants: those not judged by the point system, such as refugees fleeing persecution, war, or disease, or people who fell under the family class who had relatives in Canada who were willing to support/sponsor them until they found employment and settled down, and all other immigrants, who were judged by the point system (Baldwin 1996, 9). But it appears that even the shift to the point system in the 1960s continued to reinforce the social-engineering component of the earlier immigration policy, ensuring that the major flow of immigration was still from Europe. The majority of "skilled" immigrants up to 1967 came from Western European countries because Europe had the "push" factors that encouraged migration, such as the dislocation of war, overcrowding, and so on; Europeans could meet the Canadian legislative requirements for language, education, and training for various professions and trades (Bambrah 2005); they also had resources for mobility, and they had preexisting roots in mainstream Canadian society.

Given the more open nature of the point system, Asians in the 1960s were able for the first time to enter Canada freely (i.e., without overt and specific legislative barriers) and begin to establish some semblance of a community, but it would take another twenty years for the pattern of immigration to shift dramatically. Even after 1966, for example, South Asian immigration patterns reflected "chain migration" (Buchignani, Indra, and Srivastiva 1985). That is, usually men from the same village or kinship group in India ventured forth to Canada.

By the 1980s, however, a distinct demographic shift began to take place in Canada generally, and particularly in Toronto, where non-European skilled immigrants began to outnumber European immigrants. Now institutional barriers and structural realities are preventing nonwhite immigrants from becoming part of the national narrative. Because of economic restructuring toward outsourcing and contractual work (see TD Bank Financial Group 2005), skilled immigrants coming to Canada are finding themselves unable to access stable and skills-commensurate employment. They are increasingly filling the ranks of underemployed contingent labour whose ability to organize is limited by the very nature of their work. Self-employed and contractual workers, piecemeal workers, and temp agency workers are inherently involved in an employment relationship (by definition unstable and siloed) that is not amenable to traditional union organizing. This problem is compounded by the fact that nonwhite ethnoracial workers continue to be minoritized in the labour movement.[4] As a result, earnings among immigrants have "fallen below those of [the] native-born population, while unemployment, underemployment and poverty levels in this group have increased" (Bambrah 2005, 1).

It is interesting to note that, even though the rationale for immigration and therefore the type of immigrant coming to Canada have changed dramatically from earlier times, the marginalization of nonwhite immigrants from structures of power in society continues to persist. What was previously possible through overt racist policies is now made possible by structuring immigrant access to lower-end jobs. In both cases, the outcome is transnationalism.

## Precarious Employment and Political Participation

Canadian immigration policy, in the period since the 1960s, has been designed to meet two key nation-building needs: an aging and diminishing population needs to be supplemented, and the minimum skills required to qualify for Canadian society are moving toward higher levels of education and communication. Thus, Canada's immigration policy is meant to reap the benefits of globalization by capitalizing on the mobility and dislocation of people while allowing only the skilled and in fact elite workforce from across the globe to come to and settle in Canada. However, the deep-seated racist attitudes toward workers of colour becoming the nation are in fact stalling national plans. Internationally trained professionals are routinely denied licences in their fields because their credentials are not recognized, though the same credentials allow them to score high in the point system.

By seeking international skills for immigration but not giving immigrants access to commensurate licensing and/or employment, Canadian immigration policy and licensing regulations ensure that a surplus pool of skilled labour has been created to function in society as a contingent and precarious labour force. In a recent open letter published in the *Globe and Mail* to the prime minister, the chair of the Toronto Region Immigrant and Employment Council (TRIEC), Dominic D'Alessandro (also the president and CEO of Manulife Financial), quotes the Conference Board of Canada as calculating the impact on the Canadian economy of not recognizing immigrants' learning and learning credentials in the range of $3.42-$4.97 billion annually. He adds, "I see this as a critical issue both for successful nation building and for maximizing the economic potential of Canada" (15 September 2004, A19).

In addition to economic marginality, other laws, such as those governing access to voting, reduce the opportunity and even the desire of immigrants for political participation. Not surprisingly, then, there appears to be a growing gap between immigrants' skills and their ability to participate in Canadian society effectively both economically and emotionally. Research shows that immigrants today are better educated than before, but unlike immigrants in the past, they are not able to reach average Canadian earning capacity even within ten years; immigrant poverty is growing; people of colour, particularly women, are among the poorest (Ornstein 2000; Galabuzi 2001); and voter apathy among racialized communities is growing. Even more disturbing is the fact that underutilization of immigrant skills and domestic restructuring ensure that immigrant people (who are also people of colour) systemically end up more and more in precarious and contingent work.

Hence, the real price of Canadian immigration policy both internationally and domestically is that it seems to create disenfranchised and dislocated people who often use their transnational connections to their countries of origin to retain some semblance of belonging and influence. Today's independent immigrants are educated and skilled people who have a certain sense of entitlement to the structures of power in their countries of origin. However, degrees of marginalization from structures of power in Canada, initially through the denial of participation in democratic structures, and simultaneously and persistently from economic structures, make them by necessity transnational communities.

An example can be seen in immigrant participation in politics. Due to changes to the voting system, no immigrant or refugee is able to vote for any order of government (municipal, provincial, or federal) until he or she acquires Canadian citizenship, which requires a minimum of three years of residency. For refugees and those without status, this minimum term may be longer depending on how long it takes the government to process their claims.[5] So today's immigrants, at least initially, experience separation from the most obvious point of access for citizen participation in issues of nation building, and this separation could last for a minimum of three years. During this time, the only political connection that they retain is to their countries of origin. Juxtapose this connection with lack of access to gainful employment because of the lack of recognition of immigrant credentials/ experience/skills and the reasons for persisting transnational links become obvious.

Furthermore, increasing restrictions are being placed on the rights of citizenship, so even those who have gained the technical "right" of citizenship can either lose that right or have it curtailed in the name of, for example, the security agenda, thus continuing the disenfranchisement and dislocation of some immigrant communities in Canada. This legislatively sanctioned "exclusion" of racialized immigrants (that they could lose their right to residency or not be protected by the state in spite of having Canadian citizenship [e.g., as in the Maher Arar case]) is clearly reflected in the changes made to the Citizenship Act through Bill C-18, the new Immigration and

Refugee Protection Act (IRPA) stipulations, and the antiterrorism bill. Security certificates, ad hoc border searches, investigations and arrests without proper due process, expanding the rights of the state to detain and deport Canadian residents without disclosure, increasing the role of political rather than judicial review in immigration and refugee determination by placing political appointees on the Immigration and Refugee Board – these are just some of the legislative mechanisms marking the experiences of some immigrant communities.[6]

## Transnational Practices and Access to Professions and Trades

It is against this background of political disenfranchisement that I raise the issue of immigrant access to professions and trades. In my experience of working with, advocating for, and mobilizing internationally trained immigrant professionals, particularly doctors (Association of International Physicians and Surgeons of Ontario – AIPSO[7]) and engineers (Council for Access to the Profession of Engineering – CAPE[8]), this lacuna between the obvious benefit of "integrating" immigrant skills and the lack of structural change to accommodate that "integration" is obvious. While in the 1960s European skilled labour coming to Canada found easy access to professions or trades due to familiarity with Canadian structures of assessment and licensing, which replicated European models, today there seems to be a real barrier to access in society for immigrant people (PROMPT 2004). Part of the problem is the lack of proper planning between immigration criteria and the ability of licensing bodies to assess diverse international credentials of immigrants. But part of the problem is entrenched exclusionary notions of what is Canada. Today we have a shortage of doctors in Ontario, yet AIPSO, which has a membership of over 2,000 internationally trained medical professionals, is unable to gain access to the profession for its members. There are approximately 1,000 internationally trained engineers in CAPE's membership, out of which only 18 percent are working in their profession, and more importantly, over 50 percent are unemployed. Stories of doctors driving cabs and engineers delivering pizzas have become commonplace and part of Toronto's folklore.

However, there is a material basis for these stories in terms of the persistence of intractable institutions and policies and their costs to individual immigrant lives. An internationally trained engineer pointed out in a discussion with me that "I came here because I thought I would have protection of my rights, I would have the ability to use my high qualifications, and I would have space in public policy." Similarly, another engineer noted, "I came here to have mobility rights which were denied to me both in my country of origin due to war and in my country of training due to visa limitations. I wanted to live freely and peacefully, and my friends and Canadian consultants with whom I worked in South Asia said Canada was a good place to live and work." Both presumably scored high points on the immigration points grid for their education, language facility, international experience, and adaptability. Yet both are unable to find jobs that are commensurate with their qualifications, experience, and skills. Both said that the situation in Canada is not what they thought it would be.

According to some immigrant professionals, there is an obvious connection between the influx of immigrants in the 1980s and the changes made to Canadian legislation for licensing that are designed to limit access of internationally trained professionals to their profession. They cite, for example, the introduction of the "one year of Canadian experience" stipulation of the engineering licensing process in 1990 as a legislative mechanism that systematically created a structural barrier to entry into the profession for immigrant engineers. According to this requirement, an immigrant engineer can pass all the exams, but a licence is issued only when he or she has acquired one year of Canadian experience (even though he or she may have ten years of international experience). Until this experience is acquired, these individuals cannot call themselves engineers. The reality is that internationally educated professionals (IEPs) are stuck in a catch-22 situation. They do not get jobs because they do not have Canadian experience and/or a Canadian licence, but they cannot get Canadian experience or a licence without the job.

Presumably, Canadian immigration policy is targeting educated and skilled professionals because the Canadian economy needs skilled labour. However, knowing that the majority of immigrants are coming from nontraditional and nonwhite countries, the Canadian nation-building narrative seemingly cannot accommodate this possibility except in a diminished capacity. As one immigrant professional pointed out, the purpose is clear: "Today immigrants bring money that is used by the economy in any case, and they have higher skills than the Canadian average that are being downwardly adjusted into trades." Others agree and add, "they want our children!" They cite negative population growth in Canadian society, an aging population, and a shrinking support base, and they conclude that immigrants are encouraged to come to Canada not to make their own lives but to produce children to service those who are aging. Both of the engineers mentioned above are considering leaving Canada.[9]

These kinds of stories are common. Sohail and Rafi are both engineers too. Sohail stayed in Canada for one and a half years, paid approximately $5,000 to recruiters to find a job, sent out more than 200 résumés, received one interview, drained all his savings. Eventually, he surrendered his Canadian residency, left his family in Canada, and got work in the Middle East. Since then, his wife and children have received Canadian citizenship, but he refuses to get it and intends to retire in his country of origin. However, his children are settled in Canada and are not likely to leave, thus creating a permanently "fractured" family unit. Rafi has been living in Canada for over eight years and has never found a job that is commensurate with his skills. He works, along with other immigrant engineers, in an engineering firm but in nonengineering jobs. His most stable job was a two-year contract. The rest of the time he is hired as a contingent worker – temporary, on call, sporadic, and unstable. He is a Canadian citizen but is planning to leave Canada. Shazia is a finance expert. Her husband could not find a job in Canada, so he returned to his country of origin, while she stayed here with her daughter. She has now moved back to her country of origin to work with a new and emerging financial institution specializing in microcredit.

The same situation emerges in the medical profession. A study published by AIPSO in June 2000 states that, "during the 1980s and early 1990s, studies predicting an oversupply of physicians resulted in policy development designed to limit the supply of physicians. In Ontario, the first direct response to these reports was the recommendation of the Joint Working Group on Graduates of Foreign Medical Schools in 1986 to limit access for international physicians. The outcome was the implementation of a restricted program for the integration of international medical graduates intended and designed to act as a barrier to international physicians" (1). It is important to note that the majority of AIPSO's members are not recent graduates, as the term *international medical graduate* implies. They are fully trained physicians. The majority of AIPSO members have been in practice as licensed physicians for more than five years, and over a third have over ten years of experience (AIPSO 2002, section 3). AIPSO today has a membership of approximately 2,000 fully trained physicians in Ontario who come from approximately eighty different countries. A profile of AIPSO members shows that the majority are general practitioners or family physicians, followed by obstetricians and gynecologists, internal medicine practitioners, pediatricians, general surgeons, and anesthesiologists. This is at a time when a 1999 report by the Ontario College of Family Physicians itself points out that the shortages of family physicians and specialists in Ontario are acute, "not just in small rural and northern communities but in major southern Ontario cities like Windsor, Kitchener-Waterloo, and the Niagara Region." The report argues that "Toronto itself has a shortage of family physicians, if we take into account the unique needs of the city's large and diverse ethnocultural communities" (AIPSO 2002, section 3). The college estimates that, if the situation is not corrected, Ontario could be short 6,000 doctors by 2011 (AIPSO 2002, section 3). In the meantime, a survey of AIPSO's membership in 2000 revealed that its members were engaged in various jobs, "mostly short-term, as factory workers, waiters, telemarketers, security guards, etc. A relatively small number had found employment in health related fields as health care aides, lab assistants etc." (AIPSO 2002, section 3). As a result, almost 40 percent of AIPSO members surveyed were planning on taking US exams (Shakir 2000, 14).

Such is the transnational reality of Canada. More and more, it is the case that immigrants are returning to their countries of origin or moving on to third countries in search of work or to keep family ties intact. In fact, immigrant source countries such as India have come to recognize this situation by changing their own laws to allow their citizens to retain dual citizenship so that their nationals can access both democratic institutions and employment in their countries of origin while residing in Canada. However, this is at a cost to Canada. While nonwhite immigrants come here in a diminished capacity to service the aging nation, the country is losing their skills, their innovations, and eventually their sense of belonging to this country.

While in the past labour market needs were met through the limited utilization of immigrant skills, today the labour market needs are in fact not being met. We are wasting at least one whole generation of immigrant knowledge and skills, we are underutilizing the potential to create innovation and growth in our society, and we are jeopardizing individual and collective social and economic well-being. Why? The resistance to accommodating new immigrant skills seems to reflect the last vestiges of the same flawed and racialized thinking that propelled early Canadian immigration policies. Our nation-building ethos continues to construct non-Europeans as cheap labour but not as nation builders.

Viewing immigrant labour merely as a tool of nation building rather than as the object of nation building is neither preparing Canada for the future nor eroding immigrants' need for maintaining transnational linkages. As one immigrant poignantly said,

> When we applied, we were asked to give every single document that we have about employment, even things about the kind of proficiencies in our trade. Based on that, they accepted us. Based on that, the government thought that this person is suitable and allowed to come into this country. We land here and we try to find [a] similar kind of job in this economy. People say you don't have Canadian experience. Can anyone tell me what this means? No one has been able to ... What is so great about Canadian experience? They say you have to have worked in Canada ... Does this mean that whatever I've done for the last 20 years is inconsequential in Canada? Or, is this economy here so advanced that what we have done elsewhere is useless? (Shakir 2000, 14)

Immigration policy allows skilled knowledge workers from developing countries to come here, but domestic barriers are in effect deskilling and declassing those people, who fill contingent, temporary, and contractual jobs (Reitz 1998). Since becoming licensed is difficult, since the number of good jobs is shrinking, skilled immigrants end up in second- and third-tier jobs for which they require little retraining. Doctors are being retrained to be radiologists, engineers are eased into being technologists, and fully qualified professors and educators are becoming supply teachers or daycare attendants. The irony is that, though the immigrants are supposed to maintain the Canadian standard of living, immigrant doctors, engineers, and teachers cannot even maintain their "own" standard of living, which was their rationale for migrating in the first place. This experience of betrayed aspirations and downward mobility in fact produces, almost by necessity, transnationalist trends among immigrants today as they increasingly move home or elsewhere in search of work.

Another important factor producing transnationalism among immigrants is rooted in immigration policy itself. While immigration legislation of the early 1900s allowed white European settlers great latitude to bring their family members to Canada (including extended members), thus creating rooted communities, today the legislation defines "family" in limited terms and severely curtails the type and number of immigrants and their relations who can come to Canada. This is happening at a time when immigrants are coming from societies that have a broader notion of the family than the European norm. Thus, immigrants today at best have only their immediate family (meaning spouse and children) join them under the family reunification policy, leaving behind tangible and compelling reasons to retain transnational ties – namely, familial and kinship ties. The introduction of the financially onerous ten-year bond of sponsorship also discourages immigrants from bringing in family members. In conjunction with the level of deskilling and declassing of skilled immigrants, it is inevitable that immigrants will retain ties to their countries of origin for the sake of self-preservation and as a fall-back position should they decide to abandon their stay in Canada.

Ironically, the forces of globalization that have created the demographic shift in Canada in spite of structural resistance to that change are producing two contradictory trends in society. While they are engendering the phenomenon of transnationalism among immigrants, they are also posing a challenge to the Canada of tomorrow, which by necessity will become increasingly nonwhite and non-European. Will Canada respond to the challenge and build a stronger nation based on two types of equal Canadians – those who are born here and those who have migrated here irrespective of race or other markers – or will it continue its racist and negative history of marginalizing nonwhite people and thus creating unsettled and "transnational communities" of some Canadians?

**Notes**

1  In this chapter, I do not wish to comment on the refugee experience since it is legislatively and experientially unique and cannot be addressed in the same manner as that of immigrants.

2  It has been referred to as the Chinese Exclusion Act by groups who are waging a legal battle against the government of Canada to seek redress on behalf of families who were affected by the Chinese Immigration Act (1885). See the work of the Chinese Canadian National Council at http://www.ccnc.ca.

3  From the Citizenship and Immigration Canada website: "The most culturally acceptable immigrants came from the United Kingdom and the United States, but they did not match the businessman's concept of the ideal malleable labourer. British and American newcomers were not prepared to tolerate, for example, the low wages or the wretched working conditions of railway construction. Furthermore, they were all too familiar with unions, which could pose a problem for employers" (CIC, http://www.cic.gc.ca).

4  In the past few years, I have been invited by the workers of colour caucuses and equity units of some of the largest unions in Canada to speak to the executive and union membership about antiracist organizational change.

5  New research also shows that the immigrant/racialized vote in fact carries less "value" because of how wards are structured in terms of population density and seats allocated (see Pal and Choudhry 2007).

6  See the Canadian Council for Refugees website at http://www.web.net/ccr/ and "Comments on Bill C-18" by the Council of Agencies Serving South Asians at http://www.cassa.on.ca.

7  For more information on AIPSO, see http://www.aipso.ca.

8  For more information on CAPE, see http://www.capeinfo.ca.

9  During the past eight years, I have worked with and spoken to hundreds of immigrant professionals. Some of those discussions are reflected in this chapter.

# 5

# On Tim Hortons and Transnationalism: Negotiating Canadianness and the Role of Activist/Researcher

*Leela Viswanathan*

On a recent trip overseas, I attended a conference of urban planning academics and then indulged in a one-week holiday in nearby Netherlands. The last leg of my trip brought me back to Amsterdam's Schiphol Airport, where the process of boarding my flight back to Toronto was streamlined. Before boarding the aircraft, those passengers with Canadian passports were to stand in one line and those with non-Canadian passports in another. I suppose all of us were foreigners of one sort or another – being foreign, after all, is relative – but since I was born and raised in Canada and had a Canadian passport I stood in the designated Canadian line with my passport ready in my right hand, my thumb acting as a bookmark for the page with my passport photo. I observed how my fellow Canadian passengers ahead of me had their passports inspected by the security officer. When it was my turn, the officer first inspected my documents with her naked eyes, and then she dressed her right eye with a sort of magnifying glass/monocle-like contraption. As she inspected my passport with the eyepiece, I couldn't help but think that it was like a third cyborg eye. Without removing her eyes off the passport, she began "the interrogation":

Where were you born?
Are you going home?
Where is home?
Did you enjoy your stay in Amsterdam?
How long was your stay?

During the entire interrogation, the officer inspected the pages of my passport with her oracle eye as if she could see things with that eye that I could not, things with hidden meanings. When she finally looked up, she asked, to my utmost surprise, "what about Tim Hortons? I hear so much about Tim Hortons." My brain took a new leap from one level of irrationality to another. And as I prepared my response, I thought of other possible questions regarding Canadiana that she might pose – questions regarding curling, lumberjack shirts, doughnuts, and maple syrup. The Tim Hortons question was a trick question, or so I thought. In one fell swoop, it addressed three elements of Canadiana: hockey, coffee, and doughnuts. "Oh, yes, of course," I replied. "Tim Horton was a famous Canadian hockey player, but I suppose you are referring to the more popular chain of doughnut shops and coffee that lots of folks love." No follow-up questions ensued. The officer nodded and then chortled, "I see ... Well, enjoy your flight!" As I settled into my seat on the KLM flight destined for Pearson airport, I wondered, did my passport alone validate my Canadian citizenship and identity, or should I be thanking my knowledge of our Canadian saviour, Tim Hortons?

When I am abroad, I am Canadian, or at least I have to respond to specific questions to justify my Canadianness – questions regarding Tim Hortons but so far not about saris and samosas. When I am in Toronto, I am deemed to be a South Asian, and for all intents and purposes my cultural ancestry would reflect this designation. My parents emigrated from India to Canada in the early 1960s, and I was born in Canada; however, I realized that I was South Asian only seven years ago, when I was approached to join the board of directors of a Toronto-based network of social service agencies serving South Asians. Until then, I had thought myself to be a transplanted Montrealer in Toronto. But I soon learned that "South Asian" is a term for people who traced their roots back to the region of South Asia, a region that encompasses not just India but also Bangladesh, Nepal, Pakistan, and Sri Lanka. It is my experience that people are called South Asian, or call themselves South Asian, when they are outside the region of South Asia. For example, rather than calling oneself Indian, or Pakistani, national identities are subsumed under larger regional areas and become the basis for solidarity in a new country.

In my case, in Canada, my South Asian identity is linked to my parents' regional area of origin, or my ancestral roots, rather than to my own country or city of birth, and in calling myself South Asian I have one more basis for building common ground with folks who also trace their roots back to South Asia. This basis for a common ground becomes a point of access for belonging to communities of South Asians or a South Asian community. Even so, as noted by Aparna Sundar in this volume, subsuming oneself under the umbrella title of South Asian has been mostly unproblematic for coalitions of agencies providing services such as immigration and settlement support. However, this proves more difficult for coalitions such as the South Asian Left Democratic Alliance (SALDA) that focus on matters resulting from conflicts within specific South Asian nations, among religious groups, and along lines of class and occupation. The term *South Asian* does not necessarily address these kinds of "fractures" in the community, even though it might be used in an attempt to bridge these divides.

It is vital to consider the term *community* in terms of its use and its meaning in my research and engagement with immigrant and racialized groups; academics and nonacademics use the term a fair bit, but do they know what each other means when they use it? I consider that there must be a meaning for community that goes beyond one of belonging, coexistence, and possibly sameness. As a result of researching the term, I have come to agree with Henri Lustiger-Thaler that communities represent "ways of becoming and knowing" and that each reflects "striving for something in *common*" (1994, 21). Lustiger-Thaler suggests that communities can be seen "as ongoing practices that build and incorporate sentiments of solidarity, public spiritedness, *and* difference" (40). Thus, how community might develop, and the struggle associated with this search for commonality, not necessarily as a homogeneous endpoint, are of key concern and might involve conflict. Groups should be asked what they consider "themselves to have *in common*" (23), and it must be accepted that these so-called commonalities may change over time or circumstance.

A link can be drawn between processes of community building and Peggy Levitt and Nina Glick Schiller's (2004) suggestions regarding transnational identities and transnational practices. As noted by Luin Goldring and Sailaja Krishnamurti in the introduction to this volume, Levitt and Glick Schiller (2004) point out that a sense of transnational identity can develop – that is, a "way of belonging" – without having to engage in transnational "ways of being." Building community and transnational identity are both means by which ways of belonging are developed over space and time. While some individuals are working out what it means to be an immigrant living in Toronto, many are also coming to terms with building a new sense of home and belonging in Canada, without necessarily severing ties with friends and relatives who may still live outside Canada. Of course, like me, they too are building on their understanding of the term *South Asian,* because where they came from, "South Asian" was not necessarily part of their common language either. These experiences have taken me outside the realm of South Asian groups and have involved leaders from Chinese, Latino-Hispanic, and continental African groups in Toronto who are also working toward overcoming barriers faced by their communities in terms of underemployment, poverty, and racism, to name just a few, and their categorization as "other."

Arjun Appadurai (1996) has looked critically at the role of those deemed "other" in relation to city and nation. He laments that "racialized and minoritized" people in America continue to be relegated to tribalist categories and as such are not made welcome (171). Appadurai states that, while living in Western countries (particularly America), he has observed that the challenge presented by diasporic communities is a global phenomenon but that Westerners have not yet "come to terms with the difference between being a land of immigrants and being one node in a postnational network of diasporas" (171). So an understanding has to be reached that "emerging diaspora runs with, and not against, the grain of identity, movement, and reproduction" (171). From Appadurai I draw that governments in the West too often see their own socially and economically marginalized groups of communities as cultural and political threats at the same time that these communities face greater threats from the institutionalized practices of the state on a global scale. For example, the US War on Terror and the Canadian government's engagement in Canada-US border politics since this war was declared have further racialized Muslims and immigrants from Muslim countries. The Muslim diasporas are seen as running against the grain of a North American society, and while they may indeed be seen as a node in a global postnational network, it is not in a positive light in building cohesiveness and sharing; rather, it is deemed as a threat.

As a volunteer and activist among South Asian groups in Toronto over the past eight years, I have worked shoulder to shoulder with recent and not-so-recent immigrants to Canada. In working together, we have helped each other to better understand the larger systems of service delivery and public policy that affect our lives. The richness of our experiences and expertise fuel us in our struggles for social justice. I also know that one reason I was asked to volunteer my time with these groups was so that I might share my knowledge as a policy analyst and social planner. I have linked this part of my professional persona with my activist side and then shared this amalgamation of skills and interests with these groups. Subsequently, these groups have shared with me and with each other their own firsthand experiences and expertise regarding their various levels of engagement with their jobs, families, and government systems.

In 2001, I shifted gears from my day job as a policy analyst and social planner to a new kind of life and research responsibility – that of doctoral student. I returned to school because, rather than simply reacting to the problems experienced by racialized groups and communities in the city, I wanted to take the opportunity to think carefully about *how* to research such problems from an academic standpoint. However, I did not want to remove myself from the grassroots understandings and experiences of these problems. I have maintained my belief that these community experiences can inform my research, and in turn my research can benefit these community groups outside academia on terms that we set together. At the same time, as an academic researcher, obviously I intend for my work to be recognized *within* the academic establishment.

And now, as a result of this approach, I see that I have an opportunity to do more, to seek ways to build bridges between the world of academic research and the knowledge of groups outside academia and racialized communities within the city, in ways that respect all parties. These experiences and interactions with Toronto's South Asian groups have gone beyond informing my sense of personal and cultural belonging to contributing to my relatively new hybrid identity: that of community activist–academic researcher.

Hybridity has been noted to be a "counter-hegemonic strategy" (Lowe 1996, 66-67); however, on a personal note, a question remains: is *my* experience of "hybridity" a counterhegemonic strategy? Will my remixing of identities be embraced by the academic establishment and those outside it? This is to say that, in bridging activism among grassroots organizations and academia, I am negotiating more than just my South Asian identity; I am negotiating my role as a community activist with my role as an academic researcher, and I would like to be able to do both, thoughtfully, energetically, and professionally. My hybrid identity as a South Asian and Canadian has informed my activism and has helped me to reconcile my role as an activist with my role as an academic. One informs the other and my approach to engaging in research with racialized and aggrieved communities. By negotiating the relationship between my South Asian and Canadian identities, I am positioned to take a similar approach in reconciling my academic and activist roles and negotiating the parameters within which I, in conjunction with community groups who have helped me to define my South Asian and activist identities, choose specific issues and research them. Therefore, how the transnational is organized through research is directly linked to the bridging of my hybrid identities. Research on public policy, such as immigration and settlement, from the standpoint of an aggrieved group becomes an additional means for organizing seemingly disparate groups in a struggle to address systemic problems and illuminates individual experiences with these systems – who benefits and who pays. At the same time, these groups make a contribution to policy discourses and research processes that more often than not exclude their participation.

The term *transnationalism* has been criticized for its "lack of conceptual clarity" (Westwood and Phizacklea 2000, 10). Sallie Westwood and Annie Phizacklea point to the importance of coming to an understanding of the different and at times "unequal" ways in which transnationalism is experienced – that is, "the ways in which both nation and migration form loci of sentiments and emotions crucial to a sense of home" and in turn inform a "politics of belonging" (11). In this volume, how does transnationalism fit into such experiences and a dynamic notion of what constitutes community? Transnationalism is not a common word for the South Asian groups and other racialized groups with whom I have done activist work. For these groups, what seems to take precedence is the struggle to make a living, find belonging, and ultimately build new lives here in Canada. While negotiating one's mobility between Canada and "homeland" is often central to sustaining ties within family networks and, as many academics have pointed out, transmitting funds, goods, and information on local politics, how this ongoing negotiation relates to transnationalism has not necessarily been explored as a theoretical exercise, let alone a practical one, at the community level.

By contrast, the grassroots groups with which I have had the privilege of working have little difficulty relating to the term *diaspora*. In fact, the term enables these groups to connect with individuals and groups with similar cultural histories and experiences beyond their local geographical community in which they are living. These groups might feel a connection to other people who left the same country of origin. These groups also might relate to shared historical experiences of displacement and mobility of peoples from their homelands and reconnect with them if these connections were, at one point or another, fleeting or lost altogether. Diaspora is a term that enables these individuals and groups to relate to something bigger than themselves and their local community connections. Individual connections to diaspora may differ in level of intensity, and, frankly speaking, some may feel no connection at all. Simply knowing that such a diaspora exists may be enough – as if a connection may be built when and if an individual chooses to do so.

I see this particular phenomenon among some youth transitioning to adulthood and among adults reflecting on their youthful experiences in Canada. For example, some youth born in Canada may feel a strong connection to the Indian diaspora through their parents and might "lose touch" as adults when their relatives are no longer living back "there," back "home." Or I have seen adults renewing or discovering a connection to family and histories "abroad" when they lacked this connection in their socialization growing up in Canada. These connections to diaspora could be understood as transnational connections. The means by which these connections are built or renewed could be by cultural, educational, or political associations or through marriage or family reunification.

I recognize that communities contemplate macroissues of globalization, nationalism, and human mobility, but transnationalism and transnationality are not working terms used by community groups, in my experience, to describe their interactions between macro- and microissues. The idea of human agency in effecting social and individual change at the local level and in relation to global networks, including our own families and friends, is often on our activist minds. Agency becomes a means through which building security of justice and space for oneself and one's family can be sought out and possibly achieved (Westwood and Phizacklea 2000).

The contrast of academic interpretations and grassroots possibilities for understanding transnationalism makes me think of Aihwa Ong's (1999) contribution to transnationalism discourses. Ong suggests that, instead of focusing on globalization studies, transnationalism offers a "cultural logic" – one that refers to "cultural specificities of global processes, tracing the multiplicity of the uses and conceptions of culture" (4). For example, I have wondered whether or not the South Asian and Chinese youth I have worked with over the years would consider themselves to be living transnationally, or "operating in communities along multiple international axes," to use a phrase from an early proposal for this volume, and how this would translate into their senses of identity and belonging. Their constructions of multiple identities and belonging are dynamic, incorporating national cultural heritages of their parents with their understandings of South Asian and Chinese cultures in the Canadian context, thus constructing their personal or collective interpretations of what it means to be Canadian. They may be aware of and concerned about what is taking place in their ancestral lands, but many are also culturally aware of and engaged in the civic life of Toronto. All these elements inform who they are, and their identities can change as their understanding of "home" relative to Canada or another country, or Canada relative to the globe, changes. After all, as Stuart Hall notes, "people are not cultural dopes. They know something about who they are" (1997, 58). These youth give me hope for building a further understanding of my own hybridity and how such a multiplicity in identity may change over time, as I learn and grow as an activist and researcher.

"Transnationalism processes are situated cultural practices" (Ong 1999, 17). These processes point to the complexities and "tensions between movements and social orders," such as the movements of people and capital and their relationships to governments in particular nations, regions, or locales (Ong 1999, 6). For some governments, the cultural and racial diversity of populations becomes an economic commodity (i.e., labour) that is promoted to attract corporate investment and as a cultural asset that is celebrated under the colourful umbrella of multiculturalism (Abu-Laban and Gabriel 2002). Therefore, "diversity management," as practised by some governments, can be considered an example of transnationalism or an outcome of transnational processes.

The tensions inherent in such practices provide the basis for action or "political agency" from the very groups that they engage, namely immigrants. In my experience, many immigrants who are excluded from professional labour markets and have not yet gained formal citizenship status continue to be deemed "hot commodities" for attracting investment to the city. How can they claim their rights to the city and to their own economic and social well-being? Do immigrants benefit in some way from having their skills and education commodified, even when they are not able to obtain employment in their fields and have no formal political franchise? If so, then how? These are just some of questions linking macroissues to the local context that have surfaced in both my academic research and my activism.

In the transnationalism workshop that inspired this volume, one member of the audience declared, "I think it is high time that we talk about the ethics and morality of doing research in the community." I believe that this is a serious and very useful question to be posing for those who pride themselves on being reflexive practitioners, ones who are not just made curious by their research and research contexts but also engaged by their role as researchers in the "communities outside academia." What would it be like if academic researchers concerned themselves with conducting research not simply on their own terms or along the terms of their university settings but also in a negotiated process with the communities in which and with whom the research will be conducted? How can our work as academics run in tandem with that of our "community partners," thus building the capacity of the communities most involved with, or affected by, our joint research?

The Social Sciences and Humanities Research Council (SSHRC) in Canada has sponsored academic–nonacademic community collaborative grants such as the Community-University Research Alliance (CURA) and more recently the SSHRC-Heritage Canada joint Strategic Initiative on Multicultural Issues (see http://www.sshrc.ca). These grant programs show promise for the possibilities for academic–nonacademic research collaborations. These programs have also placed an emphasis on the distribution of research findings among both academic and nonacademic communities. However, I argue that these plausible factors should not make issues of accountability and ethics in such research collaboration an outdated concern. Namely, collaborations between academics and nonacademic "community groups" should allow for negotiations about research design, ethics, and accountability through the development of the research partnership and beyond. For example, whose ethics guidelines are applied in the development and execution of the project? Are such guidelines mutually developed and agreed upon by academic and community partners? How is the knowledge to be gained through the research beneficial to the communities involved, and in what way has the capacity of the community groups to engage in research been heightened and the potential for such research capacity become sustainable? Are the process and outcome of developing these research relationships as important as the dissemination and collection of research findings?

For researchers Robert Rundstrom and Douglas Deur, "ethics is a relational and contextual matter" that requires recognition of the ways in which the relationship among research partners (including research subjects) is shaped by the interactions among these parties (1999, 238). How are issues, rights, practices, and ethics formulated and given meaning by all research participants? Thomas Herman and Doreen Mattingly (1999) have written about some of the pitfalls and challenges associated with engaging in academic-community collaborative research, particularly from the standpoint of academics. The authors offer that in their work with community organizations they have had to negotiate their relationship with their fellow scholars *at the same time as* they negotiate their relationship with their nonacademic community research colleagues. One means for alleviating some of the tensions associated with this dual recognition, the authors suggest, is to establish long-term relations between academics and community organizations or aggrieved groups, even offering services to community participants. Herman and Mattingly also note that the time it takes to foster such relationships in tandem with their academic service and administrative work can be taxing and lengthy and "speaks to the ethical dissatisfaction many researchers feel with allowing their analytic roles to stand as their only form of public participation" (212). At the same time, internal, university community service might hold more value in consideration for tenure and promotion than active service to nonacademic community-based initiatives. As suggested by both Bose and Sundar in this volume, engagement with the transnational is not necessarily idyllic and is mired by both challenges and opportunities. In the same vein, add the layers of differences among and within transnational communities to the development of academic-community partnerships and it becomes clear that challenges and opportunities will arise; however, the resultant complexity should not deter all parties from testing the waters in building mutually beneficial relationships.

My involvement with groups of South Asian, Chinese, Hispanic, and African communities in Toronto has required negotiation of my role as a researcher and activist on a personal level and in our collective expectations for the process, outcome, and impact of our collaborative research. This is a rich experience that continues to inform the theoretical explorations in my academic research and the implications of this research on my professional and community practices. It also leads me to ask questions regarding the role of pedagogy and research involving grassroots organizations. Many universities struggle not only to reach out to nonacademic communities to build new research relations but more importantly to draw in the communities to engage with the academic community. I would posit that, while many universities are succeeding in the former, in part due to pressures by granting bodies to move away from "research for research's sake" initiatives, many universities continue to struggle with the latter. Some authors use the term *reciprocal research relations* to reflect the possibility of exchange between academics and community groups but suggest that building such relations is "time intensive and infrequently rewarded in the academy" (Herman and Mattingly 1999, 220; see also Rundstrom and Deur 1999).

Appadurai (2000) speaks to the difficulties in producing knowledge through globalization research that not only meets academic standards but also remains relevant to grassroots organizations and community groups. He raises questions regarding the nature of collaborative research, the legitimacy of new knowledge that gets produced, as well as the various "communities of judgement and accountability" that might be judged by academics as central to the pursuit of such knowledge. I would agree with him that, when it comes to debates regarding collaborative research involving communities beyond the realm of academia, grassroots organizations should be enabled to participate in these debates. This, in turn, would lead to a joint review by academics and community organizations of the ethics of engaging in community-based research. Such a review should engage community-based organizations in the development of guidelines and the documentation of expectations for collaborative research.

Does the possibility for such social and institutional change exist? Is it as complicated as advocating for changes to exclusionary national immigration policies as suggested by fellow activist Uzma Shakir? My own experience has shown that such change is possible, even if it occurs only incrementally, one negotiated effort at a time and with a long-term investment in years of effort and commitment, one researcher and one community group at a time. The realm of study of transnationalism is but one context that could allow for academics and grassroots community groups to revision the field, to learn from one another, to renegotiate the language of the field across academia and grassroots communities, and ultimately to effect a more equitable practice of joint community-based and academic research.

One morning last year, the lady at the Tim Hortons stall I frequented on campus proceeded to fill my ecofriendly mug with a double-double (coffee, with two creams and two sugars), and she apologized for having run out of cream.

"Would milk be all right with you, dear?" she asked.

"I don't mind at all; I don't usually have cream at home," I responded.

"Funny how most of the students don't either, dear," she quipped. "They just act as if they do."

I pondered her response, considering that for some, particularly cash-strapped students, cream symbolizes wealth and luxury, perhaps also some kind of First World authenticity. The conversation still lingers in my thoughts, and I wonder if being Canadian is about acting a part that is an iconic nationality officially documented while preserving one's hybridity beneath the surface *sans papiers*. I could sit in a university campus courtyard sipping my Tim Hortons coffee, contemplating the implication of my South Asianness blending with the brown sludge of cream and caffeine epitomizing Canadiana and flowing through my hybrid veins, but I digress. Instead, I think back to that day at Schiphol Airport. I wonder why some might consider that cultural symbols and my knowledge of Tim Hortons and hockey or saris and Bollywood movies and all their auxiliary commodities could supposedly reveal more about my Canadian nationality, or my South Asian identity, or variations thereof, than a passport document ever could. Or that any of these cultural objects could reveal a transnationality, a "cultural logic," that might be understood by people living outside and inside Canada, if it is not first negotiated by me, on my terms, on Canadian soil or abroad. However, I don't have answers; these are merely contemplations, leading to more questions about negotiating my own version of Canadianness. Perhaps I will find answers somewhere among the academic discourses, my activism, and my urban research or even among my class of second-year undergraduate students, who have, I'll bet two Timbits, something to contribute from their own experiences.

# Part 2
## States, Transnational Labour, and Diasporic Capital

# 6
# Globalizing Work, Globalizing Citizenship: Community–Migrant Worker Alliances in Southwestern Ontario

*Kerry Preibisch*

A defining feature of global restructuring in high-income countries has been the growing incorporation of foreign workers in various sectors of the economy. Canadian horticulture is a case in point. The profitability of farming operations in the country's key site for horticultural production – southwestern Ontario – has become increasingly reliant on a highly flexible, mobile foreign workforce facilitated by the Canadian state under the Caribbean-Mexico Seasonal Agricultural Workers Program (SAWP). The government refers to the SAWP as a seasonal, temporary work program, yet such descriptors belie the use of foreign workers in agriculture. While foreign workers were originally hired to meet seasonal shortages, they are now present in the country year round, have longer contracts, and return year after year. Furthermore, while migrant workers were initially employed in the fruit orchards and tobacco fields in southern Ontario, they now work in a wide range of production processes throughout the country. The presence of thousands of Mexican and Caribbean workers has created a new dimension to the human geography of Ontario (Cecil and Ebanks 1991), especially in regions where workers are concentrated.

As these transnational foreign workers have assumed a greater profile in the production of agrifood products, they have also increasingly become constituents of the social fabric of rural Ontario. Yet within the emerging literature on the phenomenon of temporary labour migration to agriculture, the relations between migrants and rural communities have largely been ignored. In this chapter, I explore both the structural constraints that contribute to the social exclusion of migrant workers in rural communities and the personal ties that are presenting new forms of rural inclusiveness. In particular, I examine the ways in which Canadian citizens, acting as individuals and through community groups, take an active role in advocating for the rights of foreign workers. A key consideration is the implications that these new alliances between transnational foreign workers and citizens hold for our understandings of civil society and citizenship.

## Citizenship and Power in the Global Political Economy

According to the United Nations, in 2005, some 191 million people lived outside their countries of birth or citizenship (Stalker 2006). Central to the trends differentiating global migration flows from the past is the number of people working in high-income countries under temporary work visas. This trend was particularly marked throughout the 1990s, growing at much more rapid rates than permanent immigration (OECD 2003). The incorporation of foreign workers helps to ensure global competitiveness in world markets by enhancing labour flexibility in the sectors in which they are employed. As some scholars have argued, under recent global restructuring, the nation-state assumes a key role in restructuring national labour-capital relations through global strategies that involve "reorganizing its own regulatory and political boundaries to protect its position within the globalized political economy" (Rai 2002, 97). Within this scenario, the granting or withholding of citizenship rights becomes a powerful regulatory mechanism at the disposal of labour-receiving states to create and maintain a pool of highly exploitable and socially excluded workers (Stasiulis and Bakan 1997; Baines and Sharma 2002; Ball and Piper 2004). Through immigration policy, the state is able to render "legal and legitimate discriminations based on whether individuals embody capital (e.g., as transnationalist capitalists benefiting from wealth creation in the Newly Industrialized Countries) or poverty (e.g., of the majority of those living in developing nations), as well as the dominant race/ethnicity and gender" (Stasiulis and Bakan 1997, 119).

Citizenship is thus conceptualized here as a social relation of power that acts both at the level of the nation-state and within the global political economy. Situating citizenship in this way furthers the debate beyond the conventional conceptual framework based on the sociological analysis of T.H. Marshall (1964) that distinguishes three different dimensions of citizenship (civil, political, and social rights), which developed historically. Marshall's approach has become hegemonic in the social science literature, constituting a well-used, historically dominant paradigm (Cohen 1999). Marshall's framework, however, has been criticized on a number of grounds, including its evolutionary stance, its failure to address citizenship comparatively and historically, and its lack of consideration for the differentiating elements of class, ethnicity, and gender (Turner 1990). The work of feminist scholars in particular (Pateman 1988; Williams 1989; Phillips 1991) dispelled liberal notions of the universal citizen based on white, European, propertied males to the exclusion of others (Stasiulis and Bakan 1997). While these theorists' contributions were central in emphasizing the gendered nature of citizenship, many remained limited both to Western modes of citizenship and to a fairly homogeneous understanding of women (Yuval-Davis 1999b). Nira Yuval-Davis has extended social relational analysis further, advocating for approaching citizenship in ways that take into account the multiple dimensions of social divisions and locations that include membership in dominant or subordinate groups, gender, ethnicity, origin, and urban or rural residence. Citizenship must be "understood as a multi-layered construct, in which one's citizenship in collectivities in the different layers – local, ethnic, national, state, cross- or trans-state and supra-state – is affected and often at least partly constructed by the relationships and positionings of each layer in specific historical context" (Yuval-Davis 1999b, 123). This approach finds resonance in Daiva Stasiulis and Abigail Bakan's work on foreign domestic workers that emphasizes citizenship as "a nodal point for the intersection of many other social relations" (1997, 117). Social relational approaches highlight the ways in which citizenship – as a social relation of power – undergoes constant change and (re)negotiation (Stasiulis and Bakan 1997). They allow us to recognize and explore how citizenship is reformulated through historical struggle (Turner 1990) while furthering our understanding of current trends in human mobility in the context of global restructuring.

Thinking about citizenship as a relation of power should not obscure citizenship as a set of practices carried out by social actors articulating popular demands for participation (Turner 1990). Agnes Ku (2002) notes that a growing number of scholars is reconceptualizing citizenship as "a set of cultural, symbolic and political practices through which individuals and groups claim new rights or struggle over existing rights" (543). In particular, research on the political associations of transnational migrants posits citizenship as a practice increasingly being enacted in transnational contexts and involving more than one nation-state (Levitt 2001a; Goldring 2002). While there is a long, postwar history of a broad range of marginalized groups articulating a more inclusive citizenship within the nation-state on the basis of the right to equality of treatment,[1] more recently contemporary international migration has forced a fundamental reshaping of how we think about citizenship (Castles and Davidson 2000; Stasiulis and Bakan 2003). Relevant to this chapter are the ways in which the global movement of people has opened up new forms of, and spaces for, political participation in ways that transgress national boundaries (Law 2002; Courville and Piper 2004), a debate that I return to later.

### Foreign Workers and Canadian Agriculture

The core program under which foreign workers are granted temporary employment authorization in Canadian agriculture is the SAWP. The program began operating in 1966 with a bilateral agreement between Jamaica and Canada but has since expanded to include other Caribbean countries and Mexico. The SAWP is managed and implemented at the federal and provincial levels and within bilateral frameworks of agreement between Canada and the labour supply countries (Verma 2003). In Canada, the principal federal agency managing the program is Human Resources and Skills

Development Canada (HRSDC). Day-to-day administration in Ontario is carried out by Foreign Agricultural Resources Management Services (FARMS), an employer organization. Labour supply country governments shoulder a considerable share of the administrative burden, including managing recruitment and providing officials to Canada to act as worker representatives.

The SAWP has grown significantly. From just 264 Jamaicans in 1966, the SAWP workers now number close to 20,000 nationwide. The overwhelming majority is employed in Ontario (85 percent). Establishment and growth of the program reflect transformations in the character of Canadian agriculture, including a shift away from the family farm. Rural Ontario has witnessed land consolidation, a decrease in the size of growers' households, and a declining interest among growers' children to farm (Basok 2002). Throughout the twentieth century and to date, growers have failed to attract and retain domestic sources of labour (Satzewich 1991; Wall 1992) as citizens with other employment options have been unwilling to accept the low wages and working conditions of farm labour. The SAWP's massive growth in the 1990s was also a direct result of the increased competitiveness of Canada's greenhouse production and the program's extension to new operations that were formerly excluded, such as floriculture.

The global competitiveness of Canadian agriculture hinges on the casualization and/or flexibilization of the workforce. In world markets, Canadian producers compete with their counterparts in the United States, who rely heavily on documented and undocumented migrants from Latin America and the Caribbean (Griffith et al. 1995; Martin 2003). Although foreign workers are less pervasive in Canada, they have tremendous economic importance. Some authors have argued that foreign workers constitute a structural necessity for the horticultural industry (Basok 2002), while others have linked their increased use to the rapid expansion of the greenhouse sector in the 1990s and its strong performance in international markets (Weston and Scarpa de Masellis 2003). Further, my research indicated that some employers consider their foreign crew as their core workforce, with domestic workers as supplementary (Preibisch, forthcoming). The SAWP is no longer a seasonal, temporary program. Foreign workers are present in Canada from early January to mid-December, and individual contracts may last up to eight months. In addition, foreign workers are now employed throughout the country and within a greater number of commodities.

## A Reliable Workforce

The Canadian horticultural industry believes that the limiting factor to further investment is an inadequate supply of "reliable" labour and that foreign workers fill this gap (FARMS 2003a). In industry and government discourse, this characteristic is often used to illustrate the desirability of this workforce, whereas wage differentials are rarely discussed. This discursive focus underscores the key advantage that foreign workers represent. Although they comprise a low-cost workforce and undoubtedly depress local wages, their lack of freedom and powerlessness constituting their reliability make them particularly valuable to capitalist accumulation (Basok 2002). Many scholars have argued that the SAWP is illustrative of unfree labour relations extant in modern capitalist economies (Satzewich 1991; Wall 1992; Sharma 2001; Basok 2002).

Foreign workers' vulnerability is structured primarily through the denial of legal citizenship.[2] Under the SAWP, workers enter Canada as noncitizens, nonpermanent residents. They are assigned a sole employer and thus do not enjoy the citizenship rights of labour mobility. They are further denied access to a range of services and protections that composes the social citizenship entitlements accorded to Canadians (Baines and Sharma 2002). Even though many foreign agricultural workers have been serving the Canadian labour market for decades, they are legally prevented from ever gaining citizenship status. This feature distinguishes the SAWP from the Live-In Caregiver Program (LCP), Canada's foreign worker program for domestic labour, which allows participants to apply for permanent resident status after two years of employment.

Constituting foreign workers as "reliable" includes limiting their social commitments through mechanisms that are mutually reinforcing. Paradoxically, SAWP workers enter the country as single applicants but must demonstrate that they support families in their home countries. Preference in recruitment is biased toward married workers to deter them from attempting to secure permanent residency through marriage or seeking to remain illegally. Residential arrangements that house workers on their employers' property also accord their employers a form of supracontrol over their lives. Some growers engage in measures to limit migrants' social lives, such as the sanctioned use of "farm rules" that include imposing a curfew, hiring security guards to monitor movements on and off the farm, enforcing restrictions on workers' mobility, and prohibiting the entry of visitors (Preibisch 2003).

Workers' vulnerability is further institutionalized through mechanisms of labour recruitment and retention, such as the policy allowing employers to request their workers by name each year. While the policy is beneficial to employers by reducing turnover, it also fosters a high degree of worker self-discipline and shores up worker loyalty (Wall 1992; Basok 2002; Binford 2004). The Mexican government also requires employers to submit end-of-season evaluations for workers; those who are not renamed or who receive a poor evaluation have been interrogated in Mexico, and some have been suspended for a year (Preibisch 2000). In general, workers worry that a negative evaluation or failure to be named could compromise their continued participation in the program. Some also fear losing their current placement to one that is less attractive. Mexican workers seeking better working conditions, accommodation, or a longer contract can request to be placed on another farm, but the government enforces an informal three-year rule whereby requests for transfer are denied until a worker has completed three consecutive work seasons with the assigned employer (Binford 2004). The most effective mechanism of control is employers' power to dismiss and, therefore, repatriate workers. Although deportation rates are low, fear of repatriation pervades workers every day. They have been repatriated for falling ill, refusing unsafe work, making complaints related to housing/working conditions, or having unauthorized visitors (Smart 1998; Basok 2002; UFCW 2002; Preibisch 2003). Workers consequently take measures to avoid repatriation and the loss of livelihood, some at considerable cost to themselves, such as nonreporting of injuries or illnesses (Basok 2002; Preibisch 2000; UFCW 2002; Binford 2004).

Workers' vulnerability is further institutionalized in the limited protections afforded by their home country states. As mentioned, labour supply countries post officials in Canada charged as worker representatives. Their other task, however, is to maintain their country's share of labour placements in the SAWP and thus ensure a steady stream of remittances home. Labour supply countries rely heavily on the foreign exchange earnings derived from remittances, whose impressive growth rates are eclipsing traditional sources of foreign exchange and have proved more stable than foreign direct investment inflows. Employment opportunities in high-income countries not only provide foreign exchange but also relieve labour-sending states of some of the political pressure resulting from the social costs of economic liberalization that have eroded the livelihoods of small-scale producers and waged workers. The SAWP policy that allows employers to choose the country of origin of their workers and to switch at will deprives labour supply countries of bargaining power to press for higher wages or improved working conditions and represents a deliberate strategy by the Canadian government to discipline the workforce and its representatives. When the SAWP expanded to include Mexico, a confidential government report noted that "Manpower [now HRSDC] have indicated they see this as a useful development in the sense that the competition aids Canadian producers in bargaining for conditions with the Caribbean authorities" (cited in Verma 2003, 69).

The inadequate protection provided by home country officials is compounded by failures in the governance of the SAWP on behalf of the Canadian provincial and federal governments. Provincially, HRSDC makes little effort to enforce housing standards carried out by municipal public health inspectors or to standardize inspections across the province. Employers that have demonstrated unsafe or dehumanizing employment practices are rarely sanctioned or denied foreign workers. Federally, HRSDC recently extended a new foreign worker program subject to less government regulation to agricultural producers, a move that threatens to place workers in even more vulnerable situations. These failures in governance are compounded by an absence of social programs or service provision geared at the 20,000 foreign workers within the country.[3] Finally, foreign agricultural workers face further disadvantages owing to their occupational status as farm labour. In Ontario, domestic and foreign farm workers are accorded fewer legal rights than workers in other sectors (see interview with Raper in this volume). In sum, foreign agricultural workers constitute a highly exploitable and vulnerable group within the Canadian labour market and society in general.

### Community-Worker Relations

In recent years, temporary migration to Canadian agriculture has become a topic of scholarly interest. This literature has brought to light the lived realities of these transnational migrants, explored the impact of labour migration on communities of origin, and analyzed the incorporation of foreign labour in Canadian agriculture (Satzewich 1991; Ganaselall 1992; Wall 1992; Colby 1997; Knowles 1997; Smart 1998; Basok 2002; Verduzco and Lozano 2003; Weston and Scarpa de Masellis 2003; Preibisch 2003, 2004; Binford 2004; Downes and Odle-Worrell 2003; Russell 2003). Less focus has been placed, however, on the social and economic changes in Canada's rural communities that have accompanied the agricultural sector's growing reliance on foreign workers. The few studies that have attempted to identify and articulate these relationships have tended to show the ways in which such communities are linked through transnational labour markets or document the emergence of transnational communities (Goldring 1996; Levitt 2001a), while the relationships that develop *within* labour-receiving communities remain uncharted. Yet as Amy Sim (2003) argues, a consideration of the structural inequality between foreign workers, their employers, and the host society must take into account the context of reception, particularly when migrant workers are ethnically distinct owing to deliberate government policy (see Satzewich 1991).

One exception to this general paucity in the Canadian literature is Robert Cecil and G. Edward Ebanks' (1991) research conducted in the late 1980s, before the SAWP experienced its considerable growth. These researchers found some hostility toward migrant workers but mostly ignorant indifference. They claimed that the "influx of thousands of black workers into white rural areas has created a new dimension to the human geography of Southwestern Ontario," but they contended that foreign workers were socially excluded from the rural communities in which they reside (389). In addition to this singular examination of community-worker relations, research on other dimensions of SAWP migration has made more recent observations regarding social exclusion. First, studies show that foreign workers have indeed become part of the rural social landscape in areas of high concentration.

Tanya Basok's research on the greenhouse industry describes the migrant population as a marked presence in the social geography, particularly in the "Mexican invasion of the local supermarket" and the "image of Mexican men riding their bicycles along rural roads" (2002, 3). Yet in other areas of Ontario and nationwide, foreign workers are socially invisible. Josephine Smart's (1998) research in Alberta describes minimal social interaction between the settled and the migrant communities.

Second, most authors emphasize that foreign farm workers face a series of constraints in exercising a social life. The work environment, entailing long hours of physically demanding labour, is compounded by housing arrangements that geographically isolate them from the rural population. In general, foreign workers lack transportation, constituting the weekly trip to the supermarket as their single most significant social contact with local residents (Smart 1998).

Third, existing studies describe local interactions as marked by discrimination and racism (Colby 1997; Smart 1998; Basok 2002, 2004). Catherine Colby (1997) reports that workers perceived more racism than in previous migratory experiences in the United States. In a recent article, Basok (2004) argues that foreign farm workers are denied social membership in Canadian society, which in turn limits their opportunities to gain the knowledge and skills required to claim their legal entitlements.

My research in 2002 confirmed findings in the literature that foreign workers experience social exclusion from the broader rural community and that most residents are either unaware or choose to ignore the migrant community living in their midst.[4] However, I also documented social activity involving not only migrants but also the broader Canadian community, a finding that does not fit with the dominant narrative in the literature of the socially isolated migrant. Furthermore, while many of those who have formed relationships with migrants were Caribbean or Latin American immigrants, this was not always the case. Personal ties were developing beyond these communities – some amicable, some intimate, some political – all challenging the exclusionary features of the SAWP. In particular, the latter of these, the political ties, represents a new form of inclusiveness in terms of civil society engagements and citizenship in Canada.

## Civil Society Engagements with Citizenship

The spread of global capitalism has been characterized by the growing incorporation of foreign workers into the labour markets of high-income countries but also the mobilization of social movements coalescing around this group. Sasha Courville and Nicola Piper (2004) argue that the transnational character of labour migration has stimulated "transnational networking to address issues revolving around the highly vulnerable existence of foreign migrant workers" (48). Indeed, there is evidence of civil society becoming increasingly important in ensuring that migrant workers' rights are respected and often pressuring the state to expand those rights. Organizing around migrants has historically concerned domestic workers in cities. Southeast Asia is a noteworthy site for this activity. In the Philippines, civil society is highly developed, with hundreds of NGOs engaged in monitoring the well-being and treatment of migrant workers inside and outside the country (Wee and Sim 2003; Ball and Piper 2004; Courville and Piper 2004). In Hong Kong and Japan, major receivers of Filipina migrant workers, there are dozens of NGOs geared at domestic workers that offer a range of services and engage in advocacy; furthermore, their membership shows a high involvement of Filipinos themselves (Wee and Sim 2003; Ball and Piper 2004; Courville and Piper 2004; Law 2004). Domestic worker organizing, involving external agents, immigrants, and migrants, has also occurred in Canada for close to thirty years. In Toronto, the domestic workers' rights advocacy group INTERCEDE[5] has played a central role since 1977 in lobbying around employment legislation, access to collective bargaining, and the removal of the live-in stipulation (Stiell and England 1997). INTERCEDE, together with other community organizations, has been lobbying the government for over a decade to protect and expand migrant workers' rights (Philippine Women's Center 2002). The pressure from domestic workers and their allies led · to a change in federal government policy allowing temporary workers to apply for permanent residency status (Sharma 2001). Broader-based initiatives of (im)migrants, refugees, and their allies aimed at promoting and protecting the rights of migrants have also formed in Canada's three largest immigrant-receiving cities in recent years. Toronto is the base for the STATUS Campaign to Regularize Non-Status Immigrants, a coalition formed in 2000 advocating for the regularization of status of all nonstatus immigrants in Canada, while Montreal is home to the Solidarity across Borders network.

In addition to these trends, there is growing evidence in the activities of migrant workers abroad, as well as transnational coalition groups for migrant rights, to indicate significant processes of civil transnational networking (Wee and Sim 2003; Law 2004). Some of these efforts to organize transnationally include the No One Is Illegal groups campaigning for the total abolition of immigration controls throughout Europe and North America that began forming in the late 1990s and December 18, an online organization formed by Asian migrant organizations in 1997 as a "Portal for the Promotion and Protection of the Rights of Migrants." In particular, scholars have noted how Filipino domestic worker politics are unambiguously transnational in character (Stasiulis and Bakan 2003; Courville and Piper 2004).

Farm workers in the United States are another noteworthy case of civil society organizing around migrant workers' rights. American unions have now fully adopted a strong pro-migrant stance vis-à-vis undocumented farm workers (Oxfam America 2004), and immigrant rights groups in the United

States have begun to soften their opposition to guest worker programs (Pastor and Alva 2003). Indeed, the rising incorporation of mostly undocumented workers in agricultural labour markets in the United States has undermined labour organizing and forced unions to reconsider their positions (Martin 2003). This turnaround in position has been witnessed in the two largest unions, the United Farm Workers of America (UFW) and the Farm Labour Organizing Committee (FLOC). In addition, tree planters and farm workers in Oregon founded the Pineros y Campesinos Unidos del Noroeste (PCUN) in 1985 (Stephen 2003). One of the most high-profile groups campaigning for undocumented farm workers is the Coalition of Immokalee Workers (CIW), a community-based worker organization in Florida whose members are largely (im)migrants. CIW's activities have included campaigns for higher wages through work stoppages, hunger strikes, and high-profile boycotts, such as the successful, five-year boycott of Taco Bell (CIW 2004). Other organizations include the Centro Independiente de Trabajadores Agricolas in New York, the North Carolina Justice Center, the Farmworker Support Committee (El Comité de Apoyo a los Trabajadores Agrícolas, CATA) in New Jersey and Pennsylvania, and the Sin Fronteras Organizing Project in Texas and New Mexico. A remarkable indication of heightened concern for farm workers and their position in global supply chains is the adoption by Oxfam America of farm labour as a central platform of its Make Trade Fair Campaign (Oxfam America 2004). While it is beyond this chapter's scope to comment extensively on the widespread political mobilization of farm workers in the United States and globally, these trends are indications of civil engagements with migrant workers that are increasingly transnational in character. The following section focuses on the developments that have occurred in Ontario, Canada.

### Civil Society–Migrant Worker Engagements in Rural Ontario

For at least ten years of the SAWP's thirty-eight-year history, individuals and groups in migrant-receiving communities have made efforts to provide outreach – and most recently advocacy – to foreign farm workers. The emergence of new organizations and the growing momentum of efforts have accompanied increases in the migrant labour force serving horticulture and serve to compensate for a long history of inadequate support and protection of migrant workers by their home country states and the Canadian government. In Canada, these groups are diverse in their motivations, mandates, and functions. It is still early to be creating typologies for the few organizations dealing with migrant farm workers; however, some general observations can be made (see Table 6.1). First, the groups can be sorted into faith-based and secular categories. Among the faith-based groups, most do not have an explicitly social justice perspective, with one notable exception. Second, a number of functions are shared among both faith-based and

*Table 6.1*

**Organizations targeting foreign agricultural workers**

| Service | CWOP | Springdale Christian Reform | Vineland Free Reform | Project El Sembrador | CAFFE | LINCA | SECC/SEAA | Health Bus | Community Policing | Enlace | Frontier College | Justicia for Migrant Workers | UFCW | OHCOW | Windsor-Essex Bilingual Legal Clinic |
|---|---|---|---|---|---|---|---|---|---|---|---|---|---|---|---|
| Advocacy | | | × | | | | × | | | × | | × | × | × | × |
| Rights education | | | | × | | | | | | × | × | × | × | × | × |
| Raising public awareness | × | | × | × | | | × | | | × | × | × | × | | |
| Social integration | × | × | | × | × | × | × | | | × | | | | | |
| Information resources | | | | × | × | × | × | | | | | | | × | × |
| Translation services | | | | × | × | | × | | | | × | | × | | |
| Health/safety | | | | × | | | × | × | × | × | × | × | × | × | |
| ESL/literacy | | × | | × | × | | × | | | | × | | × | | |
| Skill development | | | | × | | | × | | | | | | | | |
| Recreational activities | × | × | × | × | × | × | × | | | × | | × | | | |
| Material donations | × | × | × | × | | | | | | × | | | × | | |
| Spiritual needs | × | × | × | × | | | | | | | | | | | |

secular groups, such as providing charitable outreach, organizing recreational and leisure activities, holding English as a Second Language (ESL) or literacy classes, and promoting social integration. Third, another set of organizations focuses efforts on acting as advocates to resolve poor housing or working conditions, raising the awareness of the Canadian public, educating migrant workers on their rights, and lobbying the government.

Some of the earliest efforts to target migrant farm workers emerged from rural faith communities that were motivated to address workers' spiritual needs through invitations to worship. To better serve Jamaican workers, one ecumenical group brings pastors from Jamaica every summer to minister to them. For Mexican workers, a number of churches now offer services in Spanish. These groups believe that participating in worship allows workers to fulfill not only their spiritual needs but also a measure of companionship. Services have become popular meeting places for workers and have reunited relatives and friends who did not know they had been posted in close proximity. Catholic churches frequented by Mexican workers display portraits of the Virgin of Guadalupe, their patron saint. In a sense, churches constitute the sole social space that foreign workers can openly appropriate in rural settings where they can feel "a positive sense of community and culture in a [country] where they live with their own stigmatized foreignness on a day-to-day basis" (Law 2002, 1637). Despite increasing accessibility, many workers still do not attend religious services because they work on their days of worship or lack transportation.

In addition to offering worship services, several churches run programs to provide material outreach (food, clothing, and bicycles) and host activities that target foreign workers. A shared goal of many faith-based groups is to extend workers' experiences of Canada beyond the farm and to promote social inclusion. One of the longest-standing groups, the Caribbean Workers Outreach Program (CWOP), began bringing workers and Canadians together to worship and socialize in the early 1990s. This group also organizes "reality tours" for Canadians to Jamaica, a strategy that has had positive results in promoting social inclusion in migrant-receiving communities in the United States (Grey and Woodrick 2002). Additional faith-based initiatives have emerged more recently. Project El Sembrador was formed in 1999 to provide spiritual and social support for foreign workers under a mandate with a specific social justice perspective guided by papal teachings on migrants. Other recent groups are motivated principally by Christian evangelism, with activities centring on weekly Bible studies.

The secular groups that target migrant workers are of a similarly diverse nature, and while some have been established in the localities of high worker concentration, others are based in Toronto. Like the faith-based groups, some of the functions that these groups focus on meet perceived needs such as providing material donations or hosting recreational activities, while others attempt to equip workers with skills through literacy or technology transfer. Fostering social interaction between the permanent and migrant communities is a goal of a number of groups. For example, the rural-based Community of Agricultural Foreign Workers and Friends of Exeter (CAFFE) began in 2002 with a Friday-night drop-in centre geared at providing an alternative social space, facilitating language and skills acquisition, and promoting social integration. Furthermore, the Toronto-based Enlace Community Link gears social events, an emergency telephone line, and a monthly information newsletter towards Mexican workers.

Some initiatives at service provision have come from municipal and regional authorities, but they remain limited. The Health Department of the Regional Municipality of Niagara has included foreign workers among its target populations through its mobile Health Bus campaign since 1995. One night a week, the bus is posted in a region of high worker concentration, providing treatment for minor medical conditions as well as some dental services. In two other regions, community groups have established bicycle safety campaigns. In one area employing great numbers of workers, a community centre consolidated volunteer translation services in the police station and hospital through an on-call pager system.

Many groups provide some English-language instruction, but the central provider of ESL and literacy training is the Toronto-based, nonprofit organization Frontier College, which has placed volunteers on farms where they work alongside SAWP migrants and offer ESL and adult basic education after hours. Frontier College volunteers often facilitate communication between employers and workers, sometimes by providing translation and, on other occasions, acting as mediators.

The most openly proactive efforts to defend foreign workers and ensure that their rights are respected and expanded have come from the labour movement. While its engagement with foreign workers is relatively recent, labour has been trying to organize agricultural workers in Ontario periodically since the 1970s (Wall 1996). The union most actively campaigning for farm workers is the United Food and Commercial Workers of Canada (UFCW), a union representing about 230,000 workers in the food industry. A historic moment in provincial agricultural labour relations occurred in the early 1990s when labour's lobbying efforts were successful under a sympathetic provincial government. In 1994, Ontario passed the Agricultural Labour Relations Act (ALRA) allowing workers to unionize. This "key event in Ontario farming history" (Wall 1996, 525) came and went; the Conservative party took the provincial legislature later that year and and by 1995 had repealed the ALRA.

Since then, UFCW has directed its efforts at the courts, levelling three constitutional challenges in the Supreme Court. The first two challenges concern agricultural workers in general, both citizen and noncitizen (see interview with Raper in this volume). The third challenge against the federal government concerns noncitizen agricultural workers exclusively and takes issue with the fact that foreign workers pay premiums under the Employment Insurance Act yet cannot claim the associated benefits because they must leave the country when they are no longer working (UFCW 2004).[6] UFCW charges that this violates section 15(1) of Canada's Charter of Rights and Freedoms, which guarantees every individual's right to equality under the law and equal protection and benefit of the law without discrimination. This final challenge is convincing testimony of the UFCW's commitment to lobby for the rights of foreign workers.[7]

Direct support, however, has taken other forms. In 2001, labour activists formed the Global Justice Care Van Project, a coalition to support and enhance the rights of migrant workers (see interview with Raper in this volume). With financing from several unions, the Care Van first launched a campaign to document and expose migrants' working and living conditions. The following year, UFCW opened the first Migrant Agricultural Workers Support Centre in rural Ontario and has since opened four more centres, including one in Quebec. The centres offer a range of services to migrant workers, including assistance with social benefits, legal counselling, and translation. They also engage in raising workers' awareness of their rights.

Labour activists have also organized outside formal union structures by forming the Toronto-based Justicia for Migrant Workers (J4MW). The J4MW collective, composed of students, researchers, and social justice activists, focuses activities on raising awareness of issues surrounding migrant workers, lobbying the government, and providing outreach. A principal contribution of J4MW has been to increase the profile of foreign farm workers within the Canadian public through its electronic listserv, website, and public events.

Finally, the emergence of both secular and faith-based groups has found its echo in the mainstream media. While foreign workers were formerly the subject matter of the rural press, feature and front-page articles have appeared in newspapers such as the *Hamilton Spectator* and the *Toronto Sun*. In 2002, the provincial public broadcaster dedicated a segment of its current issues program to this topic. Highly noteworthy was the 2003 release of the National Film Board full-length documentary on Mexican workers in the greenhouse vegetable industry, *El Contrato*, which has subsequently aired on public television.

## Conclusion

The alliances being forged between foreign workers and citizens hold interesting implications for the ways in which we conceptualize citizenship and civil society. Although the rising incorporation of foreign workers lacking citizenship rights in labour-receiving countries can be seen as instigated by global capital and powerful states, citizenship can also be expanded through civil society engagements or "globalization from below" (Turner 1990; Ku 2002; Ball and Piper 2004). Citizenship, seen as a relation of power, is thus open to contestation from transnational civil society. One form that this relation can take is when citizens use the power vested in their own status – material, political, and social[8] – to take an active role in advocating for the rights of migrant workers. Bryan Turner (1990) conceptualizes a citizen as "an active bearer of effective claims against society *via* the state" and citizenship as "a set of practices which articulate popular demands for participation" (212). Experiences in Southeast Asia show how NGOs can play a role in lobbying states to ratify and implement the International Convention on the Protection of the Rights of All Migrant Workers and Members of Their Families, serve as watchdogs, and encourage political and public debate (Wee and Sim 2003; Ball and Piper 2004). Through activism, citizens of labour-receiving countries can take up an active role "to advocate for the human and labour rights of foreign migrant workers, and thereby push for the recognition of the broader rights of a 'globalised' workforce" (Ball and Piper 2004, 1015).

Furthermore, Stasiulis and Bakan (1997, 2003) document the ways in which noncitizens, together with citizen allies, negotiate creative and collective strategies to attain citizenship rights and contest the limitations on their human and worker rights. Ku (2002) argues that new conceptualizations of citizenship, rights, and civil society are necessary if we are to take into account nonstatus immigrants or, in her words, "those people who are not (yet) recognized as formal citizens or residents but who have been variously involved in civil society, whether to organize struggles for their own inclusion or to associate with other fellow citizens for other purposes" (543). She further writes that the space of civil society is negotiable: "Just as the space of civil society can be expanded vis-à-vis state despotism, it may be enlarged internally through inclusion of hitherto dispossessed groups, or diminished through exclusion and discrimination. An understanding of participation, rights, and belonging as being attached not merely to the state but also to the civil society of citizens and non-citizens remains essential" (543). She argues that prevailing theories of citizenship in both the liberal and the social democratic traditions tend to define citizenship as a set of universal rights attached to the nation-state, thus failing to understand citizenship in terms of civil society. Stasiulis and Bakan theorize citizenship as "a relationship that crystallizes many other sets of social relations" and therefore as unstable and open to active negotiation, not only from powerful gatekeepers but also from noncitizens engaging in "dissident citizenship practices," often anchored in transnational networks (2003, 166).

Since 1966, foreign workers have increasingly become constituents of the social landscape of rural Ontario, the cradle of Canadian horticulture. Researchers have made important contributions to documenting the exploitive conditions under which these migrants live and work; however, little attention has been paid to the relations between these workers and the permanent settled community. While not denying the structural constraints that contribute to the exploitation of foreign workers and their social exclusion, I have presented evidence in this chapter of the emergence of personal ties that are presenting new forms of rural inclusiveness. In particular, I have focused on the ways in which Canadians, acting as individuals and through community groups, take an active role in advocating for foreign workers' rights, in compensating for the state's failure to provide services to noncitizens that would improve their well-being and encourage social inclusion, and in raising political and public awareness of this social group.

It is important to close with some disclaimers. First, the history of civil society's engagement with foreign farm workers is fairly new. While foreign domestic workers have had advocates for over thirty years in Canada, agricultural workers are only beginning to find their allies. This fact alone, directly related to their rural location, lends further support to approaching citizenship from a social relational perspective that feminist scholars have advocated. These new alliances, furthermore, are limited to a fraction of the foreign farm workers coming to Ontario each year. Most of the groups are operating with extremely limited funding and, with few exceptions, are supported entirely by volunteers. In general, community groups are working independently of one another and only recently have begun to network.[9] Thus, the efforts of these groups, while important, cannot adequately address the shortfalls in service provision accorded to foreign workers, protect them from abuses, or facilitate social integration in rural towns.

Second, the initiatives of citizens targeting foreign workers as a social group should not be naively accepted as evidence of progressive "transnational citizenship." The goals of these organizations may not be shared by migrant workers themselves, and some may even work contrary to their interests. Some faith-based and secular initiatives that have emerged at the local level, especially those in which employers are members, have sought to promote evangelism and cultural exchange, glossing over the relations of power separating the permanent and migrant communities. On the other hand, activists in the labour movement may employ aggressive tactics in achieving their goals at the expense of individual workers, who may forfeit their transnational livelihoods and thus a fundamental opportunity to improve their well-being and that of their families. In addition, the divergent tactics and approaches of the myriad groups working with migrant workers may thwart any attempt to work together effectively.

And third, while examples from Southeast Asia show that migrant worker advocacy is not necessarily the work of external agents, with migrants forming their own transnational networks (Wee and Sim 2003), this outcome seems to be a distant prospect for foreign farm workers in Canada, who currently act as recipients rather than leaders of the advocacy organizations that have emerged. In large part, this situation is owing to their vulnerability within guest worker programs and the risk of repatriation and/or permanent suspension (see Díaz Barrero in this volume). In the United States, for example, labour brokers such as the North Carolina Growers Association allegedly circulate blacklists of H2A workers who organize for improved working conditions (Southern Poverty Law Center 2007). Similarly, Basok (2002) documents how a labour stoppage by Mexican workers in Canada led to the repatriation of some twenty "ringleaders." Interviewees in this study claimed that both their employers and their home representatives had warned against their involvement in the Migrant Resource Centres, a finding corroborated by Evelyn Encalada Grez (2006). Basok (2004) further argues that most foreign workers remain ignorant of both their rights and how to exercise them. Given these constraints, it appears that, in the short term, external agents will advocate on behalf of migrant workers.

The high degree of vulnerability that migrant workers face has led some authors to suggest that NGOs and other members of civil society are necessary partners in the vigilance of proper implementation and worker protections, particularly in the case of guest worker programs where the defence of workers rests exclusively in government hands (Pastor and Alva 2003; Courville and Piper 2004). But it is precisely this situation that may prompt genuine social change, through the forging of migrant-citizen alliances. As this chapter has illustrated, labour flexibility in horticulture rests on placing inordinate power in the hands of employers and exposing workers to extreme vulnerability. Both Canadian employers and the state take comprehensive measures to maintain the "reliability" of foreign workers. Furthermore, the state has done little to meet the human needs of foreign workers beyond providing them with jobs. The glaring injustices that have surfaced as a result have prompted citizens to intervene as service providers, watchdogs, and advocates. These engagements between the globally mobile workforce and the communities in which they are employed may thus have unanticipated outcomes for advancing a rights-based agenda through transnational networks and promote new forms of inclusiveness and mobilization.

**Notes**
1  See Stasiulis and Bakan (2003, 18-22) for a more thorough treatment of postwar social movements in Canada.

2  My treatment of foreign workers as a group should not conceal other standpoints compos-
ing individual subject positions such as gender and race that reflect differential social,
economic, and political relations of power and how they affect the nature of participation,
membership, or citizenship of those within this group.

3  SAWP workers are able to access the public healthcare system without cost. Access is com-
promised because they do not report their health needs for fear of repatriation and because
employers do not always respond to their requests for medical care.

4  This chapter is based on a study undertaken in 2002 that explored the relations between
foreign workers and the settled community in rural Ontario. Research participants (*n*=104)
included government and industry representatives, employers, foreign workers, rural residents, and members of groups engaging in advocacy and/or service provision for migrant
workers. See Preibisch (2003, 2004) for further elaboration. I wish to acknowledge the
research assistance of Lauren Classen, Courtney Denard, Sarah Groot, Luz María Hermoso
Santamaría, and Kerry Nash.

5  The International Coalition to End Domestic Workers' Exploitation.

6  The Employment Insurance Act is a social insurance scheme that provides income replace-
ment benefits to workers who become unemployed. Entitlement to benefits is based on an
employee's paying premiums into the employment insurance fund. Sections 18 and 37 of
the act require that an individual be physically in Canada and available for work in order
to receive benefits.

7  Recently, UFCW dropped this claim. Although foreign workers remain ineligible for basic
benefits under the act, over the past five years, UFCW and other organizations were able to
claim parental leave benefits for this population. UFCW estimates that it has processed
approximately 2,000 such claims to date. Furthermore, the union's challenge of the federal
government's EI program yielded a significant, and indeed historic, gain when the Ontario
Superior Court of Justice ruled that UFCW has legal standing to represent foreign agricultural workers in the courts.

8  Formal citizenship in advanced industrial countries remains a goal of many noncitizen
migrants, owing in large measure to the material wealth and political stability that it offers
relative to other regions of the world (Stasiulis and Bakan 2003). While Canadian citizenship is not universal, those enjoying formal citizenship have relatively more civil, political,
social, and economic power than noncitizen migrants, including mobility rights.

9  Some time after I wrote this chapter, KAIROS Canada, an ecumenical organization focusing
on social justice initiatives, began coordinating a national Migrant Justice Network. KAIROS
convened a Migrant Justice Gathering at York University in June 2006, bringing together
migrant workers from a diverse range of industries (agriculture, domestic work, construction) and their advocates, an extraordinary juncture in migrant worker organizing.

# 7

# Forcing Governments to Govern in Defence of Noncitizen Workers: A Story about the Canadian Labour Movement's Alliance with Agricultural Migrants

*Interview with Stan Raper by Kerry Preibisch*

Kerry Preibisch had a conversation with Stan Raper, the national coordinator of the Migrant Agricultural Worker Support Centres, about the labour movement's engagement with foreign worker issues. This is an excerpt from their conversation.

*Kerry Preibisch:* Let's start with you explaining how noncitizen agricultural workers got on the radar screen of the labour movement.

*Stan Raper:* In the early 1990s, I was the Canadian coordinator for the United Farm Workers of America [UFW], and we were doing campaigns to support agricultural workers in the United States. So we travelled across Canada and spoke to labour organizations at the conventions, raised money, hawked T-shirts, anything we could do to try to educate the labour movement about the struggle of agricultural workers in the United States.

One day we got a newspaper article faxed to us saying that there was a strike in Leamington[1] and twenty workers were on a wildcat strike and were going to be repatriated, but they were being housed at a neutral zone at a local church. So we dispersed a couple of volunteers to document their situation. When those individuals came back, we realized that there were some serious problems going on in our own backyard, and we had no idea that these things were even happening.

So we started the Global Justice Caravan Project and started travelling around, getting volunteers. We were able to raise a little bit of money from the CLC and UFCW, and Auto and Steel kicked in $5,000 each, which paid for our vans and our gas.[2] We got some volunteers who spoke Spanish and went around documenting the plight of the migrant workers. When we were done that fall, we realized there were serious, serious problems and decided to issue a report. We called it the "National Report on the Status of Migrant Workers in Canada."[3] It was the first report issued by the labour movement since the early 1970s. The OFL [Ontario Federation of Labour] had done work prior to that on migrant farm workers in the Niagara region and issued a report, so we started doing more research about who was doing what. We found out that the UFCW Canada had been trying to organize the mushroom workers in Leamington and also the Caribbean workers. So we met with some UFCW representatives and started to compile some documentation so we knew what we were talking about. And that's how it all basically started.

*What's happened since then?*

Well, a lot has happened. We lobbied the UFW of America to allow us to do more work on the Canadian problem. They felt quite strongly that they needed to concentrate their strengths and efforts on things that were happening in California, Texas, and Florida. Basically, it forced them to make their own decisions, so they made a strategic move to close down their public action offices all across North America except for in their main power bases. So in places like Seattle, New York, Detroit, Canada, they closed down all their public action offices, basically laying us off. At that point, we got a phone call from UFCW indicating that they had just received word from the Supreme Court of Canada that they had won the decision on the Rae legislation and the Harris [legislation] removing the legislation challenge [see Preibisch in this volume], and they basically didn't have a plan in place. So they asked me to try to put something together.

We did that within a very short period of time. They really liked the idea and provided a budget to continue the work we were doing. But after the first year of the Global Justice Caravan Project, we realized that driving around and talking to workers was a good thing for *us*, but it didn't do much for them. So we realized rather quickly that in order to really be able to try to assist these workers we needed to have some kind of base, a centre, where they could contact us, get information in their own language, and talk to people in their own language. So we opened the centre in Leamington, and that is the first of five now that we operate.

*How do you think the centres have made a difference?*

I think there are a couple things. First, they have access to services during hours in which they are available. Most government offices are open nine to four, and if not you have to phone and leave a message and go through a bureaucracy that most Mexican workers could not comply with. So we changed our hours from twelve to eight. We offered ESL classes with the assistance of Frontier College, volunteers, and other organizations. We networked with community agencies around getting volunteer lawyers from bilingual legal services and did a lot of work in the area of health and safety, producing booklets in Spanish and English and making them fairly easy to read. So in terms of basic knowledge about what their rights are, what health and safety problems are out there, I think that this provided them with a knowledge base that they've never had before. The links to government agencies and services like WSIB [Workplace Safety and Insurance Board], CPP [Canada Pension Plan], Employment Insurance [EI], we did a lot of that casework for them. That's something that they hadn't seen before.

But I think the biggest thing was the threat that we were there. That the labour movement was there. Farmers knew that we were there, and therefore, if there were problems, we were going to find out about it and respond. That had never been the case before. So farmers were actually put in the position where here was a new kind of watchdog type of group, an advocacy group, who set up in one of the biggest areas, in the Leamington area, where there was the most migrant workers – concentration anyways – in Ontario. We weren't going away, and they knew we weren't going away. And they knew that we wanted to do a lot of things: one, health and safety; two, advocacy; and three, promote the right to unionization and basically advocate for workers on their behalf, on the ground, right in [the farmer's] face.

They've never seen that before and responded at first with hostility. They were very angry and accused us of just wanting to take the workers' money for unionization and let them rot. We told them that all the services that we provide are free, that the union pays for the staff and the centre to be there, that we're networking with the community to make the lives better for foreign migrant farm workers who go into the Leamington area, that we're not there to collect any money, and that they can say and do whatever they want. Our basic philosophy for being there was providing free services, advocating, and speaking on behalf of people who've never had a voice before. So there was a big impact.

We now see farmers coming to the centre, dropping workers off, phoning us asking to translate for them, asking to provide health and safety courses for them. In the back of their mind, they still feel that threat of unionization, but they also see an organization that is trying to assist. If you're a farmer with moderate to liberal-type views, then you have nothing to fear. We're not there to harm anyone: we're there to help people. If you're a bad farmer, you will be dealing with the union eventually. If you're a good farmer, you will have no problem from us. If farmers understand that, then it relieves the tension.

*This is an interesting point, because people often discuss the "good" and the "bad" farmers. Why do you think we have this situation where you have such a range of experiences of the workers, these "heaven or hell" scenarios?*

There are a couple of reasons, but one of the biggest problems is the industry has been self-regulated. An industry being self-regulated for the last 100 years basically means that if you're a bad employer you can get away with it. When good employers see bad employers getting away with it, they say, "what the hell, why am I being so good, I can't compete. If I'm not treating my workers badly and not getting the most that I can out of them and not spending money on housing and health and safety training and all those things, and no one is forcing me to do it, then I can get away with it." And that is the history of Ontario. It is a self-regulated industry. They have been able to get away with it.

Now that a watchdog group is out there telling them that they should do something a little bit different, they're not too happy about it. Some are starting to comply with a set of unwritten rules: you need to have a shower, a toilet, and a stove that works. Before no one knew, no one cared: [foreign workers] were invisible, and no one gave a shit. So we're trying to enforce what little rules there are and trying to push the boundaries about what are decent living conditions, what are decent hours of work, when it is too hot to work in the greenhouse. It's not when a worker faints from heat exhaustion. There is an actual temperature, so you should be looking at it and setting some guidelines around that.

You know, those are some of the basic points around the differences between them. Some of the farmers have been around a long time and can speak a little bit of Spanish or Italian. They can communicate a little bit better with the workers. The language barrier isn't there. There are fewer problems. Because I think farmers who've been around for a long time understand that, if they aren't good to the workers, the workers aren't good to them. Now there's always the bad farmer thrown in the mix that doesn't house them properly and those types of things, but I think generally most farmers are decent people. I think the problem has been that there are no rules, and you can get away with whatever you need to. If you're having a bad year and things aren't working out, then "why should I spend money on a new toilet and shower? I can get away with it this year and maybe do it next year if someone complains."

*Tell me a little bit about the legal challenges. What are they about, and why has UFCW taken this direction?*

I was reading some articles in the United States about human rights cases and how state government and the federal government moved so slowly that you could never see progress gained. There was a lawyer in California who wrote an article about how legal actions produce better results in the short term. Whether the result of those legal actions produce[s] results in the long term, I guess we'll find out. But he was arguing that governments these days will promise just about anything to get elected. Once they are elected, they drag their feet. They hear complaints from the industry that they need to be competitive, and there's the whole globalization issue that people face.

Basically, people who are interested in establishing and securing human rights and the basic rights for the agricultural sector had to launch legal challenges and force governments to govern. Which when you think about it is pretty bizarre: to force governments to govern. One of the key principles that this guy was talking about was direct legal challenges against the lack of basic human rights or labour legislation or health and safety legislation. So I passed on that article to Mike [Fraser][4] and others at the executive at UFCW. They immediately responded by saying, "yeah, let's do something. This is bullshit. We could be waiting for twenty, thirty years before a government realizes they've signed international conventions." The United Nations has declared basic human rights protections fifty-two years ago, and still governments don't act. So we need to force them.

I give Mike Fraser a lot of credit. The UFCW has spent a lot of money implementing at this point three legal challenges: two against the Ontario government and one against the federal government. The first is the health and safety legal challenge: twenty workers have died in Ontario each year for the last fifteen or twenty years, not including lost limbs, lost time, lost fingers, lost or broken arms and legs, you name it. The WSIB stats have continued to climb. I think it was a Queen's University study that claims the agricultural sector is the most dangerous occupation. It has surpassed the construction and mining industr[ies]. Those two industries have their own specific regulations dealing with health and safety – the agricultural workers have nothing.

No one can deny the importance of health and safety legislation or the protection for agricultural workers, but governments aren't prepared to move, because the industry is very effective at lobbying. Governments want to be reelected. There are thousands of farmers in Ontario – some small farms, some big farms – and they have a lot of political power. No one wants to piss them off. So the only way you can get the governments to move is to force them to move. We worked for almost two years on the legal challenge, getting affidavits from individual farm workers, doing our research. The Cavalluzzo law firm put it together, and I think it is one of the best legal challenges that I've ever seen in terms of research and documentation. If I was the Liberal government right now, I'd be very worried and very embarrassed. I think that's what forced them to move.

The second challenge concerns the right to unionization and to bargain collectively. No one wants to see unionization rights in Ontario from the industry's perspective, but again we've signed international agreements. We go to other countries and slam them for not allowing basic human rights, yet in our backyard we're denying those rights to individuals. So I say, "shame on the federal government, shame on the provincial government." Lots of legal challenges will force them to act one way or the other. Whether we win all of them, I don't know, but if nothing else we have forced the governments to educate the industry about our side. We've produced some incredible documentation that is going to be around forever on the plight of workers in Ontario during the late 1990s and early 2000s.

The Agricultural Employees Protection Act (AEPA) is what the Harris Conservative government brought in, allowing workers to join an association. If a worker has a problem at the workplace, he or she can go before a tribunal and argue the dispute. The tribunal has limited enforcement capacities, other than maybe sending the employer a letter explaining the problem and warning him not to do it again. There are no teeth; there's nothing to it. We argue that basically the tribunal is nothing but a waste of money and a duplication of bureaucracy. When the Ministry of Labour has that role and has historically had that role since the early 1940s, why the agricultural sector is exempt from going before the ministry and the Labour Relations Act is beyond me.

The Liberals in Ontario, under Dalton McGuinty, supported the AEPA when they were in opposition. It's quite clear that they do not want to move from their position. Therefore, as a labour organization that is interested in protecting agricultural workers' rights or establishing them, the only option you have is legal challenge. So we will be in the courts fundamentally arguing that association means nothing if you don't have the right to bargain collectively, if you don't have a contract that spells out the rules, the grievance procedure, basic wages and benefits, and those types of things. Agricultural workers basically have nothing right now. They can form an association, but if there are 200 workers in an agricultural operation there could potentially be 200 different associations because each individual can form their own association. This is a "divide and conquer" type of situation with no real strength. The employer is not obliged to listen to anything the association says.

*Let's say you are successful with this legal challenge. Will that extend to noncitizen, foreign workers?*

We will make sure that it does. The [New Democratic] Rae government, when they implemented the Agricultural Labour Relations Act [ALRA] in the early 1990s, said that agricultural workers would have the right to join a union and bargain collectively, but they didn't have the right to strike; that they could go through an expedited arbitration process and resolve any problem so that farms wouldn't be shut down, letting animals and plants die; that you had to remain at work and deal with your problems through a third party; and that the third party, once they heard the dispute, would rule one way or the other or try to resolve the situation. So the foreign workers weren't included, but they weren't excluded either. It was never tested, but we always argue that, had the migrant agricultural workers wanted to be part of that process, we'd take them to the labour board, and it would have probably ruled in our favour. Any worker who works in Ontario, pays provincial taxes, is part of OHIP [Ontario Health Insurance Plan, provincially funded] and Workers' Compensation, should be also provided [with] the same basic right as any other worker. We were going to test the ALRA on the migrant farm worker situation, and we were quite confident that we were going to win. We talked with other labour relations officials in other provinces who basically have protection for agricultural workers in their labour relations act. They have told us [to] bring workers forward, and we'll certify them. We do not discriminate whether they are foreign workers or Ontario or provincial workers.

*What about the third challenge?*

The third challenge deals exclusively with foreign workers. Under the Employment Insurance Act, all foreign workers under the SAWP program pay Employment Insurance [EI] and a premium but aren't entitled to collect the basic premium or the lay-off protection. So if you're a [domestic] seasonal worker in Ontario and you get laid off in the fall, you can apply for EI premiums, and if you qualify, you get them. All foreign workers pay into the same program, but when they get laid off they return home. Their visa expires, they return home, and [they] are therefore ineligible because you can't collect from a foreign country, except for the United States. They made special rules for US citizens in order to collect employment insurance, but they won't allow Mexican or Jamaican workers to do it. We argued that, under the charter, equity under the law should apply to these workers and [that] the federal government needs to reform the EI Act to either (1) provide them with the benefit once they're laid off and let them collect from their home country; or (2) remove the premiums they're paying so they wouldn't pay into a program that they aren't eligible for; or (3) something in between.

We realize that there are *some* benefits for these workers. Right now they can access parental leave benefits and sick benefits if they qualify. Very few do; I mean .008 percent of all the foreign workers this year actually collected some kind of premium from EI. So the numbers are very, very small. So we're saying adjust – reform – the EI Act. We also argue as a labour movement that EI needs to be reformed anyway. While you're in the reforming, make some changes for the migrant workers at the same time.

We heard from the attorney general of Canada about a month ago. Their position is that we don't represent migrant farm workers, therefore we don't have standing, and the legal challenge should fall. We've responded to that stating that UFCW put forward the legal challenge on behalf of workers. It's very difficult [for workers]; they fear they will be blacklisted or repatriated or sent home. That is why they don't come forward. In our affidavits to the federal government, Mike Fraser and I talk about the intimidation and fear that these workers have, the lack of appeal process, et cetera. No individual worker was prepared to put his name on the affidavit or on the legal challenge. We argue that we *do* represent migrant workers and that we have for the last five years and beyond that. If the federal government is going to argue the point about standing, then over the 2005 year we will identify individual workers to come forward. It's a huge sacrifice for them, and we don't want to put workers in that position.

We don't necessarily want to spend a lot of money going to court. We would be prepared to try to negotiate something in regards to the EI program. But right now the federal government outright just said, "You don't represent them. The legal standing is not there; the case needs to be dropped." So we're doing cross-examination in January, and we'll see what the federal government is going to do next. We definitely have HRSDC [Human Resources and Skills Development Canada] and [then prime minister] Martin's attention around the EI premiums. The farmers pay EI premiums for each foreign worker that works for them. In fact, they pay more than the individual worker. I think two-thirds is paid by the farmer, one-third by the worker. The farmers have been arguing for over twenty years that they should be removed from the program. We argue that the workers should be removed but that the farmers should still have to pay because they are getting some benefit. The consulate officials also agree with us. Both the Jamaican/Caribbean Consulate and the Mexican Consulate have written papers and information on EI premiums and vote "unfair" as well.

*UFCW has put money into the centres and the legal challenges. Some would argue that the attitudes of the labour movement in Canada toward guest workers are very different [from those] in the United States, where the labour movement has opposed these programs because of the difficulties around organizing, focusing their efforts on undocumented workers and farm workers in general. Do you think that is true?*

The [Canadian] labour movement's position is, and has been ever since I've known for the last twenty-five years, that we support the ability of workers from other countries to fill jobs that aren't being filled by Canadians. The biggest concern that we have in the labour movement is – and the federal government talks about this all the time – when you talk about foreign worker programs, it is a "Canadian first" policy, so if there are foreign workers coming in, they need to be treated like Canadians. Whenever you talk to the government about foreign [agricultural] workers, they say, "they're being paid the same, they're treated the same." In Ontario, they're right. When a foreign [agricultural] worker comes here, they have very limited access to employment standards. They have no health and safety protections. They have no right to join a union and bargain collectively. So, yes, they are being treated like Ontario residents. All agriculture workers in this province, foreign or domestic, are being abused, are being denied their basic human rights.

It varies from province to province. If you're a foreign worker and you get sent to Quebec, you get treated differently than if you're sent to Ontario or Alberta. We're saying to the [SAWP] directors that you have the capacity to set some rules and enforce those rules at the federal government level. If provinces and industries want foreign workers to come there, then they have to abide by the rules. If there is no health and safety program in place, then they don't get foreign workers. And you watch the industry friggin' scramble in order to implement health and safety legislation if the feds put their foot down and actually enforce some of the international covenants that they've signed.

There is no enforcement. That's why we say to the federal government, "you are the biggest cause of the problem. You can blame the provinces for not having basic pieces of legislation to protect these workers, and you can hide behind the fact that they are being treated the same as all other workers in the province of Ontario, but you're denying them the basic human rights. You are not enforcing international covenants, United Nations declarations, basic human rights legislations that have been signed for years, protection that all other workers in this province have." It's embarrassing as a Canadian and an activist in the labour movement that we've allowed this to happen as long as we have. It's time to enforce some of the rules or create some new rules that force the provinces to comply with basic human rights legislation, the basic employment standards legislation, and the basic unionization legislation.

The biggest majority of foreign workers under the SAWP program come to Ontario. If the federal government said, "next year, if the Province of Ontario does not have these basic pieces in place, no foreign worker would be sent to that province," there would be legislation drafted and implemented in a hurry, and the industry would back it 100 percent because they want these workers there because they can't get anyone else to do it. There are ways of doing things, but the federal government has decided that they don't want to tell the provinces what to do. The federal and provincial governments also point fingers back and forth, and you go round and round and round, and nothing gets done. We're saying, "time's up. Legal challenges are going to force you to do some of this stuff."

We've also done an awareness campaign. We do educational campaigns. We're going anywhere and everywhere to speak about the problems and abuses. We're documenting those abuses. We're filling out the national reports, sending them to whoever will read them, and doing whatever we can to advocate.

The guest worker programs, and with the new pilot project[5] that the federal government brought, force people to go AWOL and become undocumented workers. It's *indentured servitude*. They assign workers to one individual employer. If that employer is an asshole, then their life is hell for the next umpteen months while they're working there. And there's no escape, there's no appeal process, there's nothing. The only escape is to go AWOL or to go home. For a lot of people who are impoverished from other countries, who came to make some money and look after the families, and who spent a lot of money to get their papers and medical documentation, they're not in a position to go home. They need to make money, and therefore their only option is to go AWOL and become undocumented workers. We found it with the pilot workers: out of forty workers, five of them went AWOL.

This year I saw the stats so far with the SAWP program: 119 workers went AWOL. Those numbers are down in comparison to other years – I think because they're trying to get married men with families so they don't go AWOL. But when there's a serious problem, they do. We saw a case in Bradford – the employer was brutal. He still is brutal, and he still gets foreign workers. This employer withheld all their documents, treated them like shit, housed them poorly. The workers felt so badly one tried to commit suicide, [and] the other five left, ran away. We caught up with them in Windsor, and they were trying to get across the border to try to get into the United States to maybe get a job making a little bit a month. They were at wits' end. They had nowhere to go, nowhere to turn, no one to help them. It becomes desperation.

The whole notion of assigning one individual employee to one individual employer and tying all their work permits and everything to that individual does not provide them [with] the freedom to move from one employer to the other. They're trapped. As Tanya Basok says, "free to be unfree." Under very odd circumstances, they might be transferred from one employer to the other through the consulate officials, but that's only if there's no work available. There is no appeal process ... , if a worker is being mistreated, abused, not paid properly, whatever, saying this employer mistreats the workers. There is nothing in place. So we argue for a basic appeal process. We argue about transfers. We argue about not being assigned to one individual employer, so you do have some freedom to move around, which forces employers to treat the workers better so that they can keep the workers there.

We also argue for [legal] status.[6] Similar to the United States, the labour movement has been very involved in that. Status has been denied these workers. Some of them have been coming for thirty years, even longer, and still don't have an opportunity to apply for status and get dual citizenship. That would really provide them with the freedom that they need. Then they could become an equal citizen of Canada, still have links to their home country, and be able to move from one job to the other freely. And if what Canada needs is agricultural workers and a worker has been coming for five years, he's proven to the industry, to the Canadian government, to us, that he's a good person, that he can hold down a steady job and he is needed in Canada to provide the industry with a workforce, why not give him status? We're giving people status who have a lot of money, who have a lot of education, so why not give it to agricultural workers? The Live-In Caregiver Program gives [the right to apply for residence] after three years status, [so] why are we discriminating against individual farm workers who have been in the program for thirty years? Aren't they entitled to be eligible for [the] basic status right as well?

We're not just in it to be advocates and to advocate for basic human rights and other legislative protections. We argue the whole piece. So we're trying to be holistic in terms of our approach as a labour movement. That there's a whole bunch of problems, it's a complicated situation – well, it's a complicated industry. There needs to be a whole bunch of scenarios all happening at the same time. And we've been trying to promote that through our national reports and lobbying with federal government officials and provincial government officials.

*Where do you see these guest worker programs going in Canada?*

I see them expanding. I see that the federal government may be moving to these pilot project–type situations. The employer pays for their flight here and back, guaranteeing so many hours and finding some basic accommodations, which the worker has to pay for. Less bureaucracy, very limited involvement from the government, other than the issuing of a visa and a work permit. The rest is done basically by the employer and the recruiter in the home country. I see that that's the way the federal government wants to go. I think part of the problem is that the SAWP program, in terms of the employers and most government officials, has worked. It has filled the need of supplying workers at a fairly cost-effective way over the last thirty-some years. Why change something if it's not broken?

We argue that it's not broken, but the whole design was to provide employers with workers. At no point was the worker ever involved in the process. That is a fundamental error. We're saying it's time for workers to be part of the process. Give them a seat at the table. Let them voice some of their concerns with the problems and start to make some real fundamental changes that deal with some of these problems that workers are voicing to us. So far, it's like talking to a brick wall. That's the frustration of the workers and the organizations involved with these workers ... No one wants to hear you, no one wants to provide you with a voice. You can speak and bark and wave banners and placards any way you want, but the industry is more important than individual workers. So unless you're prepared to really put your foot through the door and kick it in, and force your way through legal challenges, documenting and talking about human rights abuses, to really get attention of the media, the industry, and the governments and embarrass them, then you're not going to get anywhere.

Other groups have tried to assist migrant workers in different ways. I'm not saying that this route is the best route, but over the last five years we've seen some impact. We've seen some changes; we want to see a lot more. So far, UFCW, the labour movement, church groups, and social justice organizations are all kind of behind the same basic general principles around establishing centres, around legal actions, and around continuing to lobby and document and talk about the plight of these workers in order to effectively bring change. All we can really do is keep hammering at it, and hopefully something will change. We've seen some small changes, but there are some real fundamental changes. The two main pieces that I see [are] the legislative protection piece, the status piece, and the appeal process piece. They're fundamentals and need to be in there.

*What have been the responses of the workers themselves?*
When we were doing the Caravan Project, we were swarmed. People wanted to give us their statements. They were at the point where there were wildcat strikes in a number of different areas across the province. They got to the point where they were walking off the job saying, "send me back home, this is bullshit. I'm not putting up with this crap anymore." And that's what happened; they were repatriated back to their home countries. So when the workers make that final statement that I'm walking off, I'm done, then they've already decided in their own minds. So when we pull into an area like Simcoe or Bradford or Leamington, we're swarmed. This was the first time that workers had ever had someone want to document the situation. We were there for hours. We couldn't leave. People wanted to state their claim about why would the employer deduct this, this, and this? Why is my housing so bad that I can't even shower in the morning? Or my stove doesn't work, I can't even cook. My roof leaks. The basement's flooded where my bunk is.

We were overwhelmed. The workers wanted more. They wanted advocates. They needed someone to hear their story and do something about it. When you get back in your van and you're driving home that night, you can't live with yourself. You're leaving them, and they just told you some of the most horrendous stories that you've ever heard: a worker's problems in Ontario. You're driving back to your home, to your house that has a good roof, that has a shower, a toilet, it's not flooded. It's a sense of hopelessness. Like what the hell are you doing? You've talked to these workers and actually inspired them [into] thinking that there might be some change, and we drive away and leave them there. It wasn't going to work. And that's why we've established the centres. We needed to be in those areas, there to do something.

If there was ever a time that the labour movement or someone pulled out, I would raise the money myself to run centres. I think there are a lot of organizations around who would give us money to keep centres going. We initially were of the opinion that the federal and provincial governments, the consulate officials, and the industry should be paying for those centres. I've since changed my mind. I think it's important that the labour movement is there on the ground fighting for workers' rights. That's what the labour movement does, that's what they're for.

I'm quite proud of the fact that we were able to get the labour movement on the ground, in the five major agricultural areas in Canada to start with. I would hope that there might be more. I always like to see more funds. We need more staff. We need more health and safety training. We need more advocacy. There's so much to do. Our staff is overwhelmed. Just basically the English as a Second Language (ESL) classes alone. We have volunteers that come to do that kind of work, and they're overwhelmed. The parental leave claims alone were about 600-700 claims this year. That's HRDC's work, that's the consulate's work. They're supposed to be doing that kind of stuff. That's employers' work. We're doing it because we know that they won't. Translation and hospitals, walk-in clinics, we should be billing them for the services we provide. But we don't. We're doing that because the worker asked us to go to the hospital with him and help him get well. We can't say no and won't say no. But we need more money, more resources, more staff. We could run those centres from the time those workers get here to the time that they leave and still not be able to do our work. Right now they're operating on a five-month operating time life. It could easily be all year around. But we don't have resources to do that.

Yes, there's more to do, but I think you have to be there, on the ground. When the industry knows that you've set up camp in their little neck of the woods, they're watching you just as you're watching them. So it's pretty cool.

## Notes

1  Leamington, located in southwestern Ontario, is the greenhouse capital of North America.
2  CLC is the Canadian Labour Congress; UFCW is the United Food and Commercial Workers union; Auto is the Canadian Auto Workers union; and Steel is United Steelworkers Canada.
3  UFCW's reports on migrant farm workers can be found on its website, http://www.ufcw.ca.
4  Mike Fraser is the Canadian national director and the executive vice president of UFCW International.
5  This is the Low-Skilled Workers program; see Preibisch in this volume.
6  Status here refers to the legal citizenship rights afforded to permanent residents and immigrants.

# 8

# Transnationalism, Development, and Social Capital: Tamil Community Networks in Canada

*R. Cheran*

In the contemporary context, which is marked by globalization, the changing role of the nation-state, and a growing number of transnational migrants, policy makers and scholars have begun to take note of transnational and diasporic communities. Transnational groups that are capable of maintaining and investing in social, economic, and political networks that span the globe are of increasing relevance and interest to scholars, policy makers, development workers, and NGOs in home countries as well as host countries. This chapter analyzes Tamil ethnic community networks in Canada that are simultaneously constructed and constituted as transnational and diasporic. The networks are transnational in their social organization and operation. They are diasporic because most of their members left their places of origin as refugees. These transnational community networks and the power of their social as well as economic capital play a significant role in alternative forms of development in the war-ravaged areas of Sri Lanka.

## Multiple Belongings: Transnationalism and Diaspora

Research on transnationalism and diaspora is currently conducted from numerous perspectives, including anthropology, sociology, human geography, international migration, postcolonialism, political economy, and communications. The terms *transnational* and *diasporic communities* are increasingly used today as metaphorical definitions for expatriates, expellees, refugees, alien residents, immigrants, displaced communities, and ethnic minorities. There are also suggestions to include "military diaspora" in the study of transnationalism and diaspora.[1] The terms *transnationalism* and *diaspora* can be grouped together in the sense that both revolve around the idea of "movement." The term *diaspora* has historically been used to describe the experience of forced displacement and to analyze the social, cultural, and political formations that result from this displacement. Transnational communities can be generally defined as communities living in or belonging to more than one "national" space. However, the distinction between diaspora and transnational is not always clear in social science literature. These two terms have become floating signifiers and seem to be universally deployed.

While some scholars have argued in favour of identifying a closed set of attributes and have been only minimally concerned with the actual conditions of diasporic existence (Cohen 1997), others have preferred to use the term in the broader sense of human dispersal (Safran 1991). John Docker (2001, vii) defines diaspora as "a sense of belonging to more than one history, to more than one time and place, to more than one past and future." Avtar Brah's work (1996) on diaspora locates "diasporic space" in the intersectionality of diaspora, border, and dis/location. The broader definitions do not help us to understand the specific social, historical, and political contexts within which diasporas and/or transnational communities have emerged. In addition, the traditional naming and meaning of diasporas can be expanded to include several communities that express new identities and cultural practices as the result of displacement, hybridity, and transnationality and mediated through economic transnationalism. For example, Paul Gilroy (1992) uses the concept of diaspora to argue against ethnic absolutism and unitary ethnic culture. Stuart Hall (1990) uses diaspora to emphasize the hybrid identity formation and the processes, experiences, and practices that result from displacements and cultural shifts. While recognizing that diasporas can eventually evolve into powerful transnational communities, it is sufficient to say that *multiple* and *simultaneous* ways of belonging and multiple ways of incorporation in the "home" and "host" countries comprise the one key theme that is common to both categories and useful for us in the context of development and transnational community networks.[2]

The social sciences originated in the nineteenth and twentieth centuries as part of the project of creating modern nation-states. The terms *government, organization, citizenship,* and *rights* carry with them an embedded nationalist assumption that impairs our capacity to see and understand transnational processes and movements. In addition, the emergence of the state is designed to meet the necessities of the settled or sedentary people for whom territory was the single most important factor. The state that always expects "commitment" from its subjects and the "nation" that always demands "loyalty and faithfulness" from its members are not positively predisposed to transnationalism.

New analytical lenses are essential to understand the social and political processes that transcend traditional state boundaries and create transnationalism. In the context of Tamil transnational community networks, "homelands" – the countries from which transnationals originated – and "host lands" – the countries that the transnationals often inhabit – have to be understood as a single field (Bourdieu 1986). By a single field, I mean that those who leave and those who remain should be conceptualized as a single socioeconomic and political field transcending the traditional boundaries and boundedness of nation-states and territories.

Economic globalization and immigration have been instrumental in creating several transnational communities. There are vast disparities in the status, experience, and power of various kinds of transnational communities. Ethnicity, gender, class, religion, and caste locate people unevenly within transnationalism and diaspora. The Tamil diaspora in Canada is very different from the Tamil diaspora in Norway or Switzerland (McDowell 1996a; Fuglerut 1999; Cheran 2001). The legal status of its members is crucial in this regard. Whether they have citizenship or residency rights and the nature and modalities of incorporation in the host land are important factors that determine the power of transnational communities. These communities have influenced social, economic, and political processes and events in significant ways. They also have the potential to influence economies and wealth creation to a much greater degree. From the banking network of the Rothschilds, originating in eighteenth-century Europe, to the more recent Hinduja group – a powerful Indian business conglomerate – diasporas have been leading players in global transactions (Markowits 2000).

Sri Lanka is among the top twenty developing countries that receive large amounts of remittances from its transnational communities. In 1999, for example, the country received US $1,056 million. This amounts to 6.9 percent of the GDP (World Bank 2003d). The relatively small number of Tamils from Sri Lanka living in Canada and Europe provided substantial resources that sustained both the armed struggle for a separate Tamil state and the Tamil refugee communities that are spread across the conflict zones in Sri Lanka (Wayland 2004, 421-22).

In contrast to the conventional view of remittance as obligation to nation – in both literal and metaphorical terms – or obligation to family, I suggest that remittance should also be understood as a return from investment. Often people invest all their savings and assets to send a member of the family, in many cases a male, into the diaspora. Then the one who was sent takes on the responsibility of sponsoring other family members, thereby setting in motion a process of chain migration. For diasporas, return or the hope of return to the homeland is a major defining moment. However, as diasporic communities transform themselves into transnational communities and gain power and wealth, the mythical concept of return gives way to much more practical return: return from their investments. Wealthy diasporas and transnational communities actively contribute to projects of investment and "expansion" in their homelands.

## Transnational Circulation
It is highly unlikely that the majority of members who inhabit transnational spaces will return to their homelands on a permanent basis. The most

probable scenario is that they will circulate if/when conditions in both host and home countries are conducive to such circulation. The idea and practice of circulation together with the degree of social capital that a transnational community possesses can have enormous impact on the home as well as host countries. The idea of circulation is not new in international migration. Labour migrants have historically circulated, and the demand and supply of cheap labour have determined this circulation. However, what is new in the current conception of circulation is that the main base of the circulating population is located in the West, and the power, influence, and affluence of these new transnational communities are different from the traditional labour populations that circulated.

The global economic situation in the past several decades has given rise to the syndrome of "brain drain" from the global south to the north as well as all forms of labour migration and movements of capital on a global scale. Brain drain does not seriously affect countries with a large professional population base. China and India, for example, lose only 1 percent of their professional sector to brain drain, whereas smaller countries tend to lose almost 15-20 percent of their professional force (Carrington and Detragiache 1999). Brain drain is also fostered – indeed aggressively promoted – by skilled worker recruitment policies of immigrant-receiving states. Reversing this process is impossible. However, transnational circulation can facilitate the circulation of "human capital." Such circulation is playing a critical role in relief, reconstruction, rehabilitation, and development efforts in the northeast part of Sri Lanka. The main actors that facilitate this circulation are Tamil transnational community networks in Canada and Europe.

One characteristic that distinguishes the Tamil communities in Canada and Europe from most other communities is the existence of an elaborate network of Home Village Associations (HVAs) and Alumni Associations (AAs). They are formed on the basis of people's home villages in the northeastern part of Sri Lanka or in the high schools that these people attended in that region. In the absence of state support for education, healthcare, and relief in the conflict zones, transnational community groups are often the only mechanism for relief, reconstruction, and development. For the Tamil community in Canada, the transnational community networks and ties permit them to function within the Sri Lankan context with minimal dependence on state process or regulation and no pressure for concessions. Similarly, their nondependence on state institutions has enabled these groups to be relatively immune from the coercive and hegemonizing power of the state. I argue that the ease with which Tamil transnational community groups have functioned as viable entities in their own right has facilitated the proliferation of many parallel nonstate structures. Their work has been effective in addressing unmet needs in the conflict zones of Sri Lanka.

## Social Capital

The power and influence of Tamil transnational community networks are dependent upon the degree of social capital that a community can muster. Various understandings of social capital are possible. It refers to characteristics of social organization such as networks, social trust, and social norms that facilitate coordination and cooperation for mutual benefit (Coleman 1988; Putnam 1995). The Organisation for Economic Co-operation and Development (OECD) defines social capital as "networks together with shared norms, values and understandings that facilitate co-operation within or among groups" (2001, 41). There has been a steady development in conceptualizing social capital by states, international development organizations, and the World Bank. A number of contexts have demonstrated the extent to which a high degree of social capital can play a useful role in development.[3] Previous research has also indicated the significant role played by social capital in generating better material benefits for immigrant communities (Glick Schiller and Fouron 1999). Civic engagement, the political participation of community groups, community involvement, the presence of informal networks, and trust are some of the key factors that influence the nature of social capital. This understanding of social capital is predicated on the social cohesion of communities. However, contemporary societies are facing increased immigration and emigration. Displacement has fractured social cohesion, and communities are facing economic, social, and cultural challenges in redefining or reinventing their social connectedness. Traditional idioms of social capital have certain limitations. Until now, the debates and discussions on social capital have been centred on national populations and groups. The possibility of social capital in the transnational context and the role of community networks have not been adequately studied.

Tamil transnational community networks offer a good starting point in this area of research. For ethnic communities that are struggling to adapt in a new environment, in a new country, social capital can offset some of the strains of adaptation and mechanisms of exclusion practised by the host lands. In this context, the definition of social capital needs to be deepened to include the notion of solidarity based on identity. Social capital, then, becomes the ability of a community/group to summon resources, strengths, and networks using community or ethnic ties at times of crisis and need. It is the "ethnic solidarity" that facilitates the successful buildup of social capital in the Tamil transnational context.

Different communities exhibit different degrees of social capital. The measurement of social capital has always been a tricky issue for sociologists. The World Bank has been in the forefront in promoting discussions on social capital and the measurement of social capital in the context of poverty alleviation. It has also developed an integral approach to the measurement of social capital. However, the methods developed by the World Bank through a core set of questions are aimed at the global south and national populations.[4] In my study of social capital of Tamil transnational community groups, I have modified the core questions to better address a transnational context. Fifteen focus groups were conducted in Toronto with various Tamil transnational groups and HVAs from November 2003 to January 2004. There were six to ten participants in each group, with each of the participants representing an HVA or AA. Two focus groups were conducted with women and men separately. In addition to the focus group meetings, the participants were given a questionnaire to obtain details of their particular HVA's/AA's origin, organizational structure, amount of money remitted, membership, and status in Canada. Before I summarize the findings, a contextualization of the Tamil community in Canada is necessary.

**The Tamil Community in Canada**

Sri Lankan Tamils have become the subject of recent study by various scholars (Daniel and Thangaraj 1995; McDowell 1996a; Fuglerut 1999; Cheran 2001, 2002; Wayland 2004). The Tamil diaspora consists of an estimated 700,000 people settled in Canada, Europe, India, and Australia (Fuglerut 1999; Cheran 2001). It is therefore likely that one in every four Sri Lankan Tamils now lives in the diaspora. Furthermore, it is estimated that one Tamil family unit might be divided in the following manner by the third generation: four members in Switzerland, six in the United Kingdom, two in France, three in Sri Lanka, and three in Norway.

Tamil migration from the Jaffna peninsula was triggered in the early phases of colonialism. The arid regions where the Tamils lived were completely neglected after the colonial conquest. The colonizers were interested only in developing the plantation economy in the central part of Sri Lanka while simultaneously developing Colombo and the surrounding region as the industrial capital. From about 1850 onward, the northern and eastern regions gradually lost their economic sustainability. Tamils migrated initially to Colombo and later to other parts of the British Empire. Elite and dominant groups of Sri Lankan Tamils have also had a long history of temporary emigration for education and employment, usually to Britain and the peninsular Malaya (now Malaysia). In 1911, the city of Kuala Lumpur harboured an estimated 7,000 Tamils from Jaffna. In 1957, the number had increased to 25,000. However, the civil war in Sri Lanka triggered a large exodus of Tamils to Europe and Canada beginning in 1983. In the absence of any support by the Sri Lankan state to the Tamil community in the conflict zones, sustaining a society under stress, strain, and displacement has been the single most important function of the Tamil transnational community in the past two decades. The 2002 cease-fire agreement between the government and the Liberation Tigers of Tamil Eelam (LTTE), the organization pursuing an armed rebellion, shifted the ways in which Tamil transnational communities were operating in Sri Lanka and the diaspora.[5] In the wake of the cease-fire agreement, increasingly greater emphasis has been placed on reconstruction and development rather than on relief and rehabilitation.

The Tamil diaspora is largely made up of refugees and former refugees. According to the United Nations High Commissioner for Refugees (UNHCR), in the period 1980-99, 256,307 people of Sri Lankan origin applied for asylum in Europe, one of the top ten groups of asylum seekers during this period (UNHCR 2001-2). Between 1987 and 2001, Sri Lanka was among the top three source countries for refugee claimants in Canada (CIC 2002a). Large numbers of Tamils have been granted some form of residence status in their host countries. The acceptance rate for Tamil refugee claimants has been consistently high in Canada. Perhaps this explains why Toronto has become the epicentre of Tamil transnationalism (Cheran 2002).

A recent study (Beiser, Simich, and Pandalangat 2003, 239) provides a snapshot of the Tamil community in Toronto. Nearly half (49.8 percent) of the people surveyed entered Canada as refugee claimants. Another 32.4 percent came as family class immigrants. Forty-three percent of the study sample had experienced internal displacements before arriving in Canada, and 17.5 percent had lived in various refugee camps in Sri Lanka. Another 35 percent were separated from their families during the period of immigration. Despite these hardships, the social capital of the Tamil community has been a major force in sustaining and advancing the community both in Sri Lanka and the diaspora through its HVAs, AAs, and other transnational community networks.

## Mapping Tamil HVAs and AAs

There are about 300 Tamil HVAs and AAs in Canada. The same kind of HVA networks is a common feature of all the Tamil communities in various parts of Europe and to a lesser extent in Singapore and Malaysia. The only networks that are somewhat similar are Latin American Home Town Associations (HTAs) in the United States and the networks of Malian immigrants in France. Mexicans in the United States have around 1,500 HTAs, which have supported community development activities (Stalker 2001, 117). In the case of Malian immigrants in France, it is estimated that 70 percent of them are active in their village associations and have contributed more than US $2 million toward various development projects in a ten-year period (Libercier and Schneider 1996). However, the crucial difference is that Mexican and other Latin American HTAs are formed by migrant workers, and there is a significant degree of church and government involvement in developing and sustaining the networks. In the case of Tamil HVAs, there is no church or government involvement, and all of them are voluntary organizations formed on the basis of solidarity. Social and community networks are reinforced when they are formed in response to oppression. The experience of marginalization and discrimination in both Sri Lanka and Canada has precipitated a "double victimhood" for Tamils.

Tamil HVAs/AAs are voluntary organizations formed for various reasons. One reason could be a sense of nostalgia. However, the most important reason for their formation is to assist the people in the villages back home who are struggling to rebuild their lives. Studies in the conflict zones of Sri Lanka indicate that the presence of a high degree of social capital has enhanced the livelihood strategies of these villages. Some of the organizations were started as social clubs but eventually evolved into development organizations. Charity and philanthropy have been the major functions of most of these HVAs. However, the civil war and the continuous displacement of people and almost total destruction of several villages in the past twenty years are the main reasons that changed the mandates of these HVAs. All of them are now engaged in either relief and rehabilitation or reconstruction and development work. Most of the HVAs have a cultural program, and all HVAs and AAs publish an annual magazine for circulation among their members. One HVA from the Jaffna peninsula maintains a well-endowed archive located in Toronto. Selected materials from the archive were exhibited in Jaffna in September 2004. The involvement of second-generation Tamils in HVA/AA activities is minimal and could be a limiting factor in the future of HVAs/AAs.

Some of the areas where HVAs and AAs work in Sri Lanka are predominantly under the control of the LTTE. There is a de facto LTTE state in the northeast of Sri Lanka with separate police forces, a judiciary, armed forces, and a naval unit. This state has its own Planning and Developing Secretariat (PDS) for the reconstruction of the postconflict zones. The development activities of the de facto state are heavily funded through the economic units of the LTTE in the diaspora. Large-scale projects are carried out by other transnational community organizations such as The Economic Consultancy House (TECH), Tamils Refugee Organization (TRO), and Tamil Eelam Economic Development Organization (TEEDOR).[6] However, the HVAs and AAs have successfully maintained a parallel system of development work.

The context within which these activities take place can be compared to three other geographical areas in the world. The first area is Somalia, where no central unifying authority has been in place for over a decade. Autonomous clan-based units have been formed with separate ministates. These ministates, supported mainly by their transnational community networks, operate airlines, run universities, and engage in development work (Hamza 2004). The social capital of the Somali diaspora is remarkable in this sense.[7] The second area is the safe haven for Kurdish people in parts of Iraq. A de facto state is in place there. However, there are no HVAs or AAs supporting the development work. The third location is the autonomous Basque region in Spain. While the regional state is actively soliciting and encouraging Basque transnational communities in various parts of the world, there are only 175 Basque transnational community organizations that are currently active (Totoricaguena 2004). The modalities of development work and the capacity of social capital in each case may vary. However, the transnational community networks play a central role in national and nationalist development projects.

The numbers of HVAs and AAs are continually in flux as new associations are formed and old ones cease to function. The average monetary value of work undertaken by the HVAs in their villages in the postconflict zones ranges from CDN \$8,000 to \$20,000. Most of the development work is small in scale, and there is an emphasis on building/reconstructing educational institutions, hospitals, and village infrastructures. Scholarship programs for students are also popular among AAs. The HVAs/AAs are flexible, easily switching between relief and reconstruction modes. At the time of my fieldwork in northeastern Sri Lanka in April-May 2004, most of the HVAs and AAs were continuing reconstruction work that they had initiated in 2002.

One of the advantages of HVAs and AAs is the existence of a parallel structure or organization in the homeland. The home village will have an organization that sends detailed assessments of needs and estimated costs. The money is then collected and sent to the village organization by the HVA in Canada. This process increases the efficiency of the work, and it avoids the bureaucratic hurdles usually associated with traditional development work. Northeastern Sri Lanka has been severely damaged by the war, and rebuilding it is a big challenge. One major difficulty is the availability of knowledge capital (experts and people with diverse skills). Schools, universities, hospitals, and technical institutions are understaffed and lack qualified personnel. This is one area where the Tamil transnational community groups have been playing an important role. Projects to rebuild hospitals and supply them with modern facilities are co-sponsored by all these groups. Tromso Tamil Sangam in Norway, in collaboration with the University of Tromso, is involved in two major projects. One is establishing a faculty of medicine in the Eastern University, and the other is establishing a faculty for fisheries in Jaffna. Teachers and experts will be provided to these faculties on a rotational basis. The training of local staff members is a major component of these projects. Information technology (IT) training is the major venture of the Vanni Institute of Technology (Vannitech) in Kilinochchi. Initiated and supported by Canadian and US transnational groups, Vannitech's vision is effectively to utilize the expertise and resources available from various transnational community groups. Some of the HVAs and

AAs have similar organizations in Germany, the United Kingdom, Switzerland, Norway, France, Denmark, and Australia. The network created by these organizations largely functions as several autonomous units working in tandem.

Reconstruction of damaged schools is the primary work funded by the AAs. In addition, nutritional programs for schoolchildren are funded. Scholarships and bursaries are provided to selected students. The monetary value of scholarships varies depending on the membership of the AA. However, megaprojects are being sponsored by several AAs. For example, the Canadian and UK AAs of Mahajana College in Jaffna organized a convention for the international membership in April 2003 in Colombo. The convention pledged US $4 million for reconstruction and development. IT training, scholarships, and English-language teaching were areas that received particular attention. TEEDOR and TRO are other transnational networks active in facilitating knowledge transfer for development through circulation. The HVAs and AAs do not receive any support from international development organizations, including the Canadian International Development Agency (CIDA). However, the United Nations Development Program (UNDP) and the World Bank are facilitating these activities through TRO. The UNDP has short-term projects for expatriates.

The Transfer of Knowledge through Expatriate Nationals (TOKTEN) program enables members of the diaspora to work in home countries. The potential of TOKTEN in assisting the relief, rehabilitation, and reconstruction (RRR) efforts in the war-ravaged areas is great. However, getting a large number of transnational people and organizations working through the program will be time consuming because of the UN bureaucracy. The TOKTEN program generally provides return airfare and a monthly stipend of US $1,000. This is more than adequate for any diasporic member interested in working in the northeast for a short period. The efficiency of the HVAs and AAs is also enhanced by the timely use of available funds by their counterparts in the homeland through volunteers. This is in sharp contrast to the traditional development and donor sectors. The capacity to utilize donor funding is low in Sri Lanka. For example, less than 20 percent of the donor funding is currently being used. There are several structural and other barriers, including severe shortages of labourers, skilled labourers, policy planners, project and financial managers, and banking facilities – all of which are necessary for reconstruction and development. These are some of the areas where Tamil transnational community networks are doing good work.

The three LTTE nominees for the Northeast Needs Assessment Committee set up before the Tokyo donor conference for Sri Lanka in June 2003 were from the transnational community network. One of them was a financial consultant, the other was an irrigation expert, and the third was a senior management consultant. Skill development is an important element in the RRR of the northeast. There are a few organizations like TECH trying to address the problem. However, the demand is huge, and the availability of training and expertise is limited. There is a need for a comprehensive skills development and training program that is specially designed for postwar construction and rebuilding of the northeast. The construction industry has some attractive prospects in the war-torn areas. However, only six companies, with some help from the diaspora, have been registered so far. A few transnational community organizations from Canada, Germany, Norway, and Australia are investing in the renewable energy sector. Solar panels are being produced in parts of the Vanni region, and a project for a "self-sufficient village network" in the region is under way.

The lack of an adequate banking system is a major obstacle. Unlike other parts of Sri Lanka, the northeast does not have a regional banking system. Soft loans and credit line facilities, which are crucial for reconstruction and development, are almost nonexistent. The government of Sri Lanka has proposed that the recent offer from the Indian government in extending loan facilities should be channelled through the existing regional banks. It is clear that the northeast will not be a beneficiary. HVAs and AAs have been using informal money transfer networks for remittances. In the absence of any reliable banking institutions, an informal money transfer network, or *undiyal* (in Tamil), becomes an essential part of the social capital. In the short period of two years, the transnational community networks have transformed their work from relief and rehabilitation to reconstruction and development. The current involvement of these community networks indicates two major trends. First, there is a systematic and regular circulation of professionals, experts, and members of the HVAs/AAs and other Tamil transnational community networks. Second, even though the number of big investors is small, HVAs and AAs are moving toward creating small-scale but sustainable and self-sufficient communities.

My fieldwork in the northeast also revealed some of the limitations of the transnational community networks. In several instances, the lack of coordination among HVAs/AAs from different countries results in duplication and confusion. Some Canadian HVAs and AAs have recently formed a consortium called Transnational and Diaspora Network for Development (TDND-Canada) to address these issues and coordinate all the activities of Canadian Tamil transnational community organizations. In addition, there is a regional imbalance in the work of HVAs/AAs. Many of the transnational community groups are from the Jaffna peninsula in the northern part of the country. The eastern and northwestern parts of Tamil areas are underrepresented in the Tamil transnational community networks. However, HVAs and AAs have significant potential to support small, self-sustaining communities, and therefore expansion of their network in other regions is necessary.

Furthermore, in the case of HVAs and AAs, they operate only in their respective villages and schools. Hence, their work and impact are highly localized. The wider society is not aware of the activities of HVAs/AAs both locally and transnationally. Given the power of social capital that exists in various Tamil transnational community networks, HVAs/AAs can be positively and effectively utilized for reconstruction and development. However, their success also rests upon the political and administrative mechanisms by which the transnational community networks can effectively work with each other. Given the fragile nature of the current ceasefire, it is too early to predict meaningfully any long-term outcomes.

## Political Participation and Civic Engagement

The norms and networks of civic engagement have considerable impact on the performance of representative governments and social and political movements. The nexus between civic engagement and social capital has been an important area of research (Putnam 1995). Communities with good social capital generally have high levels of civic engagement. Two decades of war in Sri Lanka have resulted in the weakening of civil society. While the electoral participation of all communities in Sri Lanka has been high, other institutions of civil society are struggling to maintain an autonomous existence. Therefore, it should come as no surprise that "strengthening the civil society" has been a key donor theme that attracts considerable funding.[8]

However, it is crucial to note that the civil society in Sri Lanka is fractured along ethnic lines. This important issue has not been adequately addressed. There are Sinhala, Tamil, and Muslim civil societies with different degrees of power, articulation, social capital, and mobility. Although Sinhalese and to a lesser extent Muslims from Sri Lanka live in Canada, it is the Tamil community that is "visible" through its political and community articulation. The HVAs and AAs are key community organizations in the political life of the Tamil community in Canada. In the past, the Tamil community has been successful in mobilizing more than 20,000 people for various demonstrations in 1995, 1998, and 2004.[9] Together with other community groups and Tamil political organizations, the HVAs and AAs were instrumental in mobilizing their members for all the demonstrations and protest marches. Some of the community groups are active in local Canadian politics. The Toronto constituency of the Canadian minister of defence has 6,000 eligible Tamil voters. Partly due to the influence of the Tamil community, the minister, then the minister of foreign affairs, assumed responsibility for including the hitherto neglected Sri Lankan civil war in Canada's foreign policy agenda. More recently, in September 2003, the Tamil community in Ontario elected 86 Liberal Party delegates supporting the leadership bid of Paul Martin from a total of 1,434 delegates in Ontario. The Tamil delegates, drawn mainly from the Metropolitan Toronto and Markham area ridings, outnumbered the total delegates elected respectively from Prince Edward Island, the Yukon, the Northwest Territories, Nunavut, and Newfoundland.[10]

## Conclusion

How do the foregoing issues impact upon sending and receiving locations of transnational spaces? What are the policy implications? Host countries that receive migrant populations in large numbers require new perspectives and policies to deal with the emergence of different dimensions of transnationalism. Historically, suspicion of transnational and diasporic communities has been the norm for Western states. Political activities by transnational communities (in support of "homeland conflicts") have been viewed with alarm and mainly through the lens of national security by host states. In the aftermath of 11 September 2001, transnational movements and the particular links between transnationals and homelands have come under ever greater scrutiny. The contradiction in the discourse on globalization, which has favoured the free movement of goods and capital but generally not of people (especially those from the non-Western world), has become acute as governments move to adopt strict antiterrorism laws and seal or at least tighten their national borders. In this context, the loyalty of transnational actors, or transnationals, has become increasingly suspect: transnational connections and circulations are increasingly subject to surveillance by security agencies. The multiple and mixed identities of transnational members are under constant pressure to conform to the notion of a homogeneous populace in the traditional nation-state.

Governments have the necessary task of ensuring public safety and security – of preventing terrorism on their soil and abroad. In my view, this responsibility necessarily requires governments to better understand the nature of transnationalism. While the political and financial influences of transnational communities have come under closer scrutiny after 9/11, Western governments have not formulated effective policy responses to the emergence of transnationalism and global diasporas. The conventional approach, applied somewhat inconsistently, has been to view diasporic communities as potentially dangerous groups bringing their "homeland conflicts" with them and therefore a perennial threat to social cohesion in host countries. Even noted human rights advocate Michael Ignatieff has suggested that

> Diaspora nationalism is a dangerous phenomenon because it is easier to hate from a distance: You don't have to live with the consequences – or the reprisals ... Canadians, new and old, need to think about what role diasporas play in fanning and financing the hatreds of the outside world. The disturbing possibility is that Canada is not an asylum from hatred but an incubator of hatred ... So it is appropriate to say to newcomers: You do not have

to embrace all our supposed civilities. You can and should keep the memory of the injustice you have left firmly in your heart. But the law is law. You will have to leave your murderous fantasies of revenge behind. (*Globe and Mail,* 25 October 2001, A17)

The problem with this view is that it homogenizes diasporic nationalism and new immigrants. Conceptually, it also fails to appreciate the distinctions between groups such as Al Qaeda on the one hand and other nonstate actors that might be engaged in legitimate struggles of self-determination (although resorting to illegitimate tactics with greater or lesser frequency) on the other (e.g., historically South Africans under the apartheid regime and more currently Kurds, Tamils, Palestinians, and Kosovars). As the power of nation-states weakens as a result of rapid globalization, and as the power of diasporic communities grows, the logic of incorporating these communities into theories and practices of international law, international relations, development policy, foreign policy, and civil society grows as well. The circulation process has to be systematized and strengthened and should be addressed in domestic policy formulation as well as in program planning and implementation.

The other area where the home as well as host countries need immediate and important work is remittances. They have become a major source of national income for countries in the global south (IOM 2003a). Remittances are the second largest source, behind foreign direct investment, of external funding for many developing countries, surpassing inflows of official development assistance (Ratha 2003, 157). Remittances are relatively stable sources of foreign exchange.

However, significant problems exist in the financial sectors, government administration, and banking systems. Collectively, they increase the transaction costs. Long delays in cheque clearances, exchange losses, and the improper disclosure of transaction costs are some of the deficiencies that constrain transnationals from sending money through the international banking system. The average cost of transferring remittances is between 13 and 20 percent (Ratha 2003, 165). Reducing such transaction costs to 10 percent would result in an annual savings of US $3.5 billion to those who send the money. Many developing countries are without extensive banking networks in rural areas. This is one of the reasons why money transfer through informal networks is the primary mechanism by which most of the Tamil transnational community networks send money.

The post-9/11 crackdown on informal money transfer businesses has affected remittances. The opportunity is ripe for banks to focus on money transfer and make it affordable and beneficial. Industrial countries should consider reducing the transaction costs of remittances to developing countries. The developing countries need to expand their banking services in the rural sector. Furthermore, governments need to acknowledge the inherent possibilities of transnational communities. These communities should be made partners and incorporated in development policy, international trade, and foreign policy.

Citizenship policies are crucial to the incorporation of transnational populations in host states. Dual or transnational citizenship is one possibility. Transnational citizenship implies not only legal status with related rights and duties within multiple jurisdictions and across borders but also the recognition of identity and meaningful participation in multiple political communities, civil societies, and public spheres – some of which span state boundaries (Falk 1993; Wong 2002). Freedom of transnational association is at the core of transnational citizenship. A reorientation of foreign aid/ development aid is also required. Here a paradigm shift is needed. The possibility of alternative development models using transnational community networks should be explored. For example, the cost of clearing a landmine in the northeast of Sri Lanka using transnational community networks will be much less expensive than proceeding without them. In the same way, several small- and large-scale development projects can be conducted with greater efficiency. Our understanding of migration and immigration must be informed by the lifelong connection between transnationals and their homelands. In addition, the circular migration of professionals, intellectuals, and development workers will be a key element in the future. It is hoped that governments, donor agencies, policy makers, and scholars will pay more attention to the phenomenon of transnationalism and the social, political, and cultural entanglements that it generates.

## Notes

1 A paper presented by Dana Magill at the University of Windsor conference in May 2004, Imagining Diasporas: Space, Identity, and Social Change, was titled "There's No Place Like Home: Definitions of Nationalism, Allegiance, and Identity in the Military Diaspora."

2 I suggest that the notion of diasporiCity is useful in describing the Tamil communities located in urban centres in the global north. The notion of diasporiCity does not signify the origins of the community, nor does it illustrate the existential conditions of living. Rather, I use the term to capture an "enunciation" and an entanglement of a new ethnicity, cityscape, and subalternity in the transnational moment. See Cheran (2007).

3 Network capitalism of East Asia is cited as one example (Putnam 1995, 291).

4 There is no consensus on the accuracy of measuring social capital since this is an emerging field. For a useful template and information on the World Bank social capital initiative, see http://www.worldbank.org/poverty/scapital/index.htm.

5 For a detailed study with regard to how Tamil diaspora can be incorporated into current social, economic, and political processes in Sri Lanka, see Cheran (2003).

6 It is alleged that all three organizations are LTTE fronts. While TEEDOR is a unit of LTTE's development wing, TRO is a registered NGO in Sri Lanka and works with both the Sri Lankan government in territories controlled by the government and the LTTE in territories controlled by the LTTE. TRO also receives project and program funding from UNICEF, the World Bank, and other international organizations.

7 However, there is a useful study comparing Tamil and Somali social capital in a transnational setting. Oivind Fuglerut (2004) indicates that Tamils in Norway are generally

employed and self-reliant, while Somalis are unemployed and depend on social assistance. Fuglerut argues that this is due to Tamil networks, which are mainly formed on the basis of political loyalties and friendship, while Somali networks are family- and clan-based.

8  For example, CIDA has allocated CDN $15 million for such purposes in Sri Lanka in the past two years.

9  An estimated 75,000 Tamils participated in the recent Tamil meet called Pongu Thamil (Tamil Upsurge), held at Queen's Park on 25 September 2004. The event was organized by the Tamil University Students' Association of Canada.

10  The comparison of the Tamil population in Canada and Prince Edward Island and Nunavut was made by a prominent Tamil member of the Liberal Party, Professor Elagu Elagupillai, at the Tamil Upsurge festival in Toronto. He demanded that the federal government respect the representative power of Tamil and other similar communities.

# 9

# Dancing Here, "Living" There: Transnational Lives and Working Conditions of Latina Migrant Exotic Dancers

*Gloria Patricia Díaz Barrero*

At the heart of women's migration from "Third World" countries to more "developed" countries are factors such as "economic inequalities within and between regions, expanding mobility of capital, people's desire to pursue opportunities that might improve their life chances, political strife, wars and famine" (Brah 1996, 178). There can be many reasons for women to move to another country, but what is noteworthy here is precisely the fact that women are crossing borders more often than men, a phenomenon that has come to be known as the "feminization of migration." According to the *World Migration* report of 2003, half of the estimated 175 million migrants worldwide are women, and women travelling individually are considered a new kind of migrant (IOM 2003b, 6). Some argue that women are moving with the main purpose of performing service work, in particular domestic and sex work (see Ehrenreich and Hochschild 2003).

This chapter concentrates on a particular group of migrant workers: women coming to Canada from Latin America with Temporary Employment Authorizations to work in the adult entertainment industry as exotic dancers. I look at the different ways that exotic dancers create, shape, reshape, and maintain transnational links with their relatives, communities, and countries of origin. The data that inform the chapter come from research that I carried out in conjunction with the Latin American Coalition to End Violence Against Women (LACEV)[1] between 2001 and 2002. The information was collected through eleven interviews with women from six different Latin American countries who were, or are currently, working as exotic dancers in Toronto. The interviews took the form of dialogues about the women's lives in their countries, how they came to Canada, what happened after they arrived, and how their lives are now in Canada. This format allowed for spontaneity and gave the women an opportunity to explore issues important to them.[2] To get a broad range of perspectives and to complement the women's perspectives, I interviewed five "key informants," people who have had a role in shaping the topic or have expertise in an area concerning the exotic dancing industry. I also carried out observations at some clubs located in downtown Toronto, where I was able to observe changing rooms, stages, washrooms, and kitchens as well as the labour conditions and internal dynamics of the clubs. I spent many hours with the women in their work places, in their homes with their loved ones, as well as in other social settings such as cafés. Doing so gave me the opportunity to see the women not only in their roles as sex workers or workers generally but also as mothers, sisters, friends, immigrants, and activists.

As underscored in the introduction to this collection, temporary workers' issues are rarely discussed from a transnational perspective. But what defines the temporary worker is transnational movement: he or she is expected to "go home" and sometimes to "come back" to Canada, depending on the type of temporary work program, so that workers develop and maintain multistranded social relations and connections in different communities. An example of this phenomenon is presented by Ofelia Becerril in her chapter, "Transnational Work and the Gendered Politics of Labour: A Study of Male and Female Mexican Migrant Farm Workers in Canada," in this volume, where she demonstrates the interconnected processes experienced by Mexican agricultural workers in Canada.

The general objective of this chapter is to address the transnational aspects of Latin American exotic dancers in Toronto, such as the immigration process, the relationship between temporary work and labour conditions, and the different connections that the women keep with their families, friends, and communities. I begin with an overview of the concept of the "transnational" and how it can be used to understand the transnational lives of the migrant exotic dancers. I then look at the immigration regulations and procedures for exotic dancers to obtain Temporary Foreign Worker visas. Next I examine how the labour conditions for exotic dancers are directly related to their status as temporary workers and how the conditions improve as women's immigration status changes to a more permanent one, such as immigrants. The final sections focus on the transnational links that the women maintain with their home countries and explore possibilities for organizing in Canada and across borders to demand rights to improve labour and living conditions.

## Transnationalism and the Livelihoods of Latin American Migrant Exotic Dancers

FOCAL (the Canadian Foundation for the Americas), in a 2004 report, stated that, "in the last decades, a new pattern of transnationalism has emerged with Latin American and Caribbean countries becoming net exporters of labour. This pattern is likely to continue in spite of the increasing cost of migration and the introduction of more stringent immigration policies.

Labour shortages in key sectors, like agriculture, an ageing population and a low birth rate in developed countries, such as Canada and the United States, are factors that will continue to *encourage* these migration flows" (4). As noted by FOCAL, Latin America and the Caribbean have become important sources of labour for Canada, especially in relation to temporary work, within a new pattern of transnationalism. Unfortunately, temporary workers have not been a matter of attention in transnational studies. If transnationalism is generally used to describe the sense of belonging to and/or the organization of daily lives around more than one nation-state, as defined in the introduction to this volume, it is evident that temporary workers clearly exhibit those characteristics. They organize their livelihoods both "here" and "there." The unsettledness of living in two, and sometimes more, countries is exacerbated by the instability and vulnerability of temporary work where their being "here" depends on that work. Thus, temporary workers maintain a multistranded link between their "home" countries, to which they return regularly or are supposed to return, and the society in which they work, make money, and in many cases end up staying more permanently.

In *Nations Unbound: Transnational Projects, Postcolonial Predicaments, and Deterritorialized Nation-States,* the authors define the term *transnationalism* as "the processes by which immigrants forge and sustain multistranded social relations that link together their societies of origin and settlement, consequently immigrants today build social fields that cross geographic, cultural, and political borders" (Basch, Glick Schiller, and Szanton Blanc 1994, 7). These authors pay particular attention to the flow of people and their interactions and linkages with their multiple locations and relocations. From this perspective, the concept of transnationalism provides the theoretical tools to understand the relationship between places of origin and places of settlement developed by people in the diaspora. When mobile workers, in this case sex workers, cross borders, they maintain different kinds of connections to their home countries, in particular to their families and children. They do so by calling, travelling, sending money, sponsoring relatives to immigrate to Canada, bringing and carrying goods, providing contacts, and networking, among other activities, as the majority of migrants do.

In studying transnational organizing, it is important to consider the social relations in which immigrants/migrants find themselves when they move to another country. When women, and men, travel with the intention to stay either temporarily or permanently, they are inserted into a new social reality. They become part of classed, gendered, racialized, and sexualized social relations that differentiate them to include them or exclude them from the construction of the nation-state or even to participate in society (Brah 1996, 182-83). In this line of thought, Inderpal Grewal and Caren Kaplan state that "transnational linkages influence every level of social existence," and these linkages are both multifaceted and uneven and influence people differently (1994, 13). Therefore, it is important to have "categories of differentiation and analysis that acknowledge the structurally asymmetrical links" (15). This analysis allows for an understanding of the different positionalities that the individuals have and how they are impacted differently by transnational links; women are impacted differently by transnational processes from men, and "women of colour" and "Third World" women are affected differently from white women by such processes. For instance, women coming from Latin America are generally regarded as poor women with no "marketable skills"; they are undervalued and underestimated. As sex workers, they are considered deviant sexual objects; as Latin American sex workers, they incarnate the "hot Latina" stereotype.

In this study, none of the women interviewed left their countries with the intention or desire to settle down permanently in Canada. For all of them, the plan was to go to Canada, make some money, and then go back to their countries, yet they all ended up staying and thus becoming implicated in new social relations. These new relations are determined by the women's position as Latin American women working in Canada, women of colour, sex workers, and temporary workers. These social relations affect their livelihoods and their working conditions. The working conditions are directly related to transnational processes because it is within the global economic context that the programs for temporary workers are established; industrialized countries extract "cheap" labour from elsewhere on the basis of temporary work.

Gayatri Spivak (1996) argues that, in the transnational world, "developing" countries cannot oppose the neoliberal agenda that is applied through "sustainable development" programs. At the same time, the "developing" economies cannot oppose the removal of economic barriers and tariffs between themselves and stronger economies. Framed within this context of unbalanced power and economic relationship between the "developing" and the "developed" nations, any equitable social distribution is impossible. According to Spivak, it is only through consolidating structures in civil society that gender justice, and social justice, can be achieved. For Spivak, the transnational world threatens to provoke more inequality and injustice, but at the same time it provides the tools to strengthen solidarity among civil societies across borders. In this sense, transnationalism also provides a site for resistance and opens up the possibility to engage in solidarity work between women located in the global north and south. Therefore, transnational theory has the potential to provide the tools for practical action to combat the interlocking system of oppressions, as I discuss toward the end of this chapter.

Theories of transnationalism are particularly concerned with the movement of people, culture, knowledge, technology, and capital across borders.

When women and men cross borders, a process of dislocation and relocation begins. Theorists of transnationalism are interested in studying those processes and how individuals are able to link places, or ideas, of origin with the "host" spaces. These processes dramatically impact women, since crossing borders implies "leaving home behind," and "making a new home" and "homemaking" have been roles traditionally assigned to women. Theories of transnationalism, then, both provide a way to understand the multiple oppressions experienced by this group of women as subjects living in more than one nation-state and suggest possibilities for resistance to demand better working and living conditions.

### Immigration Procedures for Exotic Dancers as Temporary Workers

The *Foreign Workers Manual* is the instrument that "explains the regulations and CIC's policy with respect to temporary foreign workers. It also provides guidelines that will assist officers in interpreting the Regulations and explain the programs that fit under these Regulations" (Citizenship and Immigration Canada [CIC] 2005, 8). It explains that, when a person wants to come to Canada to work on a temporary basis, in most cases she or he needs to apply for a work permit[3] from outside Canada (9). However, the person can apply only after being offered a job by a potential employer and after Human Resources and Skills Development Canada (HRSDC)[4] has provided a labour market opinion or "confirmation" of the job offer (CIC 2004c).

The manual states that exotic/erotic dancing requires a work permit (CIC 2005, 15), and currently CIC also needs a validation or confirmation of the job by HRSDC. Until 2004, exotic dancers were exempted from the confirmation letter requirement by HRSDC. This changed in November 2004 as a result of the scandal involving then-immigration minister Judy Sgro for her issuance of an exotic dancer visa to one of her campaign workers from Romania. HRSDC issued the following statement: "Section 5.25 – HRSDC national confirmation letter for exotic dancers was removed. Reference to HRSDC low-skilled program is included" (CIC 2005, 4).

Traditionally, the exotic dancers program had enjoyed the exemption of the confirmation letter because it was considered an exchange program. According to Audrey Macklin, from 1970 there was for many years a cross-border movement of women to work as exotic dancers between the United States and Canada, and this was interpreted by the authorities as an "exchange program" (2003, 467). Thus, until November 2004, any person could arrive at a port of entry or go to a Canadian embassy or consulate with a job offer from a potential Canadian employer and be issued a work permit for which the employer is not required to have a letter of confirmation from HRSDC.

HRSDC has argued that there is a temporary shortage of workers in the exotic dancing industry in Canada; however, this shortage seems to be more permanent than temporary inasmuch as exotic dancers have been allowed into the country since the 1970s. Moreover, as argued above, temporary worker status adds another form of oppression to the women already marginalized as women of colour and as sex workers. If the Canadian government were really interested in the well-being of these women, it would allow exotic dancers to immigrate to the country as permanent workers.

The position of migrant exotic dancers as "temporary foreign workers," added to the fact that their employers are not subjected to any kind of government scrutiny or supervision, places the women in a vulnerable position as workers since the possibility of remaining in Canada depends completely on the goodwill of their employers. This situation exposes them to physical and psychological abuse by club owners, managers, and agents. As Consuelo Rubio, a key informant for this research and a lawyer, explains, "the visas that the women have are based on the demand. When the women arrive here, they can stay if the club needs, but if the club does not need them, well, they send them back. It is like an instant labour force – they come and go. Since they do not have any permanent status, the clubs do with them whatever they want to" (translated from Spanish by the author).

This study found that women's working and living conditions, as well as their emotional well-being, depend on and dramatically change according to the women's immigration status. The issue is not whether they have a regularized status but what kind of legal status they do have – if they are temporary workers, or if they have a permanent status such as a landed immigrant visa. In this reasoning, the legal categories of "landed" versus "temporary" mark the quality of life for the women. This subtle observation challenges much of the literature on transnationalism that assumes the "immigrant" as a homogenous actor who moves and develops links to different societies without taking into account that those links are directly influenced by the legal status of the "immigrant." Through the study, it was evident that working and living conditions were far better for those women who were able to acquire landed status in Canada than for those who remain with temporary worker visas. The next section explores the working and living conditions of the exotic dancers who were part of this study.

## Labour and Living Conditions for Migrant Exotic Dancers

According to the Canadian government, exotic/erotic dancing is a regularized occupation included in the National Occupational List. In Canada, there are three main instruments that shape the law in the industry and therefore affect the working conditions of the dancers: the courts, the Criminal Code of Canada, and municipal bylaws. Even though exotic dancing is a recognized occupation, it is not exempted from the marginalization and stigmatization typical of the sex work industry. "Sex workers" are regarded as a social category rather than a professional one. They are seen as women who deserve to be pitied or despised; they are excluded from the mainstream and located in low and marginal positions similar to those occupied by minority ethnic groups (Bindman and Doezema 1997, 4). What happens when these sex workers are already part of an ethnic group and are temporary workers? In the system of interlocking oppressions, where can this group of Latin American migrant sex workers be placed in relation to mainstream society? These issues will be explored in the following section.

Out of the eleven women interviewed, ten entered the country with working visas or work permits; the other one became an exotic dancer after years of being in Canada. These ten women were recruited in Latin America either by agents or by friends who told them about the opportunity to come to Canada. The most common way in which women are recruited is through agents. These agents are from the women's own countries or other countries in Latin America; they speak Spanish and know the culture. In general, the agents are in charge of finding prospective women to come to Canada. Often they recruit women who are already in the sex industry, but they also recruit them through friends, relatives, or acquaintances: "Someone who knows someone who is offering opportunities to go to Canada." These agents are generally financed by club owners in Canada who are interested in bringing new labourers for their clubs.

When the women arrive in Canada, a country that they do not know, where they do not speak the language and have no social networks, club managers and agents become their main contact, creating a relationship of dependency. For instance, they give the women contracts to renew their visas in order to remain legally in the country. As one woman explained, "the club gives me a contract, and they send it to Immigration. Immigration gives me a visa for a year, ... and they [the club] charge me $400 for the visas."

Club managers are also the ones who tell the women what is and what is not legal to do in their work, though of course this information is not always accurate. Thus, when the women make a decision to do lap-dancing, for example, they usually are ill informed and confused about the regulations. Later, with time and bad experiences, they learn how it works. One woman explained, "they never tell you that you have to sit on the client, but that is what you see in the club. They do not say anything, and everybody does lap-dancing. But they know it is illegal." Overall, women recognize that lap-dancing is illegal, but they see no other option but to do it or be out of business: "I know that you are not supposed to do lap-dancing, but, if you do not do it, you are not going to make any money. You have to sit on the client and let him touch you. We all do it." Yet this is a very contradictory position because, if they do it, they are at risk of being deported if they are caught. Undercover police looking for women who touch clients or let clients touch them are not rare in the clubs: "One night I was working in Brampton, and that day all the clients were undercover ... Later that night police with guns and masks showed up. There were policemen all over the place."

This dependency, particular to migrant exotic dancers, plus the lack of authorities' scrutiny of clubs and the fact that the women are not provided with any information by immigration authorities, provides a suitable environment for abuse. For example, in some clubs, the women have to give as much as 50 percent of their earnings to the club, another share to the agent, and keep only 25 to 30 percent. "Look, for every dance you made two dollars. The client pays six dollars: three are for the club, one is for the agent, and two for you." In some clubs, women were not allowed to handle money; they could only deal with "chips," pieces of plastic that have a currency value similar to the ones used in casinos. At least three women mentioned this situation. "We used to dance for chips. We could not have any money ... At the end of the shift, you go to the office, and they give you a piece of paper saying the number of chips you made that day, but you do not see any money until the end of the month." In other cases, women were not paid their salaries. They were told that they were going to be paid in their country of origin, and finally they were never paid. Even though all the women came to Canada with signed contracts, the contracts were not honoured. "They told us that they were going to help us save money. It did not bother me because I thought that after six months I was going to go back with my money."

Every woman reported having had some kind of problem with club managers and club owners, from physical violence, sexual abuse, and retention of documents to failure of payments. "I had a problem with the owner. I had a fight with the person I shared the room with, so I had to sleep in the manager's room. We lived in a house with many other women, and the manager lived there, but there were no more rooms left, so I had to sleep with him. I felt that I had to make love with him because I was living there."

The abuse comes not only from club managers and owners; it is not unusual for clients also to treat the women with disrespect. Sometimes they are abusive and offensive, insulting the women because of their English skills, race, or "ignorance." Women reported being witnesses to physical abuse of other women by clients and of clients refusing to pay a woman after she had danced for them. In the words of this woman, "if a client wants to abuse you, nothing happens – they can do it since the client is always right." Although violence and abuse are not exclusive to the sex trade, since they are also present in other labour sectors of "unskilled" workers (e.g., live-in caregivers or textile workers in *maquilas*), the stigma of being a sex worker is a major factor that impedes women to look for reparation or any other legal redress.

Other issues for the migrant exotic dancers include, for example, disillusionment when they arrive in Canada. Glamorization of the lifestyle waiting for them in Canada was a very important tool used by agents and recruiters. When the women arrived here, they were shocked by the conditions of the places where they were going to work. "When we arrived, we were paralyzed. We were hoping for something completely different. To start with, they told us that we were going to go to one of the most exclusive places in Toronto. Imagine, you think that you are going to go to a beautiful place, with all kinds of luxuries, and when you arrive it is a place with a bad reputation."

As it stands, the women enter the industry in a completely dependent relationship with the club and have to face the already deplorable labour conditions in the exotic dancing industry. I visited several clubs in downtown Toronto, and I verified the poor conditions of the changing rooms, washrooms, and stages. Changing rooms are the only spaces in the club where the dancers can relax and release the pressures of their job. When women arrive at the club, the first place they go is to the changing room to get ready. They undress and dress, put on makeup, and do their hair – all this in a place that is very poorly cleaned and frequently has inadequate furniture, poor lighting, and no ventilation. The physical demands of dancing are enormous, and sometimes women change their outfits twice or more. But the clubs usually do not have showers, towels, or anything that could provide some comfort to the women (see Graham 2001).

In summary, women's working conditions and emotional well-being depend on and dramatically change according to women's immigration status. When women have a temporary working visa and are working for the club that recruited them in Latin America, they are more likely to be subjected to physical, sexual, and psychological abuse as well as human and civil rights violations. Yet, when they have gained permanent status such as landed immigrant, the abuse by club owners, managers, or agents greatly decreases. The women are subjected to the abuse faced by many temporary workers in Canada as well as to stigmatization and isolation from the society at large. In spite of the difficult working and living conditions that the dancers face while living in Canada, all of them develop and maintain links and connections to their home countries; families and especially mothers and children play significant parts in their lives. The next section explores some of the transnational links that shape women's lives, their families, and their communities.

## Transnational Lives

There are many ways in which women maintain strong bonds with their families in their countries of origin. A crucial factor, and the most common one, is that of remittances. A predominant element of transnational theory is the study of capital flows. Grewal and Kaplan emphasize the economic component of transnational accumulation and challenge the conventional boundaries of national economies (1994, 9-10). This understanding of transnational capital flows provides a context for phenomena such as remittances where, for example, the well-being of many families located in Latin America depends on the money sent on a regular basis by Latinos, and more often by Latina women, situated in the north.

Most of the women interviewed mentioned that they send money on a regular basis to help with the daily expenses of the household, to educate younger relatives, to support their children, and to make small investments. When one woman was asked if she sent money, she answered, "Yes, every month. My mother lives in my home, and I send money even to my sisters because the situation in Colombia is very bad. I wish I could bring them up with me."

Another fundamental goal for most of the women is to be able to provide their families, in their home countries and in Canada, with a house: a place where their families, particularly their mothers, can live comfortably. At least four women talked about being able to build their homes in their home countries. For them, this achievement is impressive taking into account that they all are, or were, single mothers. In the words of one woman, "I was not making millions of dollars, but I started sending and sending money to build my own house." One woman has also bought property in Toronto: "Me, for example, I have bought a house for my family, [and] I have furnished it. I also bought a condo here, and I just bought this house."

Apart from building a house, some women also feel responsible for the well-being of their families in their countries since they consider themselves to be better off economically: "All these years that I have worked, the money that I have has not been for me, it has been for my family. I have paid doctors; I paid for my brother's surgery, and I bought a house for them."

Another important aspect that the women mentioned is the possibility of reuniting the family. Thus, when the women gain permanent residency, they try to sponsor their children and parents; at least one woman was able to bring her mother to Canada, and almost all the women who had children in their country, except two, have been able to sponsor their children. For example, one woman came as an exotic dancer, later got married, and recently sponsored her spouse's child. Another woman was able to bring her child and her mother: "Currently, I live with my two children and my mother."

It is remarkable to notice that, in spite of the harsh working and living conditions described in the previous section, these women maintain a high degree of connection to their home countries. They "make home" here and there, and they belong to both here and there. In the transnational experience of these women, communities are made not only in the home countries but also where the women work and live in Canada.

When I met the women, talked to them, saw them inside and outside the clubs, they were not shy in expressing their desire to organize themselves to improve their working and living conditions, to gain control over immigration issues, and to demand their rights in this country. However, Latin American migrant exotic dancers have not been able to organize in any structured fashion either among themselves or across racial lines to demand basic rights. This failure, according to Laura Agustín, makes it impossible for migrant sex workers "to fit into classic migration frameworks, in which associations are formed as an essential step to 'settling down'" (2002, 112). Because of the women's condition as temporary and stigmatized workers, their support networks are very informal and flexible, and they have to change rapidly according to women's needs and situations.

For instance, some dancers become support networks for other dancers, particularly for those who have just arrived in the country. Usually, dancers who have been in the industry longer let the new dancers know that they can work without having to pay agents, that they are overpaying boarding and food, and that they can even change clubs if they want. They give each other vital information that can help them with regard to lawyers, social services, and labour rights. These women acknowledge the crucial role that other dancers play: "I learned from other dancers and clients that there were clubs that paid much better"; "now that I know the kind of help that there is for us, I tell the other women, I give them advice."

Some other efforts to address the issues and problems faced by migrant Latin American and Caribbean sex workers have been carried out by different organizations in a transnational manner using the Internet as a tool. For example, the Women's Rights Net in August 2003 set up a webpage called Trabajadoras Sexuales Migrantes,[5] providing different kinds of information and resources for migrant sex workers. Femmigration[6] is another web resource for migrant sex workers that makes available clear information about the immigration procedures and conditions for sex workers in the European Union. Other groups work in the field with migrant sex workers, for instance, Hetaira[7] in Spain, where the majority of women coming from Latin America and the Caribbean are concentrated.

## Transnational Organizing: Some Recommendations

During this research, a number of recommendations were formulated to improve the migrant exotic dancers' conditions. These recommendations came from the dancers, the key informants, and the discussions held with the advisory committee from LACEV. Here are some of the recommendations.

- *Provide information:* The women should be provided with clear and understandable information about the regulations in the exotic dancing industry, their rights, and immigration issues. For instance, kits with complete information in the women's languages should be handed out when the women are issued their working visas. These kits should include information on immigration issues, exotic dancing regulations, criminal law, and a list of places and telephone numbers where the women can find help.

• *Facilitate access to education:* Dancers with working permits should be allowed to attend English as a Second Language classes or other types of training that could prepare them in case they want to leave the job or want to immigrate as skilled workers under the immigration point system.

• *Improve labour conditions:* If the concern with lap-dancing is to prevent harm to the women, then the current regulatory devices are not effective. A more effective solution is to regulate the industry in order to improve working conditions for the dancers. Women should be able to perform their work in a hazard-free environment, one that is free of violence.

• *Reform immigration practices:* The immigration process needs to be reviewed and changed because, as it is now, it puts the women in a very vulnerable position. Exotic dancers should be allowed to immigrate to the country as permanent workers, ideally as independent workers.

If the above recommendations were to be implemented, the working and living conditions of the migrant Latin American exotic dancers could improve, and this improvement would have a positive impact on Canadian society at large; after all, these women are transnational subjects who are able to live and build realities in more than one nation-state, Canada being one of them. They are economically involved here and in their home countries, building or buying a house for their parents, educating their children, and starting businesses. At the same time, they struggle and on occasion are able to stay permanently in Canada, buy a home, work, learn English, and get married. They maintain fluid communication that connects their home countries and Canada. Overall, they are key players in a transnationalized world.

**Notes**

1 LACEV, today known as MUJER, is a local grassroots organization of and for Latin American women emphasizing their rights and freedoms. See http://www.mujer.ca/.

2 All the interviews were in Spanish and were audiotaped with the permission of the person being interviewed; then they were transcribed verbatim and translated into English.

3 For a complete reference about the jobs that require work permits, see sections R186 and R187 of the *Temporary Foreign Worker Guidelines (FW)* (Ottawa: CIC, 2005).

4 Formerly, this task was carried out by Human Resources Development Canada (HRDC). This office was split into two departments, Social Development Canada and Human Resources and Skills Development Canada. See http://www.hrdc-drhc.gc.ca.

5 See http://www.whrnet.org/docs/tema-trabsexmigrantes.html.

6 See http://www.femmigration.net.

7 See http://www.pensamientocritico.org/crigar0703.htm.

# 10

# Transnational Work and the Gendered Politics of Labour: A Study of Male and Female Mexican Migrant Farm Workers in Canada
*Ofelia Becerril*

It is impossible to understand the dynamics of labour and the transnational lives of migrant farm workers in Canada independently of two interconnected processes: the expansion and consolidation of the Canadian agricultural industry, and the emergence of social and political organizations that seek to defend migrant workers' rights. Workers in the Seasonal Agricultural Workers Program (SAWP)[1] should not be considered an insignificant part of the industry, for they already constituted 52 percent of total employment in the fruit and vegetable sectors in Canada in 2000 and 45 percent of total person hours (Weston and Scarpa de Masellis 2003, 6). In 2002, 58 percent of these migrant workers (out of a total of 18,535) were Mexicans working in Ontario (Verma 2003, 26). Initially, only men were employed, but, in the past fifteen years, women have also been hired under the program. They work each year between six weeks and eight months in vegetable, fruit, tobacco, and flower crops on farms and in greenhouses in southwestern Ontario.

Roger Rouse (1991) showed that, when social relations intensify between a locality of origin and a new settlement area, "transnational circuits" may emerge, which far from disappearing with time may become stronger and consolidated. I would argue that transnational circuits are emerging and that they include the Canadian rural communities where more than 10,000 Mexican migrant workers travel to work. These circuits are geographically dispersed, spanning many localities in Canada and Mexico.

For Linda Basch, Nina Glick Schiller, and Cristina Szanton Blanc (1994), transnational communities may develop as immigrants encounter the exclusionary dynamics of "nation building." These transnational communities may elude the domination of the nation-state by escaping from its territorial sovereignty and transcending important categories by which the state operates (Kearney 1995). Lata Mani (1992) proposed that the points of view of subordinates, taken in the aggregate, afford a privileged place for resistance to those who deny transnational communities their own voice and their alternative point of view. Transnational communities thus offer a unique point of view and represent a privileged site for contestation precisely because, far from being a single site or "point," they constitute trans-local and transnational social processes (Besserer 2002, 21).

In my research, I address the following questions. What are workers' conditions by gender in the SAWP? What are the responses of Mexican migrant workers to changes in transnational work arrangements associated with agricultural production in Canada? Is the cultural struggle of temporary workers a process of transnationalism from below? I propose that Mexican transmigrant workers who live their daily lives in two societies, Canada and Mexico, are engaged in an everyday struggle against extant and emerging forms of inequality. They are also contesting changes in the transnational work arrangements of the Canadian horticultural sector. From this perspective, I argue that these thousands of Mexican migrant workers are a form of transnational community that organizes, using their own voices and their working lives, to articulate collective actions in transnationally constituted acts of contestation.

Recent literature on this topic recognizes that "Mexican migrants have played an integral role in the Canadian economy, [but] in social and cultural terms most are not viewed as citizens of the communities which have grown to depend heavily on their contributions" (Basok 2003, 12). While this is an important point, two key issues have been overlooked in the literature. One is the situations and experiences of female Mexican farm workers in Canadian fields; the other involves the cultural struggle performed on a daily basis by Mexican workers on farms and in Canadian rural communities.

This chapter explores the conditions, experiences, and gendered contract labour policies of the Canadian-Mexican Seasonal Agricultural Workers Program. Based on fieldwork on Mexican migrant workers employed in Leamington, I make three central arguments. First, a conceptualization focused on the gendered composition of labour and gendered division of tasks among Mexican migrant workers is needed to analyze the transnational organization of work in Canada. Second, everyday Mexican migrant workers' practices against employers' exploitation and control are expressions of an emergent cultural struggle. This struggle, in turn, has given rise to an advocacy movement aimed at improving the workers' conditions. To understand the cultural struggle among workers, it is necessary to explore the meanings that the Mexican migrant workers attach to their transnational experience while living and working in Canadian farms and communities. Third, the structural changes in the industry and flexible labour arrangements on the one hand, and the responses to them by workers and other social actors on the other, need to be studied and theorized together rather than independently.

## Methodology and Conceptual Approach

For the purposes of this discussion, the term *cultural struggle* is defined as the practices, experiences, and discourses shaped, contested, and defended in different domains of power relations, individually or collectively, by both male and female Mexican migrant workers in order to resist exploitation, control, exclusion, and racism as exerted in Canadian farms and communities. This cultural struggle arises as a response to Canadian capitalist transformation in horticulture, which increasingly relies on temporary workers. In spite of the fact that this cultural struggle may not necessarily effect change at a structural level, the transformations that the workers undergo in everyday attitudes, norms, "structures of feeling" (Williams 1972), and "practical knowledge" (Besserer 2002) constitute a broader phenomenon linked to transformation in civil society. I owe this use of the concept of cultural struggle to Aihwa Ong (1991), who uses it to replace the notion of class struggle. Ong argues that "workers' struggles and resistances are often not based upon class interests or class solidarity, but comprise individual and even covert acts against various forms of control. The interest defended, or the solidarity built, through such acts is more often linked to kinship and gender than to class" (280-81).

In his historical study of the English working class, Edward Thompson (1962) argued that class is a cultural formation. Similarly, Ong (1991, 304) proposed conceptualizing workers' experiences as cultural struggles against new and varied modes of control. According to Ong, by insisting on a single measure of class agency, we risk diluting the political significance of cultural resistance in encounters with capitalism. Ong's approach is helpful in understanding as cultural struggle the social processes that take place in the intersections between Mexican transnational communities and Mexican workers in transnationalized Canadian agroindustrial regimes of control.

"Cultural struggle" can be understood as complementary to "class struggle" rather than as opposed to it. Thus, "class struggle" is important for identifying class position, working and living conditions, and class conflict between social actors, while cultural struggle focuses attention on the cultural resistance and contestation of social agents, rooted in class positions, against previous and emerging forms of inequality associated with the prevailing and hegemonic cultural logic.

A theoretical perspective attentive to the cultural struggles associated with class transformation used alongside a conceptual framework sensitive to the emergence of transnational forms of organization (Rouse 1992, 27) is fundamental in analyzing Mexican migrant workers in Canada because it lets us restore a cultural dimension to the study of their work and lives. It is equally important to approach transnationalism from a perspective attentive to the interplay of culture, class, and power (Rouse 1992, 27). From this perspective, cultural struggles are not fixed inside communities or geographies; they emerge from social processes where "what community is" and "what space means" are part of the cultural struggle itself (Besserer 2002, 25). In this way, culture is understood as an arena where temporary workers contest meanings of work, wildcat strikes, living, sexuality, the body, feelings, inequality, and their experiences in Canadian farms and communities. The cultural struggle is simultaneously generated inside productive and reproductive fields because migrant workers work and live in the same place: on the property of the Canadian employer. This chapter documents the everyday silent struggles that take place in one form of Mexican transnational community, one constructed through cultural contestation.

My study draws on several research techniques. In Ontario, I conducted in-depth interviews with fifty-five Mexican workers who worked in Leamington's farms and greenhouses during the 2003 season. In Mexico, between February and April 2003, I interviewed twenty-eight Mexican workers who already had contracts to work at various Ontario farms at the offices of the Ministry of Labour (Secretaría del Trabajo y Previsión Social [STyPS]). Of the total of eighty-three interviews, 46 percent were conducted with women. Semistructured interviews were also conducted with Mexican workers who, having participated in the program, subsequently stayed on in Leamington with their families. Questionnaires with open-ended questions were used for interviews with a sample of Leamington's producers and with officials at the Mexican Consulate in Toronto, STyPS, and Foreign Agricultural Resource Management Services (FARMS), as well as with people from the organizations that provide services to the migrant workers (Migrant Workers Support Centre, Cultural Program for the Migrant Worker, Enlace, and Justicia for Migrant Workers). I also interviewed key informants in Leamington.

Both participant and ethnographic observation were of great value, as this allowed me to record the workers' lives and work at the farms. I was able to follow their experiences in many contexts: their housing, their eating areas, transportation to Leamington's downtown, the supermarkets and shops, the banks, the agencies to send money to Mexico, the offices to pay Canadian taxes, the locations from which they call their families, the fields where they play soccer, the organizations they attend for English classes, the church where they hear Mass, and the streets they bike and walk.

Fieldwork in Leamington was conducted between May and July 2003. I chose to conduct a case study of Leamington's horticultural industry because Leamington is the region with the largest concentration of Mexican workers. In 2002, it had 39 percent of a total of 7,553 workers in Ontario (FARMS 2002; STyPS 2002). It is also where 33 percent of the 2,109 Essex County farms are located (Municipality of Leamington 2002a, 2002b). Using a combination of both quantitative and qualitative methods allowed me to identify the sites and crops where men and women are employed and to explore the social practices and the representations constructed by the workers about their working experiences. Given that the present study is exploratory and that the sample was not designed to be representative, my results should be considered provisional and as pointing to issues that can be taken up in future research.

## Leamington's Niche in Transnational Production and Labour Arrangements

Leamington, known as "Canada's tomato capital," is a rural community in Essex County, located forty-five kilometres southeast of Windsor, Ontario. It is a region with favourable agroclimatic conditions for the horticultural industry, "but it is the tomato production that occupied a central place in the Leamington economy in the 20th century" (Basok 2003, 6).

As a result of the constant growth of the horticultural industry and its concentration in southeastern Ontario, Leamington has undergone transformations that have led it to occupy an important niche in the transnational agricultural labour market, absorbing mainly male and female Mexican migrant workers. Mexican workers are now being employed not only in small family farms but overwhelmingly in greenhouse growers' corporations. In 2001, Leamington's greenhouse vegetable industry already covered a concentrated area of 987 acres, making it the largest greenhouse vegetable production area in North America (Whitfield and Papadopoulos 2002). In 2002, almost 88 percent of the 3,000 SAWP workers in Leamington were Mexican. Based on the number of employees, the 212 farms in Leamington can be classified according to three groups: small-scale companies (62 percent), which employ from 1 to 10 Mexican workers; medium-sized companies (27 percent), with 11 to 50 workers; and big corporations (11 percent), which employ between 51 and 500 workers (FARMS 2002).

Table 10.1 shows that the production of greenhouse vegetables in Canada is concentrated among fifteen of Leamington's largest producers. In 2002, these producers employed approximately 43 percent of the Mexican SAWP workers in Leamington. The table illustrates a significant change in the organization of labour in this sector of the internationally competitive Canadian horticultural industry.

### Workers' Working Conditions by Gender

Immigrant labour is not neutral or uniform. Rather, it is stratified along racial, ethnic, and gender lines. Even though the participation of Mexican and Caribbean women is small (3 percent of 15,213 migrant workers in 2002), the past decade has seen an increase in the employment of women, specifically of Barbadian and Mexican women.

*Table 10.1*

**Greenhouse vegetable operations larger than ten acres, 1 September 2001**

| Name | Production | Mexican workers | Location | Acreage |
|---|---|---|---|---|
| Mastron Enterprises Ltd.* | Tomato | 507** | Leamington, ON | 53 |
| Great Northern Hydroponics* | Tomato, cucumber | 115 | Leamington, ON | 53 |
| DiCiocco's Farms* | Tomato, pepper | 74 | Leamington, ON | 49 |
| Houweling Nurseries Ltd. | NA*** | NA | Delta, BC | 48 |
| Amco Farms Inc.* | Tomato, pepper, cucumber, eggplant | 114 | Leamington, ON | 40 |
| Sabelli Farms* | Cucumber | 52 | Leamington, ON | 38 |
| Veg. Gro. Sales Inc.* | Pepper | 72 | Leamington, ON | 36 |
| Nature Fresh | Pepper | NA | Leamington, ON | 35 |
| Canagro | NA | NA | Delta, BC | 31 |
| Suntastic Hothouse | NA | NA | Exeter, ON | 30 |
| Mucci, Bros.* | Tomato, cucumber | 106 | Leamington, ON | 30 |
| Les Serres du St. Laurent Inc. | NA | NA | Portneuf, QC | 30 |
| Cervini's* | Tomato, cucumber | 95 | Leamington, ON | 25 |
| Delta Pacific | NA | NA | Delta, BC | 25 |
| St. Davids Hydroponics | NA | NA | St. Davids, ON | 24 |
| Gipaanda | NA | NA | Delta, BC | 24 |
| Double Diamond Acres Limited* | Tomato | NA | Leamington, ON | 24 |
| Howard Huy Greenhouses* | Cucumber, pepper | 18 | Leamington, ON | 24 |
| Hazelmere Greenhouses Ltd. | NA | NA | Surrey, BC | 21 |
| Hydro-Serre Mirabel | NA | NA | Mirabel, QC | 17 |
| MOS Enterprises* | Tomato | 26 | Leamington, ON | 13 |
| MOS Capital* | NA | 21 | Leamington, ON | 12 |
| Paul Dyck* | Pepper | 20 | Leamington, ON | 10 |
| Hillcrest Farms | NA | NA | Leamington, ON | 10 |
| **Total** | | **1,220** | | **702** |

  * Participates in the program and employs Mexican migrant workers.
 ** FARMS (2002); STyPS (2002).
*** Data not available (NA).
*Sources:* Municipality of Leamington (2002a); Whitfield and Papadopoulos (2002).

Female Mexican farm workers began participating in the Canadian agricultural labour market in 1989 with an initial group of thirty-seven women. By 2002, there were 339 female workers (STyPS 1998-2003). In 2002, fifty-seven female Barbadian farm workers were hired, a significant increase compared with the twenty-eight women employed nine years earlier (Downes and Odle-Worrell 2003). Gustavo Verduzco and María Isabel Lozano (2003, 14) explain that the growing interest in Mexican female workers shown by Canadian farmers is related to the workers' prior experience in packaging and selecting vegetables and fruits in Mexico. As a result, Canadian employers can avoid the expense of training them, and they require little supervision. As one producer commented, "Mexican workers work tirelessly and do not require any kind of supervision. They know what they are doing."

In most cases, Canadian farms demand skilled female labour for the production of specific vegetables and fruits. Some examples are Mexican female workers from Irapuato, Guanajuato, with experience in strawberry production.[2] Employers take advantage of the skills that Mexican female workers from Irapuato have developed over the years in strawberry fields. However, these employers do not recognize the workers' skills with higher wages, nor do they acknowledge that, in the absence of skilled workers, they would have to devote resources to training. From the point of view of the program, the common geographical origin of these female workers also constitutes an advantage. Sometimes these workers are asked to refer more women from their communities of origin to work in the strawberry fields.

The demand for Mexican labour and the organization of the labour process in Canadian farms and greenhouses are based on a strict gender, ethnic, and racial division of labour that also involves discrimination. While temporary Mexican male workers are employed to carry out the most dangerous, hardest, and dirtiest tasks on the farms, such as harvesting crops, most local workers (who are not in the SAWP) are employed in supervisory, management, and administrative positions. In some farms, some Canadian agricultural workers do the same work that Mexican migrants do but at a higher rate of pay. Furthermore, in their own accounts, Mexican migrants frame as voluntary the fact that they accept an extension of work hours to twelve or more per day. However, employers use this willingness as an indicator in evaluating their productivity and in deciding whether to hire them for the next season. In some greenhouses, one sees Mexican women working in harvest tasks while resident Mennonites work in packaging.

The division of labour appears to be gender-based with respect to geographical destination, crops, duties, opportunities, and employment durations. However, this gender division of labour and the low rates of female participation in the program constitute a form of workplace discrimination as greater opportunities are available for male workers compared with female counterparts.

In Canada, only a few farms employ female Mexican migrant workers (3 percent of a total of 11,000 Mexican workers in 2004). Between 2001 and 2003, thirty-five farms employed female Mexican migrants; this represented only 2 percent "of a total of 1,800 employers in all Ontario and Quebec, through the SAWP" (Weston and Scarpa de Masellis 2003, 4). Mexican women are geographically concentrated, with 60 percent working in Niagara-on-the-Lake and Leamington.

Most male and female Mexican workers are concentrated in Ontario's and Quebec's agricultural labour market (95 percent). Alberta and Saskatchewan have recently included women in the labour process. Female labour is used mainly in Ontario's and Quebec's fruit and vegetable industries, whereas male labour is also employed in tobacco fields, cutting down Christmas trees, and beekeeping in other provinces. In some of the largest greenhouses in Leamington, female workers work in their homes during the weekends on the packaging, but male workers are exempted from this arrangement. Furthermore, the majority of the eight-month contracts are assigned to male workers.

With the new system of flexible labour and stratification along the lines of race, ethnicity, and gender, workers from Mexico and the Caribbean are pitted against each other in new ways. Mexican migrant workers and Caribbean migrant workers compete for temporary work. Depending on the season, Mexican and Caribbean women are hired for specific tasks, reducing the range of activities for which each is hired. Similarly, male and female workers from both source regions compete against each other for work. The number of female workers from each source region may be increased or decreased, and female workers are substituted with Mexican or Caribbean male workers for a season or more. A detailed gendered analysis would allow us to understand the impact of the organization of male and female transnational labour on the productive process, work relations, and flexible labour regimes.

## Cultural Struggles for Social Inclusion

Paralleling the development of new systems of flexible labour in Canadian agriculture, processes of contestation and defence have arisen among Mexican migrant workers. These processes, which I describe as cultural struggles, seek to counter both the economic exploitation and control exerted by employers and the political and economic conditions imposed by the program. Ong (1991, 295-96) uses the concept of cultural struggle in her analyses of flexible labour regimes in Asia and Mexico. I use it here to explore the work experiences of Mexican migrant workers in Canada. Without denying the importance of class struggle, but using a Marxist approach to class that includes attention to consciousness, interests, and solidarity or class alliances, I argue that it is in the cultural realm that Mexican migrant workers contest meanings, values, and goals associated with their employment, gender, and ethnic experiences in the complex transnational reality of their work in Canada.

The cultural struggle of Mexican male and female workers on Canadian soil manifests in the form of workers' daily social practices on farms and in greenhouses, as well as in rural communities in Canada, especially those sites that are part of emergent transnational circuits that receive numerous workers, such as Leamington, Simcoe, Niagara-on-the-Lake, and Bradford, all in Ontario. These male and female workers are transmigrant social actors who are not only a "structural necessity for Canadian fruit, vegetable and tobacco growers" (Basok 2002, 139) but also have re-created social, economic, and cultural lives for over thirty years on the farms and in the communities.

Although economic and political conditions force Mexican migrant workers to accept exploitation and abuse in Canadian fields and communities, workers author practices of resistance. As active and thinking subjects, they employ a variety of work-related strategies to meet their economic needs.

The analysis of Mexican migrant workers' experience is fundamental in understanding how cultural systems are formed, contested, and defended by the workers. Male and female Mexican workers take a risk by coming to Canada with hopes of better lives for themselves and their families. A common statement is "we are here out of need." Some female workers declared, "we are here because of the men, who didn't take responsibility for their own children." Most of the women are single mothers or leave their children with their grandmothers, a sister, or a daughter. In contrast, married male workers leave their children with their wives.

If both male and female workers are subjected to severe exploitation and discrimination, it is also true that they enact expressions of contestation of such working conditions. A female worker with thirteen years of work experience in Canada provides an illustration of how Mexican workers engaged in verbal and nonverbal acts of resistance, refusing to remain with the same employer and using their own voices to directly defend their human dignity as workers and as women:

> I tolerated it out of need. But last year my *patrón* [boss] crossed the line; he yelled at me a lot, I burned my feet, because we bottle at 200 degrees. A scalding tomato fell, I cut my hands ... I said, "this is it, I don't want to be with this *patrón* anymore." One thing is to accept a job that they have given you, and a very different one is their crossing the line. They say one must obey, that one is obliged to let them humiliate you, awful things, which we endure out of need for a job, but this is too much.

The male workers give voice to their own experiences of resistance and their tactics to oppose work conditions. A Mexican worker with six seasons of experience said,

> We were out in the field when it began to rain ... We asked the supervisor
> for raincoats to be able to go on with our duties. Because he turned a deaf
> ear to our request, I told my fellow workers that we needed to stop working
> until the raincoats had been brought ... I stopped working and walked back
> to my place [housing] ... The supervisor ran after me and told me, "I am
> going to bring the raincoats, but you need to go back and continue work-
> ing." I waited until the raincoats were there, and only then did I resume
> working. We shouldn't have to work under those conditions.

Other forms of cultural resistance and contestation by migrant workers and
others can be seen in struggles over the construction of personal identity.
The new cultural hegemonic logic in Canada arises from a cultural politics
of social differentiation between foreign temporary migrants and the Canadian resident community. While residents and citizens are members of the
Canadian nation-state, Mexican migrant workers are denied a place of belonging in Canadian society. A stigmatized identity is given to them in a
society where they are wanted as part of the workforce but not as people. A
poem declaimed by a male worker in the context of a football game (between workers from farms in Simcoe, Georgetown, Milton, and Niagara-on-
the-Lake) expressed the way that migrants build a subaltern identity of
"double consciousness," seeing themselves as migrant agricultural workers
of two nations:

> Those who, day in and day out, manage a strained conversation with the
> strawberries, while they work. Those who, without planning to and with-
> out regrets, harvest the fruits of that land, they are the Ghesquierers [from
> Herry Ghesquiere Farms], from that large farm in Simcoe, which without
> planning has grown day by day, thanks to the labour of these Mexican
> migrants, who with their sweat and effort, have worked each day to be
> among the best ... like each and every one of us, like each and every one of
> them, who try to forge a dream by coming to Canada.[3]

This poem suggests that Canadian farms can be seen as sites in transnational
spaces, where Mexican migrant workers reinterpret their work experiences
and their identities and respond with several strategies of resistance.

### Individual Practices and Discourses

The cultural struggle materializes in individual practices and in discourses
formed, contested, and defended by Mexican migrant workers. Despite the
situation of isolation to which they are confined in Canadian farms and
communities, most of these workers have taken advantage of their job mobility as a strategy to switch employers and improve their working conditions. They denounce workplace conditions and strategize about employment

tactics, as illustrated by the narrative of a male worker – someone who spent six seasons in Canada:

> In the farm where I am working, the supervisor, who is Canadian, treats us abusively, he yells at us and has really bad manners. I tell him, "do not raise your voice, I am doing a good job here." Others may not say a thing, but I will not shut up. No more shouting, no more abuse ... This time I only need to finish the season. But next time I will look for a different farm. We always have the chance to switch employers and farms, but you just need to wait for the season to be over.

For some Mexican workers, breaking the work contract is another form of cultural resistance against the control exerted by the program and specific employers. A worker explained his reasons for not finishing his contract: "I went back to Mexico, because in Mexico someone needed me, my family comes before my work in Canada, I already fulfilled six months, [so] I broke the contract." The interests defended are more often linked with the commitment of the workers to their families than with their class interests.

Many try to remain as named[4] workers at a single farm, while others would rather change farms, crops, and communities in their attempt to extend their working stay in Canada. This is a strategy, however, that only experienced workers can implement given that they know which farms, crops, and communities need their labour. In this regard, a male worker stated that

> a worker's reference letter is his own work. If you know how to do a good job, you will be hired in almost any farm. I have been working in Canada for fifteen years. I began working for an employer in Niagara-on-the-Lake in March. I finished my contract there, and then I spoke on the phone with another farmer from Simcoe ... We always have the opportunity to seek a transfer when our contract expires. We can either call the consulate or use our own contacts. Because I have learned to work in tomato, peach, flowers, apple, grape, and tobacco fields, I can be employed in any farm ... I have already spoken over the phone with a former employer from Leamington. I sent him a fax, and he answered that I should go with him once I'm done with my job in Simcoe. The only thing we need to do is learn English. With just a little, you can already look for work. It's so as to avoid being unemployed.

Even if female workers are more isolated than their male counterparts, and their job mobility is more restricted because of the fewer employment opportunities, some of them can extend their contract through a transfer.

The cultural struggle is gendered because both strategies and meanings are different for female and male workers. I found that the practices and discourses of female Mexican workers tended to focus on their families and children. One woman's account illustrates the implications of leaving her children with relatives in Mexico: "I don't want to stay this long. I will ask for a five-month contract instead of eight. I spend too much time here, in Canada. I have spent already three seasons in this farm. I want to leave because this farm has given me no profit. It is the first time that it happens that I see no improvement. They don't give us enough hours of work. I'd better look somewhere else, under the same program, but on a different farm. I think of my children. I spend too much time away from them."

Mexican workers develop their cultural struggle in everyday attitudes, norms, "structures of feeling" (Williams 1972), and "practical knowledge" (Besserer 2002). The narrative of a male Mexican worker illustrates clearly how in his daily life a new alternative order of feeling is constructed when he experiences disagreement, loneliness, sadness, anxiety, and depression and feels the need for spiritual encounters with himself to reach some inner peace:

> We belong to the same country, but here we are unknown to each other ... We are free, we come from a free country, and everyone does what is okay for each one because we are not tied to anyone. Not even the employer can tell us, "I don't want you to go there." We make our own decisions about working hours ... I need to be spiritually good; if I am not, the storm can destroy me. You need to have some inner peace; if you cannot have it, you can die of loneliness and sadness. It is a spiritual meditation ... When it happens to me, I try to have an inner spiritual encounter with myself that day. There are no constraints on me (on the job); I try to make this spirituality, it seems to be part of me, that inner spiritual meeting seems to have been part of me all my life.

## Collective Practices and Discourses: Strikes and Sexuality

In Ontario, agricultural workers and SAWP migrant workers continue to be denied the right to unionize and collectively bargain despite the *Dunmore* decision (Verma 2003, 173; see http://www.canlii.org/ca/cas/scc/2001/2001scc94.html for the decision), and temporary workers are legally prohibited from organizing wildcat strikes. Nevertheless, Mexican migrant workers in Leamington did go on strike twice, in 2001 and 2003. The strikes took place in two of the largest greenhouse corporations.

Before the 2001 strike, Mexican workers expressed their demands through Spanish-speaking people attached to Leamington's St. Michael's church. The most common problems of which they complained were the lack of a translator when visiting the doctor, the unsatisfactory bank services used to send their remittances to their families, the lack of maintenance of their housing, and abuse by the employers. Degrading treatment by the supervisor and excessive charges for the meals received at one of the companies were the basis for the workers' protests and strike. Although the work stoppage lasted for only a day, and almost half of the workers were immediately repatriated to Mexico, it was this event that prompted the rise of today's social and community organizations.

Evelyn Encalada, an activist with the Global Justice Care Van Project in the organization's early days, describes the first strike experience: "In April 2001, Mexican migrant farm workers organized a wildcat strike in one of the largest greenhouses in Leamington ... Indeed, fear acts as the main deterrent in taking action against substandard living and working conditions. The threat of deportation and being expelled from working in Canada is too much of a risk for many. This labour stoppage confirmed these fears, as 21 workers were identified as ringleaders and promptly repatriated to Mexico" (2003, 17). One of the first outcomes of the organizing was the opening of the Migrant Workers' Support Centre only a few months after the strike. As Tanya Basok puts it, "in April 2001, the United Farm Workers of America-Canadian Office was contacted with regard to the case of some twenty migrant farm workers from Leamington facing repatriation to Mexico. This action was precipitated by a walk-out of some 50 Mexican migrants protesting against their working conditions" (2003, 15). After this, other organizations emerged, such as Enlace and Justicia. The workers who had been involved in the strike were punished by not being granted work in Canada the following year. The 2001 strike had a tremendous impact on both male and female workers. The experience of social struggle is already part of their collective memory and is a useful tool to raise consciousness among the new generations.

In April 2003, Mexican workers employed by another large greenhouse corporation walked off the job to protest against a new, computerized system of piecework payment[5] that would substitute their hourly wages. The result of the strike was the early repatriation to Mexico of thirty out of a total of sixty workers. The excuse was that there wasn't any more work to be done, but Jamaican workers were hired in their stead. Unlike the first strike, this time the Mexican migrant workers managed to return in June to finish their contracts on a different farm. A male worker with four years of experience who took part in the event told me,

there was discontent because with the piecework system you don't see the money unless you deliver. When we are with the trucks, we lose time ... fifteen to twenty seconds at a time, one hour and a quarter a week. We were asking for monetary recognition of this time. All the workers agreed to walk out of the job. It lasted only a day. That same day the manager told us to go back to work the next day and that we would get paid for the time we demanded. They began paying for half an hour, but by the time consulate officials arrived they stopped the payments. They fired thirty workers. We opposed the consulate officials. We told them, "if one goes, we all go," but they tricked us. When we went for lunch, they asked a few of us to stay because they wanted to have a word with us and dismissed the rest. They told us, "the *patrón* is not happy with what was done and already has asked for a crew of Jamaicans." The rest were told a different story, that some left because the farmer did not want Mexican workers anymore and that the rest would leave later because there were no airplane tickets. It was a great blow that they dealt us.

Mexican migrant workers organized a wildcat strike in Leamington to protest their working and living conditions. The strike was about economic issues, but it also involved contestation about cultural meanings played out in specific political contexts. Thus, the struggle for human dignity and the recovery of identity as whole human beings take place in the form of cultural struggles.

Canadian farmers and the Canadian and Mexican governments have established several disciplinary techniques that regulate and punish the sexual and social behaviours of Mexican migrants. They punish more women than men: if women get pregnant or have affairs with their employers, they are laid off from the program. The Mexican workers' response has been to develop new forms of sexuality by crossing boundaries of race, class, and nationality. The struggle to freely exercise sexuality simultaneously generates a contest for the recovery of identity as a whole human being. Thus, "what sexuality is and what sexuality means" are part of the same cultural struggle. The notion of "sexuality" is contested. To make love with someone within the grower's property, to dance in nightclubs, to have affairs with Mennonite women, with the employer, or with Canadian residents, these all become examples of contestation by Mexican migrants in the context of Canadian culture and in the political framework of the SAWP.

The multiple responses produced by Mexican transmigrant workers outline a process of self-affirmation as human beings in Canadian communities and as social beings with transnational relations deployed in transnational social fields. These responses are a reaction to the dominant society, which makes them feel that they are worthless, that they do not have rights, and that the only thing important is their work, not their person.

## Negotiating the Future

I have argued that a conceptualization focused on the gender of temporary agricultural workers is needed for analyzing the transnational organization of work in Canada. I have also argued that Mexican men and women attempt to counter employers' exploitation and control through everyday practices and discourses, which defend their dignity and personhood. These efforts need to be understood as an integral part of civil society's defence of migrant workers' labour and human rights.

For Mexican and Caribbean workers, organizing remains a great challenge due to their fear of losing their jobs. Their awareness of unemployment and poverty back home is crucial in this process. A man who had worked for twenty seasons in Canada reflected, "it is really hard to do something [make a difference]. If we protest, even if all 3,000 workers stationed in Leamington did, we'd get sent back to Mexico. They can do that because there are another 3,000 Mexican workers ready to come to Canada to work."

The persistence of temporary migration and work in Canada reflects both the serious problems of unemployment and the high levels of poverty in Mexico. If the presence of temporary Mexican workers in Canada becomes more than a short-lived phenomenon, and both the Mexican and the Canadian governments hold up the SAWP as a model of "best practices" to be followed in other Canadian industries and other countries, the program must be analyzed carefully and reformed so as to improve the terms of employment.

## Acknowledgments

This research project was made possible by the financial support granted by Mexico's National Science and Technology Council (CONACyT) and the Autonomous Metropolitan University. I am also grateful to the Mexican seasonal workers for both their trust and the time devoted to answering my questions. I would also like to thank the Ministry of Labour (Secretaría del Trabajo y Previsión Social) and the Mexican Consulate in Toronto for the information provided. I am grateful to York University, especially to Luin Goldring, Judy Hellman, Deborah Barndt, and Viviana Patroni from the Centre for Research on Latin America and the Caribbean (CERLAC) for their generous support. Marshall Beck's sustained assistance throughout my work has been invaluable. The University of Windsor's academic assistance was vital for the development of my research, particularly on the part of Tanya Basok. I am also grateful to Kerry Preibisch of the University of Guelph for her comments and suggestions. I particularly wish to acknowledge the hospitality of the Migrant Workers Support Centre during my stay in Leamington. I am extremely grateful to Artemisa Bahena for her invaluable research assistance. Finally, I would like to acknowledge Luin Goldring and Sailaja Krishnamurti for inviting me to contribute to this publication.

This chapter is part of a broader research project for my doctoral degree in anthropology. Much of the research was conducted between September 2002 and August 2003 while I was a visiting scholar at York University and the University of Windsor.

## Notes

1 Mexico, Barbados, Jamaica, Trinidad and Tobago, and the Organization of Eastern Caribbean States are part of the Canadian government's SAWP.

2 In 2000, twenty Mexican women were employed by a Quebec strawberry producer. A year later, the same company hired forty-three Mexican women. This demand for strawberry-specialized Mexican women also emerged in 2001 in Prince Edward Island, where twenty-five women were hired by a single farm (STyPS 2000).

3 Translated by Luin Goldring, from the following original: "Ellos, quienes de sol a sol en las mañanas platican a duras penas con las fresas. Ellos que sin querer y sin lamentarse nada cosechan con tanto afán el fruto de aquélla tierra, son Ghesquieres [from Herry Ghesquiere Farms], aquella gran farma que se ha establecido en Simcoe y que sin querer progresa día a

día, gracias a la mano de estos compañeros campesinos mexicanos migratorios, que con su sudor y esfuerzo, se esfuerzan por ser cada día uno de los mejores ... como todos y cada uno de nosotros, como todos y cada uno de aquéllos que se esfuerzan por forjar un sueño y venirse al Canadá." (Alberto Mejía, Mexican worker interviewed by the author, published in *El Surco* 5 [2004].)

4  The Agreement for the Employment in Canada of Seasonal Agricultural Workers from Mexico states that, effective the eighth working day, such a worker shall be a "named worker." In reality, the named worker is the one designated by the employer as a worker for the following season.

5  The computerized, barcoded system monitors how long a worker takes to perform a given task on the tomato production line. Three tasks are paid by piecework: cutting leaves, stapling, and putting on "elbows."

# 11
# Development and Diasporic Capital: Nonresident Indians and the State
*Pablo S. Bose*

This chapter seeks to explore the increasingly complex transnational relationships between immigrant, expatriate, or diasporic communities and
development in their ancestral "homelands." In recent years, such links have
become an increasing focal point of academic inquiry (Levitt 1998b;
Itzigsohn and Saucedo 2002; Nyberg-Sorensen, Van Hear, and Engberg-
Pedersen 2002; Østergaard-Nielsen 2003). Numerous national and regional
governments as well as development agencies and international monetary
institutions have similarly identified diasporas as integral components in
future developmental visions (Van Doorn 2002; Rauch 2003; Vertovec 2003).
Much of the research and discussion on development and diasporas has
focused on remittances, money sent by an individual or family living in a
(relatively) prosperous country to relatives in their country of origin. Recent figures show the global trend of remittance transfers to be both substantial and on the increase. By the end of 2001, remittances to developing
countries alone stood at between \$72.3 and \$99.5 billion US[1] (World Bank
2003a, 157). Stereotypical situations might describe migrant workers from
Latin America and the Caribbean, domestic workers from the Philippines,
or skilled craftspeople and professionals from India who work in the Persian Gulf, the United States, or Western Europe and send portions of their
incomes "back home" to help their families with specific needs: food, clothing, building a bigger (and better) house, financing a local water or electri-
fication project, donating funds toward a community hospital or school,
and so on.

Yet there are as many divisions within diasporic groups and variations in
the forms of diasporic developmental assistance as there are between sending
and receiving countries, distinctions in their identity, nature, and character,
differences based on class, gender, ethnicity, and culture that affect a given
diasporic community's relationship to development in its putative homeland. This chapter, therefore, examines several key and emerging questions
regarding diasporas and development. For example, at a time of intensified

attempts by hometown associations and national governments to court émigrés to help build neighbourhoods and nations, how do diasporic communities engage in activities that aid development? Equally important, what *types* of development do diasporic funds and influences help to enable? Moreover, while the desire to help families, friends, and communities "back home" is often an admirable one, can there be costs – social, political, ecological – associated with such assistance? In particular, what of development activities and projects that have significant population displacement effects? How, then, might diasporic communities become enmeshed in a paradoxical dilemma, one in which their own connection to "home" and desire to improve it result in turn in the disruption of another local community's equally strong link to "place"?

This chapter considers these questions in four parts. The first section places diasporas within the context of their "transnational practice" (Portes, Guarnizo, and Landolt 1999), focusing in particular on the participation of diasporic communities in development processes within "home countries." The second section focuses on the relationship between economic development and population displacement in order to examine the possible effects of diasporic involvement in development financing. The third section turns to the recent history of diasporic development in India – a country that is, along with Mexico, one of the two highest remittance-receiving regions in the world – where both the federal and the regional governments are making a concerted effort to capture the wealth of its diaspora. The fourth section explores the diaspora-development-displacement nexus by presenting some early findings of an ongoing study of new housing projects in peri-urban Kolkata, West Bengal, and the possible economic and cultural influence of Bengali-Canadian communities on such developments. The case raises several questions related to the themes discussed in the chapter as a whole. What are some of the complexities of diasporic involvement in development processes? Can the developments in India currently funded or facilitated by diasporas be perceived as sustainable? Or are they activities that are fundamentally displacing, whether socially, ecologically, or economically?

## Diasporas, Transnational Practices, and the (Re)Development of "Home"

Diasporic communities have existed for centuries and in many ways complicate modern notions of geographical and political boundaries. They are multifaceted social organizations, interwoven in the contemporary context with legacies of colonialism and emerging trends toward cultural, economic, political, and social globalization. Diasporas take many forms beyond the traditional notion of persecuted victims forced to flee their homelands. They take many names besides diasporas – transmigrants, émigrés, immigrants, and expatriates among them. Generations of communities have flourished away from their "homelands," retaining strong economic and political ties to their places of origin and often distinct cultural identities. Scholars have documented many examples, including trade, labour, imperial, and post-colonial diasporas (Cohen 1997; Van Hear 1998; Braziel and Mannur 2003; Castles and Miller 2003). There is a long history of different émigré groups not simply assimilating and disappearing into a melting pot of their new host countries but rather participating in efforts to materially and ideologically restructure their putative homelands. Some scholars have defined this dynamic as an essentially transnational one, a "process by which trans-migrants, through their daily activities, forge and sustain multi-stranded social, economic, and political relations that link together their societies of origin and settlement, and through which they create transnational social fields that cross national borders" (Basch, Glick Schiller, and Szanton Blanc 1994, 6). This participation has taken many forms, including the provision of goods and services and in-kind labour to their former communities, moral support for ideological projects, and material economic assistance in the form of remittances and direct investments.

The importance of remittances in particular for the world economy has become increasingly apparent in recent years. A growing body of literature has noted the growth of remittances in both nominal terms and as relative to the receiving countries' gross domestic products (Batzlen 2000; Gammel-toft 2002; Garza and Lowell 2002). The World Bank's *Global Development Finance 2003* report estimates that workers' remittances in 2001 accounted for nearly US $73 billion in capital flows to the developing world, second only to foreign direct investment as a source of external funding and far outstripping traditional development aid (Ratha 2003, 157). And unlike foreign aid, remittances are not "tied" to the self-interests of donor nations or the loan conditions of multinational institutions such as the IMF.

For many countries – and indeed for some entire regions – remittances have become an integral part of economic survival. As mentioned previously, the past five years have seen India and Mexico ranked alternately first and second as the countries receiving the largest shares of remittances globally. As well, Latin America and the Caribbean received over US $25 billion in remittances in 2002, while South Asia received over US $16 billion (IMF 2003). Guillermo Perry, the World Bank chief economist for Latin America and the Caribbean, states that "foreign direct investment and re-mittances are key for Latin America and the Caribbean as it remains more sensitive than other regions to external shocks due to vulnerabilities to capital flow reversals. At a time when debt flows are falling, remittances represent one of the most stable sources of income for the region" (World Bank 2003c). The flows of remittance funds from the United States to Mexico as well as the rest of Latin America and the Caribbean have grown to the extent that the US federal government has commissioned several inquiries into the phenomenon. In 2002, the Committee on Banking, Housing, and Urban Affairs of the Senate noted that Hispanic families in the United States sent an average of US $200 seven times a year to relatives in Latin America and the Caribbean.

Not everyone sees remittances and diasporic capital as an unalloyed boon, however. Susan Pozo and Catalina Amuedo-Dorantes (2002), for example, suggest that workers' remittances in fact have a negative impact on receiving countries' economies in the form of a real exchange rate appreciation, artificially inflating the value of domestic currencies and decreasing productive capacities. Remittances in particular and diasporic capital in general are also notoriously difficult to calculate and capture. Recorded in the balance of payment current account as either "private transfer receipts" or "unrequited capital transfers," most remittance numbers fail to account for more informal money transfers, for foreign exchange that is brought in personally (much of which is recorded as the receipts of tourism), and for personal goods. Some critics estimate that roughly half of the actual amount sent by foreign workers and émigrés fails to be measured by contemporary national accounting statistics (Debabrata and Kapur 2003). Similarly, given that it is impossible to tell the origins of deposits in external currency accounts and that the diasporic nature of much "foreign" direct investment is unclear, these sources of diasporic capital are likewise prone to underestimation.

Dependence on remittances to provide a stable economic support, as Perry suggests, therefore seems to be fraught with risk. Far from insulating economies against "external shocks," there is mounting evidence that in some situations diasporic capital flows can indeed exacerbate crisis situations. And, as pointed out earlier, there are serious ethical issues concerning diasporic investments and remittances in terms of their differentials and sometimes deleterious effects on a receiving country's population. Moreover, remittances are not, of course, the only part of the story. As the final sections of this chapter demonstrate, an exploration of these dynamics demands a wider understanding of the phenomenon of the diaspora-development connection beyond remittances to include both diasporic capital and cultural flows, a reading that would include investment schemes, currency deposit accounts, and property and business ownership in addition to ideological, political, and social projects.

Yet, despite these potential problems, nation-states the world over are salivating at the prospect of capturing income from departed sons and daughters. Toward what use might such diasporic capital be put? The following section, which discusses the link between economic development and population displacement, looks at some of the potential harms that might be caused by development financing aided by diasporic communities.

## Development, Displacement, and the Dilemma of Diasporic Funding

To some, it might seem that there is no downside to diasporic funding for development initiatives. Whether born of altruism, obligations to self, family, nation, religion, ethnicity, or a multiplicity of other factors, diasporic funding for development seems to have a net positive effect. To understand that there can be negative consequences to what are in most cases the best of intentions, one must examine the link between development and displacement in a global and historical perspective.

"Development" – a contentious and much-debated concept – has long been associated with ideas of modernization and economic growth and naturalized within the political-economic space of the nation-state. A central tenet of most mainstream theories of development has held that a linear, historical process is necessary for all emerging nations to undergo to become fully "developed." In the process, old traditions and superstitions, as well as cultural, social, and even political patterns, needed to be discarded or at least disciplined (Inkeles and Smith 1974; Cooper and Packard 1997). Massive upheaval would take place, involving social and economic changes, such as commercialization, industrialization, urbanization, secularization, individualization, and globalization – all of which imply, at some level, the displacement, voluntary or otherwise, of the population.

Such changes and difficult transitions have indeed been the rule across the globe, especially over the past two centuries. While displacement due to political conflict dominates public perception, it is in fact forced migration due to development that was the prime culprit in population displacements of the twentieth century. The removal – for the purposes of modernization and industrialization – of particular groups of people from geographical regions to which they have cultural and historical ties has proceeded at an alarming rate. While conflict-related involuntary or forced migration has seen upward of 20 million people displaced worldwide by both cross-border and internal strife, critics estimate that as many as 100 million people across the globe have been dislocated as a result of processes of economic development – including specific projects (e.g., dams, highways, and parks), resource extraction (e.g., logging, mining, and fishing), and broader policies (e.g., land reform and privatization schemes) (Robinson et al. 2002). The urgency of this crisis cannot be overestimated, with some experts suggesting that an additional 10 million people a year are displaced by infrastructure projects alone (Cernea and McDowell 2000).

Although the process of development-induced displacement has accelerated in the post–Second World War era, it is neither a new phenomenon nor one confined to a specific geographical region of the world. Displacement due to development can be seen in many historical examples, from the enclosure of common lands in Europe to attempts by various colonial powers to restrict indigenous peoples' access to natural resources. And while contemporary issues of development-induced displacement tend to be identified with the "Third World," industrialized nations have their own lengthy and ongoing relationship with displacement. The profound and often devastating consequences of the development of industrially advanced nations on indigenous communities as well as racialized and marginalized groups continue to be both a pressing and an underrecognized issue that affects contemporary cultures and politics in the developed world. It is important to acknowledge that development and displacement are not simply a "Third World" issue of dams and modernization. They can also be seen and felt in communities across the "developed" world as processes of gentrification and economic globalization create increasing insecurity, dislocation, and alienation for many within our societies.

If the majority of development strategies intended to modernize and industrialize societies and better the lots of their populations have instead led to massive impoverishment and the creation of a substantial number of "internal refugees," then diasporic communities that contribute financially or otherwise to such strategies find themselves in an ethical dilemma. Diasporic populations feel intimately connected to "place," hence their continued involvement with development in their "home countries." Soon-to-be-displaced populations within those "home countries" feel no less attached to such places. Should one's attachment to place take precedence over that of the others? Are there ways of balancing these competing claims on space, place, and home? The following two sections explore these questions further by looking at specific examples from the case of development in contemporary India and the involvement of its many diasporic communities.

## Wooing Diasporic Capital: India's Twenty-First-Century Developmental Visions

> Traditionally investment in the bond market is done after looking at security, liquidity, safety and returns. We will add Emotional Property to tap funds from NRIs. We would appeal to their emotions and ask them to lend for development in the motherland. (*Economic Times of India*, 6 December 2000)

With these words, the Minister for Major Irrigation and Narmada in the Indian state of Gujarat announced in December 2000 a new strategy aimed at raising money for public expenditures, in particular the massive scheme to build interlocking dams in the Narmada Valley of northwestern India. The specific objective was to tap the lucrative NRI (Non-Resident Indian) market of wealthy expatriates and loyal émigrés for financial aid to fund the project. Three years later, in his opening speech to the first Indian diaspora conference, held in New Delhi in January 2003, then Prime Minister of India Atal Behari Vajpayee again made clear that the linkage between émigrés and development was both recognized by and a priority of the federal government of India (as it is for many others elsewhere): "I have always been conscious of the need for India to be sensitive to the hopes, aspirations, and concerns of its vast diaspora. We invite you not only to share our vision of India in the new millennium but also to help us shape its contours. We do not want only your investment. We also want your ideas. We do not want your riches, we want the richness of your experience. We can gain from the breadth of vision that your global exposure has given you." Although he emphasized that it was not only the wealth of the diaspora that was so attractive to the Indian state, Vajpayee's assurances that India had a positive investment climate and was firmly entrenched on a path toward modernization and equitable development implied a clear policy of wooing diasporic capital.

Vajpayee also indicated several rewards for the Indian diaspora's support for the Indian state over a decade of tumultuous economic and political upheavals. Two years earlier, the government of India had created an NRI and PIO (persons of Indian origins) division within its Ministry of External Affairs. The Indian central government also established a High-Level Commission on Indian Diaspora, whose policy recommendations as released in January 2003 proposed the extension of dual citizenship rights to NRI and PIO individuals (Lakhilal 2003).

The attention paid by the central government (as well as regional governments) to the Indian diaspora is unsurprising if one considers the size and significance of the diasporic population. At present, Indian émigrés are estimated to number between 25 and 40 million people worldwide (depending, as always, on how one defines inclusion in a particular diasporic community). And while it is true that many new immigrants from India in countries such as Canada struggle socially and economically to adjust to their new surroundings, it is becoming equally apparent that significant sections of the Indian diaspora across the globe are highly successful and indeed prosperous in their new homes (Motwani, Gosine, and Barot-Motwani 1993). In 2002, India outpaced Mexico as the country receiving the largest volume of remittances in the world, totalling over $16 billion (IMF 2003). The Gujarati diaspora alone, which makes up less than .01 percent of the population of the United States, is estimated to control over 5 percent of that country's wealth (High Level Committee on the Indian Diaspora 2002, 169-77).[2]

The attempt by the Indian state to attract diasporic capital is not a new phenomenon. Within decades of independence, the extensively planned Indian economy, combining a strategy of heavy and commodity-based industries, teetered on the verge of collapse. In the face of massive trade deficits, the Indian rupee had been devalued by 20 percent by 1967, with its value seemingly on an inexorable spiral downward. The Indian government sought to staunch the bleeding of its domestic economy by looking to the resources of successful Indian émigrés (Seshadri 1993). The decades since the end of the Second World War and India's independence had led to a steady stream of migration toward industrialized nations such as the United States, Britain, and Canada as well as workers who flocked to the oil-rich Persian Gulf. As well, older diasporic Indian communities – many the descendants of indentured labourers – had deep roots in East Africa, the West Indies, and Southeast Asia (Motwani, Gosine, and Barot-Motwani 1993).

And the money did flow, not only in the form of remittances but also in the form of foreign currency deposits. The state-controlled Reserve Bank of India initiated two programs in the late 1970s to attract funds in foreign currency from overseas Indian communities. The first was to create Foreign Currency Non-Resident Accounts, which insured the depositor against exchange rate fluctuations by providing a fixed rate. The second scheme was called the Non-Resident (External) Rupee Account, which offered a higher interest rate without the guarantee of a fixed exchange rate. By 1982, these initiatives were further refined to make it even more attractive for NRIs to deposit their money in Indian banks and to invest in real estate in India, including offering assured repatriation of funds and a further 2 percent interest on foreign currency deposits held in India (Nayyar 1994).

The success of this strategy to woo NRI money was considerable, although ultimately it was only a temporary solution. Throughout the 1980s, NRI money helped to balance India's trade deficits – but "leakages" in the trade account and elsewhere helped to substantially offset these gains. Indeed, as V. Krishnamurty (1994) argues, to a large extent the support provided by NRI funds merely put off the economic reforms that sooner or later needed to be undertaken by the Indian state. Krishnamurty also points out that diasporic capital has a complex and often contradictory effect on the receiving country's economy. Deposit flows, he suggests, come out of savings and wealth, while remittances come out of income. There are two different trajectories and class implications for these types of diasporic assistance – and possibly two different outcomes. Krishnamurty goes so far as to suggest that "remittances bring down the measured deficit while deposits help to finance it" (7).

The differences between the nature of these forms of diasporic capital – and the risks of informally relying on the flow from remittances for financial stability – became stark when the growing economic crisis finally reached meltdown status in 1991. Inflationary pressures, coupled with overvalued exchange rates and rising fiscal deficits, had severely staggered the Indian economy. It could not, however, recover from the body blow dealt by a series of external shocks, the most severe of which was the 1991 Gulf War. Not only was the Indian state responsible (at considerable expense) for repatriating hundreds of thousands of workers threatened by war, but also the flow of foreign exchange from the gulf dried up, and the sudden spike in oil prices further crippled the economy. The credit rating of India in the international loan market plummeted as commercial lenders shied away. Furthermore, the second part of the diasporic capital equation – foreign currency deposits – abruptly abandoned ship. Nearly US $1 billion in NRI deposits exited the country. Capital flight in general was precipitous, often citing severe exchange restrictions as the motivation but also following the general trend of unease regarding the Indian economy. As a result of this economic collapse, India was eventually forced to accept a series of economic reforms (aimed at trade liberalization) as part of a loan package from the International Monetary Fund and the World Bank (Nayyar 1994).

Despite the problematic experience of looking to émigrés and their funds, the Indian government has continued its pursuit of diasporic capital. Between 1991 and 2001, the central government floated three separate savings schemes. Each followed a particular political or economic event that placed the Indian state in a precarious financial position. In 1992, the government issued India Development Bonds, following the debt crisis described above. In 1998 and 2000, the government launched Resurgent India Bonds and India Millennium Development Bonds, respectively, with the former a direct appeal for diasporic assistance following global sanctions on India due to nuclear weapons testing. Approximately US $2 billion was raised by the first set of bonds and roughly US $4 to 5 billion by the following two. Each offering targeted infrastructure financing in India, though in actual terms less than one-third of the funds was directed in this manner, with the rest entering general revenues (interview with V.C. Bajpai, 9 March 2004).

The basic assumption underlying these efforts is that, despite increasing globalization and economic, cultural, and political integration across the world, locality, place, and especially "the nation" all still matter. Preliminary studies of investment by NRIs indicate that "emotional ties with India" rank as the single highest motivating factor spurring these diasporic capital flows (Krishnamurty 1994, 11).[3] Such surveys suggest that diasporic communities demonstrate a strong desire to participate in the material as well as ideological restructuring of their places of origin.

It is not only "nation" that is of importance in the search for diasporic capital, however. Several regional governments within India – including those of Andhra Pradesh, Maharashtra, and Madhya Pradesh – have established agencies in order to woo NRI money to their states, playing up notions of not simply "Indianness" but also "Marathiness" and "Andhraness." Parallel in many ways to the nationalist appeals that laid the foundation for development projects of the early postcolonial period, these calls by regional governments for extended civic duty to departed sons and daughters tie identity not to the nation-state but to specific regions and localities.

The lure of diasporic capital is so strong that it seems to cut across even some of the most entrenched political and historical traditions. Take, for example, two of the most vigorous recruiters of diasporic capital, the states of Gujarat and Kerala. Both are well-known examples within the Indian development literature of heavily industrialized states with high literacy rates and relatively affluent urban populations.[4] Both also have long histories of internal development aided by expatriates and overseas workers, primarily situated in the Persian Gulf. Politically, however, the two are – by reputation at least – quite dissimilar. Kerala has a history of socialist traditions, including democratically elected communist state governments and a high degree of political mobilization among its population as a whole. Civil society in Kerala is heralded as particularly strong, as evidenced by a series of successful social movements that have emerged to contest issues of gender, religion, caste, and social and ecological justice. Gujarat, on the other hand, is characterized by uneven internal political development, split primarily along rural, religious, class, caste, and regional lines. Over the past decade, the state has been wracked by some of the worst communal and particularly anti-Muslim violence seen since India's partition, culminating in the pogroms of 2002 that resulted in over 3,000 deaths. Gujarat is also characterized by long-standing political conservatism, a tradition that stretches from its production of right-wing nationalist leaders such as Sardar Vallabhai Patel to its embrace of the neofascist *Hindutva* (Hindu nationalist) agenda that has been ascendant in India over the past twenty years.

Yet these two different states with such opposite-seeming local political traditions are both engaging in a very similar quest for diasporic capital. Both are firmly situated on the track of neoliberal economic expansion adopted enthusiastically by a Hindu nationalist-dominated central government that once decried globalization and championed *swadeshi*.[5] Today, the government of Gujarat proudly claims the title of "The Business State of India," while the government of Kerala declared 2003-4 to be "The Year of Investment." Both states see investment by their expatriate communities as being an integral part of their current strategies of growth. Gujarat, for example, actively solicits funds from its diasporic communities located in North America and the United Kingdom, through instruments such as bonds and direct private investment. The government of Gujarat has even initiated its own program to recognize NRIs from that state through the Gujarat State Non-Resident Gujaratis Foundation. Membership in this organization includes perks such as a Gujarat Card – somewhat similar to the Indian central government's Person of Indian Origin Card – which entitles the bearer to "special consideration by the Government of Gujarat" (Government of Gujarat 2004). Kerala has similarly embarked on an aggressive search for NRI-assisted regional development through programs such as Global Investor Meet, which boasts several millions of dollars raised over the past year from the state's émigrés for regional projects (Government of Kerala 2004).

The desire for diasporic capital extends in the Indian context beyond the central and state governments and public sector financing. While remittance-driven development has indeed played a major role in regions such as Gujarat and Kerala, and the amounts raised by investment schemes such as the India Development Bonds, Resurgent India Bonds, and India Millennium Development Bonds have been significant, there are multiple other ways in which the influence of the diaspora in India's contemporary development can be seen and felt. Perhaps one of the most apparent in the present context has been the impact of diasporic capital, aesthetics, and values on both private and public urban development throughout India's many cities. The sheer pace and scale of such urban redesign are remarkable and the political, economic, social, and ecological consequences as yet unclear. In the final section of this chapter, I describe a project that explores the refashioning of urban fringes of one of India's most populous metropolises, Kolkata. This case illustrates many of the points made throughout this chapter regarding the connections between development, displacement, and diasporas.

## Bengali-Canadian Communities and the Urban Development in Kolkata

As noted above, the impact of diasporic tastes and economic power is clearly evident in the processes of urban development and gentrification currently under way across India. In cities such as Mumbai, Delhi, Bangalore, Hyderabad, Ahmedabad, and Cochin – to name but a few – construction work is booming. "Development" in India today is more than the infrastructure projects – dams, highways, irrigation canals, resource extraction enterprises – that have traditionally been conjured up by the concept. Indeed, what is most striking about the process of urbanization in these cities is the attempted re-creation of the developed world not in the image of London, New York, or Paris but in the image of suburban California, Colorado, or British Columbia. In rapidly developing new towns such as Gurgaon (in Haryana, just outside Delhi), and on the fringes of hosts of other cities, malls, gated communities, entertainment complexes, country clubs, and all the markers of conspicuous middle-class affluence and consumption abound. Hand in hand with these developments has come the wholesale displacement of the populations that used to live there: agrarians, horticulturalists, landless labourers, migrant workers, and others. The more fortunate have found jobs as drivers, domestics, and the ubiquitous security guards for the new housing estates and their affluent denizens; others have been pushed out into city slums and rural villages and into conflicts with the working poor and marginalized in those spaces.

My own study of such processes focused on the housing development projects in and around the Eastern Metropolitan (EM) Bypass that runs along the eastern fringes of Kolkata, from the neighbourhood of Garia in the south to the township of Salt Lake in the north. Covering over 12,000 hectares, the eastern fringes of the city have long been regarded as an ecologically fragile zone. Urban development has been allowed to take place in and around them only slowly and with extensive planning by the Kolkata Metropolitan Development Authority (KMDA) and the Kolkata Municipal Corporation (KMC). Scientists, ecologists, urban planners, municipal authorities, and local farmers and fishers have worked together over many decades to create innovative waste-recycling and water management programs that made the East Calcutta Wetlands "highly regarded [worldwide] as a model for wastewater aquaculture" (Bunting, Kundu, and Mukherjee 2002). The wetlands provide approximately 150 tons of fresh vegetables daily and over 10,500 tons of fish for urban markets within Kolkata, mainly serving the working poor. Close to 50,000 people are employed in the fisheries, mainly working in cooperatives and state-run associations.

Land reclamation and mixed-use planning led to the creation of Bidhannagar (Salt Lake) in the northeast through the 1960s and 1970s, while two further planned projects were added through the 1980s and 1990s, East Kolkata Township and Baishnabhghata-Patuli Township (KMDA 2000). The 1990s and post-liberalization India saw the proposal of even more ambitious development projects along the EM Bypass, but at this point these plans were to be challenged and curtailed by a groundswell of opposition from a host of different groups. They included local farmers and fishers whose livelihoods would be lost along with the fields and working fish ponds (*bheris*) in the region. Also opposed to the project were rag pickers and workers in the garbage disposal areas known as *dhapas*. Kolkata-based environmental organizations such as Vasundhara and various governmental authorities (including the West Bengal Pollution Control Board, the Department of Fisheries, Government of India, and the Department of Environment, Government of India) worried about the massive ecological degradation that the development plans entailed (Vasundhara 2004). Social workers and social justice advocates warned that the provision of affordable protein and foodstuff from the wetlands fisheries and farms to local markets would further disadvantage the urban poor, who relied heavily on the supply (Bunting et al. 2001). Various groups protested the population displacements planned (or already under way) as part of the developments. Some of the latter, such as the People's Commission on Eviction, held extensive hearings into the ongoing economic and political disenfranchisement. Others, such as People United for Better Living in Calcutta, waged court battles and succeeded in a Calcutta High Court freeze in 1993 on further development by the Calcutta Metropolitan Development Authority and the Calcutta Municipal Corporation in the region (People United for Better Living in Calcutta 2004). On 19 August 2002, the government of West Bengal and the government of India declared the East Kolkata Wetlands to be a Ramsar site, protected by the International Convention on Wetlands against unsustainable development (Ramsar Convention on Wetlands 2004).

Despite these apparent triumphs in the region – the long history of mixed-use wetland development, the utility that the area has in helping Kolkata to deal with its waste management issues without having to develop expensive and extensive waste water treatment plants, the court cases won and the international treaties signed – development continues unabated in the East Kolkata Wetlands. Part of the problem is illegal filling of and construction on the ponds. Another is shady land deals and questionable rezoning practices. Private-public partnerships and development deals have also served to hasten the scale and pace of construction all along the corridor. Existing townships and areas are being expanded (especially Salt Lake City's New Town Centre and all throughout Baishnabhghata-Patuli). All along the EM Bypass, there are large new shopping malls in existence or under construction as well as international hotel chains, entertainment parks, playgrounds, and massive new apartment complexes of the type seen in Gurgaon. Within the city as well, several connectors and flyovers have been constructed to ease traffic congestion within the urban core and to facilitate easy access to the bypass, with such construction leading to the potential displacement of hawkers and squatters (Bhattacharjee 2003).

How are these processes of development and displacement linked to the diaspora? In the case of the housing complexes, which are now the prime engines of urban redevelopment on the fringes of Kolkata, interviews with developers and promoters indicate that between 25 percent and 75 percent of apartment ownership is by overseas Indians – that is, NRIs and PIOs (interviews with Bengal Silver Springs Projects, 27 April 2004; South City Projects, 5 May 2004; Vedic Village Projects, 12 May 2004). Promotional websites and advertisements explicitly target diasporic groups – or those who wish to live like them. A highly visible advertising campaign on billboards throughout Kolkata for the South City Projects promises would-be buyers that they can "live the way the world does." Other complexes offer "Western-style amenities" and send travelling sales caravans to diasporas in London, New Jersey, and Toronto. Shopping malls in Kolkata's peri-urban fringes are similarly constructed with assumed diasporic sensibilities and pocketbooks in mind. The best and brightest in multinational brands are represented among the retailers, and the malls replicate the "big box" concept so prevalent in suburban North America. It is the life of the wealthy middle-class North American – idealized in the figure of the successful NRI who has "made it" as an IT, medical, engineering, business, academic, or legal professional – that is being sold here, paradoxically both to Indians and to NRIs/PIOs. In the case of the diasporic Indians, seeing themselves represented as success stories through Bollywood cinema, in Indian television and song, as well as in various governments' new attraction to their capital serves to reinforce this particular image of what it means to be a member of the diaspora. One member of a local social movement in Kolkata that has challenged displacement due to urban development recently asked, as we walked by a project of thirty-six-storey apartment buildings set amid golf courses, swimming pools, country clubs, and other gated communities, "why do overseas Bengalis feel that they need to live in the wind?" (People United for Better Living in Calcutta, 16 May 2004). The phrase "living in the wind" is a play on another local advertising campaign that tells apartment buyers that they can "live in the sky" in a thirty-six-storey building (constructed on recently filled alluvial soil). It also denotes a sense of transience attributed to some members of the diaspora and their attachment to a local place, at least in the estimation of people like the speaker. To those like him, the new development complexes are clearly aimed at diasporic groups and their assumed needs and desires, a set of preferences that is removed at several levels from those of "ordinary" Bengalis, set above and apart and ephemeral all at once. Yet for many other Indians within India – particularly in the emerging and growing middle classes – the NRIs and the lifestyle associated with them have equally become objects of aspiration. Those of the diaspora, in this sense, are sustaining and transforming a somewhat idealized homeland – at the same time that they themselves are sustained and transformed by events and perceptions within their homeland.

### Conclusion

The significance of diasporic groups in financing development activities, policies, and projects in countries across the world is both considerable and on the increase. Through remittances, investments, property ownership, and cultural influences, diasporic communities continue to reshape the material, aesthetic, and ideological landscapes of their homelands. In India, diasporic capital flows have played a profound role in the country's recent history, particularly its economic history. Yet such connections are not without their costs, sometimes particularly negative ones such as population displacement. It is for these reasons that groups such as the National Alliance of People's Movements, a broad-based coalition of grassroots social justice movements spread across India, have called explicitly for diasporic communities to participate more knowledgeably and more ethically in their investments in the "homeland." Transnational solidarity and support networks based in other countries, such as the Association for India's Development, a US-based organization, have similarly urged a focus on ethical behaviour by NRIs, suggesting that members of the diaspora ask themselves, "what kinds of developments in India are the Indians in the US (and other countries) making possible?" (Association for India's Development 2004). My own ongoing study focuses on the rise of a transnational middle-class Bengali consciousness both within the diaspora and within Kolkata itself and the material impacts that it has had on the changing face of the city and its periphery in order to consider just such questions.

**Notes**

1  The variance in numbers demonstrates the difficulty in calculating remittance rates. The lower figure shows workers' remittances as recorded under "current transfers" in the current account of the balance of payments, while the higher figure adds to this compensation of employees and benefits recorded under "income" in the current account and migrants' transfers that are reported under "capital transfers" in the capital account of IMF's *Balance of Payments Statistics Yearbook*.

2  Such statistics may help to explain the steady stream of Gujarati politicians making their way to the United States in recent years as supplicants to wealthy expatriates, seeking funds for a variety of causes.

3  The second highest motivation is the prospect of higher returns on investment, followed by a stated familiarity with Indian economic conditions.

4  Gujarat, however, has a much higher rural population than Kerala, which in turn has the second highest rate of population density among Indian states.

5  Gandhian economic self-reliance and independence.

# Part 3
# Transnational Organizing and Social Change

# 12

# The Institutional Landscapes of Salvadoran Refugee Migration: Transnational and Local Views from Los Angeles and Toronto

*Patricia Landolt*

This chapter draws on ten years of research conducted by the author[1] on Salvadoran migrant organizations in three urban settings to explore the relationship between transnational practices and immigrant settlement dynamics. The detailed study of the transnational and incorporationist practices of a single refugee population settled across very different urban centres of North America offers a rich empirical basis for comparative analysis. Focusing on the Salvadoran refugee-migrant settlement experience in the cities of Los Angeles and Toronto, the chapter contributes to the comparative study of immigration by analyzing the ways in which multiple levels of contextual factors and institutional interactions contour the process of immigrant incorporation.

This chapter analyzes three dimensions of the relationship between migration, settlement, and transnational practice. First, it considers national-level differences in the conditions of exit, modes of entry, and contexts of reception that organize Salvadoran migration to Canada and the United States. Second, it considers the ways in which the urban form – a city's political and cultural history, its immigration patterns, and its labour market dynamics – emerges as a second-tier context of reception for immigrant incorporation. Third, it conceptualizes settlement as a process of institutional interlocution in which an immigrant group engages with and is engaged by different state and nonstate institutions. Tracing various constellations of institutional interactions in which Salvadorans take part, the chapter explores how these interrelationships lead to the production of different notions of collective identity and distinct patterns of transnational and incorporationist political practice.

## A Transnational, Multilevel Framework for Analyzing the Immigrant Experience

A context of social exclusion and limited economic opportunities in host societies coexists with new possibilities for sustaining meaningful relationships with people and institutions in places of origin (Basch, Glick Schiller, and Szanton Blanc 1994; Portes, Guarnizo, and Landolt 1999; Vertovec 2001). Constant exchanges and interactions between migrants and nonmigrants tie together societies of emigration and settlement. Circuits of contact between movers and stayers lead to the production of transnational social fields – sets of interlocking networks of social relationships through which ideas, practices, and resources are exchanged, organized, and transformed (Basch, Glick Schiller, and Szanton Blanc 1994; Levitt and Glick Schiller 2004). Variation in the scope and character of transnational practices across and within immigrant groups is associated with differences in the contextual factors that frame the migration process and with differences of gender, religion, race, national origin, legal status, and network resources.

A multilevel approach is required to capture the border-crossing dynamics that frame migration patterns and immigrant settlement processes. Three threads of this multilevel framework are worth identifying. First, contextual dimensions such as the conditions of exit and reception that organize a migration flow produce a guiding framework of material and symbolic resources for an immigrant group. Whether a migration is forced or voluntary, the sending state's relationship to the migrant population, the responses of the host government and civil society to the newcomers, labour market conditions in the place of settlement, and so on combine to produce different settlement outcomes across immigrant groups even when these groups have similar demographic profiles (Portes and Borócz 1989; Portes 2003).

Second, cities can be read as dynamic contexts for immigrant incorporation. Newcomers always necessarily adapt to the structure and order of the city into which they enter and in so doing transform the city's social, economic, political, and cultural landscapes (Brettell 2003b). Certain dimensions of the urban form that are particularly important for shaping immigrant settlement outcomes include a city's relationship to its immigration history and its ethnic and racial diversity; its labour market structure and the kinds of economic niches into which it channels newcomers; its political culture and traditions of civic participation and oppositional politics; and the patterns of residential settlement and social interaction produced by its built environment.

Third, immigrants are continually engaged by and interact with a variety of social, economic, and political institutions, which may originate in the country of origin, the place of settlement, or elsewhere. This includes both state and nonstate actors such as community organizations and settlement agencies, religious organizations, local school and neighbourhood organizations, professional associations, social movement organizations, lobby and advocacy groups, as well as home and host country political parties. Each such organization or institutional actor provides immigrants with a set of material and symbolic points of reference that may encourage or discourage the maintenance or revival of ties to the home country or to co-nationals settled in other locations of the globe (Levitt 2001b).

The immigrant experience is spatially complex and multidimensional. Immigrant families, the institutions they build, those in which they participate, those that engage them – each has a distinct spatiality. The settlement experience may emphasize incorporationist practices at one moment and transnational practices at another. Involvement in local institutions may be a stepping-stone toward greater involvement in the country of origin or may produce a seemingly irreparable break in an immigrant's ties to her place of origin. Transnational and incorporationist practices are rarely mutually exclusive, and their interrelationship is constantly being renegotiated. The networks that immigrants sustain can be global, transnational, and local, where the global arena is associated with networks and processes that are decentred from any specific location and the transnational with practices that are anchored in but always cross and transcend the borders of two or more nation-states (Kearney 1995; Kivisto 2003). The "local" and its boundaries are thus no longer so simple to define since people, in this case transnational migrants in Toronto and Los Angeles, can imbue it with global and transnational meanings and materiality (Gieryn 2000).

## Contrasting Salvadoran Refugee Migrations to the United States and Canada

In the 1960s, El Salvador had a century-old tradition of largely unauthorized and unregulated regional labour migration tied to the seasonal demands of Central America's agroexport economy (Vilas 1995). International migration to the United States was initiated during the Second World War when labour contractors recruited workers to fill temporary labour shortages in California's shipping industry (Hamilton et al. 1988). In the 1960s, Salvadoran women were informally recruited to work as private domestic workers, typically for US government officials based in Washington, DC (Repak 1995). In contrast, labour migration from El Salvador to Canada was effectively nonexistent.

In the late 1970s, the violence and economic disruptions of the civil war prompted a massive refugee exodus that ruptured El Salvador's regional labour migration system. Thirty percent of the country's population, estimated at just over 5 million in 1980, was forced to abandon its place of origin. The lion's share of the refugees left the region and made their way to the United States and in smaller numbers to Europe, Australia, and Canada (Zolberg, Suhrke, and Aguayo 1989; Hamilton and Chinchilla 1996). The pre–civil war networks of labour migration played a defining role in setting the pace and direction of early refugee flows. Migration networks to Washington,

DC, Los Angeles, and San Francisco served as important beachheads for refugee migration during the war.

El Salvador's refugee exodus takes place against a highly politicized backdrop. Regional and international actors – the Salvadoran government and its guerrilla opposition, the Frente Farabundo Martí para la Liberación Nacional (FMLN), the US government, the United Nations, and different international humanitarian organizations – compete to define the situation of the refugees who are alternately lauded as radicals, identified as subversives, or patronized as victims of a distant conflict. Given this hyperpoliticized context, the modes of entry of Salvadoran refugee migration to Canada and the United States exhibit dramatic differences.

In the case of the United States, the US government refused to recognize El Salvador as a refugee-producing country, financed the Salvadoran government's war effort, and questioned the legitimacy of asylum applications. As a result, Salvadoran refugees typically crossed from Mexico into the United States undetected; expecting to have their refugee claims rejected, they often applied for asylum only if and when they were apprehended by the Immigration and Naturalization Service (INS). Today, close to three decades after their initial arrival and in spite of intense lobbying by Central American immigrant rights advocates and the presentation of at least three federal government initiatives meant to facilitate the regularization of their status, an estimated 50 percent of the 2.2 million Salvadorans in the United States remain undocumented or have only secured some form of temporary immigration status (López, Popkin, and Telles 1996; Popkin 2003). In other words, more than a million Salvadorans now live and work in the United States without full legal status.

Salvadoran migration to the United States before, during, and after the civil war has been organized around the informal social networks of the migrant population and follows a classic pattern of chain migration. Migrants draw on the resources and example of friends, family, and co-villagers to make the trip north and, once in the United States, to find housing and employment. This pattern of unauthorized chain migration under conditions of resource scarcity has encouraged residential concentration and the creation of labour market niches. It has also enabled groups of extended kin and co-villagers to re-create and reinvent premigration social institutions. Contact with co-villagers, translocal social obligations to nonmigrants, and hometown nostalgias are important material and discursive points of reference that orient the process of Salvadoran identity formation.

The modes of entry and status upon entry of Salvadoran refugees entering Canada are markedly different. In the first years of El Salvador's refugee crisis, the Canadian government was reluctant to accept Salvadoran refugees and agreed to do so only in response to lobbying by Canada's unions, refugee rights advocates, and more established Latin American immigrants

(Ferris 1987; Kowalchuk 1999). In the mid-1980s, the government finally recognized El Salvador as a refugee-producing country, prompting a steady flow of regulated and authorized refugee entry into Canada. In addition to high acceptance rates for asylum seekers, the government created several emergency programs to facilitate the accelerated entrance of high-risk refugee populations, including political prisoners and refugee camp populations facing deportation from Costa Rica and Honduras (Montes 1989; Basok 1993).

Table 12.1 provides a breakdown of Salvadoran migration to Canada. There are currently an estimated 68,000 Salvadorans in Canada, of whom 38,000 entered the country legally during the civil war (CIC 1994). The remainder were either born in Canada or emigrated later under the family reunification or independent class immigration arrangements. The table shows that, of the Salvadoran population that arrived during the war, 58 percent entered Canada as convention refugees selected abroad, 17 percent arrived through family reunification provisions, 13 percent entered as independent skilled workers, and 11 percent applied for asylum at the US-Canada border. Until recently, there has been no unauthorized Salvadoran migration to Canada.

The federal government's involvement in the regulation of the refugee flow is a defining feature of Salvadoran migration to Canada. Informal chain migration is not an organizing principle of this flow. The state-assisted mode of refugee entry produces a social organization of the Salvadoran population in Canada different from that found in the United States. In Canada, few Salvadorans are bound together through informal social networks formed prior to or in the course of migration. Instead, nuclear family ties and friendships forged with co-nationals after arrival are the most common point of departure for social exchange and collective action. In this context, the symbolic common denominator for community formation is not home village ties or *paisanaje* but premigration political activism, national identity, and the refugee experience. Refugeeship and in some social settings the discourse of political exile become important elements of Salvadoran identity formation.

## Urban Landscapes as Contexts of Reception: Los Angeles and Toronto

North American cities experienced a set of dramatic structural shifts beginning in the 1970s. This sea change in urban life was characterized by an increase in international migration flows, deindustrialization, the restructuring and bifurcation of labour markets, and a reorganization of state institutions in a climate of fiscal austerity (Sassen 1991; Cross and Moore 2002). Two features of this structural transformation are of particular relevance to the context of reception that frames Salvadoran migration, including each city's immigration and labour market dynamics.

*Table 12.1*

**Salvadoran immigration to Canada, 1980-2001**

| Immigration class | Period of immigration (% of total Salvadoran immigrant population) | | | | | | | | | | | Total % | (N) |
|---|---|---|---|---|---|---|---|---|---|---|---|---|---|
| | 1980-81 | 1982-83 | 1984-85 | 1986-87 | 1988-89 | 1990-91 | 1992-93 | 1994-95 | 1996-97 | 1998-99 | 2000-1 | | |
| Refugee | .1% | 4.4% | 9.5% | 10.0% | 9.4% | 12.7% | 9.1% | 1.4% | .9% | .5% | .5% | **58.5%** | (27,494) |
| Family reunification | .4% | .5% | .7% | 1.2% | 1.2% | 2.5% | 4.5% | 2.3% | 1.4% | 1.1% | 1.1% | **16.9%** | (7,965) |
| Skilled worker/ self-employed | .4% | 2.5% | 1.3% | 2.8% | 1.3% | 1.7% | 1.9% | .3% | .3% | .2% | .5% | **13.2%** | (6,217) |
| Backlog | | | | | | 7.8% | 3.1% | .1% | .0% | .0% | .0% | **11.0%** | (5,174) |
| Deferred removal order | | | | | | | | .0% | .2% | .1% | .0% | **.3%** | (131) |
| Entrepreneur/ investor | | .0% | | | .0% | .0% | | .0% | .0% | | | **.0%** | (16) |
| Live-in caregiver | | | | | | | | | .0% | .0% | | **.0%** | (2) |
| **Total %** | **.9%** | **7.4%** | **11.5%** | **14.0%** | **12.0%** | **24.6%** | **18.5%** | **4.1%** | **2.9%** | **1.9%** | **2.2%** | **100.0%** | |
| **(N)** | (405) | (3,467) | (5,426) | (6,584) | (5,635) | (11,570) | (8,706) | (1,948) | (1,346) | (901) | (1,011) | | (46,999) |

*Source:* Longitudinal Immigration Database 1980-2001 (IMDB).

In the 1970s, Los Angeles emerged as a gateway city for international migration. The foreign-born population grew from only 11 percent in 1970 to 35 percent in 2000. Latin Americans and Mexicans in particular became an indomitable force. By 2000, Mexicans constituted 40 percent of all immigrants, followed by Salvadorans (6.2 percent) and Filipinos (5.6 percent) (Bobo et al. 2000; Halle 2003). The overwhelming presence of Mexicans and Central Americans infused Los Angeles with a distinct feel as Latin Americans imposed their social reality as undocumented refugees and workers on the city's labour markets, public spaces, and both state and nonstate institutions.

Toronto has a long history as an immigrant city and perhaps more importantly, since the promotion of Canadian multiculturalism policies in the 1970s, has become a self-consciously multiethnic city. Every year Toronto receives over 40 percent of Canada's newcomers, and unlike Los Angeles, where there is a huge concentration of Latin American immigrants, no single source country or region dominates Toronto's immigration flow (Jansen and Lam 2003). Of the immigrants granted permanent residence between 1980 and 1996, only 10 percent came from traditional source areas, 15 percent from eastern and southern Europe, and 51 percent from Asia, 18 percent from Latin America and the Caribbean, and 6 percent from Africa (Preston, Lo, and Wang 2003). Until the 1990s, the majority of Latin American immigrants entering Canada did so under either refugee provisions or refugee-like conditions (Goldring 2006). Given their small numbers and the social dispersal that tends to result from their mode of entry into the city, Latin Americans have not gained social prominence in Toronto as they have in Los Angeles (Goldring 2006). Latin Americans are easily absorbed into the city's often depoliticizing multicultural mix (Goonewardena and Kipfer 2005).

In Los Angeles and Toronto, Salvadorans have been and remain concentrated in industrial niches that are characterized by low wages, poor working conditions, and uncertainty (Wilson 2000; Landolt 2001). Salvadoran women have found work as industrial and private caregivers and domestics and in labour-intensive assembly work organized through sweatshop and homework arrangements (Repak 1995; Bobo et al. 2000; Landolt 2001). Young men perform dangerous and backbreaking work – cleaning high-rise windows, removing asbestos, landscaping, et cetera (Mahler 1995; Landolt 2000; Andrade-Eekhoff 2004). In 2000, an estimated 20 percent of Salvadorans in the United States lived below the poverty line, with mean earnings calculated at US $9,865 (Logan 2001). In Canada, 13 percent of Salvadoran households earn less than CDN $10,000, and 20 percent earn less than CDN $20,000 (Census Canada 2001). In effect, Salvadoran working families maintain high rates of labour market participation but very low wage rates (Ornstein 2000).

Structural differences across the two urban economies produce important distinctions in Salvadorans' social location in the local labour market. Undocumented immigrants are a pillar of the Los Angeles economy. They constitute one-third of the Los Angeles workforce and produce a downward pressure on working conditions (Bobo et al. 2000). In Toronto, an increase in subcontracting and temporary work arrangements signal a trend toward the deregulation of the labour process and an erosion of working conditions and workers' rights (Cranford, Vosko, and Zukewich 2003). However, because they are not undocumented, Salvadorans in Canada have access to an important set of state provisions, such as healthcare, unemployment insurance, and workers' compensation in case of injury, that are not available to a large number of Salvadoran Angelinos.

## The Local and Transnational Dimensions of Institutional Engagements

Each settlement location presents Salvadoran refugees with an institutional landscape of material and symbolic possibilities for building community. While this institutional interaction is axiomatic of the immigrant experience, perhaps because of the highly politicized character of El Salvador's refugee crisis the intensity of this interaction emerges with great clarity and poignancy in the Salvadoran case. Of particular importance is the fact that in both Los Angeles and Toronto varying constellations of local and transnational nonstate organizations loosely allied with or sympathetic to the political project of El Salvador's guerrilla opposition sought to engage with and/or assist the refugee population (Gosse 1988, 1996).

Los Angeles emerged as an active hub for the FMLN and the Central American solidarity movement. The FMLN organizations developed a successful model of local, cross-country, and transnational grassroots activism and formal political lobbying. One faction of the FMLN created the Central American Refugee Centre (CARECEN), while another founded El Rescate. These two organizations undertook fundraising, lobbying, and educational programs consistent with the strategic priorities of the guerrilla movement. In part because of the absence of state settlement assistance for Salvadoran refugees, the two organizations also provided emergency relief and legal services to refugee families. They also focused considerable resources on the political education and mobilization of Salvadoran Angelinos.

As discussed previously, chain migration and *paisanaje* or "ties to the home village" are the first and perhaps most obvious material and symbolic point of reference from which Salvadorans sustain social exchanges and construct collective identities. The effort by the FMLN – via CARECEN and El Rescate – to organize the refugees of Los Angeles around a radical political project emerges as a second element of collective identity formation. However, in contrast to the high costs associated with political loyalty to the FMLN, the expectations tied to *paisanaje* are perceived as more innocuous in part because they are easily folded into the social obligations and normative expectations associated with kinship ties.

While much less is known about the relationship between globally networked grassroots organizations and Salvadoran refugees in Canada's settlement cities, preliminary research suggests a dramatically different situation from the one found in Los Angeles. In the case of Toronto, three types of institutional engagements framed the Salvadoran refugee experience.

First, institutional engagements revolved around the FMLN, which had a weak, unstable, and often fractious institutional presence. In the mid-1970s, efforts to develop an FMLN base in Toronto produced important contacts with academics and led to the maintenance of working partnerships with Canadian unions, human rights organizations, and refugee rights advocacy groups. The institutional weakness of the FMLN reflected both its failure to "capture" the city, as it were, and a decision by the FMLN to relegate Canada to a second tier within its transnational advocacy agenda. The FMLN's relationship with Toronto's Salvadoran refugees was quite weak and sporadic. In sharp contrast to the situation in Los Angeles, and in part given generous state settlement assistance for refugees in Canada, FMLN organizations played no role in the immigrant settlement process.

Second, faith-based and ethnospecific immigrant settlement service agencies emerged as important interlocutors of the Salvadoran refugee population. Upon arrival in Canada, Salvadoran refugee families received a range of social services, including free healthcare, subsidized housing and in some cases a family spending allowance for a period of up to one year, and English as a Second Language (ESL) classes. Private organizations, particularly faith-based groups, were encouraged by the state to sponsor refugee families, and in such cases some elements of the settlement process occurred via the religious congregation. The Quaker Refugee Committee (QRC) was one such institution. It welcomed the refugees and served as a meeting place for what emerged as an active cluster of Salvadoran families that offered each other mutual aid. This group was also able to tap into the networks of the Canadian Quaker membership to expand its knowledge of the Canadian system and diversify its resource base.

Third, Salvadoran refugees received significant solidarity from Latin American political and cultural organizations, notably the city's politically savvy Chilean exile organizations. For instance, Latin American artists joined forces to organize weekly *peñas* or cultural evenings that featured poetry, live music, and plenty of political discussion. In this context, Latin American radical left politics and mobilization against dictatorships and US imperialism became central elements of Salvadoran identity for a core group of highly politicized refugees. This loosely organized, dynamic, yet underfunded cluster of grassroots political initiatives emerged as a third point of reference for

Salvadoran community organizing. It dovetailed discursively, if not institutionally, with the ecumenical and progressive religious framework that cloaked much of the Salvadoran immigrant settlement process.

## Building Community in the Postwar Era

In 1992, the government of El Salvador and the FMLN signed the UN-brokered Peace Accords of Chapultepec, ending a civil war that had claimed over 80,000 lives. The process of national reconstruction and reconciliation brought about dramatic changes in the institutional landscape of El Salvador, its migrant settlements, and the web of transnational relations that brought together these locations. Ideological polarization grew less stark, and political spaces, once sharply defined and defended with force, were more openly contested. The FMLN largely withdrew from its global network of commitments and turned to the task of reconstituting itself as a national political party. In contrast, the government of El Salvador, which had established few if any transnational contacts during the war, launched a US-centred campaign to bring the country's migrant citizens – the *hermano lejano* or "distant brother" – back into the national community (Landolt, Autler, and Baires 1999). An unplanned consulate-based strategy of holding meetings with local community activists and business leaders was eventually consolidated into a full-fledged program for migrant citizens in 2000 with the creation by the Ministry of Foreign Affairs of a new office called the General Secretariat for Attention to the Community Abroad (Dirección General de Atención a las Comunidades en el Exterior, or DGACE).

The peace accords effectively ruptured existing transnational networks, opened the doors to the proliferation of new types of transnational interests and relationships, tested well-worn local and global alliances, and rewrote the possibilities for transnational and incorporationist participation by Salvadoran immigrants. In this context, Salvadoran immigrant organizations in Los Angeles and Toronto, as elsewhere, sought to redefine their postwar role in El Salvador, their local and transnational political alliances and agendas, and their relationship to the local Salvadoran immigrant community.

## Los Angeles: Combining Local and Transnational Concerns

Two events frame the transformation of Salvadoran-Angelino organizations: the signing of the peace accord in El Salvador and the LA riots of 1992. The restructuring of Salvadoran-Angelino organizations was propelled by an effort to bring together transnational and incorporationist Salvadoran immigrant concerns into a more or less compatible platform and organizing agenda. The goal then was to guarantee a place for Salvadoran migrants not only in El Salvador but also in local LA institutions.

After 1992, Salvadoran migrants' desire to participate in the postwar project of reconstruction and reconciliation encouraged the formation of a new generation of Salvadoran-American organizations, including professional and business organizations, youth groups, workers' centres with union ties, and hometown associations that focused on financing improvement projects in the members' places of origin in El Salvador. The more established organizations – such as CARECEN and El Rescate – responded to this postwar renaissance by trying to forge relationships with the new groups. For instance, El Rescate helped Salvadoran hometown associations (HTAs) to constitute the group Communities United to Provide Direct Aid to El Salvador (COMUNIDADES). This umbrella organization brings together more than sixty HTAs and encourages them to share best practices and allows El Rescate to facilitate HTA access to project funds with US organizations and, more recently, Inter-American Development Bank loans that are disbursed through the Salvadoran government.

Old guard Salvadoran organizations also initiated a strategic dialogue with the Salvadoran government and its consular representatives, mobilizing together to regularize the migrant population's legal limbo. Joint lobbying by Central American state officials and the grassroots Central American Immigration Task Force enabled the successful passage of NACARA, the Nicaraguan Adjustment and Central American Relief Act, which allows Guatemalans and Salvadorans who had arrived in the United States prior to 1990 to apply for permanent residency (Popkin 2003).

In the period following the LA riots of 1992, new political and social concerns emerged in the city, and a new set of funding priorities was established by government institutions (Johnson, Farrell, and Jackson 1994). Salvadoran community organizations capitalized on the new context, often playing a leading role in designing community-based responses to the root causes of the riots. Given their geographical location in "troubled communities" or "riot hotspots" such as Pico-Union, the heart of the Salvadoran community in Los Angeles, Salvadoran organizations received state funding for youth leadership programs and economic development initiatives. Groups with a history of denouncing human rights abuses in El Salvador and along the border turned to denouncing human and civil rights abuses perpetrated by the INS, the Los Angeles Police Department, and the National Guard. Salvadoran organizations also became active members of several postriot coalitions, including Rebuild LA, the Coalition of Neighbourhood Developers, and the Latino Coalition for a new LA.

During a ten-year period of intense activity, the Salvadoran organizations of Los Angeles redefined their mandates and developed new alliances that bridge the local, national, and transnational concerns of Salvadoran Angelinos. The LA riots marked an institutional watershed as Salvadoran organizations were pushed to refocus their work toward inner city neighbourhoods of Salvadoran concentration, city politics, and interethnic alliance building. The simultaneous proliferation of hometown associations with strong ties to Salvadoran places of origin and the extraterritorial presence of the Salvadoran state prompted Salvadoran organizations to engage with institutions and individuals in El Salvador.

### Toronto: Bifurcated Local and Transnational Agendas

The Salvadoran community of Toronto does not exhibit the organizational renaissance and diversification of transnational exchanges that characterize Los Angeles. The Salvadoran government and the country's business sector remain remarkably absent from the Toronto scene. Perhaps because of comparatively small numbers, lack of entrepreneurial activities, and perceived political radicalism, there is little interest among the Salvadoran state or capital elites in courting or recapturing Salvadoran Torontonians as "distant brothers" of the nation. In turn, rather than a reorientation of transnational and local political engagements, in Toronto the postwar period has been characterized by a process of institutional erosion and an inability to bridge local and transnational realities to create a more coherent platform of concerns.

In 1992, there were just over a dozen Salvadoran organizations in the city. The majority were aligned with one of the five political movements that constituted the FMLN, had a small but devoted membership, and relied on informal fundraising for support. While these organizations were slowly dissolved and memory of their existence faded, Salvadorans in Toronto still considered contact with the FMLN to be an important part of their political engagement. The FMLN representatives, particularly *comandantes* and ex-combatants, continued to visit the city and would draw a sizable audience of well-informed Salvadorans anxious to continue engaging in El Salvador's political process.

Efforts to reinvent the community's transnational institutional commitments in the postwar period have tended to follow one of two paths. On the one hand, a large number of ad hoc and short-lived transnational initiatives have appeared. Without fail, natural disasters and elections in El Salvador tend to produce a flurry of fundraising activities – concerts, raffles, educational events, Sunday dinners, and so on. As they renew the cross-border exchange of resources and ideas with institutions and people in El Salvador, these projects are well received by many Salvadorans. They are also important moments for Salvadorans to stage large public gatherings, and as such they allow the group to reconnect and renew the highly politicized boundaries of membership that have been so central to their definition of "the community." However, the projects that give rise to these activities are commonly initiated and maintained through small networks of individuals. The resources of the activist cluster are often exhausted long before their work has been institutionalized or they have been able to consolidate a broad membership.

On the other hand, more institutionally stable and successful transnational grassroots projects initiated from within the Salvadoran community have ended up being absorbed into Canadian institutions or falling into Canadian hands. I offer two examples of this pattern. First, the SALVAIDE is a grassroots development organization that has its roots in the FMLN and the Salvadoran community in Canada. One of its main activities has been the coordination of sister city relationships that pair rural communities in El Salvador with a municipal or community group in Canada. Many of these sistering relationships were formed during the civil war and have continued to exist in the postwar era. The SALVAIDE survived the institutional erosion that affected most other Salvadoran organizations in Canada in part because it was able to tap into funding from the Canadian International Development Agency (CIDA). Yet as it has secured state funding, the organization has also distanced itself from Salvadorans, except for the annual fundraising party that brings out a Salvadoran crowd.

Second, a grassroots transnational partnership has been organized around the Caravan of Hope, begun by a group of Salvadorans in 2001 after earthquakes destroyed many urban and rural communities in El Salvador. The group found an institutional home in a small Anglican church in north Toronto. Their project has grown into an annual pilgrimage of buses that make the trip from Toronto to El Salvador to deliver in-kind donations to select rural communities. Unfortunately, the growth of the project has meant increasing costs for participants, increasingly hierarchical decision making, and a bureaucratic formalization of activities, with the result that the Caravan of Hope appears to have left behind its founding Central American membership. While Salvadorans continue to help meet the donation targets in Toronto, today's pilgrims are by and large white, nonimmigrant Canadians with little connection to El Salvador.

A second arena of activism has focused on local concerns such as affordable housing, children's performance in the school system, and issues associated with working poverty more generally. In this realm, two patterns of institutional development are evident. There is evidence to suggest that Salvadorans have learned to successfully navigate the Canadian system. For example, in the early 1990s, Salvadorans were able to establish two housing cooperatives in Toronto. This has been a major victory for them. The cooperatives guarantee affordable housing for a significant number of families and allow the group to finally claim a physical space as a meeting place of its own. In a city where there is limited residential concentration among Salvadorans, and hence face-to-face contact is restricted, the establishment of a gathering place is fundamental. However, neither the successful establishment of housing cooperatives nor the production of a distinctly Salvadoran gathering place has sparked any further organizing activities.

Finally, Salvadoran efforts to penetrate the social service agency sector have met with mixed results. A small number of important leaders and activists of the Salvadoran community has been able to gain employment within the city's state-funded community centres and social service and immigrant settlement agencies. Yet Salvadorans have been largely shut out of leadership positions within these organizations. This is considered a fundamental stumbling block for a long-term political voice in city politics since these organizations are seen as a training ground for political leadership (Bloemraad 2003). Salvadoran invisibility within the social service sector is a source of heated debate among Latin Americans. In particular, it is believed that South Americans and Chileans in particular have maintained an unreasonable monopoly on paid and executive board positions within immigrant service agencies. Indeed, organizations dominated by South Americans have had a difficult time analyzing and acting effectively in ways that recognize the specificities of the Salvadoran refugee experience (Chute 2004).

The postwar period of Salvadoran activism and community organizing is marked by institutional weakness and resource depletion in a context of continued political radicalism. A continued moral and political commitment to participating in El Salvador's struggle to build a more just society has produced a series of small ad hoc initiatives. But there has been a constant failure to consolidate the work of small clusters of active individuals into a more broad-based and institutionalized effort. Ironically, the institutionalization and growth of transnational projects, particularly when they involve building bridges beyond the Salvadoran community, have resulted in a loss of control over decision making and resource allocation by the group. Salvadoran organizers have also not made any explicit connections between local and transnational modes of political engagement, and participation in local issues has remained highly individualized.

**Conclusion**
This comparative exploration of Salvadoran refugee migration to Canada and the United States advances our understanding of the relationship between transnational migration and the institutional dynamics of immigrant resettlement. A transnational lens of inquiry, which considers the contexts of both exit and reception that frame a migration system, offers a more complete understanding of settlement outcomes. In this case, the forced character of the refugee flow plays into the refugees' interpretation of their migration as largely temporary or partial. In turn, differences in the contexts of reception that frame Salvadoran migration to Canada and the United States are associated with distinct modes of entry and settlement.

To summarize, Salvadoran migration to the United States was organized around the informal social networks of the migrant population and followed a pattern of chain migration based on social network ties among kin and co-villagers. These dimensions of identity become important for resource sharing and patterns of collective action. In contrast, the Canadian government's eventual willingness to accept Salvadorans as refugees and grant them settlement support upon arrival has limited the formation of chain migration patterns. In this case, nuclear family ties and political affinities form the basis for the formation of networks of friendship and mutual aid and the organization of community projects.

One of the fundamental differences across the two case studies has to do with the institutional framework within which the early years of the settlement experience are organized. This chapter suggests that state and nonstate institutional engagements with a newcomer population vary across settlement locations and are a critical determinant of outcomes. In the case of Los Angeles, settlement assistance, however limited, was organized through highly politicized, often FMLN-affiliated community organizations (e.g., CARECEN and El Rescate) that linked emergency reception assistance to political education. This kind of partisan settlement assistance initiated the construction of an important institutional bridge that bound Salvadoran refugees together with politically astute and increasingly well-connected Salvadoran community organizers. In the case of Toronto, the state plays an active role in the settlement process, which is seen as an institutional gateway to long-term civic engagement and formal political participation (Chute 2004). State mediation of settlement and its organization and delivery through Canadian institutions have not been conducive to the production or strengthening of Salvadoran-centred social networks. Instead, this mediation has tended to encourage incorporation into Canadian institutions.

Finally, a set of broader conceptual and methodological insights has emerged from this exploration of Salvadoran transnational migration and institution building. The study confirms the value of a comparative mode of analysis. This mode has allowed me to draw attention to the ways in which purportedly similar immigrant populations experience profoundly different processes of incorporation as a result of contextual and institutional differences across settlement locations. The discussion also suggests how we can begin to merge effectively our concern for global and transnational processes with a grounding in the particularities of the local.

**Note**

1 Data for this chapter come from two research projects in which I have participated: the Comparative Immigrant Entrepreneurs Project (CIEP), Principal Investigator Alejandro Portes (http://www.cmd.princeton.edu/ciep.shtml), 1996-2000; and the SSHRCC-funded project Social Cohesion and International Migration in a Globalizing Era, Principal Investigator Michael Lanphier (http://www.yorku.ca/cohesion/LARG/html/largindex2.htm), 2002-5.

# 13
# The South Asia Left Democratic Alliance: The Dilemmas of a Transnational Left
*Aparna Sundar*

The South Asia Left Democratic Alliance (SALDA) came together over the course of 1997 as a Toronto-based activist collective, with members who traced their origins to the countries of South Asia or who were interested in the region.[1] In the initial years, it consisted almost entirely of university faculty and students; appeals for new members at its own events and others led gradually to a somewhat more diverse membership. Given that several of the founding members were first-generation immigrants to Canada, it seemed inevitable that the organization would have transnational aims – seeking to intervene in the public sphere in defence of democracy and human rights in both South Asia and Canada, through educational events and other forms of activism.

One of the earliest concerns motivating the organization's founding was the growing polarization between the various South Asian diasporas, caused by the divisive politics (religious, ethnic, national) of their countries of origin. This polarization was especially evident on the campuses, where student groups were fragmented along lines of nation or religion (Indian students, Hindu students, Sikh students, Tamil students, Muslim students) and rarely made common cause. A related concern was with providing a critical and alternative perspective on history and culture to youth raised here, whose desire to learn more about "their" history and culture made them fertile soil for the educational efforts of religious chauvinists, such as the Hindu nationalist Vishwa Hindu Parishad (VHP or World Hindu Council), which, along with the Bharatiya Janata Party (BJP) and the Rashtriya Swayamsevak Sangh (RSS), make up the organized forces of Hindu nationalism. As Tapan Basu et al. note in their succinct introduction to the phenomenon of Hindu nationalism, "the VHP was specifically set up to forge a corporate Hindu identity, to unite all Hindu sects in opposition to Islam" (1993, ix). It is with this aim of constructing and strengthening Hindu identity that the VHP operates in the Hindu diaspora, conducting youth summer camps and other such programs as well as mobilizing funds for activities in India. Youth of Hindu origin in Canada, often even more than their immigrant parents, become champions of these chauvinist causes, providing the international legitimacy that the organizations need to raise funds and create supportive lobby groups in the diaspora.

Thus, from the start, transnationality – the straddling of cultural spheres, of social and political phenomena, and frequently of citizenship – was both the context (of members' lives and of several of the issues that they took up) and the challenge (of being able to organize effectively across national borders and across the different layers and enclaves of the various South Asian diasporas) for SALDA. What follows is a participant's reflection on this experience of organizing transnationally. I start by outlining some of the group's recent activities in order to give a sense of the variety of social justice issues with transnational implications. In the final section, I explore some of the difficulties of organizing within transnational spaces that are, in general, already marginal to mainstream politics. These difficulties include building a community around shared political positions in a situation where differential experiences with immigration and settlement have served to create new cleavages and tensions within already fissured societies. They also include gaining support for positions that are critical of states in both "sending" and "receiving" countries and of social elites within both the immigrant community and mainstream society, in a situation where immigrants rely heavily on states and social elites for their survival and advancement. The theoretical contribution of this chapter lies in its suggestion that the difficulties of organizing transnationally have not only to do with national borders, state policies, laws, surveillance, and policing but are also created by the diverse conditions of the transnational experience itself. Differences in the period of immigration, the nature of integration and location within the new country, and the relationship to states and social groupings "back home" compound existing social hierarchies and differences to further complicate the task of building a political community.

## Recent Activities

A review of SALDA's recent activities reveals transnational concerns of two kinds. The first is the emigrant's concern with events back home and a desire to influence them, especially when such phenomena actively recruit the transnational and the diasporic, such as in the case of Hindu nationalism. The other concern – perhaps the one that has increasingly come to dominate the group's activities, as members have been in Canada longer, and as second-generation youth have become involved – is the desire to influence events in Canada that have particular implications for South Asian immigrants. Informing these activities is the group's political mandate:

The South Asia Left Democratic Alliance (SALDA) aims to defend and extend the space for progressive politics in South Asia and Canada ... SALDA is committed to fighting for social justice, radical democracy and secularism. It works to oppose sectarianism and oppression based on religion, gender, race, sexual orientation, caste, class or ethnicity. SALDA defends and promotes civil liberties, especially by opposing state terrorism in the form of militarization, surveillance and targeted policing. SALDA also joins other groups to resist the deepening grip of global capital and challenges the entrenchment of the neo-liberal agenda in South Asia. SALDA builds alliances with individuals and groups to combat the rise of the religious right in South Asia and across the world. (SALDA 2003)[2]

Since its inception, SALDA has sought to apply this mandate through a variety of campaigns, events, and initiatives. For example, an ongoing issue in 2004-5 was that of the proposed Shari'a tribunals in Ontario. A group of Muslim Canadians had set up an Islamic Institute of Civil Justice to work as a tribunal under the Ontario Arbitration Act (1991) to resolve civil and personal (family) disputes according to the Shari'a, for those Muslims choosing to avail themselves of it.[3] SALDA joined other concerned organizations in lobbying the attorney general of Ontario not to allow the establishment of this tribunal on the ground that it was potentially harmful to a large number of Muslim women in Ontario. Our opposition was based on the premise that language and/or cultural barriers might force these women to accept decisions reached by the tribunal because they may be unaware of their rights of recourse to Canadian law, or they may be led to believe that it is their religious duty to accept a decision based on the Shari'a, or they may be coerced by family members to apply to the tribunal and accept its decision.[4]

In a somewhat unexpected response to a highly visible campaign against the tribunals waged by an assortment of otherwise often politically incompatible individuals and groups, the Ontario government decided in late 2005 to ban all faith-based arbitration. Although SALDA largely welcomed this decision, we still felt the need to examine to what extent Islamophobia had informed the decision and the actions of several members of the campaign. In the roundtable discussion on the subject,[5] members who had been active in the campaign said that their own opposition had been based on their experience with Shari'a in South Asia, on the group's position on religious politics in general as expressed in their mandate and through other campaigns, as well as on their current work with newly immigrant Muslim women in Toronto. Despite this, they had not taken this position easily, for they were keenly sensitive to a context in which any statement seen as critical of Islam could be used to further label Muslims or those with transnational identities as "antinational" in their values or loyalties. After all, it was not long ago when this was precisely what had happened to several of their South Asian brothers.

The case they had in mind occurred in 2003, with application of the Anti-Terrorism Act.[6] As an aside, it may be interesting to note that the direct authoritarianism of post-9/11 national security legislation such as this act may appear to be in some contrast to the legal pluralism of the Canadian state implied by the Arbitration Act, with the space that the latter had created for the oppressions of community. In August 2003, twenty-three Pakistani students were arrested in Toronto under the Anti-Terrorism Act on allegations of being "terrorists," held in maximum security for long periods without ever being formally charged, and then deported purely on grounds of commonplace immigration violations.[7] SALDA joined other community organizations in the formation of Project Threadbare, a campaign for the release, exoneration, and compensation of the detainees. Despite the extraordinary efforts of some of the campaign activists to have the men released on bail, most of them were finally deported to Pakistan without exoneration or compensation.

The above two involvements reflected members' attempts to bring to bear their transnational experience on events in Canada. The next two saw members taking this further, linking with other similarly located individuals and groups. In March 2003, SALDA mounted three workshops at the Toronto Social Forum, reflecting the range of interests of its members: Building Alternatives: Democratic Decentralization and Self-Sustaining Markets in Kerala, India; Showcasing South Asian Documentary Film Making; and, relevant to this account, with other Asian organizations, Sharing Asian Experiences of Globalization: Mobilizing Toward a Solidarity Network.[8] Out of the last came the founding of the Asian Solidarity Network, Toronto (ASNT), consisting of organizations from the South Asian, Filipino, and Korean communities in Toronto as well as of individuals from these and other Asian communities. The ASNT aimed to work on issues common to the Asian region – such as militarization and national security legislation in the wake of 9/11 and globalization and the rights of workers and communities – as well as to Asian communities in Canada – such as racial profiling, immigrant rights, healthcare, and access to social services.

Similarly, in January 2004, SALDA put on an event jointly with the Coalition for Aboriginal Sovereignty and the Toronto Social Forum. It highlighted the experiences of South Asian immigrants in Canada, such as the Pakistani men held under Project Thread; indigenous communities affected by Canadian capital, such as those in Kashipur, India, facing displacement by an ALCAN[9] mine; and indigenous communities in Canada, with their centuries-long history of displacement and oppression by the forces of capital, empire, and the modern Canadian state. Entitled Strangers at Home, the event combined film, spoken word, drama, and music. The packed and diverse audience that it drew, on what was possibly the coldest night of a very cold winter, indicated that the "estrangement" it spoke of resonated with many sectors of Canadian society. The event was mounted again by SALDA, in a more bare-bones form, as a workshop at the World Social Forum later the same month in Mumbai, India.

Activities informed by the first type of concern – the immigrant's concern with events back home and a desire to influence them – also continued, such as the panel discussion on Pakistan, India, and the Prospects for Peace held in August 2003.[10] Panelists Tapan Bose of the Pakistan-India People's Forum for Peace and Democracy, Teesta Seetalvad of the Mumbai-based Communalism Combat, Tarek Fatah of the Muslim Canadian Congress, and Toronto-based Kashmiri activist Hamid Bashani of the Advocacy Council discussed the implications of religious fundamentalism, militarization, Indian and Pakistani interests in Kashmir, the geopolitics of America's War on Terror, and the people's movement for secularism, democracy, and self-determination, and for peace and development in the region. Most sustained, in this context, has been the ongoing concern with Hindu nationalism.

## Religious Nationalism

Because it has been an ongoing focus for SALDA since its inception, it is important to highlight the group's concern with combating the rise of support for *Hindutva* ("Hindu nationalism") in India and in Canada.[11] SALDA has organized a variety of events to bring attention to this issue, including screenings of films such as Anand Patwardhan's *In the Name of God*, Suma Josson's *Gujarat: Laboratory of Hindu Rashtra Fascism*, M.S. Sathyu's *Garam Hawa*, and Aparna Sen's somewhat more controversial *Mr and Mrs Iyer*.[12] The organization held a vigil and public meetings to condemn the pogrom against the Muslims in Gujarat in 2002 and is currently working with the Forum of Indian Leftists (FOIL) on identifying Canadian-based sources of funding for the *Hindutva* movement.

It was in relation to the fight against *Hindutva* that SALDA had perhaps its most successful experience of organizing transnationally. This was its media intervention in 2000 against the attempt to censor the Toronto exhibition Dust on the Road. Mounted by the Canadian Hoopoe Curatorial, the exhibition contained works by Indian and Canadian artists in support of secularism and human rights. A significant participant was Safdar Hashmi Memorial Trust (SAHMAT), an Indian artists' organization well known for its work in opposing the Hindu nationalist agenda. The exhibition had received some funding from the Shastri Indo-Canadian Institute, a bilateral organization. The Indian high commissioner, upon visiting the exhibition and becoming aware of the nature of the work, thought that it was contrary to the agenda of his political bosses in the Hindu nationalist BJP and put pressure on the Shastri Institute to withdraw its funding. SALDA worked with Hoopoe Curatorial to launch a media campaign that drew significant attention from mainstream and ethnospecific print and broadcast media in Canada. This coverage, assisted by publicity through networks outside Canada, such as FOIL in the United States, South Asia Citizens' Web (SACW) based in France, and SAHMAT in India, led to media scrutiny in India, where several MPs then signed a petition raising it as a question in parliament. Although the funding was not restored, the public outcry ensured that the Indian government could not further its agenda without challenge and was forced to answer for it publicly.

### Challenges in Transnational Organizing

SALDA's experiences suggest that transnationality has allowed not so much for new forms of organizing as for new alliances and new arenas of action, with the "interests" of its transnational members becoming ever more widely defined. While the forms of organizing may not be entirely novel, the spheres that the group has entered have taken it beyond its original conception – that SALDA would focus on issues specific to South Asia, such as religious nationalism, regional and ethnic conflict, militarization and democratization, and as they affected the diaspora in Canada – to form alliances with other Asians, other immigrants, other Muslims, and others on the "left." But for every success that transnationality has made possible, there are other challenges that it has posed. Working in this transnational arena, there is no "natural" community but one that has constantly to be constructed in a number of ways.

First, SALDA's constituents are transnational in more ways than one. That is, they do not straddle just Canada and South Asia but also trace their origins to different countries in South Asia. For new immigrants, "South Asian" is an identity that meant little while they were in South Asia, and it has been argued that even here the term has little resonance for them, unlike "Indian," "Pakistani," "Bangladeshi," or even "Hindu"/"Muslim," to which they instinctively and viscerally respond. This is usually not a problem for organizations that provide necessary and valuable services applicable to all, such as those to do with immigration, settlement, or domestic violence.[13] But SALDA frequently focuses on issues that explicitly have to do with conflicts within and among South Asian nations, such as Hindu or Muslim chauvinism and discrimination against other religions, the India-Pakistan conflict, or Kashmir's right to self-determination. The divisive nature of such issues means that there is greater potential for breakdown of this tenuous new identity. Furthermore, the reality of its membership – almost entirely Indian and Pakistani, with the former numerically dominant within the context of Indian hegemony in the South Asian region – has led to charges of an implicit Indocentrism in its focus and positions, efforts to overcome which have had at best mixed success. This numerical dominance is perhaps inevitable given the relative size of the various countries of origin as well as the fact that in the 1990s Indians made up the largest number of Asian immigrants to Toronto after the Chinese, followed by people from the Philippines, Hong Kong, Sri Lanka, Pakistan, and Taiwan (Statistics Canada 2001). However, this fact does not explain the near absence of Sri Lankans and Bangladeshis in the group or eliminate the need for a more self-consciously inclusive politics.

Second, fracturing within the "community" has to do with distinctions of class and occupation. South Asians in Toronto occupy a range of occupational and class positions, depending in part on the period of their immigration. Among others, there are the Mississauga-based professionals who arrived in the 1960s, the settled working-class communities of Malton and Brampton, and the more recent refugee communities of St. James Town, a high-density, low-income apartment complex in downtown Toronto. In contrast, there is greater homogeneity among SALDA members, most of whom are drawn from academia or from social services. SALDA is not based in any particular residential community and has virtually no members from among the large and growing working-class South Asian immigrant populations.[14] The fact that all its activities are carried out only in English can be a further barrier for many new immigrants, creating a necessary unity between South Asia's linguistic diversities but opening up yet another division.

Third, there is a generational divide. As mentioned above, the need and desire to work with youth comprised a focus from the outset. An early organizational debate about the lack of resonance of the word *left* for those still children at the time of the collapse of the Berlin Wall, or their association of it solely with the authoritarian and statist variants described in their history texts, led to the addition of the word *democratic* to SALDA's name. But neither this addition nor a youth activist camp held in 2000 was enough to attract significant numbers of youth to the group.[15] Some of this failure may have to do with the original conception that those who had grown up in South Asia had an obligation to the youth raised here to tell them the truth about their history/culture – that there was no one "culture," monolithic, illiberal, that it was instead plurivocal and diverse, that it had been contested in the past and would be contested again. This obligation to impart the "truth," however, then itself set up the hierarchy of experience over innocence that is one of the "traditional" hierarchies of South Asian culture. But there are also cultural differences: generational differences in the culture of doing politics that are also common to the mainstream left, differences between those who learned their political tactics in the South Asian milieu and those for whom the milieu has always been Canadian, and differences in the issues that generate passion.

A further divide has to do with the fact that the differences in political culture within the South Asian diasporas are not only generational. Although few, if any, of SALDA's members come from the organized party left in South Asia, they come from a context in which this left has (India) or has had (Pakistan, Sri Lanka) a powerful and influential presence. Their acknowledgment of this history in their self-conscious identification as "left" isolates them from much of the larger South Asian community in Canada. For South Asian immigrants, as for other immigrants in Canada, left politics hold little attraction, persuaded as they are that official multiculturalism and the welfare state guarantee both personal and community security and advancement. In the federal election of 2004, for instance, more South Asians stood as candidates of the right-wing Conservative Party than of the social democratic New Democratic Party, with the Liberal Party remaining the party of choice for immigrants.[16] The events following 11 September 2001 – national security legislation, racial profiling, and the personal hostility experienced by many members of the South Asian, largely Muslim but also Sikh, communities – have challenged this complacency somewhat, as the initial broad-based support for Project Threadbare showed. But this has yet to translate into sustained involvement in organizing or into marked shifts in party preferences.

Finally, if forging a community of identity has not been easy, it has been no easier to forge one of opinions/values. If it is true that older and younger South Asians differ in their political schooling, and in what excites their passion, it is equally true of the immigrant left and the "mainstream" left. The Canadian left itself is complicated, fragmented along lines of ideology, political tradition, and identity. A case in point might be Rebuilding the Left, an initiative to create a "structured movement of the left" that brought together a number of organizations from Toronto and across the country and in which SALDA was involved. The fact that, despite a founding conference in October 2000 that attracted more than 700 people, by 2002 the initiative had collapsed is indicative of the fault lines mentioned above.[17] Negotiating its way through these fault lines, while trying to find a secure foothold within the community with which it has a political affinity, thus remains a challenge. The Asian Solidarity Network may be seen as a response to some of these difficulties, a way of forging a broader unity based on regional commonalities "back home" and shared immigrant positions in Canada.

The difficulties of constructing an enduring community contribute to SALDA's marginality, as do its organizational limitations: its lack of funding from the Canadian state, within whose easy multicultural calculus it does not quite fit; its voluntary activist character, so that members receive no remuneration or material benefits for their efforts; and its collective structure, which means that there are no formal hierarchies, not even elected ones – so that it teeters between an implicit hierarchy based on years in the organization, on the one hand, and a free-for-all whereby new members have often taken it off track, or initiated projects that they have not stayed to complete, on the other. Yet SALDA members continue to value this loose collective structure, arguing that it is the best way of facilitating the involvement of new members, of harnessing the talents and equal participation of all members, and of remaining open and accountable.

Despite these challenges, SALDA continues to grow, for the transnational ambit of members' concerns ensures that there is no shortage of issues. And it continues to enter new local arenas, such as the annual Gay Pride Parade, in which it marched for the first time in 2004.

**Notes**

1   Countries of South Asia include Afghanistan, Bangladesh, Bhutan, India, Maldives, Nepal, Pakistan, and Sri Lanka.
2   For the full text, see http://www.salda.org.
3   For more about the institute, see http://www.muslim-canada.org.
4   For more details, refer to http://www.salda.org/ShariaLetter.html.
5   For a report of the discussion, see "SALDA Roundtable on Faith-Based Arbitration in Ontario," *Relay* 10 (2006): 38-44, available at http://www.socialistproject.ca/relay/relay10.pdf.
6   The Anti-Terrorism Act, Bill C-36, is an omnibus bill that was passed after 9/11 that, along with other laws, such as Bills C-22, C-35, and C-42, gives the government "virtually unreviewable" power to label organizations and individuals as terrorists. This legislation, deemed to be in the interests of national security, has greatly increased the incidence of racial profiling and surveillance of specific communities.
7   See http://www.threadbare.tyo.ca.
8   For more about these workshops, and the Toronto Social Forum, refer to http://www.ryerson.ca/tsf/.
9   ALCAN is a Canadian aluminum multinational. The struggle of the Kashipur villagers is documented in Angad Bhalla's film *UAIL Go Back*. For more about this struggle, see http://www.alcantinindia.org/.
10  For a full report of the meeting, see http://www.salda.org/PeaceInitiativePanel.html.
11  See Bose in this volume for the connection between *Hindutva* and diasporic political and financial support.
12  For an indication of some elements of the controversy, see Sathyamala (2004).
13  Examples are the South Asian Women's Group (SAWG), South Asian Family Support Services (SAFSS), Alliance for South Asian Aids Prevention (ASAAP), South Asian Legal Clinic of Ontario (SALCO), and Coalition of Agencies Serving South Asians (CASSA).
14  Recent studies show that 34.6 percent of South Asian families in Toronto live below the Statistics Canada Low Income Cut-off. See http://www.salc.net/.
15  A similar youth camp, called Youth Solidarity Summer, has been run for the past several years in the United States with generally good success.
16  Immigrants credit the Liberal Party under Trudeau with introducing more liberal immigration policies and official multiculturalism and believe that the Liberals continue to be the best guardians of both sets of policies. The Liberals have also been skilled at cultivating ethnic "vote banks" by selecting candidates from the dominant ethnic group in a constituency.
17  For reports from the conference, see *Canadian Dimension* 35, 1 (2001). Authors included in that issue are Bannerji (2001) and Rosenfeld and Gianola (2001). For the origins of the idea of a "structured movement of the left," see Gindin (1998).

# 14

# Transnationalism and Political Participation among Filipinos in Canada

*Philip F. Kelly*

When Jean Chrétien was facing increasing pressure to resign as Liberal Party leader and prime minister of Canada in the summer of 2002, he made two appearances in British Columbia that were widely interpreted as attempts to consolidate support from specific communities for his continued leadership. The first appearance featured the declaration of a Sikh temple in Abbotsford as a National Heritage Site; the second was the dedication ceremony for the new millennium gate in Vancouver's Chinatown. His strategists had chosen their photo opportunities carefully. The Chinese and South Asian communities are Canada's largest designated "visible minorities." Both groups represent important sources of electoral votes in urban areas and, more importantly in this instance, were traditionally supporters and members of Liberal Party riding associations (and increasingly backing Paul Martin's challenge to Chrétien's leadership).

Had the Prime Minister's Office pursued this strategy further, it might have noted that, after China and India, the third largest stream of immigrants to Canada in the 1990s was from the Philippines. By 2001, Filipinos represented 7.7 percent of all self-declared visible minorities and the fourth largest group (after those whom Statistics Canada categorizes as "Chinese," "South Asian," and "Black"). Yet there were no Filipino events or visits on the prime minister's agenda. Perhaps the presence of Canada's only Filipino MP (Rey Pagtakhan, from Winnipeg) in his cabinet was acknowledgment enough. Perhaps Chrétien would in any case have targeted other more populous groups – ethnic Russians and Poles, for example, represent larger constituencies than Filipinos. But the omission was arguably indicative of a larger phenomenon in relation to the Filipino community – its relative invisibility on the Canadian political scene in terms of elected officials or candidates for any party. Using both statistical sources and interviews with community leaders in Toronto, this chapter explores that absence, seeks reasons for it, and notes exceptions to it. In particular, I suggest that various forms of transnational linkage are significant elements in an explanation of limited political engagement. This is not to suggest that continued engagement with social and political life in the Philippines necessarily limits engagement with Canadian society (as if a "zero sum game" were at play) but that the nature of transnational connections and obligations among Filipino immigrants tends in various ways to limit the potential for collective political engagement in Canadian politics.

To seek a Filipino imprint on the Canadian political scene in the form of elected officials is, however, to adopt a rather narrow definition of political activism and integration. In this chapter, I suggest that, if a broader conception of activism is used, there is some evidence of a vibrant, and growing, political engagement among the Filipino community. Over the past three decades, this engagement has included opposition to martial law in the Philippines in the 1970s and 1980s and attempts to change the circumstances of Filipina domestic workers in Canada in the 1980s and 1990s. These issues have not, however, necessarily united the community as a cohesive force. Thus, in this chapter, I remain attentive to the multiplicity of voices within a "Filipino community" that is often assumed, from the outside, to be coherent and unified. Just as the category "immigrant" can cover a multiplicity of diverse and contradictory identities, so too can the more specific label "Filipino."

The transnational linkages significant in this account take several forms. First, continued engagement with political processes in the Philippines has, in the past, led to divisions within the Filipino community in Canada that have precluded a united front in addressing issues of concern to the group as a whole. Second, social networks in Canada, together constituting what we might call Filipino-Canadian associational life, have a strong transnational component as they tend to be based upon commonalities of origin rather than common goals among groups of Filipinos in Canada. This too has resulted, until recently, in a limited engagement with Canadian policy issues that affect Filipinos. Third, ongoing transnational financial commitments to family members back in the Philippines have meant that the imperative for many Filipino immigrants has been to find "survival" jobs rather than employment that is appropriate to their qualifications. This imperative, along with an array of institutional barriers, has kept many professionally qualified Filipinos in marginal socioeconomic positions and with neither the time nor the resources to be politically engaged. Fourth, a network of transnational labour market institutions, such as recruiters, consultants, and training centres, collectively channel many Filipino immigrants into marginal jobs in the Canadian economy. Fifth, and finally, the larger transnational context of immigration, in what Yen Le Espiritu (2003) calls a global racial order, points to the ways in which Filipinos are racialized in Canadian society. While not a "strand" of transnational linkage in the sense implied by Linda Basch, Nina Glick Schiller, and Cristina Szanton Blanc (1994) in their classic formulation of the phenomenon, this larger conception provides an important component of the transnational "field" in which immigrant experiences are constituted.

The empirical focus here is primarily on Toronto and its region – the largest site of Filipino settlement in the country and home to 133,680 individuals who declared their ethnic origin (or part of it) to be "Filipino" (more than twice the size of the next largest community in Vancouver). The chapter is structured in the following way. In the first section, a profile of Filipino settlement in Canada demonstrates the social and economic marginalization of large segments of the Filipino community and suggests that transnational connections and a broader context of racialization must be seen as playing a part in this situation. The second section then examines Filipino involvement in the formal Canadian political process, seeking reasons for the community's low representation in the country's parliament, legislatures, and city halls. Socioeconomic marginality has played a part in this, but so have various political divisions transplanted from the Philippines and the transnational nature of Filipino associational life. The third section explores two issues that Filipino activism has vigorously addressed, as noted above: the anti–martial law campaigns in the 1970s and 1980s, and changes to various domestic worker programs since the 1980s. The chapter concludes by arguing for a more inclusive interpretation of "political integration" and by drawing connections between transnationalism and the possibilities for political engagement in Canada.

### Filipino Migration to Canada

Canada's Immigration Act of 1967 allowed nonwhite applicants an equal chance of admission for the first time. Before that watershed, the number of Filipino settlers in Canada was very small indeed. The flow of immigrants from the Philippines remained relatively small until the early 1970s. The declaration of martial law in September 1972, however, was a defining moment that led many middle- and upper-class Filipinos to reevaluate their futures in their homeland. Even those not specifically targeted as political enemies or challengers by President Ferdinand Marcos saw a suspension of political freedoms and a deterioration of economic prospects. At the same time, the Marcos regime was actively promoting overseas contract work as an economic development strategy. While such contracts took workers primarily to the booming oil economies of the Middle East, and later to the industrializing "tigers" of East Asia, many also sought permanent settlement in North America.

Table 14.1 shows the period of arrival for Filipino immigrants resident in Canada in 2001. Less than 5 percent of the population arrived prior to 1970,

*Table 14.1*

**Time of arrival for Filipinos in Canada, 2001**

| Period of immigration | Filipino immigrants | % of total Filipino immigrants |
| --- | --- | --- |
| Before 1961 | 215 | 0.1 |
| 1961-70 | 9,080 | 4.1 |
| 1971-80 | 42,875 | 19.2 |
| 1981-90 | 52,515 | 23.5 |
| 1991-95 | 63,640 | 28.5 |
| 1996-2001 | 54,715 | 24.5 |
| Total | 223,035 | 100.0 |

*Source:* Statistics Canada, 2001 Census, Metropolis Project Core Data Set Tabulations. These data refer to the arrival dates of immigrants who declared themselves to be Filipino in response to the visible minority question in the 2001 census.

more than three-quarters have arrived since 1980, and in 2001 over half of all Filipinos in Canada had arrived in just the previous ten years. It is important to note, then, that Canada's Filipino community is predominantly composed of recent immigrants – a feature that distinguishes it from the Filipino population in the United States, where a century of colonial and postcolonial ties has facilitated several waves of immigration from the Philippines.

A further distinctive feature of the migration stream from the Philippines has been the importance of special immigration categories for domestic workers – first under the Foreign Domestic Movement and then, from 1992, under the Live-In Caregiver Program (for details, see Bakan and Stasiulis 1997; England and Stiell 1997; Pratt 2004). Under the caregiver program, visas are issued to those who will work and live in the homes of their employers – usually caring for the elderly or for young children. After two years in the program, participants can apply for immigrant status. Women have comprised the overwhelming majority of participants in this program (and Filipina women have dominated the program since the mid-1990s). The result overall has been a gendered migration stream, with women comprising almost 60 percent of immigrants from the Philippines in the period 1980-2001 (CIC 2002b).

A related characteristic of Canada's Filipino population is its concentration in relatively few labour market niches (see Hiebert 1999). Clerical work, healthcare, hospitality, retail, and manufacturing in particular are prime destinations for working Filipinos, and within these sectors there is a tendency toward segmentation into lower status occupations. A numerical way of representing this phenomenon using the 2001 census is to calculate the ratio between the percentage of Filipinos in a job category and the percentage of the population as a whole in a job category. In healthcare, for example, Filipino men and women are respectively 5.3 and 3.3 times more

*Table 14.2*

**Mean earnings (CDN$) of Filipinos and others in Toronto CMA, 2000**

|  | Male income | Female income |
| --- | --- | --- |
| Filipino immigrant population | 39,295 | 31,846 |
| Entire immigrant population | 58,789 | 40,984 |
| All visible minority immigrants | 43,162 | 33,273 |
| All visible minority nonimmigrants | 46,746 | 39,088 |
| All immigrants | 50,748 | 36,198 |
| All nonimmigrants | 66,133 | 45,395 |

*Source:* Derived from Statistics Canada, 2001 Census, Metropolis Project Core Data Set Tabulations. These figures refer to average employment incomes in Canadian dollars from full-year, full-time employment in 2000 for the Toronto Census Metropolitan Area (CMA).

likely to be working in "assisting occupations" than the population as a whole. But in occupations such as physician, dentist, or surgeon, Filipinos are greatly underrepresented – using a similar calculation, there are about one-quarter as many Filipino men and about one-half as many Filipina women as there "should be" in such occupational categories.

This concentration in relatively low-paying service sector employment is reflected in statistics on the incomes of Filipino immigrants. As Table 14.2 shows, while women earn consistently less than men across all groups, Filipino men and women earn well below average earnings whether they are compared with other visible minority immigrants or with the population as a whole.

If Filipino immigrants were arriving with relatively low levels of education and professional experience, then this occupational segmentation and the low average earnings might be expected. But in fact a Filipino immigrant is far more likely to have a university education than a Canadian-born citizen. Almost 57 percent of Filipino immigrants residing in Toronto in 2001 had some university-level education. This number compares with 33 percent for all immigrant groups and just under 35 percent for all residents of Canada. To this must be added the fact that Filipinos are coming from a context in which English is widely spoken, as the lingua franca of government, the media, and the educational system, and a context in which institutions are primarily based on American models. There is, therefore, a great deal of linguistic, institutional, and cultural familiarity with a North American way of life. Yet this familiarity appears to have been rewarded with a very marginal socioeconomic status upon arrival in Canada.

A final feature of Filipino settlement is worth noting. As a group, Filipinos are unusually widely dispersed in terms of their residential settlement. In the Toronto Census Metropolitan Area, for example, nearly half (45 percent) of all Census Dissemination Areas (which comprise small neighbourhoods of 400-700 inhabitants) record a Filipino population. This confirms earlier analyses of 1996 census data showing that in both Toronto and Vancouver Filipinos exhibit among the lowest levels of statistical segregation of any visible minority group (Bauder and Sharpe 2002).

There are, then, a number of features of Filipino settlement in Canada that are, in a sense, anomalous. An unusually well-educated and culturally prepared population that has integrated well with other communities in workplaces and neighbourhoods across the urban landscape nevertheless finds itself in a marginalized social and economic position.

The reasons for Filipino socioeconomic marginalization are complex and are in the first instance related to the institutional barriers to highly qualified Filipino immigrants practising in regulated professions. While immigrants are admitted by the federal government on the basis of their professional qualifications, experience, and cultural preparedness, professional labour markets are regulated at the provincial level by largely autonomous bodies (e.g., the Professional Engineers of Ontario, the College of Nurses of Ontario) that assess foreign qualifications and prescribe the upgrading or retraining that immigrants must undergo to become certified. These barriers to entry frequently mean that mechanical engineers find themselves working as production line operators, accountants as billing clerks, and registered nurses as clinical aides or nannies. But transnational processes are also a key component in understanding this process of deprofessionalization.

First, various transnational institutions have channelled Filipino immigrants into particular segments of the Canadian labour force. A web of recruitment agencies, immigration consultancies, and training centres exists in both Toronto and the Philippines, shaping the characteristics of Filipino immigrants to Canada and directing them to particular niches in the labour market. Privately owned caregiver training institutes and nursing colleges, for example, have proliferated in the past five to ten years in Manila. This transnationalized network of institutions trains and delivers a stream of Filipino workers, inserting them into the lower rungs of Canada's urban labour market.

Second, after arriving in Canada, immigrants have ongoing transnational financial commitments to their family members or to those from whom money was borrowed to fund their immigration application. These obligations (along with the costs of living in major cities such as Toronto) create an immediate need to find "survival jobs" rather than professionally appropriate jobs. In many cases, taking courses to upgrade Philippine qualifications to a level acceptable to Canadian regulatory agencies is simply impossible.

Third, there is an element of transnationalism that relates less explicitly to the linkages between "home" and "host" areas but more broadly to the ways in which the Philippines and Filipinos are represented and racialized in Canadian society at large. In other words, we need to remain mindful of the context of transnational relationships between societies, as these relationships go beyond the transnational ties maintained by individuals. Racialization refers to the process in which a group is socially constructed as racially distinct and is attributed certain characteristics in the process. This idea has been carefully explored by several researchers who examined the Live-In Caregiver Program (England and Stiell 1997; Stiell and England 1997; Pratt 2004). Examples are numerous, cumulative, sometimes subtle, and invariably rooted in the colonial past. To illustrate the process, one need look no further than a short article that appeared in the *Globe and Mail* on 19 February 2004. The article, innocuous if not read thoughtfully, concerned an application by Philippine broadcaster ABS-CBN to launch a twenty-four-hour cable TV channel in Canada. In just a few column inches, it encapsulated many assumptions frequently made about Canada's Filipino community. Its first line read "Call it Nanny-TV," which in itself drew the ire of numerous online chat room contributors and a letter published in the paper the following day, all pointing out the conflation of Filipino-ness with domestic work. The article went on to point out that "Canada's large Filipino community, which includes many women who work in domestic jobs, makes it an attractive target audience for a network that is heavy on local news and lighter fare such as variety-style musical shows, celebrity watching and a fantasy series centred on the love life of a mermaid" (A5).

The overall impression left by the article was that most Filipinos in Canada are intellectually wanting, socially nonintegrated, and nannies doing menial housework (in fact only 6.8 percent of immigrant Filipinos in the Canadian labour force were employed in such work in 2001). The article was not, of course, a major piece of journalism, but it did provide a window on the easy thoughtlessness through which racialization can occur (even, or perhaps especially, in the newspaper of the nation's liberal establishment). Such a process of racialization must be factored into any analysis of the limited labour market options that Filipinos find themselves with and must ultimately be related back to the historically rooted relationship between white colonial societies and the colonized and racialized "other." This relationship colours the experiences of Filipinos in Canadian society and even more so in the United States (Espiritu 2003).

## Invited to the Party? Filipino Involvement in Canadian Electoral Politics

Having established the social and economic marginalization of Filipinos in Canada, and some of the transnational contexts in which it occurs, I turn now to examine the participation of Filipino immigrants in formal political processes. A number of studies have examined the participation of immigrants and visible minorities in the Canadian electoral process, but none has provided any specific data on the Filipino community (Black 1982, 1991, 2001). It is therefore difficult to assess the extent to which Filipino immigrants are actually enfranchised in the process. We do know, however, that, of 302,195 people who declared their visible minority status as Filipino in the 2001 census, 244,380 held Canadian citizenship and could therefore exercise voting rights (if over eighteen years of age).

Whatever the electoral turnout among Filipino-Canadians, with a few exceptions it has not translated into a large number of successful electoral campaigns by Filipino candidates. In Vancouver, with Canada's second largest Filipino community, there have been no electoral successes recorded. In Toronto, community leader Mel Catre sought a Liberal nomination for the federal Liberal Party in 1988 but was narrowly defeated by Yasmin Ratansi, who ultimately succeeded David Collenette in the Don Valley East riding for the party in 2004. Gene Lara stood in Toronto Centre Rosedale (a riding that includes St. James Town, which has a significant concentration of Filipino immigrants) for the New Democratic Party (NDP) in the provincial election of 2003 but was defeated by a non-Filipino Liberal candidate. For electoral success stories in Ontario, one must turn to municipal councils. Alex Chiu is a long-standing Filipino-Chinese councillor in Markham, north of Toronto, and Arturo Viola has served as lord mayor of Niagara-on-the-Lake (Cusipag and Buenafe [1993] provide further details on other, less successful, campaigns). It is worth noting, however, that some non-Filipino candidates have developed close ties with the Filipino community. Examples include Tony Ruprecht, Liberal member of the Ontario provincial legislature for Toronto-Parkdale, and Raymond Cho on the Toronto City Council. Others, such as Bill Graham, representing Toronto Centre for the federal Liberals, are less closely identified with the Filipino community but nevertheless have Filipinos working in their riding associations to garner support among the local community.

Winnipeg stands out as the sole location in which a Filipino community vote appears to have been decisive in successful electoral campaigns. In addition to two Filipino members of the Legislative Assembly (MLAs) and one city councillor, Rey Pagtakhan was a Liberal member of the federal Parliament for Winnipeg North from 1988 to 2004, including stints in various ministerial portfolios.

Notwithstanding the exception of Winnipeg, a number of reasons might be identified for low levels of Filipino representation in political office. The first factor is residential dispersal, which means that, while Filipinos are numerous across the urban regions of Toronto and Vancouver, they are not a sufficiently significant presence in any particular riding to make a decisive difference. This point is illustrated in Table 14.3, which lists all electoral

*Table 14.3*

**Filipino presence in selected Canadian electoral ridings, 2001**

| Riding | Total riding | Filipino population | Percentage |
|---|---|---|---|
| Winnipeg North, MB | 79,415 | 14,070 | 17.7 |
| Winnipeg Centre, MB | 80,930 | 10,290 | 12.7 |
| Vancouver Kingsway, BC | 115,325 | 8,325 | 7.2 |
| Scarborough Rouge River, ON | 115,430 | 7,780 | 6.7 |
| Mississauga East–Cooksville, ON | 122,565 | 7,385 | 6.0 |
| Scarborough Centre, ON | 102,810 | 7,020 | 6.8 |
| Montreal–Mount Royal, QC | 98,340 | 6,750 | 6.9 |
| Scarborough Southwest, ON | 105,435 | 6,195 | 5.9 |
| Vancouver South, BC | 113,065 | 6,115 | 5.4 |
| York Centre, ON | 113,195 | 6,100 | 5.4 |
| Mississauga–Brampton South, ON | 113,825 | 6,055 | 5.3 |
| Toronto Centre, ON | 114,680 | 5,850 | 5.1 |

*Source:* Statistics Canada, Profile of Federal Ridings, www.statscan.ca. The Filipino population is drawn from the visible minority responses in the 2001 census. Riding boundaries reflect 2003 revisions.

ridings in Canada with Filipino populations over 5 percent of the total population.

Even most ridings incorporating known "Filipino" neighbourhoods (e.g., Toronto Centre, Vancouver Kingsway, and Mount Royal in Montreal) register only a 5-7 percent Filipino population. Winnipeg, however, is different. High levels of residential concentration in certain neighbourhoods (and, it should be noted, much smaller ridings) mean that the "Filipino vote" makes a big difference. The ridings of Winnipeg North and Winnipeg Centre were home to 80 percent of Manitoba's 30,490 Filipinos in 2001. They had Filipino communities accounting for 17.7 and 12.7 percent, respectively, of their total populations. This higher residential concentration, combined with the higher turnout among the community when a Filipino is standing for office, explains in part Pagtakhan's successes over several elections. When Pagtakhan was finally defeated by the NDP's Judy Wasylycia-Leis in 2004, both had campaigned vigorously at Filipino community events, and Wasylycia-Leis even attempted to learn some Tagalog.

There are, however, other factors that community leaders identify in explaining the dearth of Filipino electoral candidates. Perhaps most obvious is the relatively recent establishment of the Filipino community. Research on voting patterns among immigrants has shown that length of residence is strongly correlated with propensity to vote – it might therefore be expected that the number of Filipino votes and candidates will increase in future elections as recently arrived Filipinos develop a sense of ownership in Canadian social institutions. However, the socially and economically marginal position of Filipino immigrants noted earlier could imply that this will develop over a longer time span than one might hope. A Filipino activist noted the connection between social marginalization and a lack of political representation:

> I feel that culturally, in terms of projection of our culture, we are very successful. There are so many cultural groups; they love to create cultural groups that would provide music or dances or cultural events ... They love to get together because they want to relax ... Maybe it's not fair for me to say this, but it is an escapist attitude about the whole situation because it's really difficult to transfer or to move from where you came from to here. And you work yourself to death, and then what do they do? You don't want to talk about politics or focus on analyzing your situation. (Interview, Community Organizer 1, Toronto, August 2004).

A further barrier, noted by some community leaders, to the emergence of candidates specifically from, and for, the Filipino community is the relative absence of wealthy individuals – entrepreneurs in particular – from whom to draw funding. The Filipino community is distinctive in its paucity of individuals earning a livelihood from self-employment in entrepreneurial activities (in Toronto in 2001, only 3.2 percent of Filipino immigrants were self-employed, compared, for example, with 13.5 percent of Chinese immigrants and 36 percent of Korean immigrants). This feature of Filipino economic integration, some argue, results in a lack of wealthy donors to support and sustain political candidacies.

Perhaps the most telling factor in limiting candidacies from the Filipino "community," however, is the absence of a coherent and unified community upon which to base an electoral campaign. While Filipino associational life is vibrant (upwards of 250 organizations are registered with the Philippine consulate in Toronto alone), so are the divisions, tensions, and rivalries within and between community groups. These may be based on competition for members or funds, or on personality conflicts between rival leaders, but they may also be rooted in political or identity differences transplanted from the Philippines.

The Philippine political landscape is a complex amalgam of ideological, class, dialect, religious, and regional differences, and many of them resurface as divisions within Filipino communities in Canada. These divisions make it difficult to establish a spokesperson for "the community" and thus a united political voice: "The Filipinos are basically [following] Filipino mentality, never united, never united" (Interview, Community Organizer 2, Toronto, August 2004).

While divisions from the Philippines may persist in Canada, a further transnational context for limited political engagement is to be found in the nature of Filipino associational life. Relatively few organizations are concerned with the political or professional goals of Filipino-Canadians, while many more are social and cultural groups founded upon connections of common towns or provinces of origin in the Philippines, university alumni associations, or religious groups transplanted from the Philippines (e.g., the Christian congregation known as El Shaddai). While associations for Filipino nurses, accountants, lawyers, realtors, and so on, and advocacy groups for caregivers (e.g., Intercede and the Philippine Women's Centre of Ontario) do exist, their numbers of active members are much smaller. Rather, the basis for associational life is largely the transposition of loyalties from the Philippines into a Canadian context. This lack of a unified institutional basis for political advocacy inevitably plays a role in limiting collective Filipino engagement in Canadian electoral processes.

While there may be reasons for Filipino candidates failing to come forward, or failing to succeed when they do, there is also another side to the story, which relates to the failure of Canadian political parties to actively cultivate and promote Filipino candidates. Some leaders in the community articulated this idea and expressed some dissatisfaction that they were seen as useful purveyors of the "ethnic vote" at election time but were not taken as seriously when nominations were sought. One activist described his role in mobilizing Filipinos and other visible minority immigrants for the provincial Liberal Party in Ontario under Premier David Peterson: "Whenever he has ethnic problems, he calls me and says, 'come to the office right now, we got a problem, you solve it' ... [But] in times of organization and appointments, they do not look at the ethnic groups, only in times of elections. Admittedly, I think they just want to use us, that's our perception" (Interview, Community Organizer 2, Toronto, August 2004).

## Activism Beyond the Ballot

If representation in electoral campaigns is limited, it does not imply an entirely disengaged attitude toward politics among the Filipino community in Canada. Activism of a nonparliamentary kind has arisen around a number of issues, although not all of them have united the Filipino community, nor have they necessarily elicited widespread involvement beyond a core group of activists. This section will explore two issues of concern to Filipinos in Canada around which activism has emerged: the first concerns continued involvement in political processes and debates in the Philippines, and the second involves engagement with policy debates in Canada over domestic worker programs since the 1980s.

### Transnationalizing the Political: Philippine Politics in Canada

Until legislative changes in 2003, Filipinos overseas were not entitled to vote in Philippine elections. With the Philippine Overseas Absentee Voting

Law, Filipino citizens living overseas could register to record an absentee ballot. The process was primarily aimed at gathering the votes of overseas contract workers who retain their Philippine citizenship and ultimately return to the Philippines. For permanent immigrants in North America, the process is considerably more difficult as it involves applying in person at a Philippine consulate, together with a signed undertaking to return to live in the Philippines. Clearly, this is not the intention of most Filipinos in North America, so in 2003 only about 900 absentee voters registered at the Toronto consulate. Of those, about 350 actually recorded a vote with the consulate in the 2004 presidential and senatorial election. Worldwide, 89,688 absentee voters registered of an estimated 7.5 million Filipinos living overseas (Editorial, *Manila Times*, 8 September 2003).

A second law, passed in 2003, extended the potential number of overseas voters further. Under the Citizenship Retention and Reacquisition Act, all natural-born Filipinos who have lost their Philippine citizenship by becoming citizens of other countries could reacquire their citizenship. Those acquiring Canadian citizenship will also be permitted to retain Filipino citizenship and voting rights. But if the conditions for exercising an electoral franchise remain as they stand at present, it seems unlikely that even Filipinos overseas who retain or regain their citizenship will actually vote. Furthermore, the bases of political allegiance in the mainstream Philippine political scene tend to be personal rather than ideological. There is no long-established party system, and loyalties tend to shift from election to election. Ongoing loyalties of an ideological or institutional nature are thus difficult to sustain from afar.

This does not imply, however, that overseas Filipinos in Toronto or elsewhere are unaware of political events back home. Many follow developments closely through websites or community newspapers that carry syndicated columns from Manila's dailies. Cable TV providers in Toronto also supply Filipino news and entertainment on community channels. For most, however, political issues in the Philippines are followed with interest rather than active engagement. Only a small core of activists in Toronto (e.g., in the Philippine Solidarity Group, established in 1989) are engaged in exchanges with politically progressive organizations in the Philippines – occasionally raising money or sponsoring visiting speakers. Such groups focus on issues of human rights, political power, economic disparity, and neocolonialism in the Philippines. Issues specific to Canadian relations with the Philippines are a particular concern – for example, the social and environmental impacts of Canadian mining activities in the Philippines. But where such groups do interact with political movements in the Philippines, it is with progressive/leftist organizations rather than those in the mainstream of political power brokering.

The engagement of Filipinos in Canada with Philippine politics has not always, however, been so limited or muted. In the 1970s and 1980s, passions ran high concerning the dictatorial rule of Ferdinand Marcos, and the Filipino community in Canada was deeply divided between those for and those against the president. A minority maintained support for Marcos until the end. Dr. Francisco Portugal, for example, a president of the Ontario Council of Filipino-Canadian Associations, was quoted three years after Marcos' overthrow, suggesting that "there's a strong pro-Marcos sentiment even now, especially among the older folks ... He's being judged guilty without proof" (*Toronto Star,* 5 November 1989, A1).

Many others, however, were passionately opposed to the Marcos regime and directed their lobbying efforts at Philippine diplomatic offices in Canada (in particular the Toronto consulate, which opened in 1978) as well as the Canadian government and Canadian public opinion. The first and largest anti-Marcos group to coalesce in Toronto was the Canada Philippine Friendship Society, formed in 1975. The group included a number of dissidents from the Philippines, several of whom had spent time in jail for political opposition to the Marcos regime. The group metamorphosed over the course of a decade, becoming successively the Anti–Martial Law Alliance, the Coalition Against the Marcos Dictatorship, and finally the Campaign for Democracy and Independence in the Philippines (CAMDI). Tensions between the anti-Marcos activists and the Philippine consulate were frequent, and by the early 1980s rival events were being organized around the annual Philippine Independence Day celebrations in June.

After the assassination of opposition leader Benigno Aquino at the Manila airport in 1983, the depth of opposition to Marcos deepened in Toronto. A series of speakers from the Philippines kept activists informed of events back home, and new organizations emerged, such as the Ninoy Aquino Memorial Institute and the Movement for a Free Philippines. By the time of Marcos' final downfall in 1986, these groups had collaborated with the CAMDI in forming the Canadian Campaign for the United Opposition (Cusipag and Buenafe 1993). Much attention was paid to informing the Canadian public of human rights abuses in the Philippines and to supporting dissident movements at home. But pressure was also exerted on Canadian political institutions in order to undermine Marcos' legitimacy on the global stage. For example, when the Canadian National Exhibition proposed inviting First Lady Imelda Marcos to a Philippine exhibit in 1978, vigorous protests resulted in the cancellation of her appearance. When rumours circulated in 1980 that Prime Minister Pierre Trudeau had informally accepted an invitation to visit Manila, a campaign was waged to protest any such implicit endorsement of the Marcos regime. When Trudeau did finally visit in 1982, pressure from anti-Marcos movements in Canada ensured that human rights abuses were explicitly raised in his meeting with the president (Cusipag and Buenafe 1993).

A key feature of the anti-Marcos movement was the breadth of the coalition among Filipino-Canadians, encompassing a range of regional, linguistic, religious, and class differences. One Filipino-Canadian activist noted that "the anti-Marcos movement really ... brought about the formation of a broad front ... Even people in what you would call the upper crust of the Philippines community [were involved]" (Interview, Community Organizer 3, Toronto, August 2004). In addition, after the fall of Marcos, many who had been active in the opposition movement turned their attention to the experiences of Filipinos in Canada. Many of the same personalities would again emerge as community leaders involved in advocacy on "Canadian" issues. Fely Villasin, for example, was a national coordinator of the CAMDI and later a coordinator of Intercede (the Toronto Organization for Domestic Workers' Rights). Carmencita Hernandez, also active in the anti-Marcos movement, went on to play a key role in the Kababayan Community Centre in Parkdale, Toronto.

In summary, the animosity between pro- and anti-Marcos groups was a major divide within the community and must be considered one of the factors behind the lack of political coherence among Filipino immigrants in Canada, at least in the 1980s and 1990s. Personal resentments across that divide still exist among some prominent community leaders. But activism around Philippine political issues has also incubated community leaders prepared to advocate and lobby within the context of Canadian political institutions.

### The Rights of Domestic Workers

As noted earlier, a distinctive feature of Filipino immigration to Canada over the past two decades has been the importance of the Foreign Domestic Movement (1982-91) and then the Live-In Caregiver Program. From 1980 to 2001, 43,664 Philippine-born immigrants (out of a total of 223,457) arrived under the Live-In Caregiver Program and its predecessor or as the dependants of those entering under such schemes (though these figures must be placed alongside those noted above, which showed a much smaller proportion of Filipinos actually engaged in the childcare and homecare occupations in the 2001 census).

These programs have allowed domestic workers to enter Canada on work visas; provided they live in the homes of their employers for two years, they may then apply for permanent residency. The programs have been widely criticized for permitting many abuses of migrant workers' rights – to privacy, to adequate food and shelter, to financial compensation, to freedom of movement, and to legal due process.

Several organizations in Toronto have been active advocates for the rights of domestic workers – they include Intercede, the Migrante Women's Collective, and the Philippine Women's Centre of Ontario. Often this advocacy has involved supporting the rights of (or providing sanctuary to) individual domestic workers against exploitative or abusive employers or against immigration authorities. In several cases, these organizations have networked with advocacy organizations across the country to work on the cases of individual Filipina domestic workers. These collaborations resulted in notable successes for Leticia Cables and Melca Salvador, Filipina domestic workers in Edmonton and Montreal, respectively. Following energetic national campaigns, both were spared deportation after being accused of violating the stringent condition of the Live-In Caregiver Program (see Velasco 2002).

Occasionally, however, this work has extended into the legislative arena. When the Foreign Domestic Movement was being reviewed in the late 1980s and early 1990s (ultimately to be replaced by the Live-In Caregiver Program), the parliamentary standing committee considering the revisions heard deputations from Intercede and other organizations. While such advocacy failed to bring about significant revisions to the program (e.g., in the live-in and nonimmigrant status required of domestic workers), it did achieve some small successes – for example, a provision requiring six months of formal training in caregiving was revised to recognize one year of relevant work experience in lieu of such an onerous and expensive requirement. This was a small but key concession, and notably it represented solidarity not with those already in the program but with those back in the Philippines attempting to enter it.

Notable in all of these moments of activism, however, has been the absence of widespread support from the broader Filipino community. While the abuses of individuals have garnered press coverage in Filipino community newspapers, the work to change the caregiver program has been undertaken by a very small group of committed activists, often with support from academics and non-Filipino human rights and church-based groups. As one Filipina activist noted, "I would say we were quite successful in terms of informing the general public, but in terms of getting the reaction and support from the Filipino community, it's always nil" (Interview, Community Organizer 1, Toronto, August 2004).

Once again it is worth highlighting the largely transnational basis of Filipino associational life – based on hometown, home province, and alumni associations more than on common concerns in Canada. But broad disengagement from the issues concerning live-in caregivers also points to the class and other divisions that exist within the Filipino immigrant "community." The rights of live-in caregivers are frequently treated as a sectoral concern rather than a "Filipino" issue. Woven into this attitude is the complex ambivalence that many in the community feel toward their caregiver compatriots (see McKay 2002 on this issue in Vancouver). On the one hand, a sense of nationalism evokes feelings of solidarity and anger, but these feelings are all too often extinguished by a sense of shame at the "menial" work that many Filipinos are doing in Canada and resentment that all Filipinos should be tarred with the same brush. These sentiments are not unique to the Canadian context – Espiritu (2003), for example, provides a fascinating study of class distinctions within the Filipino community in San Diego, California, based on different times and circumstances of arrival.

## Conclusion

The instances of activism in the Filipino community described here highlight a number of points that are often neglected in discussions concerning the political integration of immigrants. First, such integration need not solely be in the form of electoral campaigns or votes. Although representation in the Canadian political establishment is an important indicator of integration, political activity is in fact played out in many spheres. While some forms of activism (e.g., concerning revisions to the Live-In Caregiver Program) may touch on the Canadian legislative process, many do not. This highlights the need to look beyond elections and party politics to find political involvement among immigrant groups.

Second, it is all too common to find references to the "Filipino community" and its "leaders" (and this chapter has been no exception). Such references can often imply a unity of purpose, a harmony of internal relations, and a commonality of priorities. As the anti–martial law case demonstrated, this unity is often illusory. Political loyalties brought from the Philippines continue to divide the immigrant population in Canada. Even issues limited to the Canadian political context do not find unanimity in the "community." The Live-In Caregiver Program is a case in point. For various reasons, the injustices confronted by Filipina domestic workers have not elicited widespread involvement among the broader Filipino population – issues of class and other axes of identity are always in play, and "Filipino-ness" is seldom a unifying characteristic. The transnational roots of Filipino associational life in Toronto (based on hometown, home province, and alumni networks) also undermine a collective political voice in Canada around issues of concern to Filipino-Canadians.

Third, transnational processes provide an important context for understanding the limited extent of Filipino political engagement in Canada. The social and economic marginalization of many Filipinos in Canada leads to marginalization from political processes, but socioeconomic marginalization and deprofessionalization are themselves in part the result of transnational financial obligations that prevent immigrants from undertaking the expensive process of upgrading and retraining to access their professions. Marginal positions in the labour market are also shaped by the transnational institutions of training and recruitment that channel Filipinos into certain jobs in Canada, even before they arrive. More broadly, the racialization of Filipinos, historically rooted in the colonial dominance of "white" societies, and still connected to the subordinate position of the Philippines in the global economy, continues to colour the process of political marginalization.

# 15
# Transnational Organizing in the Americas
*Rusa Jeremic*

As economic globalization – a globalization that is seen as coming from above – has evolved in the past two decades, a strong and vibrant globalization from below, a people's response, has emerged. Through Structural Adjustment Programs (SAPs) and free trade, the Washington Consensus model of deregulation, privatization of social services, currency devaluation, and other neoliberal measures are being implemented throughout the hemisphere by governments and multilateral institutions. As the gap between rich and poor widened, making the poor poorer and exposing the contradictions of this economic model through economic crisis and collapse, an even deeper form of liberalization for the Americas was announced in 1994 – the Free Trade Area of the Americas (FTAA) project. In response, people have moved beyond borders, linking their national problematic to others in the region to resist this hemispheric corporate project but also to work together on viable and just alternatives. This new mode of organizing transnationally across borders and sectors has played a critical role in the struggle against the neoliberal model of free trade, which forces people to abandon their homes and move beyond borders solely to ensure their own survival. This chapter explores how this hemispheric social movement emerged and what key factors have contributed to its success.

The proposed FTAA aimed to create a free-trade zone for capital, products, and services from Alaska to the southernmost tip of South America by 2005. In glaring contradiction, the FTAA would break down tariff barriers for goods and products and facilitate the expansion of multinational corporations through lax investment rules and national treatment laws, yet the notion of free movement of peoples across borders is not even a remote possibility. Indeed, the architect of the FTAA, the United States, has staunchly refused to undertake negotiations on migrants and migrant workers. At its very foundation, the FTAA is based on the free-trade integration model established by the North American Free Trade Agreement (NAFTA) implemented in 1994 between Canada, Mexico, and the United States. As such, it is much more than a commercial agreement and has the potential to have far-reaching negative consequences on national sovereignty, democracy, and respect for human rights. Moreover, the close monitoring of NAFTA by civil society demonstrates that in fact the free-trade model induces migration.

In response, citizens have joined together across sectors and borders to stop the FTAA. Moreover, the nature of NoFTAA organizing in the Americas has rapidly evolved and grown from a small critical group of concerned analysts representing civil society to a more inclusive social movement. And the large majority of those who identify themselves within the movement resisting the FTAA has always been clear in the conviction that it is not against trade per se. Rather, it is the nature of the free-trade integration model, based on the ideology of neoliberalism, that needs to be challenged and stopped.

## Setting the Stage: Northern Reasons for Resistance

In the late 1980s, a broad grouping of Canadian labour, environment, church, community, and cultural activists emerged in response to the announcement of plans for a Free Trade Agreement with the United States (CUFTA). It was a spontaneous upsurge that worked to protect Canadian sovereignty and culture under the banner of local municipal and provincial anti–free-trade coalitions. They later came together as the Pro-Canada Network (Foster 2005, 211). Shortly after the Mulroney government signed off on CUFTA, plans for a North American Free Trade Agreement involving Canada, the United States, and Mexico were announced. Again in Canada critical voices came together across sectors to resist NAFTA through a coalition called Common Frontiers.[1] It is a national coalition of labour, church, student, and international development NGOs, and other social organizations. Together with a similar national network in the United States – the Alliance for Responsible Trade (ART) – a cross-border convergence of trade activists went to Mexico. Excluded from an official NAFTA trade ministerial meeting, these church, labour, environmental, and community activists met with their Mexican counterparts, putting their experiences with CUFTA on the table. Shortly thereafter, the Mexican Action Network on Free Trade (RMALC) was formed, and a new cross-border activism emerged.

Throughout the struggles against both CUFTA and NAFTA, protecting Canada's social programs from erosion under trade agreements was a strong concern of the Canadian churches and the Canadian labour movement. In Canada, trade and investment agreements, like other economic liberalization policies before them, have yielded some new jobs, but the nature of the work is vastly different. There has been a significant shift away from formal, unionized, steady work to informal, temporary, nonunionized work for less pay. Moreover, usually women hold these unstable, low-quality jobs. A study of labour market conditions in Canada under NAFTA found that "part-time workers – overwhelmingly women – earn just two-thirds the wages of equivalent full-time workers and less than 20% receive benefits from their employers" (CLC 2003).

Another way in which Canadian society and particularly workers have been impacted by these policies is through the push for downward harmonization of social policy to conform to other NAFTA country standards. For example, the unemployment insurance program was cut and dramatically altered by both the Conservative and the Liberal governments to conform with lower US standards. Ideologically, in a bid to garner public support, the name was changed from Unemployment Insurance Program to the Employment Insurance (EI) Program. In 1989, 87 percent of the unemployed in Canada qualified for insurance, compared with 52 percent in the United States. By 2001, only 39 percent of unemployed Canadians could collect employment insurance (Foster and Dillon 2003, 93).

More women lost employment insurance protection than men since they frequently work part time and enter and leave the workforce more often due to unrecognized responsibilities such as elder care or childcare. A Canadian Labour Congress study found that the EI Program pays insurance to just one-third of working women who lose their jobs (CLC 2003). Laws like these are easily linked to rising poverty rates in Canada. They directly affect people's – usually women's – ability to ensure their families' survival and access to basic necessities such as food, clothing, and shelter.

### Setting the Stage: Southern Reasons for Resistance
In the global south, citizen movements have been struggling against austere economic restructuring in the form of Structural Adjustment Programs (SAPs) dictated by the International Monetary Fund (IMF) and the World Bank (WB) for over two decades. To get loans, southern governments sign onto agreements that generally require changing laws to facilitate corporate expansion and the privatization of public resources and services, with most of the money going back into the hands of creditors. At the end of 2001, Latin American and Caribbean countries had a total external debt burden of US $787 billion, three times higher than in 1982 when these policies were first implemented. This tripling of external debt occurred even though these countries made US $1.4 trillion in debt payments between 1982 and 2001 (Jubilee South 2002).

SAPs have facilitated similar changes to the nature of work and working conditions in the south that, in some ways, mirror the Canadian experience. In particular, for Canada's NAFTA partner, Mexico, there has been an upsurge of free-trade zones and *maquila* factories[2] as manufacturing dropped in Canada and the United States. These types of factories generally operate under tariff-free and tax-free conditions. Located all across the global south, generally each *maquila* participates in piecemeal work focusing on one aspect of putting together an electronics item or a piece of clothing. This approach provides a certain level of leverage to the multinational corporation as it can jump from *maquila* to *maquila* in search of the lowest production costs. In addition to putting very little back into the local economy so that a healthy domestic economy could evolve, these *maquilas* are often cited for the poor working conditions that affect the predominantly female workforce. Women are expected to work long hours for little pay, with no job security, forced overtime, a high risk of health problems due to unsafe working conditions, and the real possibility of sexual harassment and verbal and sometimes physical abuse (Wiggins 2003, 5).[3] In Mexico, *maquilas* are predominant in northern border towns such as Ciudad Juarez. Migrants from other parts of Mexico and Central America, who were forced to migrate for economic reasons, make up the majority of the town's population. This massive migration thus leads to an oversupply of labour, which in turn leads to the harsh working conditions and low pay described above.[4]

Moreover, NAFTA policies accelerating the liberalization of tariffs on key agricultural products such as maize and beans, among other changes such as the relaxation of communal landholding laws, have had a disastrous effect on small-scale producers, indigenous small-scale producers, and farm workers. This crisis has led to unprecedented levels of migration both internally and toward the north, including to Canada under the Seasonal Agricultural Worker Program (SAWP). For example, "over the last three years [2002-5] Chiapas has gone from being the 27th to the 11th state with the greatest migration as more and more farmers lose hope in subsistence farming" (Miguel Pickard, cited in KAIROS 2005, 12).

Given the deterioration of social and economic conditions in Latin America contributing to the widening gap between the rich and the poor, and combined with the Mexican experience of free trade under NAFTA, it is no wonder that recent attempts to further privatize services in Latin America have been met with strong national resistance. In the past several years, governments in Peru, Uruguay, El Salvador, Bolivia, Colombia, Argentina, Ecuador, and Paraguay have all tried unsuccessfully to privatize a variety of public services, including electricity, telecommunications, water, and healthcare.

The economic and social crises in the south, while resulting in increased levels of migration, have also spawned diverse forms of national resistance that have given energy and impetus to people to come together in transnational spaces to resist the proposed FTAA. If passed, it will clearly mean more of the same policies. However, people simply have no more to give and nothing left to lose.

In response, broad popular cross-sector resistance at home combined with the immediate need to counter the all-encompassing agenda found in the

FTAA has led to the recognition of the need for cross-sector, cross-border struggle. Building on the work of Common Frontiers, ART, and RMALC, a movement was born.

### The Hemispheric Social Alliance: Evolution of a Movement

In 1997, trade ministers from across the Americas met to discuss and advance the FTAA behind closed doors in Belo Horizonte, Brazil. At the same time, several hundred concerned citizens from across the hemisphere came together in an open and participatory forum. They joined together in this parallel people's forum to discuss alternatives, strategies, and actions related to the FTAA. In 1998, more than double the activists in Belo Horizonte, from a number of different social movements, came together in Santiago, Chile, the site of the next official trade ministers conference, to begin developing alternative economic, social, and cultural models for the hemisphere. Through workshops, panel discussions, and debates, a set of common issues began to emerge. By 1999, this diverse group came together to form the Hemispheric Social Alliance (HSA), a broad-based network that brings together both national coalitions such as Common Frontiers and regional networks such as Jubilee South Americas. Excluded from official negotiations, the HSA began to gather at each trade ministers summit to create a space for an alternative voice on trade. National sectors and regional networks of labour, environmental, women's, antipoverty, indigenous, and migrant workers' groups all came together to develop an all-encompassing set of alternatives that respects human rights, workers' rights, women's equality, indigenous rights, and ecological justice.

In 2001, during the Summit of the Americas, resistance to trade liberalization and its nature of excluding people reached new heights as more than 60,000 people from all walks of life and from across the hemisphere marched in the streets of Quebec City, with the HSA at the forefront. Shortly thereafter, it launched the NoFTAA campaign, thus providing a means by which the excluded from across the Americas could have their voices heard on the proposed FTAA. They called on national coalitions and regional networks to hold *consultas* – "popular consultations" – on the FTAA in their countries.

The campaign quickly gathered momentum, spurred on by the conditions described above but also due to a number of new ways of doing politics. Given the rapid growth of resistance, a more fluid approach recognizing the diversity of action and participation was needed. Given this new moment, campaign organizers proposed that a "network of networks" be created. Called the Continental Campaign to Stop the FTAA, this loose network of networks is open and participatory and brings together a rich and vibrant number of individuals and organizations from all thirty-five countries (including Cuba) in the hemisphere.

Although it began as an organized campaign with defined start and finish times, the NoFTAA campaign has become a broad-based people's movement. As such, it maintains the necessary fluidity and diversity to expand and react according to the political moment. The NoFTAA movement builds on a number of new and not-so-new ways of doing politics, starting with linking local and global struggles and using specific strategies and tools to succeed in transnational organizing such as convergences, the Internet, coordinated actions, and strategies vis-à-vis governments.

## Local and Global Unite

Living in the reality of the social and economic conditions described above has certainly contributed to people's abilities to make the connections between NAFTA and the FTAA, SAPs and the FTAA. The issue of stopping the FTAA and the identification of common experiences that go beyond borders enable activists to traverse the physical boundaries of the nation-state and join others in a common struggle, often without ever leaving their countries.

A challenge is presented to us in how we think of the local and the emphasis or importance we place on the local within transnational organizing. NoFTAA organizing is an interesting mix of local and global. Each country defines its own priorities and struggles, just as it defined its own *consulta*. For example, in 2003 there were massive mobilizations in El Salvador to stop the privatization of healthcare. At the same time, that struggle was directly linked to the proposed FTAA and its counterpart, the US-Central America Free Trade Agreement (CAFTA). In Colombia, the struggle against the FTAA is linked to the struggle against Plan Colombia and exposing the complex links between militarization, violence, and the FTAA. In Canada, Common Frontiers focused its *consulta* on Canadian healthcare and how the FTAA facilitates changing rules that will probably open the door to sweeping privatization of Canada's prized healthcare system.

In this way, the Continental Campaign to Stop the FTAA works to coordinate all local actions, transcending the local and the localization of struggle while validating this as the starting point. In November 2003, when the trade ministers met in Miami, the HSA produced plain-language printed resources, media communications, and public events that linked all of the popular consultations or *consultas* from across the Americas together. In that way, these events became interlinked as parts of a total and cohesive struggle. The unofficial referendum held in Brazil in September 2002 in which 10 million people came out and cast ballots against the FTAA; the October 2002 marches against the FTAA during the trade ministers meeting in Ecuador that saw 15,000 people marching in the streets while another 5,000 marched in Montreal and another 500 in Toronto; the November

2003 popular caravans that travelled throughout Argentina and garnered 2.5 million ballots against free trade; and the year-long Canadian petition campaign that called for safeguards to protect public healthcare and an end to the FTAA and was signed by close to 65,000 Canadians: all of these actions were seen as part of one joint struggle.

### New Strategies: Convergence at International Events

In addition to local actions that symbolically cross borders, a significant number of activists are able to physically traverse boundaries. Generally, there is a high level of recognition within the movement of the importance of a physical counterpresence at official meetings and of the strategic importance of building opportunities for face-to-face organization, coordination, and solidarity. The official FTAA negotiating meetings, such as the trade ministers meetings, have provided some of those opportunities, but several "gathering points" over the past several years have facilitated the growth of a social movement. One key event has been the annual (three years running) NoFTAA conference held in Havana, Cuba, under the umbrella of the Cuban Chapter of the Hemispheric Social Alliance. Each year approximately 1,000 people attend this event, which above all provides the space for divergent groups and movements from across the Americas to come together to discuss, debate, and strategize around the FTAA. It has been a critical space of convergence that has facilitated the growth and cohesion of the movement. Ironically, due to the insistence of the United States, Cuba has been officially excluded from FTAA negotiations. The World Social Forum held for three years in Porto Alegre, Brazil, and in Mumbai, India, in 2004 is also a key event that gathers many in one place and provides an opportunity for activists to meet and expand their circles of resistance.

As global trade talks moved beyond the FTAA to a more complicated bilateral and plurilateral agreement level, moments of convergence provided opportunities to advance a common analysis and understanding of global trade liberalization and thereby a common level of action. In the case of NoFTAA organizing, identification of commonalities enables activists to traverse the boundaries of the nation-state.

### New Tools: The Internet

The NoFTAA transnational network undeniably has been aided by Internet technology. It has proven to be a crucial organizing tool that not only facilitates information sharing but also provides a quick and effective method of mobilizing. Now, when NoFTAA activists face repression nationally or national governments announce a policy position regarding the FTAA, the information is shared across the Americas, instantaneously leading to rapid and forceful responses.

Recently, a small group of the HSA Monitoring Team decided to go beyond civil society convergences at trade ministers meetings to shadow the more technical Trade Negotiating Committee (TNC) meetings of the FTAA, which are closed-door and thereby secret sessions. Through a variety of means, HSA members were successful in gaining extensive insight into what was happening behind closed doors. Daily reports were written and immediately sent out on the Internet to the Continental Campaign members. These reports were posted on websites originating in Canada, Costa Rica, Ecuador, Colombia, Bolivia, El Salvador, Mexico, Brazil, Argentina, the United States, and reportedly even Europe. Where these reports landed demonstrated not only how far reaching and effective a tool the Internet is in disseminating information but also how that small group of analysts linked thousands across the hemisphere and globally in coordinated action and access to information.

## New Ground

The question of engagement is open to both national and conjunctural contexts. During the Quebec City Summit in 2001, it was clear that governments such as Canada's were regularly engaging in superficial consultations with certain sectors of civil society that did not dispute the FTAA or its impending implications. Moreover, when they did consult with a broader cross-section of society, they did not incorporate any of the recommendations or alternatives presented. The HSA, with involvement from across the Americas and through consensus, has produced a lengthy and detailed alternative to the FTAA titled *Alternatives for the Americas,* which incorporates respect for human rights, ecological justice, and national sovereignty and includes a chapter on migration, which calls for "respect for migrants' human and labour rights" and an end to the "criminalization of migrants."[5] The chapter, like all the others, goes on to provide a detailed alternative to forced underground migration that is the direct result of neoliberal economic globalization. Frustrated by the lack of an official response from government representatives, the HSA and its many members refused to participate in so-called consultations and were labelled "bad" civil society. Moreover, government representatives did not hesitate to categorize all opposition as violent despite the reality that only a small fragment of those opposed to the FTAA actually believe in using violent methods to advance their struggle. Indeed, the idea of a people's consultation or *consulta* emerged to counter and provide an alternative to the government-sponsored superficial consultations. It provided a way in which those most impacted by these policies would have their voices heard.

In light of this, progressive governments in Brazil, Argentina, and Venezuela have returned to age-old questions of how civil society relates to government. Levels of engagement, direct dialogue, and strategic alliances all take on new meaning when a government appears to share civil society concerns. The Brazilian government has played a critical part in validating the role that civil society plays as a key stakeholder in FTAA negotiations. For the first time ever, in Miami in November 2003, the Brazilian FTAA delegation began to include several spots designated for civil society observers. Venezuela as well has a large contingent of civil society members participating in its delegation, and it has openly promoted the use of TV/radio broadcasts of negotiations to ensure transparency and accountability. These instances are significant because, at a minimum, the Brazilian and Venezuelan governments are committed to giving the same amount of political space and perhaps political power to a degree to both the corporate elite and those representing the people.

In other instances, due to the work of the HSA, there is a growing opposition to the FTAA within Latin American parliamentarians and other country negotiators, such as those in Bolivia and the Caribbean Common Market (CARICOM), who are heeding civil society warnings on how the FTAA is nothing less than a corporate take-over of the Americas and looking to the HSA alternatives for solutions.

Although the US and Canadian governments continue to dismiss civil society concerns, civil society continues to call them to account, demanding authentic consultation, transparency, and accountability.

## The Challenge before Us

Recent developments in the FTAA negotiations show that the cracks in the trade liberalization wall are fast becoming gaping holes. The FTAA has been stalled since the last trade ministers summit in November 2003 due to a number of factors in which the NoFTAA movement has played a critical role. More and more southern governments are questioning the nature of the agreement. At the same time, they are proposing alternatives similar to the HSA documents and refusing to move forward with a deal that benefits only the north and, in particular, large transnational corporations and businesses. In addition, as the Continental Campaign to Stop the FTAA has grown and strengthened, lessons have been learned about new ways of doing activism. These new transnational spaces demand participatory approaches that are based on consensus decision making; can ally north and south activists, *campesino* activists with trade unionists, church groups with agnostics, and indigenous small-scale farmers with Latina *maquila* workers; and reach across borders and beyond nations in the same moment. Indeed, at the right time and place, the coming together of different sectors across gender, race, class, and borders provides us with the potential to effect social change in ways that might take us beyond our immediate goal of stopping the FTAA to building a more just society.

## Notes

1 For more information on Common Frontiers, see http://www.commonfrontiers.ca/.
2 A *maquila* or *maquiladora* factory refers to a company's taking advantage of tariff exemptions to produce goods in low-wage and often nonunion environments. Under typical *maquiladora* production, goods are assembled using imported parts or materials obtained without paying duties and using some domestic inputs. Once products are assembled, they are exported without being subject to taxes or tariffs. *Maquila* operations generally do not produce multiplier effects in the economies of the countries where they are located as they use few inputs, pay no taxes, and do not contribute to local infrastructure or service development.
3 There are numerous books, articles, and videos documenting the phenomenon of the *maquila*. For recent developments, resource information, and ideas on what you can do, contact the Maquila Solidarity Network at http://www.maquilasolidarity.org.
4 In solidarity with Mexican partners, Canadian churches, through the work of KAIROS, have closely monitored the impacts of NAFTA on Mexico. Canadian church leaders undertake periodic visits to Mexico to meet with partners, analyze impacts, and make recommendations to the Canadian government. Their most recent visit was March 2005. For more information, see http://www.kairoscanada.org.
5 For more information on the Alternatives Project and to download the *Alternatives for the Americas* document, see http://www.asc-hsa.org.

# 16

# The Challenges of Extraterritorial Participation: Advisory Councils for Peruvians Abroad

*Interview with Gaby Motta and Carlos Enrique Terry*
*by Luin Goldring*

During the late 1980s and 1990s, the governments of a number of migrant-"sending" countries began to implement policies to reach out to their populations abroad. While specific policies vary, particularly in terms of whether migrants have the right to vote from abroad or not, most of these initiatives involve outreach programs in one or more of the following areas: culture, education, investment, community development (including matching-funds programs), and consular protection.

A more recent form of government outreach, and state-mediated transnationalism, involves the development of formal institutions for the participation of emigrants in a transnationalized or extraterritorial sector of civil society. These institutions have been initiated in countries that have just begun to implement mechanisms for emigrants to vote from abroad, such as Mexico, and countries such as Peru, which not only allows for the vote but has also held elections in which overseas Peruvians voted for the president.

This conversation with Gaby Motta and Carlos Enrique Terry, two Peruvians who have made Toronto their home, provides their perspectives on the challenges faced by emigrants and sending-country functionaries as they become involved in the implementation of state policies aimed at promoting greater emigrant or diasporic participation.[1]

*Luin Goldring: Please give us some general background on migration from Peru and Peruvians in Canada and Toronto.*
Gaby Motta (GM) and Carlos Enrique Terry (CET): Peruvians started coming to Canada in the 1960s and 1970s when the economic and political situation in Peru became increasingly difficult. Nowadays, Peruvians live and work in Europe as well as North America. According to the World Bank, in 2003, Peru's population was 27.1 million people. But there are about 2 million Peruvians abroad, in countries such as the United States, Spain, Japan, Chile, and Canada. Over 60 percent of Peruvian migrants

are women. Like many migrants, Peruvians send money back to relatives. According to the Migration Dialogue website, in 1999 Peruvians sent home US $712 million in remittances. A study by the Inter-American Development Bank and the IMF estimated the amount sent home by Peruvians was US $1,295 million in 2003 [IADB-MIF 2004].

During the 1970s, the population of Lima grew very rapidly. But there were few opportunities for education or employment, so people started leaving the country. An estimated 70 percent of migrants went to neighbouring countries such as Chile, Ecuador, and Argentina, while 20 percent went to the United States, and the remaining 10 percent went to European countries and Canada. During the 1980s, the crisis of corruption and employment led to higher migration, with Peruvians looking for better opportunities in the United States and Canada. Many of those who came to Canada did so as refugees. After Fujimori's coup in 1992, migration increased, and the proportion of migrants going to Canada rose as well. It went from 1.5 percent of migrants during the 1970s to 12 percent during the 1990s. The proportion of Peruvian professionals leaving the country also increased.

The Hispanic Congress of Canada reports that there are about 15,000 Peruvians in Ontario, based on data from the Canadian census. This includes immigrants who arrived since the 1960s and 70s with their children as well as children and grandchildren born here. The Peruvian Consulate in Toronto has about 6,000 Peruvians registered in their database. This consulate has jurisdiction over Ontario and Manitoba.

*Please describe the relationship between the Peruvian government and Peruvian citizens living abroad before the implementation of the* Consejos de Consulta [Advisory Councils, hereafter referred to as Advisory Councils or CCs] ... *In particular, what was the relationship between the consulate and the Peruvian community here in Toronto?*

GM: The Peruvian government deals with Peruvians abroad through the consulates and the Ministry of Foreign Affairs. In Toronto, the consulate has sponsored Independence Day celebrations, cultural events, sports, and worked to attract investors interested in projects in Peru, such as mining ventures. If a Peruvian community organization was having an event, consular staff would attend.

The consulate expected the community to approach them, not the other way around. People could propose projects, for example, donations for Peru. However, when donors wanted to get tax exemptions, there was no support. The relationship was top down and not participatory: the consulate did not take into account people's expertise in designing projects or activities; they just wanted to make decisions without involving the community.

CET: Peru had a constitutional change in 1979. After that year, Peruvians living abroad have been able to vote in presidential elections. More specifically, we had to vote. After voting, one's electoral card was stamped. Not voting meant one would receive a fine.

GM: Yes, I have been voting from abroad since 1980. That year, I was in the Soviet Union. Everyone had to travel to the capital to vote.

*Peruvian state policy toward Peruvians abroad shifted in 2001, with the creation of Advisory Councils. Please tell us about the* Consejos de Consulta, *how they began, why, and what they were supposed to do.*

GM: Civil society in Peru understands that times have changed. People have become more involved in national affairs domestically and externally in foreign affairs. People are more involved in decision making within Peru, and this has also led to greater participation in politics outside the geographic limits of Peru. The introduction of the Advisory Councils was a government initiative implemented through a ministerial resolution. The minister of foreign affairs, Diego García Sayán, and his team of foreign policy advisors had been reviewing relations between Peruvians abroad and the Peruvian government, and they wanted to strengthen this link. In particular, they wanted to increase the flow of remittances from Peruvians abroad to their relatives and families in Peru. They passed a law on September 29, 2001, establishing *Consejos de Consulta* all over the world. Now there are eighty Advisory Councils throughout the world (Ministry of Foreign Affairs n.d.). In Canada, there are three Advisory Councils, in Toronto, Montreal, and Vancouver. According to the Peruvian Ministry of Foreign Affairs, the Advisory Councils were established to "improve consular services, [to] evaluate the efficiency of consular services, to improve consular protection, strengthen the connection between Peruvians and their homeland, maintain and improve the image of Peru abroad, cultural-artistic and economic promotion, and to improve the integration of Peruvians and their institutions in Canadian society" (Consulado General del Perú en Toronto 2002).

We have a document from a speech given by the vice minister of foreign affairs for the inauguration of the First International Seminar on Peruvian Communities Abroad held in Lima (Rodríguez Cuadros 2003). This document states that the government wanted to reorganize and decentralize consular services. The document also talks about the need to improve services, eliminate discrimination, and create ways for Peruvians to participate in identifying existing problems with consular services and finding solutions to these problems. The general message was that the government wanted better dialogue with Peruvians abroad and promised to improve consular protection and services, with input from us.

*At the time of these changes in 2001, who was in power? How did the idea for the councils develop, and how was this related to who was in office?*

GM: Alejandro Toledo was in power; it was after Fujimori's resignation. But the idea of reforming the consulates and the Foreign Service must have come before and has to be understood in a broader context. García Sayán was pushing this agenda, which included professionalizing the Foreign Service. But it was also part of the broader process of globalization, increasing trade, and economic and social linkages with other countries. It was not presented as a partisan policy, with one party backing it over the objections of others. Rather, it was part of modernizing the relationship between the government and Peruvians abroad. And we can't forget remittances, which were increasing. The remittances were very important.

As I noted earlier, after Fujimori's coup in 1992, middle-class professional emigration increased. After Fujimori resigned, and after Humala's insurgency, Toledo called on civil society to come together. The transitional government of Valentín Paniagua developed a model of citizen participation that was not limited to Peruvians inside the country but also included Peruvian migrants. This was a model in which civil society participated in designing various programs for the improvement of its citizens. The participation of Peruvians abroad was considered critical because, at that time, the latest statistics indicated that over 10 percent of the population was living outside the country.

*Do you know how the government came up with this model?*

CET: Not specifically, but there was consultation with other governments, particularly in Mexico. In 2003, I went to one of the early meetings of the Advisory Councils in Lima, Peru. One of the speakers, Mr. Cándido Morales, was from the Institute for Mexicans Abroad. He gave a speech describing how that organization worked. At around that time, the Peruvian consul in Toronto, Mr. Carlos Gamarra, mentioned that the Advisory Councils were following the Mexican model. The Mexican model was developed in the context of migration between Mexico and the United States, which is different. It has probably strengthened Mexican civil society, but models sometimes need to be adapted to fit other contexts.

*How did you first learn about the Advisory Councils, and what was your early involvement?*

GM: In December of 2001, the consulate in Toronto mailed out letters inviting Peruvians to a general meeting to be held in January. There were 6,000 Peruvians registered at the consulate, but not all of us received invitations. Two hundred Peruvians showed up for the meeting.

The consul came with his agenda already in mind. For example, he said we should have seven committees and said that, since there were four Peruvian immigrant organizations represented at the meeting, members of these groups should be included as representatives on the Advisory Councils. People did not agree because there were more organizations than those represented there, maybe seven or eight, and over thirty in total, if you include cultural, sports, and other organizations.

The consul was supposed to circulate information about the Advisory Councils *before* the general meeting for Peruvians held in Toronto since it was at this meeting that the Advisory Council was going to be established. A three-page document had been prepared with this information. However, the letter of invitation for the general meeting in Toronto had only a small paragraph about the councils. During the meeting, people asked for clarification on the Advisory Councils and their role. Members of Grupo Transparencia were there.[2] They noted that the information on the Advisory Councils was not complete, and after being asked to do so by the general assembly, they proceeded to read a document sent by Foreign Affairs. One of the key things missing from the consul's presentation was that part of the Advisory Councils' role was to evaluate consular services. This is something that even now has been overlooked and purposely forgotten. This has generated controversy about the role of the Advisory Councils, particularly among current conservative diplomatic representatives, not only in Toronto but around the world.

A month later, there was a second meeting for the formation of seven committees to focus on youth, culture-arts, sports, community, social action, communications, and business and professional issues. Only seventy people came to the second meeting to elect the committee heads and members. Most of the committees were to have a president, vice president, and secretary. I was on the social action committee, and Carlos Terry was on the communications and media committee. We were also supposed to elect a general Advisory Council coordinator, but I argued against that so as not to create a hierarchy. Ironically, I was elected as the coordinator of the Advisory Council in Toronto.

*What was the background of the people who went to the meetings, and did you all know each other?*

GM: Most were professionals, people from Lima. In my group, out of thirteen people, there was one woman who was not a professional. All had been professionals in my country, and three were active in our community here in Toronto. Most of us did not know each other, at least not on my committee. I knew two people out of thirteen.

*Please describe the activities of the Advisory Council in actual practice. What is your analysis of what the councils accomplish for the government, for Peruvians who are on the councils, and for Peruvians abroad?*

GM: The councils were supposed to provide a space for dialogue; they were also supposed to evaluate and improve consular services. We wanted our council to stand for greater support, better services, particularly for new-comers or recent Peruvian migrants, and to evaluate how the consular services were working. Someone at the meeting said that one of the first things to do was to decrease or reduce the fees charged to get documents (passports, military cards, tax forms, etc.). These have been reduced be-cause of the demands made by many of the Advisory Councils and also by participants at the First Seminar for Peruvian Communities Abroad, held in Lima, in March 2003.

Representatives from twenty Advisory Councils were invited to partici-pate in that seminar, out of a total of eighty councils. The ones chosen were the ones with good working relationships between the council, the local community, and the consulate's local diplomats. The invitation came to the Toronto Advisory Council after a failed election, in February 2003, which was due to the interference of the consul, the misunderstanding and misinformation of some co-nationals concerning the goals of the Advisory Councils, and the ongoing defensive attitude some people had which led them to protect the consul. The consul acted in an authoritar-ian manner and not as someone working with a set of clients, in the sense of people who deserve fair and equitable treatment. He wanted to treat people as subjects, not as citizens.

Getting back to the question of what the councils have done, one re-markable experience was when we made a call to about ten Peruvian or-ganizations for the First Encounter of Peruvian Organizations in Toronto. Representatives of four organizations came, as did the Advisory Council. It was good to have everyone together at the same table.

That meeting took place after the Toronto Advisory Council partici-pated in the First Seminar for Peruvian Communities Abroad, held in Lima, in 2003. The purpose of that meeting was to brief and update the Advisory Council membership about the goals and accomplishments of the CCs around the world. The idea was welcomed.

The councils have also succeeded in getting a reduction in consular fees, which was implemented in Supreme Decree No. 045-2003-RE.

The council has formed a program of humanitarian assistance for Peru-vians abroad who are extremely poor to repatriate bodies. Recently (Sep-tember of 2004), a family approached the consulate to request monetary help to repatriate the remains of their sister, who was extremely poor. We went to the funeral, and the woman had no casket and no flowers. Their request was denied based on the assumption that this woman had relatives in Toronto and thus would not qualify for this humanitarian fund. This young Peruvian woman had been a Canadian resident for the last three years and was the sole supporter of her six-year-old daughter. We are going to contact the consulate in Toronto and our Ministry of Foreign Affairs to come up with some solutions.

In addition to the Advisory Councils, the government also has a series of programs aimed at fostering investment in Peru and strengthening people's ties back home. For example, there is a home ownership program, called Mi Vivienda, which allows Peruvians abroad to buy houses in Peru at low costs and with very low mortgage rates. To qualify, people need to have been sending remittances for at least five months prior to applying. There is also a social security agreement, with which I am not very familiar.

In the period since the Advisory Councils were established, the government began to issue an identity card for all Peruvians abroad, regardless of their legal or migratory status, something similar to the Mexican identity card.

From the Peruvian government's perspective, the best it can achieve with the creation of the Advisory Councils would include the professionalization of the diplomatic corps; enhancing service delivery to Peruvians abroad by analyzing their feedback through an ongoing evaluation process; for civil society to assume greater responsibilities and experience a new period of social unity; increase the level of remittances which would be positive for the country's foreign exchange; increase small-business development; and promote tourism among emigrants and other visitors.

Although there have been accomplishments, the cultural promotion program and the effort to strengthen links between Peruvians in Peru and Peruvian communities abroad through these programs need to take place with a clear and transparent budget. Right now we do not know how much is in the budget nor the guidelines governing it. As a result, there cannot be community participation in the planning of the cultural events or the decision making of this program.

An important mandate of the Advisory Councils was the enhancement of interaction between the "diplomats and Peruvians abroad, by creating a space for dialogue to improve the consular services" (Rodríguez Cuadros 2003). Given that we have been following the CC process in Toronto for three years, I think it is fair to say that it is still very difficult to implement this part of the mandate, and others, because of inadequate dissemination of the rules of the initial mandate as stated in the Ministry of Foreign Affairs decree of September 2001 and the subsequent addition of bylaws in November 2002. These regulations were sent to the CCs some time ago, but even now they are still under discussion in many CCs around the world. The process does not reflect the spirit of the CCs and instead shows the lack of sensitivity and leadership of many diplomats with respect to these changes implemented by the Peruvian Chancellery.

In the case of Toronto, a formal evaluation of the consular services has not been conducted due to a lack of support by the consulate. The first Advisory Council (January 2002-May 2003) proposed the development of a jointly designed evaluation survey. However, this did not happen. I think this was due to a misunderstanding of the CC mandate regarding "evaluation and accountability" in the eyes of the diplomats and some CC members and the community at large, who continued with the old model of the consul as government and authority, as opposed to the new model, of consul as public servant. There was also misunderstanding of the idea that the CC was supposed to constitute an open space for dialogue and consultation but without the interference of the consulate in the designation of its members. This is public information that can be seen on the ministry's website [http://www.rree.gob.pe/portal/misrree.nsf/CC], but at the time the information was not widely available, nor was it clear.

In a way, one could say that the way the consul was implementing the Advisory Council was contributing to the maintenance of the very Peruvian cultural custom of creating and reproducing cultural and social barriers. As a Peruvian woman of indigenous descent, who left Peru at the age of seventeen and lived abroad since then, I have acquired more knowledge about ethical, multiethnic, professional, and social issues, based on justice and equity, and have a strong vision of the achievements of the Latino American and Canadian heritage we will leave our children and grandchildren and of the great capacities in each of the individuals that make up Toronto, Peru, and the whole world. So it is very sad to write about "our Peruvian cultural and social customs."

Pretty early on, we saw that the people who were heads of committees did not want to use the term *fiscalización* [financial accountability]; they did not want to hear about accountability or evaluation. They just wanted to go ahead with the status quo and only hold national holiday celebrations.

The committees had plans for great projects. The community and social action committee planned to come up with bulletins and fact sheets for new immigrants, and we accomplished this when we produced the first bulletin of the first Advisory Council. It contained relevant information on services for newcomers as well as contact information, websites with information and support, and all the names, e-mail addresses, and phone numbers of the people in charge of the secretariat for Peruvians abroad in Foreign Affairs. We wanted to be able to make photocopies and receive other support. But we could not use the facilities or get any support from the consulate or, more specifically, from the consul, Mr. Gamarra. So we never had a good working relationship with him and could never plan or strategize for improvements for the community in Toronto. We could not take advantage of all the professional and institutional experience that our members had accumulated, from abroad and in Canada. Of course now, if we visit the Foreign Affairs website, we would find more than ten pages of information on the area of culture, with the names of activities, events, the planning, implementation, stakeholders, and stewardship, and with an assigned budget.

Out of seventy consulates around the world, fifteen were working well with their Advisory Council and the local communities on gastronomic festivals, agreements with universities and professional bodies to accredit academic and professional programs, and so forth. Some of these activities were included in proposals presented by the first and second presidents of the Advisory Council here, with copies going to the consulate and Foreign Affairs. It outlined the projects and listed the contact information of the Canadian ministers and the members of the Advisory Council who were involved locally with Hispanic institutions. Unfortunately, our local diplomats again did not even consider it.

CET: I made a presentation to the then minister of international affairs, Mr. Pettigrew, outlining ways of supporting the Latin American community in Canada. It included the issue of improving the accreditation of professional degrees obtained abroad and the consular identification card. This card can be useful, particularly for people without legal status and for youth. For youth, the card would represent an acknowledgment from the consulate that they are Peruvians, regardless of where they were born. I also presented this at the First Seminar for Peruvian Communities Abroad held in Lima, in March 2003, along with a discussion of cases of discrimination by the police and other local Canadian authorities. I also spoke of a specific case about which the consulate was advised, but very little or nothing was done to support the students in question. The consular official thought that the Advisory Council was interfering with their support, but the Advisory Council did provide support, whereas the consulate officials only visited the detainees a couple of times and didn't really help.

GM: Another initiative was to use the consulate's space to provide free legal advice to new immigrants one day a week, another day a week to provide counselling, and another day to provide information on new Canadian laws and regulations. It didn't make sense not to support it, because in Milan, Italy, the Advisory Council was doing this. They had a counsellor and a lawyer and provided four days of free services for Peruvians by

Peruvians. It was a way to give back to the community through a community capacity-building exercise. Worst of all, the Foreign Affairs website had a communiqué discussing legal support, and the topic was also mentioned in a speech by the Foreign Affairs minister during the Third Seminar for Peruvians Abroad (held in May 2004). The Toronto consulate's website only lists a few of the Hispanic and Canadian institutions that provide some legal advice, but it is not in their institutional mandate. As a result, it does not include the community legal clinics that provide support and advice to newcomers and people without financial security.

This consul is in his fourth year, and we have not been able to work with him. His term is coming to an end. Unfortunately, we don't have much hope.

During the first Advisory Council's term, the one I was on, we made trouble for the consul. We weren't able to conduct our evaluation survey, but we showed him one from Los Angeles and wanted to have a meeting with him to take a look at their evaluation model. Our planned meeting never took place as there was a change in his schedule.

When we understood that he was never going to support the activities of the council, we started to send him letters, with copies to Foreign Affairs. For example, we would say we are having an educational activity with children in one of the TDSB [Toronto District School Board] elementary schools, with a class of more than thirty children from different ethnic backgrounds from grades two to eight that attend the Spanish-language classes as one of the international languages being taught in some of the schools in Toronto, because they had been working for two months learning about the Inca civilization, including the *quipus*,[3] and making crafts, such as painting llamas, alpacas, and vicuñas, learning anthems, and many other words in Spanish related to the Inca civilization. The displays were there for three days, and the consul was obliged to attend due to all the publicity that the Advisory Council generated. For those of us on the Advisory Council, the event on Inca culture was a great success, and we provided many objects for the display, arts and crafts, ceramics, leather objects, and different regional costumes. There were many instances where the consul did not attend or simply boycotted, as was the case with an event to pay homage to Simon Bolivar, because he represents unity for Latin Americans. There was the unveiling of a small bust in one of the biggest parks in Toronto [Trinity-Bellwoods Park], followed by a mass in a Hispanic church. The Peruvian Consulate downplayed the event, but fortunately there was a celebration and full participation by other Latin American consulates.

Another interesting thing to point out regarding the Advisory Councils and why the government has promoted them has to do with the Peruvian government's desire to have contact with Peruvians who are well integrated into the host societies. The people who tend to become involved in something like the CCs may also be civically and politically active in other areas of community leadership. For example, in the United States, we have two municipal councillors in different states and one senator as well and one recently elected city councillor in Milan, Italy.

There have been some divisions within the Peruvian community because of the Advisory Council's name: "Advisory Council of the General Consulate of Peru of the City of Toronto." Some thought it was too official. Other divisions stem from Peruvians' partisan involvement, as members are affiliated with several political parties, class differences, and people's frustration over the devaluing of their participation. I believe people would agree that the creation of the Advisory Council showed the need for changes in the mandates, structures, and strategies of existing Peruvian institutions.

*Why do you think the government started this process of reaching out to Peruvians abroad?*

GM: There are 2 million Peruvians abroad. Remittances are the second-highest source of foreign exchange, after mining. Currently, remittances come to nearly US $1,300 million a year. So the bottom line is the remittances.

*Can you tell us something about your family's experience in relation to the Advisory Council?*

GM: For my family, this experience was catastrophic in terms of time I devoted to the Advisory Council. It took me a long time to understand "our cultural issues." That is, to learn to be tolerant when faced with the negativity and lack of leadership of the consul, to be able to remain in the council in spite of the resignations and the negative newspaper coverage, and to learn that we are still many years behind other recent communities that migrated after us.

*How would you characterize relations between the Peruvian government and the Toronto consulate on the one hand and Peruvians in Canada on the other hand? Did the introduction of the Advisory Councils change things?*

GM: There certainly is more communication, which is good. A lot is up to the specific councillors. If all they want is to be named to and hold public office, they can do that for a year, and that's it. But I can't say that there is really much change in terms of how we are dealt with at the consulate. Even people from the Advisory Council now say they encounter problems. There is no easy access to consular staff.

In spite of the problems, it has been positive. The increase in dialogue and communications is good. People feel important; they feel like they count. So they will try to send a bit more money. This holds for all Peruvians, regardless of their occupation here. Another positive thing, in my view, is that the Advisory Council has made other organizations grow. Now there is competition, people raise questions about an organization's activities. One of the other achievements is that we had a meeting of all the Peruvian organizations in the Toronto area, which gave everyone a chance to come together. The process is still fairly recent, and we've managed to make a few changes, so now it is up to subsequent councils to follow up.

*Do people in the Peruvian community really know that the Advisory Council exists here, what it does, and, if so, how do they obtain this information?*

GM: Only a small proportion of Peruvians here knows about the Advisory Council, but sometimes CC members try to disseminate information through bulletins and journalist members through newspapers. The consulate provides very little information. It really depends a lot on the members of the CC, and the pressure that they can bring to bear on the consulate, while staying within the mandate of the CC.

*Do Peruvians here maintain contact with their country? What are the main ways that Peruvians in Toronto do this? (For example, families maintaining ties with relatives, reading newspapers, voting, business).*

GM: Yes, we maintain contact. Technology helps. Phone cards are cheap, there is the Internet, satellite TV, Internet phone and camera, and remittances. We also buy copies of *Panorama,* a TV show from Lima.

CET: Voting is mandatory, and it is a good mechanism for popular participation. Through democracy, institutions become stronger and can create better bridges between the government and citizens. We as Peruvians abroad do not need consular paternalism, only operational and clear rules of the game. When Peruvians are abroad, we want to participate in civil society, we want to vote, but we also want broader participation.

*Do the Advisory Councils play an important role in terms of how people maintain ties with Peru? Has it strengthened people's feeling of being Peruvian as well as Canadian? Does it make any difference to the way you feel in relation to your country?*

GM: The Advisory Council should play an important role; that is the idea, but not the reality, except in some cases like the Advisory Councils in Geneva, Switzerland, New York, Caracas, and Venezuela. I do think the councils have strengthened people's feeling of being Peruvian. But at this point in time, it is very difficult to measure this. In Toronto, the consulate has not supported the Advisory Council adequately. The consulate does not really include the Advisory Council among its list of officially recognized Peruvian organizations. For example, if one of the Peruvian organizations is having an event, the consulate officials are there; these officials will congratulate the organization and mention a few other organizations and people but without including the Advisory Council. Also, at meetings for the election of new Advisory Councils, the consular staff actively discouraged the reading of earlier minutes, which would list the accomplishments of the Advisory Council. This reinforces the lack of information about what the Advisory Council has done.

CET: They say "the road to hell is paved with good intentions" [*de buenos deseos está empedrado el infierno*]. The problem is that they [the consulate] do not really know how to facilitate interaction between Peruvians living in Peru and those living abroad.

*Do either of you envision having future links with the Advisory Councils? If so, what kind of role? If not, why?*

CET: As a Peruvian, I long for a united community, but the autocracy and centralization of power continue, along with discrimination among Peruvians. I do not think the councils are viable in the long term, nor do I think they can meet the mandates for which they were created.

GM: Yes, I could see doing some work. I was approached to work in one of the committees of the third Advisory Council of Toronto. However, I could only accept if some changes took place so that we could sit together at a roundtable that would include the staff from Foreign Affairs, community stakeholders, and Advisory Council members and the administrative staff from the local consulates. We would also have to leave the protocols and rhetorical language aside, and more than anything I would want to work on implementing the process of documented evaluations of the consular services by neutral parties. I would also want to see some real follow-up on the findings and recommendations. Without these changes, I will continue to feel that the Advisory Council, because it is not really autonomous, but includes the very people responsible for the design and implementation of the Advisory Council, in this case Foreign Affairs, is only a pretty model or "exercise" of so-called participation for Peruvians abroad. As such, it will continue to fund employment opportunities for government staff and lend credibility to the so-called democratic and transparent era of Peruvian politics, once again, for decades to come.

**Notes**

1  This chapter began as a conversation aimed at reconstructing Gaby Motta's presentation at the YCAR-CERLAC workshop in 2003. It developed into a face-to-face conversation between Gaby Motta and Luin Goldring, followed up with an e-mail exchange with Gaby Motta and Carlos Enrique Terry. Luin Goldring supplemented the conversation with data from the IADB-MIF and the World Bank.

2 Grupo Transparencia ("Transparency Group") is an election-monitoring group established in Lima for the 1995 presidential elections.

3 The term *quipus* refers to a traditional Inca oral and written form of preserving and recounting history, stories, and legends.

# Conclusion: Questions for Future Research and Action

*Sailaja Krishnamurti and Luin Goldring*

The contributors to this book show us, in a variety of ways, that transnational social engagements are not the result of a single set of historical and political situations but produce and are produced by interconnected global currents of people, capital, and power. Thus, the *transnational* is constituted by a variety of disparate mechanisms and social, political, and cultural issues, and it operates at multiple scales and levels. Although the contributors to this volume differ in exactly how they define the *transnational*, they agree that people, groups, and institutions in transnational situations are doing important organizing work. More importantly, they remind us that those who live transnational lives, and those who are doing the work of organizing transnationally, can contribute to the understanding of these processes and activities just as the scholars who research them.

In the introduction to this volume, we outlined some of the issues that have driven the burgeoning field of transnational studies in Canada and elsewhere. In this conclusion, we underscore some of the significant questions that arise from the chapters here, and we consider which directions for future research and collective work they may signal.

## What Is Transnationalism?

The contributors to this book differ widely in their approaches to what the "transnational" means for them. Is it a matter of identity, location, or strategy? For some, the transnational is experienced by people who live and work in multiple locations, while for others it is a way of remaining connected with a "home" (Díaz). For some, it is characterized by the actions and policies of states and supranational institutions (Henders) or is inevitably and forcibly produced by differentiating forms of immigration status, racism, and social exclusion (Shakir). Some contributors write about the ways in which people lead transnational lives, as in the case of migrant farm workers who shift locations seasonally (Preibisch, Becerril). Other authors comment on the ways that the transnational becomes an organizing feature of people's identities (Viswanathan, Kelly). The ways in which communities organize themselves across national borders as a strategy for dealing with particular political and social issues are also discussed by contributors (Cheran, Wayland).

Underlying these different approaches to transnationalism is another question: what explains the origin of transnational organizing? Does it arise as a response of people against the changing nature of capital, international politics, and world markets? Or is it primarily produced by and through the policies and structures of states? For example, while Bose writes about the Indian government's attempts to harness the money and political power of transnational migrants, Jeremic's chapter outlines the ways in which people in the Americas, including nonmigrants, organize transnationally to resist the inequities produced by relaxing international trade restrictions, and Cheran describes the transnational institutionalization of Tamil village associations. These cases point to a different ontology for transnational organizing, showing that transnationalism can be a mode of organizing that is structured by states and state policies, but it can also be a counterhegemonic strategy of nonstate actors, including migrants and nonmigrants.

## Who Does Transnationalism?

Scholars in the social sciences have thus far tended to view "transnational" in terms of institutions, policies, states, and migrants. In the arts and humanities, explorations of "diaspora" tend to focus on representations, texts and images, and the cultural dynamics of transnational life. People living and working in transnational contexts tend to talk about interpersonal and political relationships as the most immediate and daily facet of transnationalism with which they deal. So who does transnationalism? The chapters in this book point toward the importance of broadening transnational studies to look beyond nations and migrants, to consider other actors, such as communities, media, regulatory regimes, and family networks (Siemiatycki and Preston, Henders, Díaz). Transnational practices are enacted by states, by institutions, by people, and by communities. This book also makes clear that people in transnational social fields are often as interested in their own practices as academics (Sundar, Viswanathan, Motta). They are engaging in thinking and writing about transnationalism, and a fruitful direction for scholarly research on transnationalism would include an examination of these perspectives, considering how people talk and think about their transnational lives, how they define transnationalism, and how they represent themselves.

## Why Does Transnationalism Matter?

Transnational practices affect and are affected by issues of politics, immigration, trade, and security and include cultural, social, religious, and familial practices. Researching these practices and listening to people in communities can be an extremely helpful tool in building law and policy. Many contributors to this volume point to issues that should be of note to Canadian policy makers, particularly in the area of immigration and labour policy. Chapters by Landolt, Díaz, Raper, Wayland, and Shakir offer insights into the ways in which current Canadian policies are affecting the lives of transnational people. The policies of sending states also affect people living transnationally, and as Bose and Motta show, these states may also attempt to mediate transnational organizing practices. Several other chapters expose the ways in which transnational social and cultural practices emerge as a response to state and interstate policies (Raper, Preibisch, Becerril, Jeremic).

Although only a small portion of the people of the world move across borders (3 percent of the world's population, according to the World Bank), the issues faced by migrant people can tell us a great deal about the world. The study of transnational political, social, and cultural practices is important to scholars and policy makers who attempt to chart the effects of globalization, the changing role and function of nations and states, and shifts in international law regarding citizenship. Henders' chapter draws our attention toward gradual shifts in the international conceptualization of citizenship as states attempt to account for migration in new ways.

Another important element in the study of transnational practices is the historical and social context that it provides in understanding people's political beliefs and commitments; their art, culture, and representations; and the tensions between the production of "hybrid" cultural practices and the maintenance of traditions. While research in the humanities on diasporic and transnational cultural productions and practices can benefit from attending to the lived and embodied experiences of migrant people, social scientific research can be nuanced by attention to issues of identity, representation, and subjectivity.

### What Is the Researcher's Role?

One of the most important justifications for an increased awareness of community interests is that transnational communities and researchers sometimes speak different languages. Viswanathan points out that people in transnational communities or social fields may not use the language of transnationalism to describe themselves and that some see it as an academic discourse with little relationship to them. Some of the chapters in this volume articulate the different ways in which the *transnational* is understood by activists: as a reaction to social conditions, a continuation of family and community life across borders, and a strategy for social change.

Whether or not the transnational is seen as a result of forces from above, or as a response to them, the "objectivity" associated with classic social scientific approaches may be questioned within transnational communities. What is the work of the researcher in transnational organizing? Communities are responding that it is not sufficient for researchers to remain on the sidelines as passive observers. Many of the situations described in this book are pressing matters of livelihood to the people involved in them. Immigration status, citizenship, personal safety, access to services, fair wages, and job security are issues around which strong and forceful transnational organizing is taking place. These emerging forms of organizing are also troubling the lines between activist and researcher as more people are finding that their work involves both modes. To this end, some of the authors in this volume encourage the active and ethical participation of researchers in the movements that they study, while others acknowledge the skepticism with which some communities react to distanced, observational research (Raper, Díaz, Shakir).

## What Makes Canada Different?

One of the most significant aims of this volume is to assist in this dialogue between communities and researchers. Another and related aim has been to contextualize this multifaceted conversation within Canada's transnational communities. All of the contributors to this book write about cases in which there is some Canadian connection. Each node in a transnational network influences its shape. Canada's immigration history and policies form a significant context and background for the unique formations of transnational organizing that we encounter. Moreover, the centrality or marginality of migrant groups in Canada in relation to their numerical and social location in other sites in their transnational social fields can shape the experience of the groups in Canada. As Landolt shows for the case of Salvadorans, local contexts still matter in our age of globalization. Salvadorans in Toronto have had very different experiences of the transnational compared with those of their co-nationals in Los Angeles or in Washington, DC.

Multiculturalism, for example, is a policy that directly affects the way in which transnational organizing takes place. Public funding support for community activities such as religious services and cultural training provides unique opportunities for transnational organizing. But multiculturalist policies can also mask systemic racism in Canada. Shakir writes in detail about this in her chapter and points to transnationalism as a forced reaction to the conditions of social exclusion produced by multiculturalism and Canadian immigration policy.

The Canadian immigration context, cultural landscape, and global political situation are different from those of the United States or the countries of the European Union, sites from which a great deal has been written on the subject of transnational studies. Opening up this field of study to the

Canadian context of transnational organizing also prompts us to consider how these cases might contribute to our understanding of transnational practices in general.

### Transnational Organizing and Future Research

The questions outlined here briefly are not conclusively answered in this book, but the contributors have provided many interesting suggestions for further research and thought. It may be difficult to predict what emerging forms of transnational organizing might lead to in the future, but we can acknowledge that this kind of organizing is now a regular feature of world politics. Questions of international security, migration, and trade will shape the future of transnational communities, as will changing national attitudes and policies on these questions.

In this volume, we have attended primarily to the experiences of Asian and Latin American migrants as a means of narrowing our focus. But attention to the practices of people in other Canadian communities, such as those from Africa, the Caribbean, or the Middle East, offer other interesting and useful insights. None of these broad communities is homogeneous, and their experiences cannot be generalized, but the cases that we present here and anticipate for the future provide interesting food for thought for both researchers and activists.

# References

Abu-Laban, Yasmeen, and Christina Gabriel. 2002. *Selling Diversity: Immigration, Multiculturalism, Employment Equity, and Globalization.* Peterborough: Broadview Press.

Adamson, Fiona B. 2002. "Mobilizing for the Transformation of Home: Politicized Identities and Transnational Practices." In *New Approaches to Migration? Transnational Communities and the Transformation of Home*, ed. Nadje Al-Ali and Khalid Koser, 155-68. London: Routledge.

Agnew, Vijay, ed. 2005. *Diaspora Memory and Identity: A Search for Home.* Toronto: University of Toronto Press.

Agustín, Laura María. 2002. "Challenging 'Place': Leaving Home for Sex." *Development* 45, 1: 110-17.

Airport Authority, Hong Kong. 2000. http://www.hkairport.com/eng/flight_info/FlightInfo Frame.jsp.

Al-Ali, Nadje, Richard Black, and Khalid Koser. 2001. "The Limits to 'Transnationalism': Bosnian and Eritrean Refugees in Europe as Emerging Transnational Communities." *Ethnic and Racial Studies* 24, 4: 578-600.

Anderson, Bridget. 2001. "Different Roots in Common Ground: Transnationalism and Migrant Domestic Workers in London." *Journal of Ethnic and Migration Studies* 27, 4: 673-83.

Andrade-Eekhoff, Katharine. 2004. "Las Dinámicas Laborales y la Migración en la Region: Entre la Inclusión y la Exclusión." Paper read at the conference La Transnacionalización de la Sociedad Centroamericana: Nuevos Retos Planteados a Partir de la Migración Internacional, San Salvador, El Salvador, 13-14 May.

Anzaldúa, Gloria. 1987. *La Frontera/Borderlands: The New Mestiza.* San Francisco: Aunt Lute.

Appadurai, Arjun. 1996. *Modernity at Large: Cultural Dimensions of Globalization.* Public Worlds 1. Minneapolis: University of Minnesota Press.

–. 2000. "Grassroots Globalization and the Research Imagination." *Public Culture* 12, 1: 1-19.

Aruliah, Arul S. 1994. "Accepted on Compassionate Grounds: An Admission Profile of Tamil Immigrants in Canada." *Refuge* 14, 4: 10-14.

Association for India's Development. 2004. "Projects: Rights and Social Justice, Your Voice Counts." http://www.aidindia.org/hq/misc/vcounts/voice_counts.shtml.

Association of International Physicians and Surgeons of Ontario (AIPSO). 2000. "Barriers to Licensing in Ontario for International Physicians." http://www.aipso.ca.

–. 2002. "Integrating Canada's Internationally-Trained Physicians: Towards a Coherent, Equitable, and Effective National System." Submission to the Commission on the Future of Healthcare in Canada, section 3. http://www.aipso.ca.

Baines, Donna, and Nandita Sharma. 2002. "Migrant Workers as Non-Citizens: The Case Against Citizenship as a Social Policy Concept." *Studies in Political Economy* 69: 75-107.

Bakan, Abigail, and Daiva Stasiulis. 1997. *Not One of the Family: Foreign Domestic Workers in Canada.* Toronto: University of Toronto Press.

Baldwin, Douglas. 1996. "Promoting Multiculturalism: Canada's Immigration Policies." In *Some Missing Pages: The Black Community in the History of Quebec and Canada.* Rev. ed. http://www.learnquebec.ca/en/content/curriculum/social_sciences/features/missingpages/.

Ball, Rochelle, and Nicola Piper. 2004. "Globalisation and Regulation of Citizenship: Filipino Migrant Workers in Japan." *Political Geography* 21: 1013-34.

Bambrah, Gurmeet. 2005. "Canadian 'Experiments' in Diversity: The Case of Immigrants with Engineering Backgrounds Who Settle in Ontario." CERIS Working Paper 41.

Bannerji, Himani. 2000. *The Dark Side of the Nation.* Toronto: Canadian Scholar's Press.

–. 2001. "Rebuilding, Rethinking: Towards a Truly Inclusive Left." *Canadian Dimension* 35, 1: 22.

Basch, Linda, Nina Glick Schiller, and Cristina Szanton Blanc. 1994. *Nations Unbound: Transnational Projects, Postcolonial Predicaments, and Deterritorialized Nation-States.* Amsterdam: Gordon and Breach.

Bashi, Vilna. 2004. "Globalized Anti-Blackness: Transnationalizing Western Immigration Law, Policy, and Practice." *Ethnic and Racial Studies* 27, 4: 584-606.

Basok, Tanya. 1993. *Keeping Heads above Water: Salvadoran Refugees in Costa Rica.* Montreal: McGill-Queen's University Press.

–. 2002. *Tortillas and Tomatoes: Transmigrant Mexican Harvesters in Canada.* Montreal: McGill-Queen's University Press.

–. 2003. *Human Rights and Citizenship: The Case of Mexican Migrants in Canada.* Working Paper 72. La Jolla: Center for Comparative Immigration Studies.

–. 2004. "Post-National Citizenship, Social Exclusion, and Migrants' Rights: Mexican Seasonal Workers in Canada." *Citizenship Studies* 8, 1: 47-64.

Basu, Tapan, Pradip Datta, Sumit Sarkar, Tanika Sarkar, and Sambuddha Sen. 1993. *Khaki Shorts, Saffron Flags: A Critique of the Hindu Right.* New Delhi: Orient Longman.

Batzlen, Christof. 2000. *Migration and Economic Development: Remittances and Investments in South Asia: A Case Study of Pakistan.* New York: P. Lang.

Bauböck, Rainer. 1991. *Immigration and the Boundaries of Citizenship.* Vienna: Institute for Advanced Studies.

–. 2002. "How Migration Transforms Citizenship: International, Multinational, and Transnational Perspectives." IWE Working Paper Series 24.

–. 2005. "Citizenship Policies: International, State, Migrant, and Democratic Perspectives." *Global Migration Perspectives* 19: 1-28.

Bauder, Harald, and Bob Sharpe. 2002. "Residential Segregation of Visible Minorities in Canada's Gateway Cities." *Canadian Geographer* 46: 204-22.

Beiser, Morton, Laura Simich, and Nalini Pandalangat. 2003. "Community in Distress: Mental Health Needs and Help-Seeking in the Tamil Community in Toronto." *International Migration* 41, 5: 233-44.

Besserer, Federico. 2002. "Contesting Community: Cultural Struggles of a Mixtec Transnational Community." PhD diss., Department of Social and Cultural Anthropolgy, Stanford University.

Bhabha, Homi K. 1994. *The Location of Culture.* London: Routledge.

Bhattacharjee, Ashok. 2003. "Seminar on Accelerated Housing and Construction Industry in Bengal." Keynote address by Minister of Urban Development, Government of West Bengal, to Federation of Indian Chambers of Commerce, 25 August, Kolkata.

Bindman, Jo, and Jo Doezema. 1997. *Redefining Prostitution as Sex Work on the International Agenda.* Network of Sex Work Projects. http://www.walnet.org/csis/papers/redefining.html.

Binford, Leigh. 2004. "Contract Labor in Canada and the United States: A Critical Appreciation of Tanya Basok's *Tortillas and Tomatoes: Transmigrant Mexican Harvesters in Canada.*" *Canadian Journal of Latin American and Caribbean Studies* 29, 57-58: 289-308.

Bissoondath, Neil. 2002. *Selling Illusions: The Cult of Multiculturalism in Canada.* Toronto: Penguin.

Black, Jerome. 1982. "Immigrant Political Adaptation in Canada: Some Tentative Findings." *Canadian Journal of Political Science* 15: 3-27.

–. 1991. "Ethnic Minorities and Mass Politics in Canada: Some Observations in the Toronto Setting." *International Journal of Canadian Studies* 3: 129-51.

–. 2001. "Immigrants and Ethnoracial Minorities in Canada: A Review of Their Participation in Federal Electoral Politics." *Electoral Insight* 3: 8-13. http://www.elections.ca/eca/eim/pdf/insight_2001_01_e.pdf.

Blais, André, Louis Massicotte, and Antoine Yoshinaka. 2001. "Deciding Who Has the Right to Vote: A Comparative Analysis of Election Laws," *Electoral Studies* 20, 1: 41-62.

Bloemraad, Irene. 2003. "Institutions, Ethnic Leaders, and the Political Incorporation of Immigrants: A Comparison of Canada and the United States." In *Host Societies and the Reception of Immigrants,* ed. J. Reitz, 193-228. San Diego: Center for Comparative Immigration Studies.

–. 2005. "Much Ado about Nothing: The Contours of Dual Citizenship in the United States and Canada." Paper presented at the conference Dual Citizenship: Rights and Security in an Age of Terror, University of Toronto, 17-19 March.

Bobo, Lawrence, Melvin Oliver, James Johnson, and Abel Valenzuela, eds. 2000. *Prismatic Metropolis: Inequality in Los Angeles.* New York: Russell Sage Foundation.

Bose, Sumantra. 1995. "State Crises and Nationalities Conflict in Sri Lanka and Yugoslavia." *Comparative Political Studies* 28, 1: 87-116.

Bottomore, Tom. 1992. "Citizenship and Social Class, Forty Years On." In *Citizenship and Social Class,* ed. T.H. Marshall and Tom Bottomore, 55-93. London: Pluto Press.

Bourdieu, Pierre. 1986. "The Forms of Capital." In *Handbook of Theory and Research in the Sociology of Education,* ed. John G. Richardson, 50-61. New York: Greenwald Press.

Brah, Avtar. 1996. *Cartographies of Diaspora: Contesting Identities.* London: Routledge.

Braziel, Jana Evans, and Anita Mannur, eds. 2003. *Theorizing Diaspora: A Reader.* Oxford: Blackwell.

Brettell, Caroline B. 2003a. *Anthropology and Migration: Essays on Transnationalism, Ethnicity, and Identity.* New York: Altamira Press.

–. 2003b. "Bringing the City Back In: Cities as Contexts for Immigrant Incorporation." In *American Arrivals: Anthropology Engages the New Immigration,* ed. N. Foner, 182-203. Santa Fe: School of American Research.

Brubaker, William Rogers, ed. 1989. *Immigration and the Politics of Citizenship in Europe and North America.* Lanham, MD: University Press of North America.

–. 1992. *Citizenship and Nationhood in France and Germany.* Cambridge, MA: Harvard University Press.

Buchignani, Norman, Doreen Indra, and Ram Srivastiva. 1985. *Continuous Journey: A Social History of South Asians in Canada.* Toronto: McClelland and Stewart.

Buckley, Roger. 1997. *Hong Kong: The Road to 1997.* Cambridge, UK: Cambridge University Press.

Bunting, S.W., N. Kundu, and M. Mukherjee. 2002. "Renewable Natural Resource-Use in Livelihoods at the Calcutta Peri-Urban Interface: Literature Review." Working paper. Stirling, UK: Institute of Aquaculture.

Bunting, S.W., N. Kundu, S. Punch, and D.C. Little. 2001. "East Kolkata Wetlands and Livelihoods: Workshop Proceedings." Working paper. Stirling, UK: Institute of Aquaculture.

Canadian Labour Congress (CLC). 2003. "EI Program Robs Workers, Especially Women." Press release, 3 September. Ottawa: CLC.

Canadian Policy Research Network (CPRN). 2005. "Peopling Canada: Immigration Policy since 1867." http://www.cprn.org/en/diversity1_1-origins-topic1_1.cfm.

Cannon, Margaret. 1989. *China Tide: The Revealing Story of the Hong Kong Exodus to Canada.* Toronto: HarperCollins.

Carrington, William J., and Enrica Detragiache. 1999. "How Extensive Is the Brain Drain?" *Finance and Development* 36, 2: 46-49.

Carty, Linda, and Dionne Brand. 1993. "'Visible Minority' Women: A Creation of the Canadian State." In *Returning the Gaze: Essays on Racism, Feminism, and Politics,* ed. Himani Bannerji, 207-22. Toronto: Sister Vision Press.

Castles, Stephen, and Alastair Davidson. 2000. *Citizenship and Migration: Globalization and the Politics of Belonging.* New York: Routledge.

Castles, Stephen, and Mark J. Miller. 2003. *The Age of Migration: International Population Movements in the Modern World.* 3rd ed. New York: Guildford Press.

Cecil, Robert, and G. Edward Ebanks. 1991. "The Human Condition of West Indian Migrant Farm Labour in Southwestern Ontario." *International Migration* 29, 3: 389-404.

Census Canada. 2001. *Census Statistics on Selected Ethnic Origin Populations.* Ottawa: StatsCan.

Cernea, Michael, and Christopher McDowell, eds. 2000. *Risks and Reconstruction: Experiences of Resettlers and Refugees.* Washington, DC: World Bank.

Cheran, R. 2001. "Changing Formations: Nationalism and National Liberation in Sri Lanka and the Diaspora." PhD diss., Department of Sociology, York University.

–. 2002. *The Sixth Genre: Memory, History, and the Tamil Diaspora Imagination.* Colombo, Sri Lanka: Marga Institute.

–. 2003. *Diaspora Circulation and Transnationalism as Agents for Change in the Post Conflict Zones of Sri Lanka.* Colombo, Sri Lanka: Berghof Foundation for Conflict Studies. http://www.berghof-foundation.lk/scripts/DiasporaCirc.pdf.

–. 2007. "Citizens of Many Worlds: Theorizing Tamil Diasporicity." In *History and Imagination: Tamil Studies in the Global Context,* ed. R. Cheran, D. Ambalavanar, and C. Kanaganayakam, 150-68. Toronto: TSAR Publications.

Chinese Canadian National Council (CCNC). 2003. "Submission to the Standing Committee on Citizenship and Immigration with Respect to the Bill C-18, an Act Respecting Canadian Citizenship."

Chow, Rey. 1993. *Writing Diaspora.* Bloomington: Indiana University Press.

Chute, Tanya. 2004. "Seguir Luchando/The Struggle Continues: Salvadoran Political Participation in Toronto." Master's thesis, University of Toronto.

Citizenship and Immigration Canada (CIC). N.d. "Forging Our Legacy: Canadian Citizenship and Immigration 1900-1977." http://www.cic.gc.ca/english/department/legacy/index.html.

–. 1994. *Immigration Statistics 1992.* http://www.cic.gc.ca/english/pdf/pub/1992stats.pdf.

–. 1997. *Immigration Statistics (1987-1996): Facts and Figures: Immigration Overview (1997).* Ottawa: Government of Canada.

–. 2002a. *Facts and Figures.* Ottawa: CIC.

–. 2002b. Landed Immigrant Data System. Ottawa: CIC.

–. 2004a. *Common HRDC Confirmation Exception Categories of Work 2004.* http://www.cic.gc.ca/english/work/exempt-2.html.

–. 2004b. *Temporary Foreign Worker Guidelines (FW).* http://www.cic.gc.ca/manuals-guides/english/fw/fwe.pdf.

–. 2004c. *Work Temporarily in Canada.* http://www.cic.gc.ca/english/work/index.html.

–. 2005. *Foreign Workers Manual.* Ottawa: CIC.

Coalition of Immokalee Workers (CIW). 2004. http://www.ciw-online.org/.

Cohen, Jean. 1999. "Changing Paradigms of Citizenship and the Exclusiveness of the Demos." *International Sociology* 14, 3: 245-67.

Cohen, Robin. 1997. *Global Diasporas: An Introduction.* Seattle: University of Washington Press.

Colby, Catherine. 1997. *From Oaxaca to Ontario: Mexican Contract Labour in Canada and the Impact at Home.* Davis, CA: California Institute for Rural Studies.

Coleman, James. 1988. "Social Capital in the Creation of Human Capital." *American Journal of Sociology* 94: 95-120.

Committee on Banking, Housing, and Urban Affairs, United States Senate. 2002. Senate Hearing 107-909: Issues Regarding the Sending of Remittances, 28 February.

Consulado General del Perú en Toronto. 2002. "Consejo de Consulta del Consulado General del Perú en Toronto." http://www.tamcotec.com/conperu.toronto/consejo/#CC.

Coomaraswamy, Radhika. 1987. "Myths without Conscience: Tamil and Sinhalese Nationalist Writings in the 1980s." In *Facets of Ethnicity in Sri Lanka,* ed. Charles Abeysekera and Newton Gunasinghe, 72-99. Colombo: Social Scientists Association.

Cooper, Frederick, and Randall Packard. 1997. *International Development and the Social Sciences: Essays on the History and Politics of Knowledge.* Berkeley: University of California Press.

Council of Europe. 1950. Convention for the Protection of Human Rights and Fundamental Freedoms.

–. 1992a. European Charter for Regional or Minority Languages.

–. 1992b. Convention on the Participation of Foreigners in Public Life at the Local Level.

–. 1993. Convention on Reduction of Cases of Multiple Nationality, Second Protocol.

–. 1995. Framework Convention for the Protection of National Minorities.

Courville, Sasha, and Nicola Piper. 2004. "Harnessing Hope through NGO Activism." *Annals, American Academy of Political and Social Sciences* 592: 39-61.

Cranford, Cynthia J., Leah F. Vosko, and Nancy Zukewich. 2003. "Precarious Employment in the Canadian Labour Market: A Statistical Portrait." *Just Labour: A Canadian Journal of Work and Society* 3 (Forum on Precarious Employment): 6-22.

Craven, Matthew. 1995. *The International Covenant on Economic, Social, and Cultural Rights.* Oxford: Oxford University Press.

Cross, Malcolm, and Robert Moore, eds. 2002. *Globalization and the New City: Migrants, Minorities, and Urban Transformations in Comparative Perspective.* New York: Palgrave.

Cusipag, Ruben, and Maria Buenafe. 1993. *Portrait of Filipino Canadians in Ontario (1960-1990).* Toronto: Kalayaan Media.

Daniel, E. Valentine. 1996. *Charred Lullabies: Chapters in an Anthropology of Violence.* Princeton: Princeton University Press.

Daniel, E. Valentine, and Y. Thangaraj. 1995. "Forms, Formations, and Transformations of the Tamil Refugee." In *Mistrusting Refugees*, ed. E.V. Daniel and J.C. Knudsen, 226-56. Berkeley: University of California Press.

Das Gupta, Tania. 1994. "Political Economy of Gender, Race, and Class: Looking at South Asian Immigrant Women in Canada." *Canadian Ethnic Studies* 26, 1: 59-73.

Debabrata, Michael, and Muneesh Kapur. 2003. "India's Worker Remittances: A User's Lament about Balance of Payments Compilation." Paper presented at the Sixteenth Meeting of the IMF Committee on Balance of Payment Statistics, Washington, DC, 1-5 December.

December 18. N.d. "UN Migrant Workers' Convention Country Positions." http://www.december18.net.

Dei, George Sefa. 1996. *Antiracism Education, Theory, and Practice.* Toronto: Fernwood.

De Mont, John, and Thomas Fennell. 1989. *Hong Kong Money: How Chinese Families and Fortunes Are Changing Canada.* Toronto: Key Porter Books.

de Silva, K.M., and R.J. May, eds. 1991. *The Internationalization of Ethnic Conflict.* London: Pinter.

Docker, John. 2001. *1492: The Poetics of Diaspora.* London: Continuum.

Dolin, Benjamin, and Margaret Young. 2002. "Bill C-18: The Citizenship of Canada Act." Ottawa: Parliamentary Research Branch.

Downes, Andrew, and Cyrilene Odle-Worrell. 2003. *Barbados, Trinidad and Tobago, OECS Workers' Participation in CSAWP and Development Consequences in the Workers' Rural Home Communities.* Research report. Ottawa: North-South Institute.

Duval, David Timothy. 2004. "Linking Return Visits and Return Migration among Commonwealth Eastern Caribbean Migrants in Toronto." *Global Networks* 4, 1: 51-67.

Ehrenreich, Barbara, and Arlie Russell Hochschild. 2003. *Global Woman: Nannies, Maids, and Sex Workers in the New Economy.* New York: Metropolitan Books.

El Surco. 2004. *Boletín Mensual para los Trabajadores Agrícolas Mexicanos en Ontario, Canadá* (Monthly Bulletin for Mexican Agricultural Workers in Ontario) 5, 3: 1-4.

Encalada Grez, Evelyn. 2003. "Exclusion and Exploitation of Migrant Farm Workers in Ontario and Community Organizing for Inclusion." Unpublished manuscript, University of Toronto.

–. 2006. "Justice for Migrant Farm Workers: Reflections on the Importance of Community Organizing." *RELAY: A Socialist Project Review* 68-69: 23-25.

England, Kim, and Bernadette Stiell. 1997. "'They Think You're as Stupid as Your English Is': Constructing Foreign Domestic Workers in Toronto." *Environment and Planning A* 29: 195-215.

Espiritu, Yen Le. 2003. *Home Bound: Filipino American Lives across Cultures, Communities, and Countries.* Berkeley: University of California Press.

European Union. 2002. Consolidated Versions of the Treaty on European Union and the Treaty Establishing the European Community.

–. 2004. Treaty Establishing a Constitution for Europe.

Faist, Thomas. 1999. "Transnationalism in International Migration: Implications for the Study of Citizenship and Culture." Centre for Migration, Policy, and Society (COMPAS), Working Paper WPTC-99-08.

–. 2000. *The Volume and Dynamics of International Migration and Transnational Social Spaces.* Oxford: Clarendon Press.

Falk, Richard. 1993. "The Making of Global Citizenship." In *Global Visions: Beyond the New World Order,* ed. J. Brecher, J. Childs, and J. Cutler, 39-50. Boston: South End Press.

Ferris, Elizabeth. 1987. *The Central American Refugees.* New York City: Praeger Press.

FOCAL. 2004. *Final Report: Hemispheric Integration and Transnationalism in the Americas.* Guatemala: Canadian Foundation for the Americas.

Foner, Nancy. 1997. "What's New about Transnationalism? New York Immigrants Today and at the Turn of the Century." *Diaspora* 6, 3: 355-75.

Foreign Agricultural Resource Management Services (FARMS). 2001-4. *Employer Information Package.* Mississauga: FARMS.

–. 2001a. *Ontario Region: Caribbean/Mexican Seasonal Agricultural Workers Programs Year-to-Date Report.* Mississauga: FARMS.

–. 2001b. *Report of Migrant Farm Workers in Canada.* Mississauga: FARMS.

–. 2003a. *The Quest for a Reliable Workforce in the Horticulture Industry.* Research report prepared by Stevens Associates. Mississauga: FARMS.

–. 2003b. *Statistical Reports for 2002.* Mississauga: FARMS.

Foster, John. 2005. "The Trinational Alliance Against NAFTA: Sinews of Solidarity." In *Coalitions across Borders: Transnational Protest and the Neoliberal Order,* ed. Joe Bandy, 209-30. Oxford: Rowman and Littlefield.

Foster, John, and John Dillon. 2003. "NAFTA in Canada: The Era of a Supra-Constitution." In *Lessons from NAFTA: The High Cost of "Free Trade,"* 83-116. Ottawa: Canadian Centre for Policy Alternatives.

Fuglerut, Oivind. 1999. *Life on the Outside: The Tamil Diaspora and Long Distance Nationalism.* London: Pluto Press.

–. 2004. "Culture, Networks, and Social Capital: Tamil and Somali Immigrants in Norway." Paper presented at the Eighth Biennial Conference of the European Association of Social Anthropologists, Face to Face: Connectivity, Distance, Proximity, Vienna, 8-12 September.

Galabuzi, Grace-Edward. 2001. "Canada's Creeping Economic Apartheid." Toronto: CSJ Foundation. http://www.socialjustice.org/pdfs/economicapartheid.pdf.

Gammeltoft, P. 2002. "Remittances and Other Financial Flows to Developing Countries." *International Migration* 40, 5: 181-211.

Ganaselall, Indira. 1992. "Technology Transfer among Caribbean Seasonal Farmworkers from Ontario Farms into the Caribbean." MSc thesis, University of Guelph.

Garza, Rodolfo O. de la, and Briant Lindsay Lowell, eds. 2002. *Sending Money Home: Hispanic Remittances and Community Development.* New York: Rowman and Littlefield.

Giddens, Anthony. 1982. "Class Division, Class Conflict, and Citizenship Rights." In *Profiles and Critiques and Social Theory,* ed. A. Giddens and F.R. Dallmayr, 164-80. London: Macmillan.

Gieryn, Thomas. 2000. "A Space for Place in Sociology." *Annual Review of Sociology* 26: 463-96.

Gilroy, Paul. 1992. *The Black Atlantic: Modernity and Double Consciousness.* Cambridge, MA: Harvard University Press.

Gindin, Sam. 1998. "The Party's Over." *This Magazine* November-December: 13-15.

Glick Schiller, Nina. 2005. "Transnational Social Fields and Imperialism." *Anthropological Theory* 5, 4: 439-61.

Glick Schiller, Nina, and Georges Fouron. 1999. "Terrains of Blood and Nation: Haitian Transnational Social Fields." *Ethnic and Racial Studies* 22, 2: 340-65.

Goldring, Luin. 1996. "Blurring Borders: Constructing Transnational Community in the Process of Mexico-U.S. Migration." *Research in Community Sociology* 6: 69-104.

–. 2002. "The Mexican State and Transmigrant Organizations: Negotiating the Boundaries of Membership and Participation in the Mexican Nation." *Latin American Research Review* 37, 3: 55-99.

–. 2006. "Latin American Transnationalism in Canada: Does It Exist, What Forms Does It Take, and Where Is It Going?" In *Transnational Identities and Practices in Canada,* ed. Vic Satzewich and Lloyd Wong, 180-201. Vancouver: UBC Press.

Goonewardena, Kanishka, and Stefan Kipfer. 2005. "Spaces of Difference: Reflections from Toronto on Multiculturalism, Bourgeois Urbanism, and the Possibility of Radical Urban Politics." *International Journal of Urban and Regional Research* 29, 3: 670-78.

Gosse, Van. 1988. "'The North American Front': Central American Solidarity in the Reagan Era." In *Reshaping the US Left: Popular Struggles in the 1980s,* ed. M. Davis and M. Sprinker, 11-50. New York: Verso Books.

–. 1996. "'El Salvador Is Spanish for Vietnam': A New Immigrant Left and the Politics of Solidarity." In *The Immigrant Left in the United States,* ed. P. Buhle and D. Georgakas, 302-30. Albany: SUNY Press.

Government of Canada. 2003. "Responses to Specific Questions: Question 7." Ottawa: Canadian Heritage, Human Rights Program. http://www.pch.gc.ca/progs/pdp-hrp/docs/questionnaire/question07_e.cfm.

–. 2004. "Dual Citizenship." Ottawa: Citizenship and Immigration Canada. http://www.cic.gc.ca/english/citizen/dualci_e.html.

Government of Gujarat. 2004. NRI Division website, http://www.nri-gujarat.com/.

Government of Kerala. 2004. Global Investor Meet Program website, http://www.kerala.gov.in/invest/invest.htm.

Graham, Amanda. 2001. "Strip Clubs Bare All to Councillor." *Eye Magazine,* 29 November. http://www.eye.net/eye/issue/issue_11.29.01/news/stripclubs.php.

Green, Alan G., and David A. Green. 1993. "Balanced Growth and the Geographical Distribution of European Immigrant Arrivals to Canada, 1900-1912." *Explorations in Economic History* 30, 1: 31-59.

Grewal, Inderpal, and Caren Kaplan. 1994. *Scattered Hegemonies: Postmodernity and Transnational Feminist Practices.* Minneapolis: University of Minnesota Press.

Grey, Mark, and Anne Woodrick. 2002. "Unofficial Sister Cities: Meatpacking Labor Migration between Villachuato, Mexico, and Marshalltown, Iowa." *Human Organization* 61, 4: 364-76.

Griffith, David, and Ed Kissam, with Jeromino Camposeco, Anna García, Max Pfeffer, David Runsten, and Manuel Valdes Pizzini. 1995. *Working Poor: Farmworkers in the United States.* Philadelphia: Temple University Press.

Guarnizo, Luis E., and Michael Peter Smith. 1998. "The Locations of Transnationalism." In *Transnationalism from Below,* ed. Michael Peter Smith and Luis Eduardo Guarnizo, 3-34. New Brunswick, NJ: Transaction.

Gurr, Ted Robert. 1993. *Minorities at Risk.* Washington, DC: US Institute of Peace.

Hackett, Robert, and Richard Gruneau. 2000. *The Missing News: Filters and Blind Spots in Canada's Press.* Aurora, ON: Garamond Press.

Hall, Stuart. 1990. "Cultural Identity and Diaspora." In *Identity: Community, Culture, Difference,* ed. J. Rutherford, 222-37. London: Lawrence and Wishart.

–. 1997. "Old and New Identities, Old and New Ethnicities." In *Culture, Globalization, and the World System: Contemporary Conditions for the Representation of Identity,* ed. A.D. King, 41-68. Minneapolis: University of Minnesota Press.

Halle, David, ed. 2003. *New York and Los Angeles: Politics, Society, and Culture in Comparative View.* Chicago: University of Chicago Press.

Hamilton, Nora, J. Frieden, L. Fuller, and M. Pastor, eds. 1988. *Crisis in Central America: Regional Dynamics and U.S. Policy in the 1980s.* Boulder, CO: Westview Press.

Hamilton, Nora, and Norma Stoltz Chinchilla. 1996. "Global Economic Restructuring and International Migration: Some Observations Based on the Mexican and Central American Experience." *International Migration* 34, 2: 195-227.

Hamza, Buri. 2004. "Somali Transnational Networks and Development." Paper presented at the Tamil Refugees Organization Workshop, Colombo, Sri Lanka, 17-18 June.

Harrison, Trevor. 1996. "Class, Citizenship, and Global Migration: The Case of the Canadian Business Immigration Program, 1978-1992." *Canadian Public Policy* 22: 7-23.

Henders, Susan. 1997. "Cantonisation: Historical Paths to Territorial Autonomy for Regional Cultural Communities." *Nations and Nationalism* 3, 4: 521-40.

Herman, Thomas, and Doreen J. Mattingly. 1999. "Community, Justice, and the Ethics of Research: Negotiating Reciprocal Research Relations?" In *Geography and Ethics: Journeys in Moral Terrain*, ed. James D. Proctor and David M. Smith, 209-21. London: Routledge.

Heyman, Josiah M., and Hilary Cunningham. 2004. "Introduction: Mobilities and Enclosures at Borders." *Identities* 11, 3: 289-302.

Hiebert, Daniel. 1999. "Local Geographies of Labour Market Segmentation: Montreal, Toronto, and Vancouver." *Economic Geography* 75: 339-69.

Hiebert, Daniel, and David Ley. 2003. *Characteristics of Immigrant Transnationalism in Vancouver.* Working Paper Series 03-15. Vancouver: Vancouver Centre of Excellence, Research on Immigration and Integration in the Metropolis (RIIM).

High Level Committee on the Indian Diaspora. 2002. "Report of the High Level Committee on the Indian Diaspora."

Hiwatashi, Motomichi. 2004. "Redefining Japanese Nationality: Pluralism and the *Zainishi*-Korean Struggle for Citizenship Rights." Major research paper, MA program in political science, York University.

Hyndman, Jennifer, and Margaret Walton-Roberts. 2000. "Interrogating Borders: A Transnational Approach to Refugee Research in Vancouver." *Canadian Geographer* 44, 3: 244-58.

Inkeles, Alex, and David Horton Smith. 1974. *Becoming Modern: Individual Change in Six Developing Countries.* Cambridge, MA: Harvard University Press.

Inter-American Development Bank – Multilateral Investment Fund (IADB-MIF). 2004. "Sending Money Home: Remittances to Latin America and the Caribbean." Washington, DC: IADB-MIF. http://www.iadb.org/mif.

International Monetary Fund (IMF). 2003. *Balance of Payments Statistics Yearbook.* Washington, DC: IMF.

International Organization for Migration (IOM). 2003a. "Facts and Figures on International Migration." *Migration Policy Issues* 2: 1.

–. 2003b. *World Migration.* Geneva: IOM.

Ireland, Patrick. 1994. *The Policy Challenge of Ethnic Diversity: Immigrant Politics in France and Switzerland.* Cambridge, MA: Harvard University Press.

Isin, Engin, and Patricia K. Wood. 1999. *Citizenship and Identity.* Thousand Oaks, CA: Sage.

Itzigsohn, José. 2000. "Immigration and the Boundaries of Citizenship: The Institutions of Immigrants' Political Transnationalism." *International Migration Review* 34, 4: 1126-54.

Itzigsohn, José, Carlos Dore Cabral, Esther Hernandez Medina, and Obed Vazquez. 1999. "Mapping Dominican Transnationalism: Narrow and Broad Transnational Practices." *Ethnic and Racial Studies* 22, 2: 316-39.

Itzigsohn, José, and Silvia Giorguli Saucedo. 2002. "Immigrant Incorporation and Sociocultural Transnationalism." *International Migration Review* 36, 3: 766-98.

Jansen, Clifford, and Lawrence Lam. 2003. "Immigrants in the Greater Toronto Area: A Sociodemographic Overview." In *The World in a City*, ed. Paul Anisef and Michael Lanphier, 63-131. Toronto: University of Toronto Press.

Johnson, James H., Walter C. Farrell, and Maria-Rosario Jackson. 1994. "Los Angeles One Year Later: A Prospective Assessment of Responses to the 1992 Civil Unrest." *Economic Development Quarterly* 8, 1: 19-27.

Jubilee South. 2002. International Peoples Tribunal on Debt. Porto Alegre, Brazil. http://www.jubileesouth.org/news/EpFZVAAyEkuEdFUfZg.shtml.

KAIROS. 2005. "A Cry for Justice: The Human Fact of NAFTA's Failure in Mexico." Presented by Canadian Church Leaders Delegation to Mexico, 11-19 March.

Kallen, Evelyn. 1995. *Ethnicity and Human Rights in Canada*. 2nd ed. Toronto: Oxford University Press.

Kearney, Michael. 1995. "The Local and the Global: The Anthropology of Globalization and Transnationalism." *Annual Review of Anthropology* 24: 547-65.

Keck, Margaret, and Kathryn Sikkink. 1998. *Activists beyond Borders: Advocacy Networks in International Politics*. Ithaca, NY: Cornell University Press.

Kelly, Philip F. 2003. "Canadian-Asian Transnationalism." *Canadian Geographer* 47: 209-18.

Keohane, Robert O., and Joseph S. Nye, eds. 1971. *Transnational Relations and World Politics*. Cambridge, MA: Harvard University Press.

Khagram, Sanjeev, James V. Riker, and Kathryn Sikkink. 2002. "From Santiago to Seattle: Transnational Advocacy Groups Restructuring World Politics." In *Restructuring World Politics: Transnational Social Movements, Networks, and Norms*, ed. Sanjeev Khagram, James V. Riker, and Kathryn Sikkink, 3-23. Minneapolis: University of Minnesota Press.

Kivisto, Peter. 2003. "Social Spaces, Transnational Immigrant Communities, and the Politics of Incorporation." *Ethnicities* 3, 1: 5-28.

Knop, Karen. 1993. "Re/Statements: Feminism and State Sovereignty in International Law." *Transnational Law and Contemporary Problems* 3: 293-344.

Knowles, Kim. 1997. "The Seasonal Agricultural Workers Program in Ontario: From the Perspective of Jamaican Migrants." MA thesis, University of Guelph.

Knowles, Valerie. 2000. *Forging Our Legacy: Canadian Citizenship and Immigration, 1900-1977*. Ottawa: Public Works and Government Services Canada. http://www.cic.gc.ca/english/department/legacy/index.html.

Kobayashi, Audrey, et al. 2000. "Transnationalism, Citizenship, and Social Cohesion: Recent Immigrants from Hong-Kong to Canada." See http://geog.queensu.ca/transnat/.

Kolkata Metropolitan Development Authority (KMDA). 2000. *Calcutta Development: Programmes and Projects*. Kolkata: KMDA Publications.

Koopmans, Ruud, and Paul Statham, eds. 2000. *Challenging Immigration and Ethnic Relations Politics: Comparative European Perspectives*. Oxford: Oxford University Press.

Kowalchuk, Lisa. 1999. "Salvadorans." In *Encyclopaedia of Canada's Peoples*, ed. R.P. Magocsi. Toronto: University of Toronto Press. 1109-15.

Krasner, Stephen D. 2000. *Sovereignty: Organized Hypocrisy*. Princeton: Princeton University Press.

Krishnamurty, V. 1994. *Study of Investment Preferences of Expatriates from India*. New Delhi: National Council of Applied Economic Research.

Ku, Agnes S. 2002. "Beyond the Paradoxical Conception of 'Civil Society without Citizenship.'" *International Sociology* 17, 4: 529-49.

Ku, Jane. 2000. *Constructing a Community in Diversity: The South Asian Experience*. Toronto: Council of Agencies Serving South Asians (CASSA).

Lakhilal, Prasanth. 2003. "Dual Citizenship Greeted with Mixed Feelings." *India Tribune*, 18 January. http://www.globalpolicy.org/nations/citizen/2003/0118india.htm.

Landolt, Patricia. 2000. "The Causes and Consequences of Transnational Migration: Salvadorans in Los Angeles and Washington, D.C." PhD diss., Department of Sociology, Johns Hopkins University.

–. 2001. "Salvadoran Economic Transnationalism: Embedded Strategies for Household Maintenance, Immigrant Incorporation, and Entrepreneurial Expansion." *Global Networks: A Journal of Transnational Affairs* 1, 3: 217-41.

Landolt, Patricia, Lilian Autler, and Sonia Baires. 1999. "From *Hermano Lejano* to *Hermano Mayor*: The Dialectics of Salvadoran Transnationalism." *Ethnic and Racial Studies* 22, 2: 290-315.

Laroche, Isabelle. 2001. "The Inter-American Human Rights System and the Protection of the Rights of Migrants." http://www.december18.net/OAS.htm.

Law, Lisa. 2002. "Defying Disappearance: Cosmopolitan Public Spaces in Hong Kong." *Urban Studies* 39, 9: 1625-45.

–. 2004. "Sites of Transnational Activism: Filipino Non-Governmental Organisations in Hong Kong." In *Gender Politics in Asia,* ed. B. Yeoh. London: Routledge. 205-22.

Lee, Chin-Chuan, Joseph Chan, Zhongdang Pan, and Clement So. 2002. *Global Media Spectacle: News War over Hong Kong.* Albany: SUNY Press.

Levitt, Peggy. 1998a. "Local-Level Global Religion: The Case of U.S.-Dominican Migration." *Journal for the Scientific Study of Religion* 37, 1: 74-89.

–. 1998b. "Social Remittances: Migration Driven Local-Level Forms of Cultural Diffusion." *International Migration Review* 32, 4: 926-48.

–. 2001a. *The Transnational Villagers.* Berkeley: University of California Press.

–. 2001b. "Transnational Migration: Taking Stock and Future Directions." *Global Networks: A Journal of Transnational Affairs* 1, 3: 195-216.

–. 2003. "You Know, Abraham Was Really the First Immigrant: Religion and Transnational Migration." *International Migration Review* 37: 847-74.

Levitt, Peggy, and Nina Glick Schiller. 2004. "Transnational Perspectives on Migration: Conceptualizing Simultaneity." *International Migration Review* 38, 3: 1002-40.

Levitt, Peggy, and Ninna Nyberg-Sorensen. 2004. "The Transnational Turn in Migration Studies." Global Commission on International Migration Research Paper Series 6, Geneva. http://www.gcim.org/en/.

Ley, David. 2003. "Seeking *Homo Economicus*: The Canadian State and the Strange Story of the Business Immigration Program." *Annals of the Association of American Geographers* 93: 426-41.

Ley, David, and Audrey Kobayashi. 2005. "Back to Hong Kong: Return Migration or Transnational Sojourn?" *Global Networks* 5: 111-27.

Li, Peter. 1998. *The Chinese in Canada.* 2nd ed. Toronto: Oxford University Press.

Libercier, M., and H. Schneider. 1996. *Migrants: Partners in Development Co-operation.* Paris: OECD.

Linklater, Andrew. 1998. *The Transformation of Political Community: Ethical Foundations of the Post-Westphalian Era.* Oxford: Blackwell.

Logan, John R. 2001. "The New Latinos: Who They Are, Where They Are." Albany: Lewis Mumford Center for Comparative Urban and Regional Research.

López, David, Eric Popkin, and Edward Telles. 1996. "Central Americans: At the Bottom, Struggling to Get Ahead." In *Ethnic Los Angeles,* ed. R. Waldinger and M. Bozorgmehr. Newbury Park: Russell Sage Foundation Press. 25-56.

Lowe, Lisa. 1996. *Immigrant Acts: On Asian American Cultural Politics.* Durham, NC: Duke University Press.

Lustiger-Thaler, Henri. 1994. "Community Social Practices: The Contingency of Everyday Life." In *Urban Lives: Fragmentation and Resistance,* ed. Vared Amit-Talai and Henri Lustiger-Thaler. Toronto: McClelland and Stewart. 20-42.

Macklin, Audrey. 2003. "Dancing across Borders: 'Exotic Dancers,' Trafficking, and Canadian Immigration Policy." *International Migration Review* 37, 2: 464-501.

Mahler, Sarah. 1995. *American Dreaming: Immigrant Life on the Margins.* Princeton: Princeton University Press.

Mandaville, Peter. 2002. "Reading the State from Elsewhere: Towards an Anthropology of the Postnational." *Review of International Studies* 28: 199-207.

Mani, Lata. 1992. "Multiple Meditations: Feminist Scholarships in the Age of Multinational Reception." In *Knowing Women: Feminism and Knowledge,* ed. H. Crowley and S. Himmelweit, 306-22. Cambridge, UK: Polity Press.

Manogaran, Chelvadurai, and Bryan Pfaffenberger, eds. 1994. *The Sri Lankan Tamils: Ethnicity and Identity.* Boulder, CO: Westview Press.

Markowits, Claude. 2000. *The Global World of Indian Merchants (1750-1957).* London: Oxford University Press.

Marshall, Thomas Humphrey. 1964. *Class, Citizenship, and Social Development.* Garden City, NY: Doubleday.

–. 1992 [1950]. *Citizenship and Social Class.* London: Pluto.

Martin, Philip. 2003. *Promise Unfulfilled: Unions, Immigration, and the Farm Workers.* Ithaca: Cornell University Press.

McAdam, Doug. 1982. *Political Process and the Development of Black Insurgency, 1930-1970.* Chicago: University of Chicago Press.

McAdam, Doug, John McCarthy, and Mayer Zald, eds. 1996. *Comparative Perspectives on Social Movements: Political Opportunities, Mobilizing Structures, and Cultural Framings.* New York: Cambridge University Press.

McDowell, Christopher. 1996a. *A Tamil Asylum Diaspora: Sri Lankan Migration, Settlement, and Politics in Switzerland.* Providence: Berghahn Books.

–, ed. 1996b. *Understanding Impoverishment: The Consequences of Development-Induced Displacement.* Providence: Berghahn Books.

McKay, Deirdre. 2002. "Filipina Identities: Geographies of Social Integration/Exclusion in the Canadian Metropolis." Vancouver Centre of Excellence: Research on Immigration and Integration in the Metropolis, Working Paper Series 02-18.

Meyer, David. 2000. *Hong Kong as a Global Metropolis.* Cambridge, UK: Cambridge University Press.

Migration Dialogue. N.d. "Peru." http://www.migration.ucdavis.edu/mn/data/remittances/remittances.html.

Migration Policy Institute (MPI). 2004. "Comparing Migrant Stock: The Five Largest Foreign-Born Groups in Australia, Canada, and the United States." http://www.migration.information.org/DataTools/migrant_stock_groups.cfm.

Miller, David. 2000. *Citizenship and National Identity.* Cambridge, UK: Polity Press.

Ministerio de Relaciones Exteriores del Perú (Ministry of Foreign Affairs of Peru). N.d. http://www.rree.gob.pe/portal/misrree.nsf/077.

Montes, Segundo. 1989. *Refugiados y Repatriados en El Salvador y Honduras.* San Salvador: UCA Editores.

Morris, Nomi. 1995. "The Canadian Connection: Sri Lanka Moves to Crush Tamil Rebels at Home and Abroad." *Maclean's* 27 November: 28-29.

Motwani, Jagat, Mahin Gosine, and Jyoti Barot-Motwani, eds. 1993. *Global Indian Diaspora: Yesterday, Today, and Tomorrow.* New York: Global Organization of People of Indian Origin.

Municipality of Leamington. 2002a. *The Greenhouse Industry: Leamington Area Greenhouse Directory.* Leamington, ON: Development Services Department.

–. 2002b. "The Greenhouse Sector: Leamington's Agricultural Industry." http://www.leamington.ca/Business_Overview/Agricultural_Directory/Leamington_s_Agricultural_Industry.html.

Nagel, Caroline. 2001. "Nations Unbound? Migration, Culture, and the Limits of the Transnational-Diaspora Narrative." *Political Geography* 20: 247-56.

Nayyar, Deepak. 1994. *Migration, Remittances, and Capital Flows: The Indian Experience.* New Delhi: Oxford University Press.

Ng, Wing Chung. 1999. "Canada." In *The Encyclopedia of the Chinese Overseas*, ed. Lynn Pan, C1-C13. Cambridge, MA: Harvard University Press.

Nolin, Catharine. 2004. "Spatializing the Immobility of Guatemalan Transnationalism in Canada." *Canadian Journal of Latin American and Caribbean Studies,* 29: 267-88.

–. 2006. *Transnational Ruptures: Gender and Forced Migration.* Aldershot, UK: Ashgate.

Nyberg-Sorensen, Ninna, Nicholas Van Hear, and Paula Engberg-Pedersen. 2002. "The Migration-Development Nexus: Evidence and Policy Options." *International Migration* 40, 5: 49-73.

Ong, Aihwa. 1991. "The Gender and Labor Politics of Postmodernity." *Annual Review of Anthropology* 20: 279-309.

–. 1999. *Flexible Citizenship: The Cultural Logics of Transnationality.* Durham, NC: Duke University Press.

Organization of American States. 1969. American Convention on Human Rights.

Organisation for Economic Co-operation and Development (OECD). 2001. *The Well-Being of Nations: The Role of Human and Social Capital.* E-book. Paris: OECD.

–. 2003. *Trends in International Migration.* Paris: OECD.

Organization for Security and Co-operation in Europe. 1990. *Document of the Copenhagen Meeting of the Human Dimension of the Conference for Security and Co-Operation in Europe.* Third Conference on the Human Dimension of the CSCE, 5 June-29 July. Copenhagen: CSCE. http://www.wunrn.com/reference/pdf/Copenhagen_Conference_Human_Dimension.pdf.

Ornstein, Michael. 2000. "Ethno-Racial Inequality in the City of Toronto: An Analysis of the 1996 Census." Toronto: Access and Equity Unit, Strategic and Corporate Policy Division, City of Toronto.

Orozco, Manuel. 2003. "The Future Trends and Patterns of Remittances to Latin America." Paper presented at the Inter-American Development Bank Conference on Remittances as a Development Tool in Mexico, Washington, DC, 28 October.

–. 2005. "Transnationalism and Development: Trends and Opportunities in Latin America." In *Remittances: Development Impact and Future Prospects,* ed. S.M. Maimbo and D. Ratha, 307-30. Washington, DC: World Bank.

Ossiander, Andreas. 2001. "The Westphalian Myth." *International Organization* 55: 251-88.

Østergaard-Nielsen, Eva. 2000. "Trans-State Loyalties and Politics of Turks and Kurds in Western Europe." *SAIS Review* 20, 1: 23-38.

–. 2001a. "Diasporas in World Politics." In *Non-State Actors in World Politics,* ed. Daphne Josselin and William Wallace, 218-34. Houndmills, Basingstoke, UK: Palgrave.

–. 2001b. "Transnational Political Practices and the Receiving State: Turks and Kurds in Germany and the Netherlands." *Global Networks* 1, 3: 261-81.

–. 2002. *Transnational Politics: Turks and Kurds in Germany.* London: Routledge.

–. 2003. *International Migration and Sending Countries: Perceptions, Policies, and Transnational Relations.* Basingstoke, UK: Palgrave; New York: Macmillan.

Owusu, Thomas Y. 2003. "Transnationalism among African Immigrants in North America: The Case of Ghanaians in Canada." *Journal of International Migration and Integration* 4, 3: 395-413.

Oxfam America. 2004. *Like Machines in the Fields: Workers without Rights in American Agriculture.* http://www.oxfamamerica.org/pdfs/labor_report_04.pdf.

Pal, Michael, and Sujit Choudhry. 2007. "Is Every Vote Equal? Visible-Minority Vote Dilution in Canada." *IRPP Choices* 13, 1: 3-30.

Pan, Lynn, ed. 1999. *The Encyclopedia of the Chinese Overseas.* Cambridge, MA: Harvard University Press.

Pastor, M., and S. Alva. 2003. "Guest Workers and the New Transnationalism: Is a Progressive Program Possible?" Paper presented at the Latin American Studies Association International Congress, Dallas, 27-29 March.

Pateman, Carole. 1988. "The Patriarchal Welfare State." In *Democracy and the Welfare State,* ed. Amy Gutmann, 231-60. Princeton: Princeton University Press.

People United for Better Living in Calcutta. 2004. http://www.bengalonthenet.com/community/nonprofit_organisation/public.shtml.

Philip, M. Nourbese. 1992. "Why Multiculturalism Can't End Racism." In *Frontiers: Essays and Writings on Racism and Culture,* 181-86. Stratford, ON: Mercury Press.

Philippine Women's Center. 2002. "Overseas Filipinos in Vancouver Celebrate Gains and Look Ahead to Advancing Their Struggle for Social Justice!" http://www.december18.net/web/papers/view.php?menuID=41&lang=EN&paperID=708.

Phillips, Anne. 1991. "Citizenship and Feminist Politics." In *Citizenship,* ed. G. Andrews, 76-88. London: Lawrence and Wishart.

Policy Roundtable Mobilizing Professions and Trades (PROMPT). 2004. "In the Public Interest: Immigrant Access to Regulated Professions in Today's Ontario." Policy paper. Toronto: PROMPT.

Popkin, Eric. 2003. "Transnational Migration and Development in Post-War Peripheral States: An Examination of Guatemalan and Salvadoran State Linkages with Their Migrant Populations in Los Angeles." *Current Sociology* 51, 3-4: 347-74.

Portes, Alejandro. 2003. "Conclusion: Theoretical Convergences and Empirical Evidence in the Study of Immigrant Transnationalism." *International Migration Review* 37, 3: 874-92.

Portes, Alejandro, and József Böröcz. 1989. "Contemporary Immigration: Theoretical Perspectives on Its Determinants and Modes of Incorporation." *International Migration Review* 23, 3: 606-30.

Portes, Alejandro, Luis E. Guarnizo, and Patricia Landolt. 1999. "The Study of Transnationalism: Pitfalls and Promise of an Emergent Research Field." *Ethnic and Racial Studies* 22, 2: 217-37.

Portes, Alejandro, William J. Haller, and Luis E. Guarnizo. 2002. "Transnational Entrepreneurs: An Alternative Form of Immigrant Economic Adaptation." *American Sociological Review* 67, 2: 278-98.

Pozo, Susan, and Catalina Amuedo-Dorantes. 2002. "Workers' Remittances and the Real Exchange Rate: A Paradox of Gifts." http://www.homepages.wmich.edu/~pozo/remit. real.feb6.pdf.

Pratt, Geraldine. 2004. *Working Feminism*. Philadelphia: Temple University Press.

Pratt, Geraldine, and Brenda Yeoh. 2003. "Transnational (Counter) Topographies." *Gender, Place, and Culture* 10, 2: 159-66.

Preibisch, Kerry. 2000. "Tierra de los no-libres: Migración temporal México-Canadá y dos campos de reestructuración económica." In *Conflictos migratorios transnacionales y respuestas comunitarias,* ed. L. Binford and M. D'Aubeterre, 45-66. Puebla: Benemérita Universidad Autónoma de Puebla.

–. 2003. *Social Relations Practices between Seasonal Agricultural Workers, Their Employers, and the Residents of Rural Ontario.* Research report. Ottawa: North-South Institute.

–. 2004. "Migrant Agricultural Workers and Processes of Social Inclusion in Rural Canada: Encuentros and Desencuentros." *Canadian Journal of Latin American and Caribbean Studies* 29, 57-58: 203-39.

–. Forthcoming. "Local Produce, Foreign Labor: Labor Mobility Programs and Global Trade Competitiveness in Canada." *Rural Sociology.*

Preston, Valerie, Lucia Lo, and Shuguang Wang. 2003. "Immigrants' Economic Status in Toronto: Stories of Triumph and Disappointment." In *The World in a City,* ed. Paul Anisef and Michael Lanphier. Toronto: University of Toronto Press. 192-262.

Preuss, Ulrich K. 2003. "Citizenship and the German Nation." *Citizenship Studies* 7, 1: 37-55.

Pries, Ludger, ed. 1998. *Migration and Transnational Social Spaces.* Aldershot, UK: Ashgate; Copenhagen: Danish Center for Migration and Ethnic Studies.

Puri, Shalini. 2006. "After the Fact: A Response to My Critics." *Small Axe* 10, 1: 218-29.

Putnam, Robert. 1995. "Bowling Alone: America's Declining Social Capital." *Journal of Democracy* 6, 1: 65-78.

Rai, Shirin. 2002. *Gender and the Political Economy of Development.* London: Polity Press.

Ramsar Convention on Wetlands. 2004. http://www.ramsar.org.

Ratha, Dilip. 2003. "Workers Remittances: An Important and Stable Source of External Development Finance." In *Global Finance Report.* Washington, DC: World Bank. 157-75.

Rauch, James. 2003. "Diasporas and Development: Theory, Evidence, and Programmatic Implications: A Special Study of the US Agency for International Development Trade Enhancement for the Services Sector." Washington, DC: USAID.

Reitz, Jeffrey. 1998. *The Warmth of the Welcome: The Social Causes of Economic Success for Immigrants in Different Nations and Cities.* Boulder: Westview Press.

Repak, Terry. 1995. *Waiting on Washington: Central American Workers in the Nation's Capital.* Philadelphia: Temple University Press.

Research Directorate, Documentation, Information, and Research Branch, Immigration and Refugee Board. 1996. *Sri Lanka: Alien Smuggling.* Question and Answer Series. Ottawa: IRB.

Robinson, Jenny, David Turton, Giles Mohan, and Helen Yanacopulos. 2002. *Development and Displacement.* Oxford: Oxford University Press; Milton Keynes: Open University Press.

Rodríguez Cuadros, Manuel. 2003. "A New Vision of the Foreign Policy for Protection of Peruvian Communities Abroad and the Re-Construction of Consular Services." Paper presented at the First International Seminar on Peruvian Communities Abroad, Lima, 24 March.

Rosenfeld, Herman, and Jayme Gianola. 2001. "Prospects for a New Left? A Report on the Rebuilding the Left Conference." *Canadian Dimension* 35, 1: 18.

Rouse, Roger. 1991. "Mexican Migration and the Social Space of Postmodernism." *Diaspora* 1, 1: 7-23.

–. 1992. "Making Sense of Settlement: Class Transformation, Cultural Struggle, and Transnationalism among Mexican Migrants in the United States." In *Towards a Transnational Perspective on Migration,* ed. L. Nina Glick Schiller, Linda Basch, and Cristina Blanc-Szanton, 25-52. New York: New York Academy of Sciences.

Rundstrom, Robert, and Douglas Deur. 1999. "Reciprocal Appropriations: Toward an Ethics of Cross-Cultural Research." In *Geography and Ethics: Journeys in Moral Terrain,* ed. James D. Proctor and David M. Smith. London: Routledge. 237-50.

Rushdie, Salman. 1991. *Imaginary Homelands: Essays and Criticism, 1981-1991.* London: Granta; New York: Viking.

Russell, Roy. 2003. *Jamaican Workers' Participation in CSAWP and Development Consequences in the Workers' Rural Home Communities.* Ottawa: North-South Institute.

Ryan, Stephen. 1990. *Ethnic Conflict and International Relations.* Aldershot, UK: Dartmouth.

Safran, William. 1991. "Diasporas in Modern Societies: Myth of Homeland and Return." *Diaspora: A Journal of Transnational Studies* 1, 1: 83-99.

Samaddar, Ranabir. 1999. *The Marginal Nation: Transborder Migration from Bangladesh to West Bengal.* London: Sage.

Sambandan, V.S. 1999. "'Cyberwave' Sweeps over Tamils the World Over." Tamil Circle, Online Posting, 1 December. (Also posted in the *Hindu,* online edition of India's national newspaper, 2 December.)

San Martin, Ruth Magali. 2004. "Unwanted in Paradise: Undocumented Migrant Women Sex-Workers in Toronto." In *Calculated Kindness,* ed. Rose B. Folson, 71-83. Black Point, NS: Fernwood Press.

Sandoval, Chela. 2000. *Methodology of the Oppressed.* Minneapolis: University of Minnesota Press.

Sassen, Saskia. 1991. *The Global City: Tokyo, London, and New York.* Princeton: Princeton University Press.

–. 1994. *Cities in a World Economy.* Thousand Oaks, CA: Pine Forge Press.

–. 2003. "The Participation of States in Global Governance." *Indiana Journal of Global Legal Studies* 10, 1: 5-28.

Sathyamala, C. 2004. "Love in the Time of Genocide." *Psychological Foundations: The Journal of the Psychological Foundation of India* 6, 1: 12-21.

Satzewich, Vic. 1991. *Racism and the Incorporation of Foreign Labour: Farm Labour Migration to Canada since 1945.* London: Routledge.

Satzewich, Vic, and Lloyd Wong, eds. 2006. *Transnational Identities and Practices in Canada.* Vancouver: UBC Press.

Secretaría del Trabajo y Previsión Social (STyPS). 1998-2003. Reportes del Programa para las Temporadas 1998-2003. Mexico City: STyPS.

Seshadri, R.K. 1993. *From Crisis to Convertibility: The External Value of the Rupee.* Bombay: Orient Longman.

Shakir, Uzma. 2000. *Brain Drain, Brain Gain: Session Proceedings.* Ottawa: Caledon Institute of Social Policy.

Sharma, Nandita. 2001. "On Being Not Canadian: The Social Organization of 'Migrant Workers' in Canada." *Canadian Review of Sociology and Anthropology* 38, 4: 415-39.

Sherrell, Kathy, and Jennifer Hyndman. 2006. "Global Minds, Local Bodies: Kosovar Transnational Connections beyond British Columbia." *Refuge* 23, 1: 16-26.

Sim, Amy. 2003. "Organising Discontent: NGOs for Southeast Asian Migrant Workers in Hong Kong." *Asian Journal of Social Science* 31, 3: 478-510.

Simmons, Alan. 1998. "Racism and Immigration Policy." In *Racism and Social Inequality in Canada,* ed. Vic Satzewich, 87-114. Toronto: Thompson Educational Publishing.

Singh Brar, Sandeep. 1997. "Century of Struggle and Success: The Sikh Canadian Experience." http://www.sikhs.org/100th/part2a.html.

Skeldon, Ronald. 1994. "Hong Kong in an International Migration System." In *Reluctant Exiles? Migration from Hong Kong and the New Overseas Chinese*, ed. Ronald Skeldon, 21-51. Armonk: M.E. Sharpe.

–. 1999. "The Case of Hong Kong." In *The Encyclopedia of the Chinese Overseas*, ed. Lynn Pan, 67-70. Cambridge, MA: Harvard University Press.

Smart, Josephine. 1998. "Borrowed Men on Borrowed Time: Globalization, Labour Migration, and Local Economies in Alberta." *Canadian Journal of Regional Science* 20, 12: 141-56.

Smith, Jackie, and Hank Johnston, eds. 2002. *Globalization and Resistance: Transnational Dimensions of Social Movements*. Lanham, MD: Rowman and Littlefield.

Smith, Michael Peter. 2001. *Transnational Urbanism: Locating Globalization*. Oxford: Blackwell.

Smith, Michael Peter, and Luis Eduardo Guarnizo, eds. 1998. *Transnationalism from Below*. New Brunswick, NJ: Transaction.

Smith, Robert C. 2003a. "Migrant Membership as an Instituted Process: Transnationalization, the State, and the Extra-Territorial Conduct of Mexican Politics." *International Migration Review* 37, 2: 297-343.

–. 2003b. "Diasporic Memberships in Historical Perspective: Comparative Insights from the Mexican, Italian, and Polish Cases." *International Migration Review* 37, 3: 724-59.

Snow, David A., E. Burke Rochford, Jr., Steven K. Worden, and Robert D. Benford. 1986. "Frame Alignment Processes, Micromobilization, and Movement Participation." *American Sociological Review* 51: 464-81.

South Asia Left Democratic Alliance (SALDA). 2003. http://www.salda.org.

Southern Poverty Law Center. 2007. *Close to Slavery: Guestworker Programs in the United States*. Montgomery, AL: Southern Poverty Law Center. http://www.splcenter.org/pdf/static/splcguestworker.pdf.

Soysal, Yasemin. 1994. *Limits of Citizenship: Migrants and Post-National Membership in Europe*. Chicago: University of Chicago Press.

–. 2000. "Citizenship and Identity: Living in Diasporas in Post-War Europe?" *Ethnic and Racial Studies* 23, 1: 1-15.

Spivak, Gayatri Chakravorty. 1996. "Diasporas Old and New: Women in the Transnational World." *Textual Practice* 10: 245-69.

Stalker, Peter. 2001. *The No-Nonsense Guide to International Migration*. Toronto: Between the Lines.

–. 2006. *Stalker's Guide to International Migration*. http://pstalker.com/migration/.

Stasiulis, Daiva, and Abigail Bakan. 1997. "Negotiating Citizenship: The Case of Foreign Domestic Workers in Canada." *Feminist Review* 57: 112-39.

–. 2003. *Negotiating Citizenship: Migrant Women in Canada and the Global System*. Houndmills: Palgrave; New York: Macmillan.

Statistics Canada. 1997. *The Daily*. 4 November.

–. 2001. *Canada's Ethnocultural Portrait: The Changing Mosaic*. Census Analysis Series. Ottawa: Statistics Canada.

–. 2003. *The Ethnic Diversity Survey: Portrait of a Multicultural Society*. http://www.statcan.ca/english/freepub/89-593-XIE/pdf/89-593-XIE03001.pdf.

Stephen, Lynn. 2003. "Cultural Citizenship and Labor Rights for Oregon Farmworkers: The Case of Pineros y Campesinos Unidos del Nordoeste (PCUN)." *Human Organization* 62, 1: 27-38.

Stiell, Bernadette, and Kim England. 1997. "Domestic Distinctions: Constructing Difference among Paid Domestic Workers in Toronto." *Gender, Place, and Culture: A Journal of Feminist Geography* 4: 339-59.

Szonyi, Michael. 2002. "Paper Tigers." *National Post Business* July: 34-44.

Tambiah, Stanley J. 1986. *Ethnic Fratricide and the Dismantling of Democracy*. Chicago: University of Chicago Press.

Taran, P.A. 2000. "Human Rights of Migrants: Challenges of the New Decade." *International Migration* 38, 6: 7-52.

Tarrow, Sidney. 1994. *Power in Movement: Social Movements and Contentious Politics*. Cambridge, UK: Cambridge University Press.

–. 2001. "Transnational Politics: Contention and Institutions in International Politics." *Annual Review of Political Science* 4: 1-20.

Tatla, Singh Darshan. 1999. *The Sikh Diaspora: The Search for Statehood.* London: UCL Press.

Taylor, Charles. 1999. "Conditions of an Unforced Consensus on Human Rights." In *The East Asian Challenge for Human Rights,* ed. Joanne R. Bauer and Daniel A. Bell, 124-44. Cambridge, UK: Cambridge University Press.

TD Bank Financial Group. 2005. "Offshore Outsourcing of Services: Not Just a Passing Fad." TD Economics Special Report.

Thompson, Edward P. 1962. *The Making of the English Working Class.* New York: Vintage.

Tölölyan, Khachig. 1991. "The Nation-State and Its Others: In Lieu of a Preface." *Diaspora* 1, 1: 3-7.

–. 1996. "Rethinking Diasporas: Stateless Power in the Transnational Moment." *Diaspora* 5, 1: 3-36.

Totoricaguena, Gloria. 2004. "Ethnic Diasporas as Non-State Actors in Foreign Policy: The Trajectory of Basque Transnational Networks." Paper presented at the conference Imagining Diasporas: Space, Identity, and Social Change, University of Windsor, 14-16 May.

Tsang, Steve. 1997. *Hong Kong: An Appointment with China.* London: I.B. Tauris.

Tully, James. 1995. *Strange Multiplicity: Constitutionalism in an Age of Diversity.* Cambridge, UK: Cambridge University Press.

Turner, Bryan S. 1990. "Outline of a Theory of Citizenship." *Sociology* 24, 2: 189-217.

UFCW. 2002. *National Report: Status of Migrant Farm Workers in Canada.* http://www.ufcw.ca/ Theme/UFCW/files/National%20ReportENG.pdf.

–. 2004. "Agricultural Workers Take Ontario Government to Court." Press release. http:// www.ufcw.ca.

United Nations. General Assembly. 1948. Universal Declaration of Human Rights.

–. 1966a. International Covenant on Civil and Political Rights.

–. 1966b. International Covenant on Economic, Social, and Cultural Rights.

–. 1990. International Convention on the Protection of the Rights of All Migrant Workers and Members of Their Families.

–. General Assembly. 1992. Declaration on the Rights of Persons Belonging to National or Ethnic, Religious, and Linguistic Minorities.

–. Economic and Social Council. 1993. Draft Declaration on the Rights of Indigenous Peoples.

United Nations High Commissioner for Refugees (UNHCR). 2001-2. Statistics. http://www. unhcr.ch/cgi-bin/textis/vtx/statistics.

Vajpayee, A.B. 2003. Address to the First Indian Diaspora Conference, New Delhi, 9 January.

Van Doorn, Judith. 2002. *Migration, Remittances, and Development.* Migrant Workers, Labor Education 2002, No. 129. Geneva: ILO.

Van Hear, Nicholas. 1998. *New Diasporas: The Mass Exodus, Dispersal, and Regrouping of Migrant Communities.* Seattle: University of Washington Press.

Vasundhara. 2004. http://www.vasundhara.cjb.net.

Velasco, Pura. 2002. "Filipino Migrant Workers amidst Globalization." *Canadian Women's Studies* 21-22: 131-36.

Verduzco, Gustavo, and María Isabel Lozano. 2003. *Mexican Workers' Participation in CSAWP and Development Consequences in the Workers' Rural Home Communities.* Research report. Ottawa: North-South Institute.

Verma, Veena. 2003. *CSAWP Regulatory and Policy Framework, Farm Industry-Level Employment Practices, and the Potential Role of Unions.* Research report. Ottawa: North-South Institute.

Vertovec, Steven. 2001. "Transnationalism and Identity." *Journal of Ethnic and Migration Studies* 27, 4: 573-82.

–. 2003. "Migrant Transnationalism and Modes of Transformation." Centre for Migration and Development Working Paper Series, Princeton University. http://cmd.princeton.edu/ papers/wp0309m.pdf.

–. 2004. "Cheap Calls: The Social Glue of Migrant Transnationalism." *Global Networks* 4, 2: 219-24.

Vertovec, Steven, and Robin Cohen, eds. 1999. *Migration, Diasporas, and Transnationalism.* Cheltenham, UK: Edward Elgar.

Vilas, Carlos. 1995. *Between Earthquakes and Volcanoes: Market, State, and the Revolutions in Central America.* New York: Monthly Review Press.

Waldinger, Roger, and David Fitzgerald. 2004. "Transnationalism in Question." *American Journal of Sociology* 109, 5: 1177-96.

Wall, Ellen. 1992. "Personal Labour Relations and Ethnicity in Ontario Agriculture." In *Deconstructing a Nation: Immigration, Multiculturalism, and Racism in 90s Canada,* ed. Vic Satzewich, 261-75. Halifax: Fernwood Publishing.

–. 1996. "Unions in the Field." *Canadian Journal of Agricultural Economics* 44, 4: 515-26.

Walton-Roberts, Margaret. 2001. "Embodied Global Flows: Immigration and Transnational Networks between British Columbia, Canada, and Punjab India." PhD diss., Department of Geography, University of British Columbia.

"The War the World Is Missing." 2000. *Economist,* 5 October: 32.

Waters, Joanna. 2002. "Flexible Families? 'Astronaut' Households and the Experiences of Lone Mothers in Vancouver, British Columbia." *Social and Cultural Geography* 3: 117-34.

–. 2003. "Flexible Citizens? Transnationalism and Citizenship among Economic Immigrants in Vancouver." *Canadian Geographer* 47: 219-34.

Wayland, Sarah. 1993. "Mobilising to Defend Nationality Law in France." *New Community* 20, 1: 93-110.

–. 2004. "Ethnonationalist Networks and Transnational Opportunities: The Sri Lankan Tamil Diaspora." *Review of International Studies* 30: 405-26.

Wee, Vivienne, and Amy Sim. 2003. "Transnational Labour Networks in Female Labour Migration: Mediating between Southeast Asian Women Workers and International Labour Markets." Working Paper Series 49. City University of Hong Kong.

Werake, M., and P.V.J. Jayasekera, eds. 1992. *Security Dilemma of a Small State: Part Two, Internal Crisis and External Intervention in Sri Lanka.* Kandy, Sri Lanka: Institute for International Studies.

Weston, Ann, and Luigi Scarpa de Masellis. 2003. *Hemispheric Integration and Trade Relations: Implications for Canada's Seasonal Agricultural Workers Program.* Research report. Ottawa: North-South Institute.

Westwood, Sallie, and Annie Phizacklea. 2000. *Transnationalism and the Politics of Belonging.* New York: Routledge.

Whitfield G., and A.P. Papadopoulos. 2002. "Introduction to the Greenhouse Vegetable Industry." http://res2.agr.gc.ca/harrow/publications/Introduction_ e.htm.

Wiggins, Cindy. 2003. "Women's Work Challenging and Changing the World." CLC Research Paper 23. Ottawa: CLC.

Williams, Fiona. 1989. *Social Policy: A Critical Introduction.* Cambridge, UK: Polity Press.

Williams, Raymond. 1972. *Marxism and Literature.* London: Verso.

Wilson, A. Jeyaratnam. 2000. *Sri Lankan Tamil Nationalism: Its Origins and Development in the 19th and 20th Centuries.* Vancouver: UBC Press.

Winland, Daphne. 1995. "'We Are Now an Actual Nation': The Impact of National Independence on the Croatian Diaspora in Canada." *Diaspora* 4, 1: 3-29.

–. 1998. "'Our Home and Native Land'? Canadian Ethnic Scholarship and the Challenge of Transnationalism." *Canadian Review of Sociology and Anthropology* 35, 4: 555-77.

Wong, Lloyd L. 2002. "Transnationalism, Diaspora Communities, and Changing Identities: Implications for Canadian Citizenship." In *Street Protest and Fantasy Parks: Globalization, Culture, and the State,* ed. David R. Cameron and Janice Gross Stein, 49-87. Vancouver: UBC Press.

–. 2004. "Taiwanese Immigrant Entrepreneurs in Canada and Transnational Social Space." *International Migration* 42, 2: 113-52.

Wong, Lloyd L., and Michele Ng. 2002. "The Emergence of Small Transnational Enterprise in Vancouver: The Case of Chinese Entrepreneur Immigrants." *International Journal of Urban and Regional Research* 26, 3: 508-30.

Wong, Madeleine. 2000. "Ghanaian Women in Toronto's Labour Market: Negotiating Gender Roles and Transnational Household Strategies." *Canadian Ethnic Studies* 32, 2: 45-75.

–. 2003. "Borders that Separate, Blood that Binds: The Transnational Activities of Ghanaian Women in Toronto." PhD diss., Department of Geography, York University.

World Bank. 2003a. *Global Development Finance, I: Analysis and Statistical Appendix*. Washington, DC: World Bank.

–. 2003b. *Global Development Finance, II: Summary and Country Tables*. Washington, DC: World Bank.

–. 2003c. "Foreign Investment and Remittances Outpace Debt as Sources of Finance for Latin America and the Caribbean." News release 2003/266/S. 2 April.

–. 2003d. "Global Development Finance: Striving for Stability in Development Finance." http://www.worldbank.org/prospects/gdf2003.

Young, Iris Marion. 2000. *Inclusion and Democracy*. Oxford: Oxford University Press.

Yuval-Davis, Nira. 1999a. "National Spaces and Collective Identities: Borders, Boundaries, Citizenship, and Gender Relations: Part I." *Nivedini: A Sri Lankan Feminist Journal* 7, 1: 1-7.

–. 1999b. "The 'Multi-Layered Citizen': Citizenship at the Age of 'Glocalization.'" *International Feminist Journal of Politics* 1, 1: 119-36.

Zolberg, Aristide, Astri Suhrke, and Sergio Aguayo. 1989. *Escape from Violence: Conflict and the Refugee Crisis in the Developing World*. New York: Oxford University Press.

# Contributors

**Ofelia Becerril** has a PhD in anthropology from the Autonomous Metropolitan University, Iztapalapa, Mexico City. A specialist in the anthropology of gender, women's rural employment, and Mexican agricultural workers, she was a visiting fellow at York University's Centre for Research on Latin America and the Caribbean in 2003-4. Her doctoral research on Mexican migrant farm workers in Canada was supported by scholarships from Mexico's National Council of Science and Technology and the International Council for Canadian Studies. She has conducted several research projects on Mexican agriculture and labour in Mexico and Ontario and is a member of Enlace and Justicia for Migrant Workers, two human rights organizations.

**Pablo S. Bose** is currently the George Washington Henderson and SSHRCC postdoctoral fellow of the Department of Geography at the University of Vermont. His ongoing research looks at relationships between diasporic communities and international development, especially in the context of South Asia, urbanization, and global cities. He is undertaking a comparative study of diasporic identity formation in the United States and Canada, with a focus on immigrant Indian Bengali communities in both countries.

**R. Cheran** is an assistant professor in the Department of Sociology and Anthropology, University of Windsor, and is a senior research fellow with the International Center for Ethnic Studies, Colombo, Sri Lanka. He is the editor of *Writing Tamil Nationalism* and is co-editor of *History and Imagination: Tamil Studies in the Global Context*.

**Gloria Patricia Díaz Barrero** is a PhD candidate in social and political thought at York University. She emigrated from Colombia to Canada, where she is an active member of the Latin American women's community. Her current research is on Latin American migrant sex workers and Latinas' identity in

Canada. Her latest publications include "Strippers, Erotic, and Exotic Dancers: Immigration and Identity in the Construction of the Canadian Nation-State," published in *Cuadernos Pagu,* and "Bailarinas Exoticas, Striptease, e Inmigración en Canadá," in *Colombia Internacional.*

**Luin Goldring** is an associate professor of sociology and a fellow at the Centre for Research on Latin American and Caribbean Studies at York University. She has published articles on several aspects of Mexico-US migration, including state-migrant relations and market and gendered citizenship. Her current collaborative research is on the institutional incorporation and transnational engagements of Latin Americans in Canada and on precarious employment among Caribbean and Latin American immigrants in Toronto.

**Susan Henders** teaches international relations and Asian politics at the Department of Political Science, York University. Having completed her DPhil at St. Anthony's College, Oxford, she has taught at St. John's College, Oxford, and was a visiting professor at the University of Leuven (K.U. Leuven), Belgium. Among her publications are *Democratization and Identity: Regimes and Ethnicity in East and South-East Asia* (editor, contributor), *Macau* (co-editor, contributor, translator), and articles in journals such as *Pacific Affairs, Nations and Nationalism,* and the *Journal of Human Rights.* She is currently completing a book entitled *Diversity and (A)Symmetry: The Politics of Special Status Regions.*

**Rusa Jeremic** is the program coordinator, Global Economic Justice, for KAIROS: Canadian Ecumenical Justice Initiatives. KAIROS is a member of Common Frontiers, which participates in the Hemispheric Social Alliance (HSA). Rusa sits on the Coordinating Committee, the Technical Team, and the Women's Committee of the HSA. She has an MA in political science from York University, where she focused her studies on popular movements and transformative change. A strongly committed social justice activist, Rusa has written extensively on international trade issues and is often found speaking at local, national, and international events.

**Philip Kelly** is an associate professor of geography at York University. His research has included studies of labour, industrialization, and urbanization in the Philippines and elsewhere in Southeast Asia as well as representations of globalization and economic space in the region. He is currently working on Filipino transnational migration and labour market experiences. He is the author of *Landscapes of Globalization: Human Geographies of Economic Change in the Philippines* and a co-editor of *Globalization and the Asia Pacific: Contested Territories.*

**Sailaja Krishnamurti** is a PhD candidate in social and political thought at York University and a graduate associate at the York Centre for Asian Research. Her dissertation research is on popular culture and nationalism in the South Asian diaspora. She has been a member of several community and activist groups, including SALDA (South Asia Left Democratic Alliance) and CASSA (Council of Agencies Serving South Asians).

**Patricia Landolt** is an assistant professor of sociology at the University of Toronto and a research associate of the Centre for Urban and Community Studies (http://www.urbancentre.utoronto.ca/). Her current research and publications integrate issues of citizen and worker rights into an analysis of transnational migration, migrant labour market incorporation, and immigrant political participation and sociocultural adaptation in places of origin and cities of resettlement.

**Gaby Motta** was born in Peru, studied medicine in the Soviet Union, and came to Canada in 1989. She works at Harbourfront Community Centre as a family program manager for the Growing Up Healthy Downtown Project, which serves families with children under the age of six in the Greater Toronto Area. She has a history of volunteer work with Latin American and other community organizations. Currently, she is a member of the board of the Hispanic Development Council and Casa Doña Juana. Gaby served on the Social Action Committee of Toronto's first Peruvian Advisory Council (2001-2).

**Kerry Preibisch** is an associate professor in the Department of Sociology and Anthropology at the University of Guelph. Her research areas include Mexican rural development, global restructuring and agrifood systems, and gender and migration. Her current work focuses on temporary labour migration to Canada.

**Valerie Preston** is a professor of geography at York University, where she teaches several courses on urban social geography. Her current research examines citizenship issues associated with transnational migration, the integration of immigrant women in urban labour markets, and the housing circumstances of refugees and immigrants in Canadian cities.

**Stan Raper** is an organizer with the United Food and Commercial Workers (UFCW) Canada and the coordinator of the Global Justice Care Van program in Leamington, Ontario. The program was created to assist farm workers for the 2001-2 growing season and has continued since then. Stan is a former Canadian coordinator of the United Farm Workers of America (UFWA) and the author of the UFWA *Report of Migrant Farm Workers in Canada,* presented to the federal minister of labour in 2001.

**Uzma Shakir** is the executive director of the South Asian Legal Clinic of Ontario and the former executive director of the Council of Agencies Serving South Asians in Toronto. She is an advocate of greater representation for all immigrant communities in policy, institutions, service delivery, and societal participation on the principles of access and equity. As a community activist, she has worked extensively to create alliances among many of Toronto's newcomer communities.

**Myer Siemiatycki,** a professor of politics, is director of the MA Program in Immigration and Settlement Studies at Ryerson University. His research interests explore urban citizenship – the civic engagement of immigrant and minority communities.

**Aparna Sundar** is an assistant professor in the Department of Politics and Public Administration, Ryerson University, and a PhD candidate in political science at the University of Toronto. She is a founder and member of SALDA (South Asian Left Democratic Alliance).

**Carlos Enrique Terry** received a law degree in Peru and is now a journalist for the daily Spanish-language newspaper *El Popular* in Toronto. He is also a legal advisor for newcomers in the Spanish Catholic Church. Before coming to Canada in 1992, he worked as a legal advisor for the Dutch Embassy and in its Chamber of Commerce. Carlos was the president of Toronto's second Peruvian Advisory Council (2002-3).

**Leela Viswanathan** has a PhD from the Faculty of Environmental Studies at York University. Her scholarly interests bridge urban research with her professional and activist experiences. From 2001 to 2003, she was president of the Board of Directors of CASSA (Council of Agencies Serving South Asians).

**Sarah V. Wayland** is a research associate at the Joint Centre of Excellence for Research on Immigration and Settlement – Toronto (CERIS). She has published articles on various aspects of immigration, citizenship, and transnational politics. She obtained her PhD in government and politics from the University of Maryland and lives in Hamilton, Ontario, where she is the owner of Wayland Consulting and a director of the St. Joseph Immigrant Women's Centre.

# Index

Printed and bound in Canada by Friesens
Set in Stone by Artegraphica Design Co. Ltd.
Copy editor: Dallas Harrison
Proofreader: Jillian Shoichet
Indexer: Patricia Buchanan